Cambridge Imperial and Post-Colonial Studies Series

Series Editors
Richard Drayton
Department of History
King's College London
London, UK

Saul Dubow
Magdalene College
University of Cambridge
Cambridge, UK

The Cambridge Imperial and Post-Colonial Studies series is a collection of studies on empires in world history and on the societies and cultures which emerged from colonialism. It includes both transnational, comparative and connective studies, and studies which address where particular regions or nations participate in global phenomena. While in the past the series focused on the British Empire and Commonwealth, in its current incarnation there is no imperial system, period of human history or part of the world which lies outside of its compass. While we particularly welcome the first monographs of young researchers, we also seek major studies by more senior scholars, and welcome collections of essays with a strong thematic focus. The series includes work on politics, economics, culture, literature, science, art, medicine, and war. Our aim is to collect the most exciting new scholarship on world history with an imperial theme.

More information about this series at
http://www.palgrave.com/gp/series/13937

Penelope Edmonds
Amanda Nettelbeck
Editors

Intimacies of Violence in the Settler Colony

Economies of Dispossession around the Pacific Rim

Editors
Penelope Edmonds
School of Humanities
University of Tasmania
Hobart, TAS, Australia

Amanda Nettelbeck
School of Humanities
University of Adelaide
Adelaide, SA, Australia

Cambridge Imperial and Post-Colonial Studies Series
ISBN 978-3-319-76230-2   ISBN 978-3-319-76231-9   (eBook)
https://doi.org/10.1007/978-3-319-76231-9

Library of Congress Control Number: 2018941557

© The Editor(s) (if applicable) and The Author(s) 2018
This work is subject to copyright. All rights are solely and exclusively licensed by the Publisher, whether the whole or part of the material is concerned, specifically the rights of translation, reprinting, reuse of illustrations, recitation, broadcasting, reproduction on microfilms or in any other physical way, and transmission or information storage and retrieval, electronic adaptation, computer software, or by similar or dissimilar methodology now known or hereafter developed.
The use of general descriptive names, registered names, trademarks, service marks, etc. in this publication does not imply, even in the absence of a specific statement, that such names are exempt from the relevant protective laws and regulations and therefore free for general use.
The publisher, the authors and the editors are safe to assume that the advice and information in this book are believed to be true and accurate at the date of publication. Neither the publisher nor the authors or the editors give a warranty, express or implied, with respect to the material contained herein or for any errors or omissions that may have been made. The publisher remains neutral with regard to jurisdictional claims in published maps and institutional affiliations.

Cover illustration: S.T. Gill, Stockman's Hut, 1856. © National Library of Australia

Printed on acid-free paper

This Palgrave Macmillan imprint is published by the registered company Springer International Publishing AG part of Springer Nature.
The registered company address is: Gewerbestrasse 11, 6330 Cham, Switzerland

Contents

1. Precarious Intimacies: Cross-Cultural Violence and Proximity in Settler Colonial Economies of the Pacific Rim   1
Penelope Edmonds and Amanda Nettelbeck

Part I   Moral Economies and Labour Relations in the Pastoral Sector   23

2. The Australian Agricultural Company, the Van Diemen's Land Company: Labour Relations with Aboriginal Landowners, 1824–1835   25
Lyndall Ryan

3. Ambiguity and Necessity: Settlers and Aborigines in Intimate Tension in Mid-Nineteenth-Century Australia   45
Angela Woollacott

4. Intimate Violence in the Pastoral Economy: Aboriginal Women's Labour and Protective Governance   67
Amanda Nettelbeck

5   The 'Proper Settler' and the 'Native Mind': Flogging
    Scandals in the Northern Territory, 1919 and 1932   89
    Ben Silverstein

Part II   Emotional Economies and Cultural Hybridities   113

6   Eliza Batman's House: Unhomely Frontiers and Intimate
    Overstraiters in Van Diemen's Land and Port Phillip   115
    Penelope Edmonds and Michelle Berry

7   Women's Work and Cross-Cultural Relationships on Two
    Female Frontiers: Eliza Fraser and Barbara Thompson
    in Colonial Queensland, 1836–1849   139
    Victoria K. Haskins

8   'Murder Will Out': Intimacy, Violence, and the Snow
    Family in Early Colonial New Zealand   159
    Kristyn Harman

9   'Tangled Up': Intimacy, Emotion, and Dispossession
    in Colonial New Zealand   179
    Angela Wanhalla and Lachy Paterson

Part III   Economies of Colonial Knowledge   201

10 Arctic Circles: Circuits of Sociability, Intimacy,
    and Imperial Knowledge in Britain and North America,
    1818–1828   203
    Annaliese Jacobs

11 Mrs Milson's Wordlist: Eliza Hamilton Dunlop
    and the Intimacy of Linguistic Work   225
    Anna Johnston

12 'A Frivolous Prosecution': Allegations of Physical
    and Sexual Abuse of Domestic Servants and the Defence
    of Colonial Patriarchy in Darwin and Singapore,
    1880s–1930s   249
    Claire Lowrie

Index   273

Notes on Contributors

Michelle Berry has a BAppSc (Heritage Conservation, University of Canberra) and a Grad. Dip. History (University of Melbourne). She is currently completing a Masters degree on Eliza Batman and colonial women and the law in History and Classics, Humanities School, University of Tasmania, Australia. She has a professional background in heritage and public history, and has worked in the museum sector for thirty years.

Penelope Edmonds is an Associate Professor of History, School of Humanities, University of Tasmania, Australia. Her research and teaching interests include colonial/postcolonial histories, humanitarianism and human rights, Australian and Pacific-region transnational histories, performance, visual culture, and museums. Her latest book, *Settler Colonialism and (Re)conciliation: Frontier Violence, Affective Performances, and Imaginative Refoundings* (2016), was shortlisted for the 2017 Ernest Scott Prize in Australian and colonial history.

Kristyn Harman is a historian in the School of Humanities, University of Tasmania, Australia. She specialises in cross-cultural encounters across Britain's nineteenth-century colonies, and twentieth-century Australasia. She is the author of *Cleansing the Colony: Transporting Convicts from New Zealand to Van Diemen's Land* (2017), and was the winner of the 2014 Australian Historical Association Kay Daniels award for her book *Aboriginal Convicts: Australian, Khoisan, and Māori Exiles.* Her work has been published in journals including *The Journal of Imperial and Commonwealth History, Journal of Colonialism and Colonial History, Aboriginal History, History Australia*, and the *Journal of New Zealand History*.

Victoria K. Haskins is a Professor of History at the University of Newcastle, Australia, and Director of the Purai Global Indigenous and Diaspora Research Studies Centre. She has published widely on Indigenous history, and is the co-author, with John Maynard, of *Living with the Locals: Early Europeans' Experience of Indigenous Life* (2016).

Annaliese Jacobs is a University Associate in History and Classics, Humanities School, at the University of Tasmania, Australia. Originally from Alaska (where she worked as a historian for the National Park Service from 2001 to 2006), she received her PhD from the University of Illinois at Urbana-Champaign in 2015. Her work examines the interactions between polar explorers' families, Indigenous intermediaries, and vernacular agents in the early-to-mid nineteenth century.

Anna Johnston is an Australian Research Council Future Fellow in the Institute for Advanced Studies in the Humanities and Associate Professor in English Literature, School of Communication and Arts at the University of Queensland, Australia.

Claire Lowrie is a Senior Lecturer in History at the University of Wollongong, Australia. She works on the history of labour and colonialism in Southeast Asia and northern Australia and specialises in the history of Asian and Indigenous domestic service. Her book *Masters and Servants: Cultures of Empire in the Tropics* was published in 2016. She has also published in *Modern Asian Studies*, *Pacific Historical Review*, the *Journal of Colonialism and Colonial History*, and *Gender and History*.

Amanda Nettelbeck is a Professor in the Department of History, University of Adelaide, Australia. Her research centres on the history and memory of frontier violence, colonial race relations, and the legal governance of Indigenous people. She is co-author or co-editor of several books, most recently *Fragile Settlements: Aboriginal Peoples, Law and Resistance in Southwest Australia and Prairie Canada* (co-authored with Russell Smandych, Louis Knafla, and Robert Foster, 2016) and *Violence, Empire and Colonialism in the Modern World* (co-edited with Philip Dwyer, 2017). A new book project titled Indigenous Rights and Colonial Subjecthood is contracted by Cambridge University Press.

Lachy Paterson is an Associate Professor in Te Tumu: School of Māori, Pacific and Indigenous Studies, University of Otago, Aotearoa, New Zealand, where he teaches te reo Māori (Māori language) and Māori history. He draws on reo-Māori texts, such as newspapers, to explore aspects of Māori social, cultural, and political history. He has published numerous articles and book chapters on Māori history and is the author of *Colonial Discourses: Niupepa Māori, 1855–1863* (2006), co-editor of *The Lives of Colonial Objects* (2015), and co-author, with Angela Wanhalla, of *He Reo Wāhine: Māori Women's Voices from the Nineteenth Century* (2017).

Lyndall Ryan is Conjoint Professor in the Centre for the History of Violence at the University of Newcastle, Australia. She has a long interest in the role played by the major agricultural companies in shaping labour relations on the Australian colonial frontier and is the author of two books on the history of the Tasmanian Aboriginal people and of the first digital map of Aboriginal massacre sites across Australia.

Ben Silverstein is a Postdoctoral Research Fellow in the School of History at the Australian National University, Australia. His book examining crisis and hegemony in the government of Aboriginal people in the interwar Northern Territory of Australia, *Governing Natives: Indirect Rule and Settler Colonialism in Australia's North*, is forthcoming in 2018 with Manchester University Press.

Angela Wanhalla is an Associate Professor in the Department of History and Art History, University of Otago, Aotearoa, New Zealand; co-director of the Centre for Research on Colonial Culture; and a Rutherford Discovery Fellow. She has published widely on New Zealand history, with a particular focus on gender and colonialism. Her recent publications include *Matters of the Heart: A History of Interracial Marriage in New Zealand* (2013) and *He Reo Wāhine: Māori Women's Voices from the Nineteenth Century* (2017), co-written with Lachy Paterson.

Angela Woollacott is the Manning Clark Professor of History at the Australian National University, Australia, and Immediate Past President of the Australian Historical Association. Her latest monograph, *Settler Society in the Australian Colonies: Self-Government and Imperial Culture* (2015), was shortlisted for the 2015 Queensland Literary Awards University of Southern Queensland History Prize. Her chapter 'Imperial Conquest, Violent Encounters and Changing Gender Relations in the Colonies: The Social Impact of Colonial Warfare, 1830s–1910s' is forthcoming in Karen Hagemann et al. (eds.), *Oxford Handbook on Gender, War and the Western World since 1650* (2017).

List of Figures

Fig. 3.1	S.T. Gill (1818–1880), *Captain Davison's house 'Blakiston' near Mount Barker*, 1848, Adelaide, watercolour on paper, 21.3 × 33.8 cm; South Australian Government Grant 1979, Art Gallery of South Australia, Adelaide	54
Fig. 3.2	Katherine Kirkland, 'Life in the Bush: By a Lady,' *Chambers's Miscellany of Useful and Entertaining Tracts* 1, no. 8 (Edinburgh: William and Robert Chambers, 1845), 1	57
Fig. 6.1	'Pellonymyna' (Pellenominer) as recorded in Walker's unpublished journal. George Washington Walker diaries, Flinders Island, 1832, Mitchell Library, SLNSW	130
Fig. 12.1	Burns Philp Steamship Line between Singapore and Darwin. *Picturesque Travel*, Burns Philp and Company, no. 6, 1925, National Library of Australia	253
Fig. 12.2	*Chinese Boy on Duty*, Lambert and Co, Singapore, c. 1900, Royal Netherlands Institute of Southeast Asian and Caribbean Studies	258
Fig. 12.3	Margaret Gilruth sitting on steps outside Government House with an unnamed Aboriginal maid servant and Billy Shepherd, Darwin, c. 1912–1918, Jean A. Austin Collection, Northern Territory Library	260

CHAPTER 1

Precarious Intimacies: Cross-Cultural Violence and Proximity in Settler Colonial Economies of the Pacific Rim

Penelope Edmonds and Amanda Nettelbeck

Precarious Intimacies in Colonial Economies

Violence and interracial intimacy were intertwined at all levels of the settler colonial encounter and, in equal measures, were fundamental to the shaping of modern settler states. The development of settler colonial cultures was deeply dependent upon the everyday proximity of Indigenous and settler workers, and yet we know surprisingly little of how the intimacies arising from that proximity were intrinsically connected to forms of colonial violence. Inspired by new insights derived from feminist and postcolonial perspectives, this collection sets out to interrogate the nexus between violence and intimacy and to explore their intermixed place in the formation of settler colonial societies around the Pacific Rim. In particular, it charts the precarious intimacies of cross-cultural violence in various

---

P. Edmonds (✉)
History and Classics, University of Tasmania, Hobart, TAS, Australia

A. Nettelbeck
University of Adelaide, Adelaide, SA, Australia

© The Author(s) 2018
P. Edmonds, A. Nettelbeck (eds.), *Intimacies of Violence in the Settler Colony*, Cambridge Imperial and Post-Colonial Studies Series, https://doi.org/10.1007/978-3-319-76231-9_1

Pacific Rim settler economies, and the ways that they both enabled multiple forms of Indigenous dispossession and gave rise to new and complex social relations.

In so doing, the collection aims to move beyond familiar understandings both of 'intimacy' as primarily domestic or sexual relations and of 'colonial economies' as primarily the domain of labour relations. The notion of intimate empires has been highly influential in reorienting studies of colonial contact, as has scholarship re-evaluating the kinds of intercultural negotiations and accommodations that took place in settler colonial settings.[1] Historian Ann Laura Stoler's incisive observation that intimate and often violent bonds could be by turns ambivalent 'tense and tender ties', and that these ties figured influentially 'in the making of racial categories and in the management of imperial rule', is a signal cue for this volume.[2] Work such as Stoler's has revealed the key role of the 'domains of the intimate' in the consolidation of colonial power. As she asserts, the intimate domain reveals how 'the categories of difference underlying colonialism—the distinctions advanced as the justification for the colonizer's rule of the colonized—were enacted and reinforced in intimate realms from the bedroom to the classroom'.[3]

Such scholarship has extended analyses of colonial contact and relationships to show how colonial governance and power were strongly inflected by affect and personal connections as well as moulded by policy. It has highlighted the inadequacy of any neat division between public and private realms in explaining the imperial state and its interest in regulating all spheres of life. In particular, scholarship on the intimate empire has been highly influential in re-examining colonial cross-cultural relationships in terms of gender, domesticity, and mixed relationships.[4] Yet it also points towards the many ways in which colonial intimacies and cross-cultural proximities developed and evolved through unequal distributions of power far beyond the domains of colonial domestic and sexual life. As scholars have also argued, intimate connections in colonial settings must be understood as being embedded across the wider social and political structures of colonial life.[5] They were also central to the performances of friendship and diplomacy—failed, true, or feigned—that over the course of centuries provided a starting point for the colonial endeavour itself.[6] The sites of intimacy and violence considered in this volume are as diverse as cross-cultural maritime communities, the pastoral station, the mission, Indigenous cultural spaces, networks of exploration, and the frontier colonial home.

In a similar way, this volume takes an expansive approach to the intimate forms of violence that were embedded in economies of the settler colony. As elaborated in the key work of settler colonial scholars, the distinctive place of settler colonialism within broader histories of colonialism is shaped by the fact that settlers came to stay as founders of a transplanted political and cultural order who 'carr[ied] their sovereignty with them'.[7] Settler colonialism thereby became a transnational phenomenon that took on global scale through its assumed possession of diverse colonial territories.[8] While other, exploitative forms of colonialism extracted economic wealth from colonial territories in fixed forms such as mining and labour, settler colonialism extended the jurisdiction of empire outwards through the coterminous processes of permanent settlement and Indigenous replacement and dispossession.

In this respect, Patrick Wolfe has famously argued, settler colonialism has a more enduring and eliminative logic than other forms of colonialism: it was, and remains, a 'structure' rather than an 'event', for it entails the ongoing alienation of Indigenous peoples from their land, their polities, and their cultures.[9] Rather than experiencing the dramatic rupture of decolonization and the move to a postcolonial state that are characteristic of many colonies, settler colonies and their structures of power and dispossession endure today, and are thus marked by their historical continuity. Not only do settlers never go home, but the settler colony is notorious for its 'ever vanishing endpoint', as Elizabeth Strakosch and Alissa Macoun write provocatively.[10]

Despite such thoroughgoing vectors of dispossession, Indigenous labour was required and was often crucial to the formation of settler colonies and their economic viability. Although for Wolfe the requirement for 'native labour' would always be 'subordinate to territorial acquisition', he registered the exploitative, gendered, and sexualised nature of colonial conquest and importantly its biopolitical exigencies in nominally 'white' settler colonies', arguing that 'settler colonization relied on Indigenous labor at every stage and in every site of its development'.[11] This collection shows the variegated and strategic importance of Indigenous workers and their agency within the settler colonies in question, through the lens of an always-precarious intimacy that arose from both proximity and gendered relations.

Yet it is also clear that examinations of intimate violence in the settler colony need to account for a wider range of colonial economies of dispossession beyond the economic dynamics of formal labour relations. In addition to colonised people's labour, the settler colonial world was shaped by the powerful discursive effects of ideological and moral economies that helped structure the nature of colonial relationships. The British historian E.P. Thompson has familiarised the workings of a moral economy through his analysis of group rights that played out in tension with economic forces.[12] This understanding, however, has been revisited in recent scholarship to revive a wider conceptual history of moral economy as the ideological forces that underpinned civil society, including economic forces.[13] In the nineteenth-century settler colonial world, for instance, a vigorous moral economy circulated through humanitarian calls for the 'protection' of Indigenous peoples in ways that sought to mitigate the impacts of the empire but not necessarily threaten its economic development. As work in this volume shows, a counter-moral economy also worked to establish the boundaries of acceptable violence.

Alongside new analyses of the moral economies of colonialism, scholars have also turned to closer exploration of how an economy of colonial knowledge circulated around the British Empire, and have come to understand the exchange of colonial knowledge as another form of imperial and cross-cultural intimacy, well beyond sexuality and family formation.[14] Along with people, goods, and new technologies of the industrial era, new economies of colonial knowledge burgeoned around the nineteenth-century Anglophone settler world, influenced by wider colonial market forces and political ideas, absorbing or reinscribing Indigenous knowledge systems and in other ways taking inspiration from them. Likewise, new kinds of domestic economy formed a backbone to colonial political and economic systems, and were infused with emotional economies that traversed these histories. In these ways, the dynamics of broader kinds of colonial economies filtered through all economic settings where labour was required. The range of contexts for cross-cultural exchange considered here, then, include not only those that involved paid, unpaid, or indentured labour, but also the exchange of material culture, language, emotional life, and colonial knowledge in which the working currencies were rather different and sometimes far less tangible than money.

As we know, the mass movement of people worldwide generated by settler colonialism gave rise to new, plural modernities.[15] These modernities were frequently defined by exploitative regimes based on the usurping of Indigenous people's lands, resources, and labour, and resulting in the displacement of their diverse nations and cultures. From the late eighteenth century, Anglophone settlers of the Pacific Rim—including British colonies but also the newly acquired territories of the Pacific coast, to the south and north of North Amercia—secured control over large tracts of Indigenous land, harnessed Indigenous resources, and sometimes articulated entire Indigenous economies for their own use in ways that gave rise to new global commodity markets and economies. In this 'second empire', new Pacific Rim colonial cultures were established, built out of the foundations of earlier colonial ventures and existing cross-cultural networks of labour and trade.[16] Purportedly free of imperial restrictions, they were distinctively marked by mobility, racial intermarriage, and intercultural exchange.[17] They were also marked by coercion, exploitation, and the repression of Indigenous political and legal autonomy. In this respect, settler colonial modernity was grounded both in the violence of dispossession and subjugation, and in the movement and resignification of Indigenous cultures and bodies in new, mixed, and fragile colonial polities. Such relations were shaped by what Damon Salesa terms 'strategic intimacies': that is, the importance of managing intimacy in colonial spaces in ways that could yield strategic benefit.[18]

Through the second half of the nineteenth century and into the twentieth century, the global world of empire changed again as settler societies moved to forms of self-government and eventually to nation-state status.[19] Key to such developments were questions around the position, role, and treatment of Indigenous peoples in their relationship both to non-Indigenous colonial society and to the apparatuses of state government. These developments gave rise to new, mixed polities that were increasingly regulated through powerful discourses of race, which by the latter part of the nineteenth century became thoroughgoing in their promulgation of ideas of white superiority and of the colonial desire for the realisation of 'white men's lands'.[20] Colonial violence was deployed at all stages of evolution in settler states of the Pacific Rim, hand in hand with the forces of intercultural proximity. The effects and legacies of intimate exchange and proximate violence structured the character of labour relations, influenced the nature of gendered relationships and cross-cultural domestic lives, and stretched across families, generations, and cultures.[21] The effects of violence were always in part destructive; yet they were also productive of new situations, subjectivities, and revolutionary or resistive actions.[22]

Colonial Exchange and Proximate Violence

Scholars now generally agree that diverse processes of violence—from cultural repression to labour coercion to sexual exploitation—were fundamental to the creation of empires and to their economic and political development.[23] Even so, more work remains to be done to assess the myriad ways in which the economic and political capacities of empires were dependent upon appropriating new lands, resources, and supplies of labour.[24] This project has become more complicated in the early twenty-first century with a return by some political conservatives to progressivist histories of empire. Renewed arguments in favour of the political and cultural achievements of imperialism indicate something of a backlash against the late twentieth-century rise of critical histories of empire, and point to some of the obstacles historians still face in unpacking the complex ways that violence insinuated itself as an inherent part of the colonial project. The popular appeal of such progressivist histories has helped revive notions that the forms of cultural and coercive violence on which colonial expansion relied were overall more positive than negative in their effects. Similarly, in contemporary settler nations, renewed political appeals to unifying accounts of national history have produced denials or rationalisations of colonial violence as an unavoidable part of the civilising dimensions of modernity.[25]

In the last two decades, however, critical scholarship on settler colonialism has been vitally important in changing the ways that Western democracies with often dark colonial heritages now regard and remember themselves in a globalised political climate, especially in the 'age of apology', redress, and reconciliation.[26] Some of this scholarship has focused on 'big picture' political evolutions of Anglophone colonialism, whether forged through martial violence from below or directed by imperial policy from above.[27] Yet, in the last three decades, Indigenous, feminist, and new imperial and counter-colonial scholars have produced more detailed analyses of colonial relations in efforts to move beyond accounts of empire primarily as large-scale political or military systems driven by global economic and technological forces. While the evolution of empires undoubtedly occurred through the momentum of such large-scale forces, they were also messy and incoherent entities, influenced by the shifting political and economic priorities that unfolded at colonial peripheries.[28] By examining at closer range the interactions between global imperial forces and localised colonial pressures, recent scholarship has enabled new interpretations of how intimate and everyday encounters were implicated with different forms of colonial violence. At the same time, such scholarship has shown how these quotidian encounters, with their roots in both intimacy and violence, set the stage for the development of global imperial networks.[29] This kind of scholarship has sought to think transnationally but also 'with and through the nation', in line with Antoinette Burton's injunction to understand the ways globalised imperial pasts are carried forward into equally problematic and structurally exploitative postcolonial nations.[30]

Just as colonial and imperial scholars have been concerned to complicate the relationship between local and global, between intimacy and violence as commingled forces in the making of colonial systems, recent scholarship has radically reassessed the notion of the colonial 'frontier' to expand its meaning from either a delimited moment in time or a spatial borderland between strangers. As Deborah Bird Rose and Richard Davis argue, the culturally interdependent space of the colonial frontier demands more recognition than as the site of colonial capitalism and Indigenous dispossession, although it is also those things. Additionally, they point out, the frontier requires reimagining as a more complicated reflection of the extended histories of Indigenous and settler encounter, a site of violence and nation-building but also one of productive, sometimes unexpected, forms of 'cultural action'.[31]

Mirroring Patrick Wolfe's well-known construction of settler colonialism as a structure rather than an event, however, they stress that the intertwined, often fraught histories of the colonial frontier do not simply come to an end with the apparent end of colonialism itself.[32] As Bird has persuasively argued elsewhere, the frontier has traditionally been seen as 'a time and place' where modern culture creates itself in a sequential way, 'an historical moment of encounter that will be overcome by civilisation'. Yet such a view obscures 'the coevalness of the frontier, the formative interactions of destruction and creation'. Instead, she posits a view of the frontier as a space of 'tension-laden and interactive' colonial relationships, one that continues to offer a 'key site for reflexive critique of contemporary society'.[33] Other scholars share in this interrogation of the political amnesia wrought by a backward-looking construction of the colonial frontier and its pivotal role in the settler colonial project. Legal scholars, for instance, have shown how a historical conception of the frontier can imprint an artificial line between colonial violence and its legal control. According to this perception, the extra-legal violence that marked colonial frontier cultures might appear resolved by the consolidation of colonial legal institutions, which simultaneously absorbed Indigenous laws into a more legally uniform settler colonial world.[34] Yet, as we know, colonial violence was not limited to the space of the frontier, and neither did its structural forms come to an end with the waning of a frontier culture.

In this collection, we deploy this extended understanding of the 'frontier' as a contested concept and as a starting point at which to engage the interactions of intimacy and violence in dynamic colonial settings. We are mindful here that the shadow of the colonial frontier forms an integral part of settler colonial dynamics that are constantly being renegotiated today. In this volume, for instance, Ben Silverstein cautions against naming the frontier in a way that distances its historical violence from settler societies of the present. Following Deborah Bird Rose, he observes that partitioning the concept of the frontier from colonialism's ongoing legacies reproduces a logic in which conflict appears to be resolved by the emergence of the nation and by the removal of legible Aboriginal political life. Drawing upon the idea of the frontier as a structuring feature of nationhood, Silverstein asks how we can frame the 'recurring and enduring distributions of force that are transformed but not concluded by assertions of sovereign completion'.

In Patrick Wolfe's words, a historical tendency to relegate colonial violence 'behind the screen of the frontier' locates it as the subject of regretful disavowal.[35] A historical construction of frontier is therefore purposeful; its naming permits an asymmetrical violence that inscribes a settler colonial teleology on bodies and on land, but it can also circumscribe the boundaries of that violence.[36] Rather than localising violence in this way, we might re-imagine it as part of an everyday continuum that reached from acts of physical punishment or terror to something more prosaic. After all, colonial violence was embedded in everyday bureaucratic, social, and discursive domains; it was mobilised through a diverse, often normalised, means of coercion and control; and it was enacted across an array of settings that included colonial workplaces, domestic arrangements, legal cultures, and governmental policies.[37] As scholars have also pointed out, colonial violence was not only confined to large-scale racial contestation and military campaigns. It was equally gendered, intimate, and all too often enacted between those well known to each other.[38]

Settler, Indigenous, and Gendered Economies

The complex nature of intimate violence around the developing settler colonial world of the Pacific Rim cannot be considered without reference to the critical role of Indigenous peoples in shaping the nature of colonial economies. It is indisputable that colonialism flourished on the back of slave, indentured, and myriad other forms of unfree or coerced labour. Yet it is only two decades since Ann Curthoys and Clive Moore pointed to the earlier failure of labour historians to acknowledge the long history of Indigenous labour in Australia's colonial economic enterprise, noting that 'too often the very existence of a history of Aboriginal labour is quite unknown', at least to non-Aboriginal peoples.[39] Since then, a plethora of scholarship has examined the long and entangled history of cross-cultural and settler colonial labour relations, stretching beyond Aboriginal–settler relations to Pacific and Asian peoples in colonial economies around the Pacific rim.[40] Nonetheless, it is important to ask, as Tracey Banivanua Mar does in her book *Violence and Colonial Dialogue*, what forms of Indigenous agency might be recovered from the multiple systems of violence that were central to the experience of colonised labour forces and that were embedded in the very structures of a colonial state.[41] In the Australian pastoral sector, for instance, Indigenous people's labour provided the foundations for the production of immense colonial wealth. But while their labour was in many ways exploited and unrewarded, Indigenous people themselves had significant leverage in crafting the colonial relationship. Scholars have variously sought to trace how Indigenous people incorporated the systems and resources of pastoralism into their world. Indeed, in some important ways, their embedded place in that sector provided them with some capacity to determine terms in the colonial exchange and a means to remain attached to their own country.[42] As Tim Rowse has argued, while the pastoral world was threaded through with violent histories of dispossession and asymmetrical power, it was a world in which Indigenous knowledge and agency still carried significant weight, requiring pastoralists to make concessions to keep their work forces.[43]

The importance of Indigenous labour for the pastoral economy made the pastoral enterprise itself a potential space for colonial diplomacy and conciliation, as Lyndall Ryan explores in this collection. Comparing the approaches of the Australian Agricultural Company and the Van Diemen's Land Company, she charts two different paths in how private pastoral companies perceived the employment of Indigenous people as a desirable strategy (or not) in the development of the pastoral frontier. For the colonial humanitarians who were stakeholders in the Australian Agricultural Company, Indigenous employment was not only a convenient path to profit but also a means to further the agendas of conciliation and eventual 'civilisation'. In contrast, the Van Diemen's Land Company investors, less influenced by humanitarian discourse, avoided the potential advantages of Indigenous employment and instead actively supported the program of dispossession. In such early pastoral settings, Ryan shows, the turn to conciliation or to fear and violence sat precariously side by side.

Similarly, Angela Woollacott's chapter on the moral economy of settler pastoralism reveals just how much intimacy and violence remained in tension as equal possibilities in the early colonial relationship. Even as settlers lived in intimate proximity with Indigenous people and were dependent upon their labour, she argues, they nurtured a moral economy that justified racialised violence as a legitimate necessity and as part of their wider defence of imperial values. This was a moral code gendered as masculine and, as Ben Silverstein shows here, it endured well into the twentieth century. On the one hand, it supported the view that settler men should practice restraint as a sign of their racial superiority; on the other, it determined when and how they could practice necessary violence. In contrast to moral legitimisations for settler practices of colonial violence, Anna Johnston's chapter on practices of linguistic collection draws out both a knowledge economy and, importantly, a counteractive moral economy that was just as powerful in its implication for imagining the nature of colonial race relations. This was a moral economy grounded in the circulation of humanitarian energy, driven by an agenda to offset the impacts of colonial violence through the affective identification with Indigenous people. Such sympathetic practices were inescapably wound through with the discourses of colonialism they challenged, as Johnston notes, and they were distinctively gendered.

As many of the chapters in this collection also explore, the moral economies of colonialism were otherwise gendered in complex ways that crossed and complicated the racial divide. In her chapter on Indigenous women's labour in the pastoral sector, Amanda Nettelbeck considers the vulnerability of Indigenous women who worked in colonial industries and the uncertain place they occupied at the intersection of raced and gendered forms of labour relations. She demonstrates that even in a late colonial age when legally empowered policies of protection were becoming normative across Australia's colonies, an Indigenous woman's rights from sexual exploitation were constrained by a culture of economic paternalism which positioned her as a contracted servant to a settler master or as a husband's wife. As an institution that was embedded in and modified to serve colonial culture, the law helped to circumscribe the scope and rights of Indigenous servants in general and Indigenous women in particular.

Indigenous peoples were widely employed across colonial economies and were vital to how future colonial ventures developed.[44] For instance, in Australia's tropical north, where some 62,000 Pacific Islander labourers were imported between 1863 and 1904 to work in Queensland sugarcane plantations, the pastoral sector and colonial households, the mixed world of Aboriginal, Pacific Islander, Japanese, other Asian workers, and Europeans confounded all governmental attempts to create a white polity.[45] Again, this racially mixed world created particularly gendered forms of colonialism. In her chapter on the moral codes surrounding male domestic servants, Claire Lowrie shifts the focus from discussions about colonial servitude and violence against Indigenous women to re-centre on two colonial settings where race dynamics were shaped by the rather different logics of settler colonialism (Darwin) and exploitative colonialism (Singapore). Here Lowrie considers how moral codes about acceptable colonial violence worked to protect the reputation of ruling-class men and the wider logic of colonial patriarchy, but in rather different ways. In the settler-colonial context of Darwin, race emerged as the most important determinant of coloniser status; in contrast, in Singapore the economic imperatives of class, and associated values of masculine worth, worked to protect English and Chinese masters equally as 'good' colonial masters.

Of course, colonial economies did not only emerge from European enterprises but grew on the back of pre-existing Indigenous economies and trade networks, such as the trepang fisheries that generated cross-Pacific exchange between Indigenous Australians and Macassans well before the arrival of European colonisers.[46] In New Zealand, where practices of cross-cultural exchange and trade were well established long before the arrival of colonial government and its infrastructure, Māori actively absorbed European entrepreneurs and other colonial incomers into their economic life, prompting the early flourishing of culturally hybrid colonial economies. Alan Ward notes that a full generation before New Zealand became a British Crown Colony, Māori were providing a place for migratory Europeans in their communities 'as sources of trade, as armourers and ironworkers, as advisers in the cultivation of crops, as symbols of prestige and, in the 1830s, as teachers of reading and writing'. As they did this, new cross-cultural enterprises took root.[47] In her exploration in this collection on the Snow family murder case in early colonial New Zealand, Kristyn Harman draws out some of the tensions that arose from this economic empowerment of Māori, in a way that unsettled the normative alignments of race and class. As Harman shows, the case of the violent European Joseph Burns brought to life deep-seated fears of cultural 'backsliding' in the mixed and tense colonial port city of Auckland. A working-class white man who was employed as a labourer by the high-ranking Māori leader and government intermediary Patuone, Burns committed a murderous act and attempted to shift blame to the Māori neighbours on whose charity he largely relied. In this close cross-cultural environment, where the lines between class, labour relations, and power were not racialised in one direction, Indigenous authority and the racialised status of the white working poor were complex, potentially fraught matters.

Likewise, in her chapter on Indigenous women's 'adoption' of rescued white women, Victoria Haskins turns the tables on the colonial economy to explore the place of white settler women inside domestic and labour relations of Indigenous society. Recasting the orthodox colonial 'captivity narratives' of Eliza Frazer and Barbara Thompson, Haskins begs a different set of questions about the social, economic, and emotional economy between Indigenous women and the white women who were compelled to negotiate a place there. While Frazer clung to her own fears and belief in racial superiority, Thompson's easier experience reveals the possibilities for coexistence and mutually sustaining relations between women, through shared labour and contribution to the collective. Indigenous people, it is clear, were central to just about every kind of colonial encounter, and yet, as we know, their rich contributions to the production of an interactive colonial culture has historically been significantly overlooked. In seeking to explain this, Jane Carey and Jane Lydon make note in their work *Indigenous Networks* of a historical tendency to regard Indigenous people as being bound to local place and static time, in comparison to a tendency to see colonial cultures as globally mobile and actively transformative. The rejection of this outdated orthodoxy, they note, requires greater attention to the ways in which Indigenous peoples actively engaged with the global networks that constituted the transnational colonial world.[48]

Indeed, Indigenous people not only contributed to the making of new commercial economies in the Pacific Rim colonial world but were also essential to its mobile economies of colonial knowledge and the affective lives of its cross-cultural societies. With reference to Samoa, Damon Salesa discusses how this process occurred in the space of colonial and Indigenous interaction, within what Ann Laura Stoler has famously termed the 'domain of the intimate'.[49] Similarly, many of the chapters in this volume draw out ways in which Indigenous work sat at the very centre of exchange in colonial knowledge and emotion economies, and how intimacy and violence were wound together at their heart. For instance, Annaliese Jacobs's chapter on circuits of sociability across the colonial Pacific Rim draws out the particular kind of classed mobility that underpinned practices of scientific exploration and imperial adventuring, and the forms of social and economic patronage that enabled them to function. Through those practices, a transatlantic economy of colonial knowledge was accrued and disseminated through Indigenous objects and associated knowledges that were commodified and understood by those at 'home' through imperial discourses of exploration, science, and ethnography. Through this transfer of colonial 'trophies' from explorer men to European women at 'home', Indigenous women and European women came implicitly together, connected by the objects they either produced or interpreted. In this way, Jacobs argues, Indigenous women to some degree controlled the kinds of souvenirs and specimens that would travel back to England, while white women established themselves at the heart of a new traffic in colonial knowledge.

As this indicates and as a number of chapters in this volume explore, the domestic household sat front and centre of colonial relations as a space where different forms of intimacy and violence were negotiated. In their chapter on the administrative and affective life of George Thomas Wilkinson, civil servant in the Land Purchase Branch of the New Zealand Native Department, Lachy Paterson and Angela Wanhalla explore how the protocols of Māori sentiment structured Wilkinson's cross-cultural household, at the same time as his work served to alienate Māori from their proprietary rights to their lands. In this way, they argue, within the space of Wilkinson's own colonial household, his bureaucratic attention to the 'minutiae of dispossession' was bound together with matters of the heart and obligations of kinship with Māori women.

Such dynamics of the colonial household remind us, as Victoria Haskins and Claire Lowrie have observed, that in the nexus between domesticity, labour, and colonisation we see 'the construction and maintenance of the power relations that underpinned colonial rule'.[50] Likewise, Antoinette Burton has observed that the colonial household opens onto a space where 'contests over colonial dominion can be discerned and historicised'.[51] Penelope Edmonds and Michelle Berry's chapter on the cross-cultural pastoral household of Eliza and John Batman explores the uncertain domestic borderlands of both extreme violence and sometimes-forced intimacy, where decidedly 'unhomely' relationships were forged. As such, the Batman pastoral enterprise reveals how the theft, removal, or 'adoption' of dispossessed Aboriginal children into European homes as labourers and servants added to the destruction of Aboriginal families and contributed to a wider culture of frontier aggression. In a process that Edmonds and Berry term 'affective redescriptions', they show how gendered and intimate affective economies served to recast acts of aggression as acts of kindness and the dispersal of Aboriginal families as care. Crossing the lines between intimacy, appropriation, and possession, such actions position the domestic colonial space as the extension of a zone of frontier violence.

The central place of the colonial household in the production of colonial economies and societies invokes the complex role of gender in the making of colonial relations. James Belich's much-cited 'settler revolution' focuses primarily on the economic and political vectors of imperial expansion, leaving in the shadows the crucial forces of gender, reproduction, and biopolitics that were centrally constitutive of settler colonialism. In contrast, feminist scholars have pointed out how the settler 'revolution' in new colonies was dependent on Indigenous and white women's bodies, with a particular focus on white women's reproductive capacities.[52] As Adele Perry has argued, when we pay attention to the forces of immigration and land acquisition as the foundational forces of new settler societies, we must acknowledge that 'gender is where the abiding bonds between dispossession and colonisation become most clear'.[53] Jane Carey also makes this point concisely: if the history of settler colonialism was 'driven by the "logic of elimination" in relation to Indigenous populations, then the imperative of vigorous white propagation was its necessary corollary'.[54]

Conclusion: Intimacy and Violence Across the Pacific Rim

The essays collected here ask what kinds of relationships were possible between mistresses and servants, labourers and supervisors, colonial ethnographers and their native informants, between colonial judiciaries, settler landholders, explorers and Indigenous competitors. In turn, they query how Indigenous peoples resisted or utilised the colonial relationships that were shaped by these new settler economies. In exploring these questions, this work aims to extend an analysis of intimacy and violence as foundational aspects of colonial economies beyond delimited national frameworks or discrete historical moments. The volume's scope is transnational and longitudinal. Stretching from the early nineteenth century to the mid-twentieth century, its frontiers of encounter and exchange move from Australia's southern and tropical northern colonies to Aotearoa New Zealand, and from the shores of the Canadian Arctic to the mixed Asia-Pacific cities of Darwin and Singapore.

Alongside these localised settings, transcolonial connections appear in the mobility of colonial work forces and the ideological constructions of race and empire across the Pacific Rim. The British Empire itself, as historians have often pointed out, constituted a loosely constructed and ever-changing 'web'.[55] It generated multiple colonial economies that often overlapped with each other, and in which fragile forms of intimacy were by necessity imbricated in the evolutions of economic and political power. In examining the nature of these evolutions within the economies of settler colonialism, this collection sets out to draw out connections between the excesses of violence and the agendas of protectionism and humanitarianism; it seeks the agency of Indigenous peoples in the development of moral, domestic, and economic relations; it attempts to untangle the sexual, gendered, and racialised politics of economic exchange. Integral to an exploration of these contexts, it follows the curious mobility of texts, objects, and frameworks of knowledge, aiming to tease out the diversity of ways in which violence and intimacy, brutality and proximity, were expressed in everyday encounters on the ground. Its overarching goal is to broaden the horizon of debate about the nature of colonial economies and the intercultural encounters that were enmeshed within them. By drawing out the connections between the broad-scale dynamics of colonial rule and the violent and intimate domains of its implementation on the ground, we might better understand the legacies of settler colonialism that remain structurally embedded within contemporary democracies of the Pacific Rim.

Notes

1. For instance, Antoinette Burton and Tony Ballantyne, *Bodies in Contact: Rethinking Colonial Encounters in World History* (Durham and London: Duke University Press, 2005); Ann Laura Stoler, ed. *Haunted by Empire: Geographies of Intimacy in North American History* (Durham and London: Duke University Press, 2006).
2. Ann Laura Stoler, 'Tense and Tender Ties: The Politics of Comparison in North American History and (Post) Colonial Studies', *Journal of American History* 88, no. 3 (2001), 829.
3. Ann Laura Stoler, ed. *Haunted by Empire: Geographies of Intimacy in North American History* (Durham and London: Duke University Press).
4. For instance, Lyndall Ryan, 'The Struggle for Recognition: Part-Aborigines in Tasmania in the Nineteenth Century', *Aboriginal History* 1, no. 1 (1977), 27–52; Sylvia Van Kirk, *Many Tender Ties: Women in Fur Trade Society in Western Canada 1670–1870* (Norman: University of Oklahoma Press, 1983); Antoinette Burton, ed. *Gender, Sexuality, and Colonial Modernities* (London and New York: Routledge, 1999); Adele Perry, *On the Edge of Empire: Gender, Race, and the Making of British Columbia, 1849–1871* (Toronto: University of Toronto Press, 2001); Katherine Ellinghaus, *Taking Assimilation to Heart: Marriages of White Women and Indigenous Men in the United States and Australia, 1887–1937* (Lincoln and London, University of Nebraska Press, 2006); Ann Curthoys and Marilyn Lake, *Connected Worlds: History in Transnational Perspective* (Canberra: ANU E Press, 2006); Penelope Edmonds, *Urbanizing Frontiers: Indigenous Peoples and Settlers in 19th-Century Pacific Rim Cities* (Vancouver: University of British Columbia Press, 2010); Victoria Haskins, *Matrons and Maids: Regulating Indian Domestic Service in Tucson, 1914–1934* (Tucson: University of Arizona Press, 2012); Angela Wanhalla, *Matters of the Heart: A History of Interracial Marriage in New Zealand* (Auckland: Auckland University Press, 2013); Angela Wanhalla, *In/visible Sight: The Mixed Descent Families of Southern New Zealand* (Wellington: Bridget Williams Books, 2013); Durba Ghosh, *Sex and the Family in Colonial India: The Making of Empire* (Cambridge: Cambridge University Press, 2008); Sarah Carter, *The Importance of Being Monogamous: Marriage and Nation Building in Western Canada to 1915* (Edmonton: University of Alberta Press, 2008); Adele Perry, *Colonial Relations: The Douglas-Connolly Family and the Nineteenth-Century Imperial World* (Cambridge: Cambridge University Press, 2015); Ann McGrath, *Illicit Love: Interracial Sex and Marriage in the United States and Australia* (Lincoln: University of Nebraska Press, 2015).
5. For instance, Tony Ballantyne and Antoinette Burton, eds. *Moving Subjects: Gender, Mobility, and Intimacy in an Age of Global Empire* (Urbana and Chicago: University of Chicago Press, 2009).

6. For instance, Patricia Seed, *Ceremonies of Possession in Europe's Conquest of the New World* (Cambridge: Cambridge University Press, 1995); Leela Gandhi, *Affective Communities: Anticolonial Thought, Fin-de-Siecle Radicalism, and the Politics of Friendship* (Durham, NC: Duke University Press, 2006); Vanessa Smith, *Intimate Strangers: Friendship, Exchange and Pacific Encounters* (Cambridge: Cambridge University Press, 2010).
7. Lorenzo Veracini, *Settler Colonialism: A Theoretical Overview* (London: Palgrave Macmillan, 2010), 3; Patrick Wolfe, *Settler Colonialism and the Transformation of Anthropology* (London: Cassell, 1999), 1–3 and 'Settler Colonialism and the Elimination of the Native', *Journal of Genocide Research* 8, no. 4 (2006), 387.
8. Veracini, 'Settler Colonialism', 2.
9. Wolfe, *Settler Colonialism and the Transformation of Anthropology*, 2.
10. Elizabeth Strakosch and Alissa Macoun, 'The Vanishing End Point of Settler Colonialism', *Arena Journal* 37/38 (2012), 40–62.
11. Wolfe, *Settler Colonialism and the Transformation of Anthropology*, 29.
12. E.P. Thompson, 'The Moral Economy of the English Crowd in the Eighteenth Century', *Past and Present* 50 (February 1971), 76–136.
13. Norbert Götz, '"Moral Economy": Its Conceptual History and Analytical Prospects', *Journal of Global Ethics* 11, no. 2 (2015), 147–162.
14. Richard Drayton, 'Knowledge and Empire', in *The Oxford History of the British Empire: Vol II: The Eighteenth Century*, ed. P. Marshall (Oxford: Oxford University Press, 2001). See also Jane Kenway, Elizabeth Bullen, Johannah Fahey with Simon Robb, *Haunting the Knowledge Economy* (Abingdon: Routledge, 2006); Anna Johnston, *The Paper War: Morality, Print Culture, and Power in Colonial New South Wales* (Perth: UWA Press, 2011); Tony Ballantyne, 'Strategic Intimacies: Knowledge and Colonization in Southern New Zealand', *Journal of New Zealand Studies* 14 (2013), 4–18.
15. Paul Gillen and Devleena Ghosh, *Colonialism and Modernity* (Sydney: UNSW Press, 2007). On alternative or peripheral modes of modernity built from imperial foundations, see also Paul Gilroy, *The Black Atlantic: Modernity and Double-Consciousness* (Harvard: Harvard University Press, 1995); Luke Gibbons, 'Peripheral Modernities: National and Global in a Post-Colonial Frame', *19th-Century Contexts* 29, no. 2/3 (2007), 271–281.
16. Matt Matsuda, *Pacific Worlds: A History of Seas, Peoples, and Cultures* (Cambridge: Cambridge University Press, 2012); David Armitage and Alison Bashford, eds. *Pacific Histories: Ocean, Land, People* (Basingstoke: Palgrave, 2014).
17. Perry, *Edge of Empire*; Edmonds, *Urbanizing Frontiers*; Damon Salesa, *Racial Crossings: Race, Intermarriage and the Victorian British Empire* (Oxford: Oxford University Press, 2011); Anna Johnston, '"Greater

Britain": Late Imperial Travel Writing and the Settler Colonies', in *Where All Things Are Possible: Oceania, the East and the Victorian Imagination*, ed. Richard Fulton and Peter H. Hoffenberg (Farnham, UK: Ashgate, 2013), 31–43.
18. Damon Salesa, 'Samoa's Half-Castes and Some Frontiers of Comparison', in *Haunted by Empire: Geographies of Intimacy in North American History*, ed. Ann Laura Stoler (Durham: Duke University Press, 2006), 72.
19. For instance, Peter Burroughs, 'Colonial Self-Government', in *British Imperialism in the Nineteenth Century*, ed. C.C. Eldridge (London: Macmillan Education, 1984), 39–64; Ann Curthoys and Jessie Mitchell, 'The Advent of Self-government, 1840s–90', in *The Cambridge History of Australia*, vol. 1, ed. Alison Bashford and Stuart Macintyre (Melbourne: Cambridge University Press, 2013), 149–169.
20. Marilyn Lake and Henry Reynolds, *Drawing the Global Colour Line: White Men's Countries and the Question of Racial Equality* (Melbourne: Melbourne University Press, 2008); Katherine Ellinghaus, *Re-orienting Whiteness: Transnational Perspectives on the History of an Identity* (Basingstoke: Palgrave UK, 2009); Patrick Wolfe, *Traces of History: Elementary Structures of Race* (London: Verso, 2016).
21. Tracey Banivanua Mar, *Violence and Colonial Dialogue: The Australia-Pacific Labor Trade* (Honolulu: University of Hawai'i Press, 2007).
22. Frederick Cooper and Ann Laura Stoler, *Tensions of Empire Colonial Cultures in a Bourgeois World* (University of California Press, 1997).
23. For instance, J.R. Ward, 'The Industrial Revolution and British Imperialism, 1750–1850', *Economic History Review* 47, no. 1 (1994), 44–65; Antoinette Burton, *The Trouble with Empire* (Oxford: Oxford University Press, 2015); Angela Woollacott, *Settler Society in the Australian Colonies: Self-Government and Imperial Culture* (Oxford: Oxford University Press, 2015); Philip Dwyer and Amanda Nettelbeck, eds. *Violence, Colonialism and Empire in the Modern World* (Basingstoke: Palgrave, 2017).
24. On the correlation between colonial expansion and the economic development of empire, see, for instance, Ralph Austen and Woodruff Smith, 'The Economic Value of British Colonial Empire in the Seventeenth and Eighteenth Centuries', *History Compass* 4, no. 1 (2006), 54–76.
25. For instance, Niall Ferguson, *Empire: The Rise and Demise of the British World Order and the Lessons for Global Power* (New York: Basic Books, 2002); Stuart Ward, 'The "New Nationalism" in Australia, Canada and New Zealand: Civic Culture in the Wake of the British World', in *Australia and the World: A Festschrift for Neville Meaney*, ed. Joan Beaumont and Matthew Jordan (Sydney: Sydney University Press, 2013), 191–214.
26. Elazar Barkan, *The Guilt of Nations: Restitution and Negotiating Historical Injustices* (New York and London: W.W. Norton, 2000); Mark Gibney,

Rhoda E. Howard-Hassmann, Jean-Marc Coicaud and Niklaus Steiner, eds. *The Age of Apology: Facing Up to the Past* (Philadelphia: University of Pennsylvania, 2008); Paulette Regan, *Unsettling the Settler Within: Indian Residential Schools: Truth Telling and Reconciliation in Canada* (Vancouver: UBC Press, 2010); Penelope Edmonds, *Settler Colonialism and (Re)conciliation: Frontier Violence, Affective Performances, and Frontier Violence* (Basingstoke: Palgrave, 2016).

27. Christopher Bayly, *The Birth of the Modern World, 1780–1914 Global Convections and Comparisons* (Malden, MA: Blackwell Publishers, 2004); James Belich, *Replenishing the Earth, the Settler Revolution and the Rise of the Anglo World* (Oxford: Oxford University Press, 2009).

28. For instance, Lindsay Proudfoot and Michael Roche, eds. *(Dis)Placing Empire: Renegotiating British Colonial Geographies* (London: Ashgate, 2005); Lauren Benton and Lisa Ford, *Rage for Order: The British Empire and the Origins of International Law* (Cambridge, MA: Harvard University Press, 2016).

29. Laura Doyle and Laura Winkiel, eds. *Geomodernisms: Race, Modernism, Modernity* (Bloomington, IN: Indiana University Press, 2005); John Marx, *Geopolitics and the Anglophone Novel, 1800–2011* (New York: Cambridge University Press, 2012); Tony Ballantyne, *Webs of Empire: Locating New Zealand's Colonial Past* (Wellington: Bridget Williams Books, 2012); Zoë Laidlaw, *Colonial Connections 1815–45: Patronage, the Information Revolution and Colonial Government* (Manchester: Manchester University Press, 2005); Alan Lester, *Imperial Networks: Creating Identities in Nineteenth-Century South Africa and Britain* (London and New York, Routledge, 2001).

30. Antoinette Burton, ed. *After the Imperial Turn: Thinking with and through the Nation* (Durham, NC: Duke University Press, 2003).

31. Deborah Bird Rose and Richard Davis, 'Preface' in *Dislocating the Frontier: Essaying the Mystique of the Outback*, ed. Deborah Bird Rose and Richard Davis (Canberra: ANU ePress, 2006), iv.

32. Patrick Wolfe, *Settler Colonialism and the Transformation of Anthropology: The Politics and Poetics of an Ethnography* (London: Cassel, 1999), 2–3.

33. Deborah Bird Rose, 'The Redemptive Frontier: A Long Road to Nowhere', in *Dislocating the Frontier: Essaying the Mystique of the Outback*, ed. D.B. Rose and R. Davis (Canberra: ANU ePress, 2006), 49.

34. Lisa Ford, *Settler Sovereignty: Jurisdiction and Indigenous People in America and Australia* (Cambridge, MA: Harvard University Press, 2010); Aileen Moreton-Robinson, *Sovereign Subjects: Indigenous Sovereignty Matters* (Sydney: Allen and Unwin, 2007); Heather Douglas and Mark Finnane, *Indigenous Crime and Settler Law: White Sovereignty After Empire* (Basingstoke: Palgrave, 2012).

35. Patrick Wolfe, 'Settler Colonialism and the Elimination of the Native', *Journal of Genocide Research* 8, no. 4 (2006), 391–392.
36. Deborah Bird Rose, 'Hard Times: An Australian Study', in *Quicksands: Foundational Histories in Australia and Aotearoa New Zealand*, ed. Klaus Neumann, Nicholas Thomas, and Hilary Ericksen (Sydney: UNSW Press, 1999), 6; Julie Evans, 'Where Lawlessness is Law: The Settler-Colonial Frontier as a Legal Space of Violence', *Australian Feminist Law Review* 30 (2009).
37. Johan Galtung, 'Cultural Violence', *Journal of Peace Research* 27, no. 3 (1990).
38. Jan Critchett, 'Encounters in the Western District', in *Frontier Conflict: The Australian Experience*, ed. Bain Attwood and Stephen Foster (Canberra: National Museum of Australia, 2003), 54; Philip Dwyer and Lyndall Ryan, 'Introduction', in *Theatres of Violence: Massacre, Mass Killing and Atrocity throughout History*, ed. Philip Dwyer and Lyndall Ryan (New York: Berghahn Books, 2012), xi–xxiii; Amanda Nettelbeck, 'Proximate Strangers and Familiar Antagonists: Violence on an Intimate Frontier', *Australian Historical Studies* 47, no. 2 (2016), 209–224.
39. Clive Moore and Ann Curthoys, 'Working for the White People: An Historiographic Essay on Aboriginal and Torres Strait Islander Labour [online].' *Labour History*, special issue, no. 69, Nov. 1995, 1–29. See also Rae Frances, Bruce Scates, B. and Ann McGrath, 'Broken Silences? Aboriginal Workers and Labour Historians', in *Challenges to Labour History*, ed. T. Irving (Kensington: UNSW Press, 1994).
40. Likewise see more recently Diane Kirkby and Sophie Loy-Wilson, eds., Special issue, 'Labour History and the Coolie Question', *Labour History* 113 (Nov. 2017).
41. Tracey Banivanua Mar, *Violence and Colonial Dialogue: The Australian-Pacific Indentured Labor Trade* (Honolulu: University of Hawai'i Press, 2007).
42. Ann McGrath, *Born in the Cattle: Aborigines in Cattle Country* (Sydney: Allen and Unwin, 1987); Dawn May, *Aboriginal Labour and the Cattle Industry: Queensland from White Settlement to the Present* (Cambridge: Cambridge University Press, 1994).
43. Tim Rowse, '"Were You Ever Savages?"; Aboriginal Insiders and Pastoralists' Patronage', *Oceania* 58, no. 2 (1987).
44. For instance, Henry Reynolds, *With the White People* (Melbourne: Penguin, 1990); Shino Konishi, Maria Nugent, and Tiffany Shellam, eds. *Indigenous Intermediaries: New Perspectives on Exploration Archives* (Canberra: ANU Press, 2015).
45. For instance, Henry Reynolds, *North of Capricorn: The Untold Story of Australia's North* (Sydney: Allen and Unwin, 2003); Regina Ganter, *Mixed Relations: Asian–Aboriginal Contact in North Australia* (Perth: UWA Publishing, 2006).

46. For instance, Anne Clarke, '"The Moorman's Trowsers": Macassan and Aboriginal Interaction and the Changing Fabric of Indigenous Social Life', in *East of Wallace's Line: Studies of Past and Present Maritime Societies in the Indo-Pacific Region*, ed. Sue O'Connor and Peter Veth (Rotterdam: A.A. Balkema, 2000), 315–335; Marshall Clark, 'Tangible Heritage of the Macassan–Aboriginal Encounter in Contemporary South Sulawesi', in Marshall Clark and Sally May, *Macassan History and Heritage: Journeys, Encounters and Influences* (Canberra: ANU ePress, 2013), 159–182.
47. Alan Ward, *A Show of Justice: Racial 'Amalgamation' in Nineteenth-Century New Zealand* (Canberra: ANU Press, 1974), 13. See also Tony Ballantyne, *Webs of Empire: Location New Zealand's Colonial Past* (Wellington: Bridget Williams Books, 2012).
48. Jane Carey and Jane Lydon, 'Introduction: Indigenous Networks: Historical Trajectories and Contemporary Connections', in *Indigenous Networks: Mobility, Connections and Exchange*, ed. Jane Carey and Jane Lydon (New York: Routledge, 2014), 1–26.
49. Salesa, 'Samoa's Half-Castes', 72; Stoler, 'Tense and Tender Ties'.
50. Victoria Haskins and Claire Lowrie, 'Decolonizing Domestic Service: Introducing a New Agenda', in *Colonization and Domestic Service: Historical and Contemporary Perspectives*, ed. Victoria Haskins and Claire Lowrie (New York: Routledge, 2015), 7, 1–18.
51. Antoinette Burton, *Dwelling in the Archive: Women Writing House, Home and History in Late Colonial India* (Oxford: Oxford University Press, 2003), 5–6.
52. Penelope Edmonds and Jane Carey, 'Australian Settler Colonialism over the Long Nineteenth Century: New Insights into Gender and Biopolitics', *The Routledge Handbook of the History of Settler Colonialism*, ed. Edward Cavanagh and Lorenzo Veracini (United Kingdom: Routledge, 2017), 371–389.
53. Perry, *Edge of Empire*, 19.
54. Jane Carey, '"Wanted! A Real White Australia": The Women's Movement, Whiteness and the Settler Colonial Project', in *Studies in Settler Colonialism: Politics, Identity, Culture*, ed. Fiona Bateman and Lionel Pilkington (New York: Palgrave, 2011), 136.
55. On how this process emerged in the early modern age of expansion, see Alison Games, *The Web of Empire: English Cosmopolitans in an Age of Expansion, 1560–1660* (New York: Oxford University Press, 2008).

PART I

Moral Economies and Labour Relations in the Pastoral Sector

CHAPTER 2

The Australian Agricultural Company, the Van Diemen's Land Company: Labour Relations with Aboriginal Landowners, 1824–1835

Lyndall Ryan

In January 1826, Robert Dawson, the colonial agent of the Australian Agricultural Company (AAC), employed two Aboriginal guides, Bob and Tony from the Worimi nation, to take him to their traditional lands at Port Stephens and assist him in selecting the best site to serve as the Company's headquarters for its one million acre grant in New South Wales (NSW). Dawson later wrote:

> As soon as we had raised the frames of some of our intended habitations, we were sadly at a loss for bark to close the sides and cover the roofs with. Ben and Tony [our Aboriginal guides] … could not do all that was required; and the former, therefore, made an offer to go in search of the tribe and bring them to me, promising to return in two days with such a number as would soon finish all our huts. This promise he faithfully kept by bringing, within the prescribed time, a dozen good-natured, able-bodied friends, who having

L. Ryan (✉)
University of Newcastle, Callaghan, NSW, Australia

© The Author(s) 2018
P. Edmonds, A. Nettelbeck (eds.), *Intimacies of Violence in the Settler Colony*, Cambridge Imperial and Post-Colonial Studies Series, https://doi.org/10.1007/978-3-319-76231-9_2

each received a small hatchet, set to work on good earnest, and brought back in two or three days as would have taken our party a month to procure.[1]

In Van Diemen's Land, meanwhile, Edward Curr, the newly appointed chief agent of the Van Diemen's Land Company (VDLC) was crafting his view of the Aboriginal people in the northwest of the colony before he had even met them. The Company was about to take up its 250,000-acre grant in their homelands and Curr reported:

> the well-known character of the [Aboriginal] people must be kept in view and treachery must be guarded against. No person must suffer himself to be surprised by them at a disadvantage or without arms or be seduced by any appearance of friendliness to trust him in their power; the surest way to prevent bloodshed is to be always prepared to repel and punish aggression.[2]

Eighteen months later, the agents' different approaches to Aboriginal employment were even more starkly displayed. In November 1827, a leading colonist from New South Wales reported to the board of directors of the AAC in London of his recent visit to Port Stephens:

> Mr Dawson's treatment of the Natives is most excellent, that there were about 600 around him, that they came down in tribes—that he does not appear to apprehend depredation from them. They have not even taken a cob of corn. That he does not constrain them in any way, that he endeavours to create wants among them; which wants are supplied in exchange for labour—their labour is useful in various ways—nearly 60 of the women are employed in picking leaves out of the Company's Wool about to be sent home—they row in Boats and they peel bark for Buildings—this Bark is not found in all situations—it is fetched 17 miles by the Native Blacks to the principal Settlement. The remuneration to them is very trifling, consisting often of a handful of Corn, or a bit of Tobacco, but he gives nothing to them without an equivalent in labour. His influence over them is very great—it has enabled him to bring together in harmony hostile tribes.[3]

In Van Diemen's Land, however, Edward Curr was grappling with reports that between December 1827 and February 1828, VDLC employees had massacred forty two Aboriginal people in two separate incidents.[4] In his initial report on the incident that took place in February 1828, now known as the Cape Grim massacre, Curr stated to the Court of Directors in London: 'the shepherds fell in with a strong party of Natives who, after a long fight, left six of their number dead on the field, including their chief, besides several wounded. I have no doubt that this will have the effect of intimidating them, and oblige them to keep aloof.'[5] A later investigation, however, revealed that far from a 'long fight', the Aboriginal men were ambushed and that more than twenty Aboriginal women and children were also killed.[6]

What were the circumstances that led each agent to take a completely different view of Aboriginal employment? On the surface their differences appear difficult to fathom. Their colonial agents were employed by the boards of very similar kinds of chartered companies that were established in the same city at virtually the same time and operated in adjoining colonies for the same purpose: the production of raw wool for export to the textile mills of northern England. Were other factors at play?

The AAC and the VDLC are the oldest and longest-surviving chartered agricultural companies in Australia today; yet until the transfer of their records from London to Australia from the 1970s, most accounts of their operation were produced by senior company officers and tended to ignore Aboriginal issues.[7] The extensive records of their employment practices still await a comprehensive comparative analysis, although John Perkins started the process with an analysis of convict labour in the AAC followed by Deirdre Baistow's study of Aboriginal and convict relations at Port Stephens and Mark Hannah's landmark study of Aboriginal workers in the company, 1824–1857.[8] Hannah's study makes a vital intervention in the debate about the use of Aboriginal labour before 1850, based on Charles Rowley's view that the widespread availability of convict labour in Eastern Australia obviated the need for Aboriginal labour.[9] Richard Broome, in his general study of Aboriginal workers in southeastern Australia, tended to agree—although in special industries like sealing where convict labour was forbidden and in areas where convict labour was scarce, Aboriginal workers certainly were employed; and Alan Pope's more specific study of Aboriginal labour patterns in South Australia indicated that in colonies where convict labour was not available, some Aboriginal labour was used.[10] By contrast, most scholarly studies of the VDLC have tended to focus on the violent relations between Tasmanian Aboriginal people and company employees.[11]

Yet Hannah considers that Aboriginal male and female workers were increasingly valued by the AAC between 1826 and 1857, and cites several factors to support his case. The most important was that as workers in their own country they were less likely to leave, unlike other workers who had to make a 'psychic' adjustment to the Australian climate and the company's remote outstations. They were also more reliable as shepherds and stockmen in remote locations than convict workers; were generally more 'mentally well attuned to the tasks required of them'; enjoyed better health than other company employees; and their knowledge of the country was invaluable in tracking down absconding employees and lost sheep and cattle. Further, they were less expensive to employ than other non-convict workers, although Hannah insists that their low labour cost was secondary to their 'outstanding work performance'.[12]

Even so, Hannah considers that Dawson's employment of Worimi people was largely based on the dichotomy of protection and intimidation and that when they resisted his demands for co-operation, he 'countered in a retributive way'.[13] Although Dawson did not use 'sustained physical force' against them, he certainly tried to capitalise on their 'fears and expectations' about violence, and his 'protection' depended on their deference. Despite these misgivings, Hannah acknowledges that Dawson's determination to employ the Worimi enabled them to survive as an intact Aboriginal group far longer than most other Aboriginal communities in the region. More importantly, he argues that Dawson was instructed by the AAC to employ the Worimi and that after his dismissal in 1828, the policy of Worimi employment continued until the company abandoned Port Stephens in 1859. But although Hannah shows that Aboriginal employment was an integral part of AAC policy, he does not offer any insights into how it emerged.

By contrast, the VDLC never seriously pursued an Aboriginal employment policy. Deploying Hannah's analytical model to the VDLC's employment practices, however, it could be argued that Tasmanian Aboriginal labour would have been of immense value. Only one aspect of Hannah's model is not applicable to the VDLC's English employees, whether convict or free, and that is the island's cooler climate. The other factors would certainly have been in play. They include the 'psychic' adjustment that was required of them to survive on the VDLC's remote outstations. When the Quaker travellers James Backhouse and G.W. Walker visited the company's outstation at the Hampshire Hills in the summer of 1832–1833, they were overwhelmed by its remote location on a high plateau more than eighty kilometres inland from the headquarters on the coast. The outstation was surrounded by impenetrable forests and even in summer was subject to long periods of fog, rain, and snow. Backhouse noted that several male employees had been lost in the forests searching for straying sheep and cattle, and others had drowned trying to cross fast-flowing rivers. Yet they appeared more afraid of being killed by Tasmanian Aboriginal warriors, who were probably from the Noeteeler clan and seeking revenge for the abduction of their wives or in search of flour, sugar, and tea.[14] In the summer of 1829–1830, four VDLC servants were speared by Noeteeler warriors, and in the winter of 1831 two others were killed. In retaliation, it appears that the servants shot dead at least ten Noeteeler people.[15] Added to Curr's policy of no alcohol, many workers on the VDLC's lands experienced a far more lonely and miserable existence than on the AAC lands in New South Wales. All these factors would suggest that the employment of Tasmanian Aboriginal men and women as guides, shepherds, and hut keepers would have greatly improved the VDLC's efficiency.

Ian McFarlane, the most recent historian of the VDLC, considers that Curr alone was responsible for the failure to consider Tasmanian Aboriginal labour—on the grounds that he never appeared to show any real interest in them. As evidence, he cites the book Curr produced about his experiences as a settler in Van Diemen's Land before his appointment as the VDLC's colonial agent.[16] The book made no mention of the Tasmanian Aboriginal people even though many of them were 'still intact and in possession of their traditional lands' at the time that he wrote it.[17] As further evidence, McFarlane notes that within twelve months of the VDLC establishing a presence at Cape Grim, 'the employees under Curr's direct control had gained a reputation for brutal treatment of the local Aboriginal population'.[18] McFarlane also considers that Curr not only concealed from the directors in London the extent of several violent killings of Tasmanian Aboriginal people but, when called upon to do so, responded by deliberately reducing the number of deaths. Rather than promoting peaceful contact with the Tasmanian Aboriginal people and seeking to employ them, McFarlane contends that Curr actively sought to destroy them.[19]

But this assessment does not explain the contradiction noted at the beginning of the chapter. How was it that the AAC had success in employing Aboriginal people in New South Wales and the VDLC did not even bother with them? Curr's dismissive approach to the Tasmanian Aboriginal people would suggest that the VDLC held a very different view of Aboriginal employment. For despite the directors' concern about the Cape Grim massacre and other violent incidents involving VDLC employees, they never considered that Curr should be held accountable.

The directors' apparent lack of interest in employing Tasmanian Aboriginal labour would suggest that a broader approach to the question of Aboriginal labour is required. This chapter takes up the challenge by deploying Pennie Pemberton's analytical model of each company's capital formation and political influence.[20] It then examines the ideas and beliefs held by shareholders and directors and how they influenced the appointment of their first colonial agents, Dawson and Curr. It then moves to each company's colonial location to explore the responses of the Aboriginal people in their jurisdiction as a way of understanding the preconditions for Aboriginal employment and longer-term survival. In taking this approach, new insights emerge that could help to explain the extraordinary differences in views towards and outcome for the Aboriginal people in each jurisdiction.[21]

* * *

The establishment of the AAC and the VDLC took place in London within twelve months of each other in 1824–1825.[22] Formed in response to the Bigge Report of 1822–1823, which recommended opening up the Aboriginal homelands of New South Wales and Van Diemen's Land to sheep grazing, the promoters saw that the collapse of the Spanish wool market during the Peninsular Wars, together with the promise of cheap convict labour, made both colonies attractive locations for producing raw wool for export to the textile mills of northern England. By virtue of their land entitlements, each company was formally granted a charter by an act of Parliament. The AAC was promised a land grant of a million acres to conduct its operations in New South Wales, on condition it raised a million pounds in capital, and the VDLC was promised 500,000 acres in Van Diemen's Land on the same condition, with the argument that land in the island colony was more expensive and there was little good grazing land left. The grant was further reduced to 250,000 acres, and then later increased to 350,000.[23] In each case, the grants were to be taken up beyond the boundaries of official settlement.[24]

In view of the similarities in origins and purpose, it has long been assumed that the shareholders of each company were broadly similar.[25] But as Pemberton has found, this was far from the case. The AAC was a much larger company, and its first board of fifteen directors, which included six members of Parliament (MPs), five Bank of England directors, and four East India Company directors, reflected its considerable political influence. Most of the other shareholders were also from London and included thirty MPs and an important cluster of bankers and merchants, but there was also a significant component of wealthy free settlers and officials from New South Wales.[26]

By comparison, the VDLC was far less diverse in social composition and far less influential politically. Pemberton found that there were only two MPs on the VDLC's original share list and the fifteen-member court of directors largely comprised 'wool brokers and merchants in London and a group of West county clothiers'.[27] There were very few colonial investors on the share list, and the only overlapping investors that I could find were the MP James Brogden, who sold his five hundred shares in the VDLC in 1828; George Harrison, Permanent Secretary at Treasury, who held twenty shares in both companies; and wool brokers Henry Hughes and John Marsh, who appear to have originally held more shares in the VDLC but later sold them.[28]

The most important difference was that AAC investors could not sell their shares for five years, suggesting a commitment to long-term stability. The VDLC was far more volatile, with many of the original investors selling their shares within the first three years to the four men who would eventually control the company.[29]

Of the 490 investors in the AAC identified by Pemberton, thirty-six were either serving or former MPs, including Henry Grey Bennet and Thomas Potter Macqueen, both of whom had close connections with New South Wales. Bennet had led the campaign against Governor Macquarie's emancipist policies and laid the groundwork for the Bigge Commission of Inquiry into Macquarie's administration; and Macqueen had recently sponsored the first shipload of free settlers to New South Wales.[30] Forty-one others were Australian-based investors comprising the cream of the 'exclusives' class, including the Macarthur family; Phillip Parker King, the explorer son of an earlier governor of the colony, Philip Gidley King; and leading settlers in the Hunter Valley, such as magistrate Edward Close and the brothers Helenus and Robert Scott. Eight other London-based investors held important colonial connections, including the 'exclusives' London agent, Edward Barnard, and John Thomas Bigge, author of the reports into the future development of New South Wales. Other investors included influential civil servants in Whitehall with policy responsibility for the Australian colonies, such as the solicitor-general, William Wetherill, who assisted in the swift passage of the AAC legislation; the chief clerk at the Colonial Office, Henry Short; and permanent secretary of the Treasury George Harrison.[31] All these groups were exemplars of the ruling Anglican Establishment.

The most influential group of investors were those identified with the anti-slavery lobby in London. They included at least half the thirty-six listed MPs, such as John Copley, Richard Hart Davis, Sir Alexander Gray Grant, William Haldimand, Frederick Hodgson, Stephen Lushington, Benjamin Shaw, William Smith, and William Wilberforce. Other anti-slavery investors included the printer Charles Baldwin; the family of brewer and banker Charles Barclay; merchant bankers Charles Bosanquet and John and Thomas Henry Buckle; the Quaker family of merchant Charles Compton; solicitors William Scott, George Spence, and Thomas and William Tooke; merchant Henry Traill; the Quaker sisters Anne and Sophie Turner; the tea merchants George and Richard Twining; hop merchant William Woodhouse; and the family of merchant banker Henry Thornton, who was a key member of the Clapham Sect.[32]

Put together with the Tory investors from the Anglican Establishment, most AAC shareholders appear to have been in the forefront of promoting the humanitarian discourse of 'protection and civilisation' of Indigenous peoples across the Empire in the 1820s.[33] Their interconnections in business and government—as Alan Lester, the leading historian of the British humanitarians, points out—were an integral component of the British imperial project in this period.[34]

If this is the case, then many of the AAC investors would have been very interested in proposals for the 'protection and civilisation' of the Aboriginal people who lived on the company's grant in New South Wales; and the appointment of Robert Dawson in 1824 as the first colonial agent appears to reflect this view. Then aged forty-two years, Dawson was selected for the position from twenty-one candidates on the grounds that he had 'extensive experience' as an estate manager, was of the 'most excellent character', and had attended the same school in London as John Macarthur Jnr, the driving force behind the company's formation.[35] Even so, at the interview for the position it would have been almost impossible for the selection committee not to have been aware of his apparent enthusiasm for Aboriginal 'protection and civilisation'. Indeed, the fact that he was recalled for interview several times indicates that his commitment to Aboriginal conciliation was an important, if unstated, factor in his appointment to the position on a five-year contract with a salary of £600 per annum.[36] His clearly defined duties included the 'protection and civilisation' of the Aboriginal people in the company's jurisdiction. He was expected to carry these duties out under the aegis of a colonial committee whose members comprised the most powerful family in New South Wales, that of the High Tory John Macarthur.[37] And although the committee sacked Dawson a year early in 1828, they were fulsome in praise of his success in employing Worimi people.

This is not surprising. The Macarthurs saw themselves as the protectors of the Aboriginal people from the Gundungurra nation on their Camden estate, and John's son James acknowledged that Aboriginal people should have rights of access to their ancestral lands, with food rations, as part of their 'inheritance'.[38] He also recommended that some of the Gundungurra men should be employed as constables in the local police force. As their 'protector', however, he did not feel that those who worked on the Camden estate should be remunerated beyond the provision of food rations.[39] The Macarthurs saw themselves as the 'inheritors' of the ancestral lands of the Gundungurra, and it is likely that they expected that the AAC in their occupation of Worimi ancestral lands would also observe the ancient obligation of 'protecting' the original owners and training them in 'civilised' pursuits such as shepherding and stock work as well as domestic service. In this context, the colonial committee considered that Dawson was simply following the traditions of enfeoffment practised by the Macarthurs. Although the London directors agreed that Dawson's successor should exercise more direct power in the colony and abolished the colonial committee, they also continued to promote the policy of Aboriginal employment.[40]

By contrast, the 280 original investors in the VDLC were largely associated with two families, that of the wool broker Joseph Cripps from Cirencester in Gloucestershire, who initially bought 460 shares at £100 each, and John Pearse MP from Woodford in Essex, who originally held 500 shares. They appear to have taken the lead in establishing the VDLC, based on the advice of ship owner and merchant John Ingle, who had lived in Van Diemen's Land between 1804 and 1818, although he does not appear to have purchased any shares.[41] By 1832, the Cripps and Pearse families held 20,000 of the Company's 100,000 shares and, together with the managing director James Inglis and company secretary James Bischoff, exercised full control of the Company.[42] None of them had any previous connection with the island colony, which could have been a critical factor in the appointment of Edward Curr as the chief colonial agent.

Then aged twenty-seven years, Curr had just returned to London in 1824 when he heard of the VDLC's proposed formation. Never one to lose an opportunity, he strode into the Company's office armed with two important documents: his newly published book of his experiences as a new settler in Van Diemen's Land, and a letter of recommendation from the Colony's former lieutenant-governor, William Sorell. He so completely dazzled Cripps and Pearse with his confident demeanour and detailed knowledge of the Colony that they appointed him on the spot as the company's temporary secretary.[43] He then made himself indispensable to the company's future by purchasing a large block of shares and taking the lead in negotiations with the Colonial Office about the subscription of capital that was required before the government would grant the charter.[44] By then, Curr had secured the coveted appointment of chief colonial agent at an annual salary of £800 and no fixed contract.[45] There is no evidence that any other candidates were interviewed for the job, and it would appear that he simply slid into the position by virtue of his negotiating skills with the Colonial Office and his vision for the company's future.

Before Curr left London in November 1825 to take up his new appointment in Van Diemen's Land, he appears to have advised the directors that the company was not required to offer land grants to Tasmanian Aboriginal people whose homelands were on the Company's any more than the 'protection' required by Colonial Office policy as set out in Bathurst's despatch of July 1825. This stated that if Aboriginal people were aggressive towards the settlers, they should be treated as if they were 'enemies of an accredited state'.[46] The despatch represented a marked departure from the discourse of humanitarianism that pervaded the AAC's policy of employing Aboriginal people and integrating them into the company's social order. Rather, it was more like a return to the 'distance and fear' policy that Lieutenant Governor David Collins had brought to Van Diemen's Land at the outset of colonisation in 1804.[47]

Unlike Dawson in New South Wales, there is no evidence that Curr sought to employ Tasmanian Aboriginal people from the North West to guide him across their homelands, let alone advise on a site for the VDLC's headquarters. Yet a close reading of the journals of two of the company's surveyors, Henry Hellyer and Jørgen Jørgenson, indicates that had Tasmanian Aboriginal people been employed to guide them in the search for pastoral land, their quest would have been more readily accomplished. As it was, they were frequently lost in thick forests.[48]

Thus it was only when rumours of the Cape Grim massacre reached London in late 1827 that Curr felt the need to defend his policy. In his despatch to the directors about the massacre, he wrote:

no one could feel more anxious than I have been, to avoid any kind of contention with these people, and I have always enjoined the men to have no communication with them what-ever, friendly or otherwise, knowing that their friendly visits, are only paid for the purpose of ascertaining our means of defense and weak points, and are generally the forerunners of attacks. They have been the aggressors and strife, once begun with any of these tribes, has never been terminated, nor will, according to present appearances, but by their extermination.[49]

When the directors received the despatch, they were forced to respond to Curr with a policy more in keeping with that of the AAC. Every effort, they said, should be made to 'conciliate and civilise the natives to make them your friends instead of your enemies', no matter how difficult, for 'it is the duty of the Company to attempt it, and if they can be brought into a state of comparatively social comfort it will be conferring upon them a greater boon than the value of their range and hunting of the Lands of which they will be deprived, and of which the Company will have possession. The Court [of directors] cannot too strongly urge these attempts upon you.'[50]

But it was too late. By then, Curr was in sole control of the company's operations in Van Diemen's Land, having forced the resignation of his deputy, Stephen Adey, and another senior officer, Alexander Goldie.[51] It is unlikely that he would have accepted a directive from London to seriously consider the prospect of Aboriginal employment.

* * *

How is it possible to compare the experiences each Aboriginal group—the Worimi at Port Stephens in New South Wales and the North West and North peoples in Van Diemen's Land—had with British colonists before the two companies arrived in their country? By an odd irony, each group had had long experience with the intruders, but with vastly different outcomes. The Worimi first encountered the British in 1795 when they welcomed five male convict runaways as ancestors who had fallen in battle and returned to visit them. They conferred Worimi names on them and offered them Worimi women as their wives.[52] During the period from 1804 to 1823 when the nearby town of Newcastle was a penal settlement, some Worimi men were employed by the station superintendents to track down and return absconding convict men. In 1822, the penal station relocated north to Port Macquarie and a military post was established at Port Stephens to check for runaways moving south. The soldiers appear to have established friendly relations with the Worimi.[53] By the time Dawson arrived at Port Stephens in January 1826, the Worimi had had more than thirty years' interaction with the colonists yet about six hundred of them remained in full control of their country. Many of them spoke English, others were expert sailors, and still others were used to being hired as guides to settlers arriving in the Hunter River area in search of good grazing land for their flocks and herds. In January 1826, when Dawson sought out the Worimi guides Bob and Tony to select the headquarters of the AAC grant, he was simply following a practice that was well established in the region.

In this case, however, the Worimi leaders invited the AAC to their own country and in return expected protection from their traditional enemies at Myall Lakes and further north at the Manning River. Dawson was quick to understand this. He employed several Worimi men as guides to introduce him to their country in his quest for good land to pasture sheep and cattle. And although he treated these men with extreme paternalism, he also ensured that they had access to rations and shelter and that they were part of the AAC establishment. During his time as colonial agent, he also ensured that Worimi women were protected from sexual assault by the male convict workers. Dawson and his successors—Sir Edward Parry (1830–1834), Edward Dumaresq (1834–1838), and Phillip Parker King (1838–1848)—regularly attended Worimi ceremonies, and all the company officers at the Port Stephens establishment became proficient in the Worimi language. Of course there were disputes and, on several occasions, a breakdown in communications; and by the late 1830s, there was extensive sexual interaction between Worimi women and convict men. Yet the Worimi survived and, as Hannah points out, their labour was highly valued by the company.[54]

The experiences of the Tasmania Aboriginal nations from northwest Van Diemen's Land with the British began from about 1810 when small groups of sealing men landed on the coastline in search of Aboriginal women they could hire to catch seals.[55] McFarlane cites several instances of violence: when a group of sealers in 1815 shot men of the North West people who were trying to prevent them from taking their wives by force, and in 1820 when nine sealers attacked a group from the Parperloihener clan who were mutton-birding and seven women were abducted and taken to Kangaroo Island.[56] He is wary of judging the long-term impact of abduction on the people as a whole before the arrival of the VDLC in

1826.[57] Nevertheless, the Tasmanian Aboriginal people in northwest Van Diemen's Land appear to have experienced greater levels of violence from 'outsiders' than the Worimi at Port Stephens, although no attempts were made to drive them from their homelands. When the VDLC arrived in the region in 1826, it is estimated that fewer than two hundred people from the North and North West nations were still alive.[58]

It could be argued that the violent conditions enabled Curr to offer the Tasmanian Aboriginal people the same kind of protection the Worimi sought from the AAC, and he could certainly have employed them as guides to the surveyors in their search for pastures for sheep and cattle at Hampshire and Surry Hills. When he established the company headquarters at Circular Head, he would have known that Tasmanian Aboriginal women and boys were forcibly working with the sealers and, like government agent G.A. Robinson in the island's northeast, he could have worked with local chiefs to seek the return of the women and children and become their protector against further abductions.[59] He certainly required Aboriginal guides to assist the surveyors in locating pastoral land and good boatmen in assisting with the transport of supplies. But he did not attempt to implement any of these measures.

It is not known whether Curr formally met any Aboriginal people when he arrived at Circular Head in 1826, although it is known that the area was on the boundary of the two powerful clans—the Plairhekehillerplu from the North Nation at Emu Bay and the Tommeginer from the North West nation at Table Cape. With a combined estimated population of about eighty in 1826, they were the survivors of more than two decades of violent conflict with the sealers and were struggling to maintain their cultural existence.[60] In other areas of the VDLC grant, such as the remote west coast, the surveyor Jørgen Jørgenson encountered several parties of the Tarkiner clan of the North West nation near Sandy Cape in 1826–1827 and reported that they were 'intact' as family groups, were 'inoffensive and friendly' and 'frank and generous treatment may render them of some service to white men who should visit this quarter'.[61] He also warned Curr that company servants in the remote stations at the Hampshire Hills, the homeland of the Noeteeler clan of the North nation, were 'taking liberties' with Noeteeler women which had led to the shooting of a Noeteeler clan chief, but Curr did nothing about it.[62] He never sought out Aboriginal people, even on the grounds of protection, although it is possible that some Aboriginal youths, such as Pevay (Tunnerminnerwait), from the Parperloihener clan at Robbins Island, could have visited the company's headquarters at Circular Head with the AAC boatman Alexander McKay.[63] It is known that the stockman James Cubit, who assisted Hellyer in marking the track from Launceston to the Company's wharf at Emu Bay in 1826, 'dropped a few' Aboriginal warriors when they harassed the road workers' camp.[64] The company's leading surveyors, Joseph Fossey and Henry Hellyer, never reported employing Aboriginal youths to assist them in their work, suggesting that they adhered to Curr's policy of 'distance and fear'. But the government surveyor John Helder Wedge was known to have employed at least three Aboriginal boys to help him in identifying the boundaries of the company's grant in 1828 and to have 'rescued' another from the surf after his party shot at sixteen Aboriginal people in a sand dune on the west coast.[65]

McFarlane is not sure whether Curr ever knew about this incident, and suggests that the white men in Wedge's party were veterans of the Vandiemonian War then raging in the settled districts.[66] Such incidents certainly would have made forging productive relations with the Aboriginal people in the region very difficult to negotiate but not altogether impossible. Rather it would appear that the company's officers were simply unwilling to do this. When the government agent G.A. Robinson arrived in the region in June 1830, he found little evidence of genuine interaction between the company officers and Aboriginal people.[67] Yet there were ample opportunities for Aboriginal employment in the company as boatmen, guides, shepherds, and hutkeepers, and it is possible that from time to time some were hired to perform these tasks.

One possible reason for Curr's apparent refusal to engage with Aboriginal people is the absence of legal backup. Whereas Dawson could call on a magistrate who lived just outside the company's grant to deal with issues arising in the AAC's workplace, Curr was the only magistrate in the entire northwest region of Van Diemen's Land until 1830, with the nearest magistrate located at Norfolk Plains more than one hundred kilometres sixty miles away by road, or at George Town by ship. He was expected to resolve incidents of petty crime by himself, and his dual position of chief employer and law officer meant that he could rarely take a dispassionate view of workplace disputes. As Curr himself noted: 'the power I exercise here is both master and magistrate, party and judge'.[68] With company settlements scattered across the entire northwest of Van Diemen's Land, he was flat out controlling the convict workers. Civil officers also lacked the legal power to maintain authority. So it is not surprising, as McFarlane points out, that

Curr would minimise reports of frontier violence, including massacre, and place any blame entirely on the Aboriginal victims.[69]

McFarlane concludes that 'Curr was definitely not the man to be entrusted with the task of negotiating a relationship with the Aborigines'.[70] The model of close integration of the Aboriginal people that was eventually adopted by the directors in London was not promulgated until October 1829, by which time Curr's practice of 'distance and fear' had become, in reality, a policy of Aboriginal extermination.[71] This dreadful outcome was only prevented by the forced removal of more than fifty Aboriginal people from the Company grant to Flinders Island between 1832 and 1834.

There is no doubt that the Company's reputation was severely tarnished by reports of massacre, and the publication of a history of the Company in 1832 by James Bischoff, the company secretary, was clearly an attempt to restore its reputation.[72] The inclusion of an extended appendix of copies of the official correspondence between Lieutenant-Governor Arthur and the secretaries of state for the Colonies about the Vandiemonian War was an attempt to place the company's actions in the broader context. Yet their operations were located far from the killing fields in the settled districts and the infamous military operations of 1830.[73] Rather than restoring the company's reputation, the book appeared to place it at the centre of the violence.

As this chapter has demonstrated, comparing the investors in the AAC and the VDLC as a way of understanding their economic and social backgrounds and political influence, and comparing the experiences of the Aboriginal communities before the companies took up their land grants, allows new insights to emerge about each company's policies and practices towards Aboriginal labour. The humanitarian presence among the AAC shareholders, together with the High Tory influence of the major colonial investors, suggests that from the outset the AAC was firmly committed to promoting Aboriginal employment and expected their colonial agent to implement it. As a result, the Worimi people on whose lands the company settled until 1859 survived, albeit in small numbers. They remain a strong community today.

The VDLC investors, however, were less influenced by humanitarian discourse, far less interested in promoting Aboriginal employment, and exercised fewer controls over their colonial agent Edward Curr. When directed to adopt an employment policy in 1829, he simply ignored the order. Rather, he actively supported the removal of the Aboriginal people from their homelands on the company grant and became an active promoter of the idea of a 'native-free' colony.[74]

The experiences of the AAC indicate that there is every reason to expect that the VDLC could have implemented an Aboriginal employment policy, which in turn could have enabled the survival of more Aboriginal people in northwest Tasmania. Curr missed a golden opportunity to promote the employment of Tasmanian Aboriginal people at a critical point in the Colony's history. Like Dawson, he could have been remembered as a champion of Aboriginal survival. But the opposite is the case: he is remembered today as an active proponent of Tasmanian Aboriginal extermination.

Notes

1. Robert Dawson, *The Present State of Australia; A Description of the Country, its Advantages and Prospects, with Reference to Emigration; and a Particular Account of the Manners, Customs, and Condition of its Aboriginal inhabitants*, 2nd ed. (London: Smith, Elder and Co., 1831), 19.
2. VDL Co Orders, No. 4, 22 March 1826: VDL C, 1826, Tasmanian Archive and Heritage Office, Hobart (hereafter TAHO). See also Ian McFarlane, *Beyond Awakening: The Aboriginal Tribes of North West Tasmania: A History* (Launceston: Fullers Bookshop, 2008), 76.
3. Information given by Lt Col Dumaresq on Friday 30 November 1827: AA Co Correspondence A, 78/9/1 Australian National University Archives, Canberra.
4. Ian McFarlane, 'Cape Grim', in *Whitewash: On Keith Windschuttle's Fabrication of Aboriginal History*, ed. Robert Manne (Melbourne: Black Inc., 2003), 279.
5. Curr to Directors, 28 Feb 1828, Despatch No. 11, 1828: VDL Co Papers, VDL 5/1, TAHO.
6. N.J.B. Plomley, ed. *Friendly Mission: The Tasmanian Journals and Papers of George August Robinson 1829–1834*, 2nd ed. (Launceston and Hobart: Queen Victoria Museum and Art Gallery, 2008), 216, 236–237.
7. The AAC is currently owned by the Tavistock Group, based in the Bahamas; the chairman and major shareholder, Joe Lewis, is the sixth wealthiest person in the UK. The company operates several cattle stations in the Northern Territory and owns seven million hectares of land. The VDLC is currently owned by the New Zealand company Fontera. The best-known history of the AAC before 1970 is by Jesse Gregson: *The Australian Agricultural Company 1824–1875* (Sydney: Angus and Robertson, 1907). The earliest histories of the VDLC include Jørgen

Jørgenson, *History of the Origin, Rise, and Progress of the Van Diemen's Land Company* (London: Robson Blades, 1829), and James Bischoff, *Sketch of the History of Van Diemen's Land and an Account of the Van Diemen's Land Company* (London: J. Richardson, 1832).
8. John Perkins, 'Convict Labour and the Australian Agricultural Company' in *Convict Workers: Reinterpreting Australia's Past*, ed. Stephen Nicholas (Sydney: Cambridge University Press, 1988); Deirdre Bairstow, 'With the Best Will in the World: Some Records of Early White Contact with the Gampignal on the Australian Agricultural Company's Estate at Port Stephens', *Aboriginal History* 17, no. 1 (1993), 1–21; Mark Hannah, 'Aboriginal Workers in the Australian Agricultural Company 1824–1857', *Labour History* 82 (May 2002), 17–33.
9. C.D. Rowley, *The Destruction of Aboriginal Society: Aboriginal Policy and Practice*, vol. 1 (Canberra: Australian National University Press, 1970), 17.
10. Richard Broome, 'Aboriginal Workers on Southeastern Frontiers', *Australian Historical Studies* 26, no. 103 (1994), 203–220; Alan Pope, 'Aboriginal Adaptation to Early Colonial Labour Markets: The South Australian Experience', *Labour History* 54 (1988), 1–20.
11. Geoff Lennox, 'The Van Diemen's Land Company and the Tasmanian Aborigines: A Reappraisal', *Papers and Proceedings, Tasmanian Historical Research Association* 37, no. 4 (1990), 165–208; McFarlane, *Beyond Awakening*.
12. Hannah, 'Aboriginal Workers', 28, 30.
13. Hannah, 'Aboriginal Workers', 20.
14. James Backhouse, *A Narrative of a Visit to the Australian Colonies* (London: Hamilton, Adams and Co., 1843), 107–130.
15. Lennox, 'Van Diemen's Land Company', 207–208.
16. Edward Curr, *An Account of the Colony of Van Diemen's Land Principally Designed for the Use of Emigrants* (London: George Cowie and Co., 1824).
17. McFarlane, *Beyond Awakening*, 70.
18. McFarlane, *Beyond Awakening*, 89.
19. McFarlane, *Beyond Awakening*, 89–95.
20. P.A. Pemberton, 'The London Connection: The Formation and Early Years of the Australian Agricultural Company' (PhD thesis, Australian National University, 1991).
21. Pemberton, 'The London Connection', Appendix A: Australian Agricultural Company Shareholders Lists, 346–353; VDL Co Shareholders List: VDL Co Papers, 206, TAHO.
22. Pemberton, 'The London Connection', 40.
23. McFarlane, *Beyond Awakening*, 252, note 97.
24. The AAC gained its charter in the Act of Parliament 5 Geo. IV, cap. 86 (6 December 1824) and the VDLC by the Act 6 Geo. IV, cap. 39 (10 November 1825).

25. Pemberton, 'The London Connection', 42.
26. Pemberton, 'The London Connection', 43.
27. Pemberton, 'The London Connection', 47.
28. See Pemberton, 'The London Connection', Appendix A, 346–353; for VDL Co shareholders lists, see VDL Co Papers, 206, TAHO.
29. Pemberton, 'The London Connection', 39–40, 66; VDL Co shareholders list: VDL Co papers, 206, TAHO.
30. For Bennet, see C.M.H. Clark, *A History of Australia*, vol. I (Melbourne: Melbourne University Press, 1962), 332–333, 339, 367; for MacQueen, see E.W. Dunlop, 'Thomas Potter MacQueen' in *Australian Dictionary of Biography*, vol. 2, ed. A.G.L. Shaw and C.M.H. Clark (Melbourne: University of Melbourne Press, 1967), 195–196.
31. Pemberton, 'The London Connection', Appendix A, 346–353.
32. Pemberton, 'The London Connection', Appendix A, 346–353.
33. Zoe Laidlaw, 'Investigating Empire: Humanitarians, Reform and the Commission of Eastern Inquiry', *The Journal of Imperial and Commonwealth History* 40, no. 5 (December 2012), 750.
34. Alan Lester and Fae Dussart, *Colonization and the Origins of Humanitarian Governance: Protecting Aborigines across the Nineteenth Century British Empire* (Cambridge: Cambridge University Press, 2014), 1–36.
35. AA Co Minutes, 26 November 1824, cited in Pemberton, 'The London Connection', 185.
36. Pemberton, 'The London Connection', 196.
37. Dawson, *Present State of Australia*, 1–2.
38. See Alan Atkinson, *Camden* (Melbourne: Oxford University Press, 1988), 21, 208.
39. Atkinson, *Camden*, 21, 208.
40. Hannah, 'Aboriginal Workers', 40.
41. K.A. Green, 'John Ingle (1781?–1872)', in *Australian Dictionary of Biography*, vol. 2, ed. A.G.L. Shaw and C.M.H. Clark (Melbourne: University of Melbourne Press, 1967), 3.
42. VDL Shareholders list: VDL Co Papers, 206, TAHO.
43. McFarlane, *Beyond Awakening*, 68.
44. R.W. Horton to Curr, 14 April 1825 and Bathurst to Curr, 15 April 1825: VDL Co Papers 173/1/1, TAHO.
45. See entry on Edward Curr in *Australian Dictionary of Biography*, vol. 1, ed. A.G.L. Shaw and C.M.H. Clark (Melbourne: University of Melbourne Press, 1967), 269–272.
46. Bathurst to Darling, 12 July 1825, *Historical Records of Australia*, series I, vol. xii (Sydney: Commonwealth of Australia, 1919), 21.
47. See Australian Joint Copying Project National Archives (UK) Public Record Office (PRO) Colonial Office (CO) 201/25; see also Lyndall Ryan, *Tasmanian Aborigines: A History Since 1803* (Sydney: Allen and Unwin, 2012), 47.

48. Diary and Field Book of Henry Hellyer, VDL 341, TAHO; Jørgen Jørgenson, *History of the Origin, Rise and Progress of the Van Diemen's Land Company* (London, 1829; facsimile edition, Hobart: Melanie Publications, 1979).
49. Curr to Directors, 28 February 1828: VDL Co Papers, Inward Despatch No. 11, VDL 5/1, TAHO. See also McFarlane, *Beyond Awakening*, 93–94.
50. Court to Curr, 28 October 1828 and 8 October 1829: VDL Co Papers, Outward Despatches No 83 and 93, VDL 6/1, TAHO; see also McFarlane, *Beyond Awakening*, 94–95.
51. Adey resigned in 1828 and Goldie resigned at the end of 1829.
52. Charles E. Bennett, *Early Days of Port Stephens* (Newcastle, n.d.), 4.
53. Bennett, *Early Days of Port Stephens*, 5.
54. Hannah, 'Aboriginal Workers', 17.
55. McFarlane, *Beyond Awakening*, 54.
56. McFarlane, *Beyond Awakening*, 49, 52, 55.
57. McFarlane, *Beyond Awakening*, 63.
58. Author's estimate.
59. Plomley, *Friendly Mission*, 295–320.
60. Ryan, *Tasmanian Aborigines*, 22–25, 34–37.
61. N.J.B. Plomley, *Jorgen Jorgenson and the Aborigines of Van Diemen's Land* (Hobart: Blubber Head Press, 1991), 9.
62. Plomley, *Jorgen Jorgenson*, 9.
63. Plomley, *Friendly Mission*, 214.
64. 6 June 1826: VDL Co Papers, 540, TAHO.
65. John Crawford, W.F. Ellis, and G.H. Stancombe, eds. *The Diaries of John Helder Wedge 1824–1835* (Hobart: Royal Society of Tasmania, 1962), 48.
66. McFarlane, *Beyond Awakening*, 87–88.
67. Plomley, *Friendly Mission*, 214.
68. Quoted in McFarlane, *Beyond Awakening*, 80.
69. McFarlane, *Beyond Awakening*, 91.
70. McFarlane, *Beyond Awakening*, 76.
71. McFarlane, *Beyond Awakening*, 91.
72. James Bischoff, *Sketch of the History of Van Diemen's Land* (London: John Richardson, 1832).
73. Bischoff, *Sketch*, Appendix, 185–260.
74. James Boyce, *Van Diemen's Land* (Melbourne: Black Inc., 2008), 308.

CHAPTER 3

Ambiguity and Necessity: Settlers and Aborigines in Intimate Tension in Mid-Nineteenth-Century Australia

Angela Woollacott

In the middle decades of the nineteenth century, settler pastoralism spread rapidly across the Australian colonies. This was a core part of the settler colonialism expanding around the globe, a form of colonialism that shared features with colonies of direct rule, such as reliance on militarism, even as it had land-grabbing and dispossession at its heart. In this chapter I ponder questions of morality under settler pastoralism, with the goal of tracing connections between the economics of colonialism, violence, and intimacy. To contend with such questions, we need to place settler colonialism and pastoralism in global context.

As is well known, by the 1830s European imperialism was deeply entrenched, already controlling much of the globe. The following decades would see the rapid further expansion of the British and French empires in particular, with settler colonialism spreading across vast territories including in southern and northern Africa and the western United States. Violence structured the contact zones of aggressively expanding colonialism, from the British settler colonies of Canada, Australia, and New

A. Woollacott (✉)
Australian National University, Acton, ACT, Australia

© The Author(s) 2018
P. Edmonds, A. Nettelbeck (eds.), *Intimacies of Violence in the Settler Colony*, Cambridge Imperial and Post-Colonial Studies Series, https://doi.org/10.1007/978-3-319-76231-9_3

Zealand, to crown colonies of various European empires including British India, the Netherlands East Indies, and French Indochina. Warfare was fundamental to imperial expansion, while colonies of direct rule such as French Indochina and British India violently put down rebellions and anti-colonial wars, consolidating their grip through militarism and the threat of violence.[1] Insurrections and uprisings commonly characterised colonial societies. Thus, militarised violence pervaded frontier zones and the daily life of colonial societies. The ubiquitous presence of troops, their continual availability to colonial regimes, and the strategic deployment of indigenous men as soldiers and police all sustained the rule of colonisers. Warfare in diffuse and chaotic forms characterized imperial expansion and indigenous resistance.[2] This was the broader context for Australian settler colonialism of the early-mid nineteenth century. Importantly, British settlers in Australia were aware of at least some of these developments elsewhere.

Settler morality was put under scrutiny by the 1835–1836 British Parliamentary Select Committee on Aborigines, whose work has been analysed by Elizabeth Elbourne through the committee's account of the 'sinfulness of settlers'. Elbourne argues that a particular form of evangelical Christianity had been forged in the preceding battle for the abolition of slavery and now drove the committee's work. She canvasses the committee's views of expanding settler control in New South Wales, the Cape Colony, Canada, and New Zealand, and its attempt to find redemption for the problematic morality of colonialism. In the face of expanding capitalist agriculture, Elbourne contends, which in the case of New South Wales was driven by white settlers who were 'peculiarly corrupt and immoral', the committee sought ways forward for British colonial policy that would redeem both settlers and Aborigines. In relation to New South Wales, she suggests:

> Court evidence speaks to the relationship on the ground between intimacy and violence (as interaction and violence co-existed), as well as to central importance of violence to frontier relationships. It also hints at ways in which at least some settlers thought of violence, perhaps as regrettable but also as a necessity.[3]

I shall pursue some of the interlinked factors Elbourne considers, including settler morality, intimacy, and violence, though my concern is not with the committee's views but with relations between settlers and

Indigenous people on the ground on the pastoral frontiers of southern Australia in the early to mid-nineteenth century. In particular, I will focus on how, as settler territorial control expanded, interracial relations became at once immediate and fraught, as the economic requirements of pastoralism made moral ambiguity a staple of settler life. While Elbourne briefly alludes to 'capitalist agriculture', I shall focus on the immediacies of settler pastoralism, whose specificities justify attention.

Recent debates over the nature of settler colonialism have revised Patrick Wolfe's thesis that it involved a logic of elimination, to emphasise instead both the coexistence of settlers and Aborigines and the latter's exploitation.[4] It is, of course, relevant to pay attention to the economic basis of specific modes of settler colonialism, such as settler pastoralism. In his study of capitalism and the changing economy of the Australian colonies, Philip McMichael points to the effects of land dispersal in this expansionist phase of settler pastoralism. In contrast to the mixed-use, developed estates of the coastal regions, the squatters of the 1830s and 1840s were often semi-nomadic. Pastoralism produced good financial returns, such that some mixed-use farmers relied on squatting and pastoralism to develop their older estates. But the squatter who had no other estate usually developed a credit relationship with a coastally based merchant to sustain their enterprise. Squatters' runs varied greatly in size, as did their financial resources. Smaller-scale squatters supervised their own runs, while larger-scale operators might include several partners, or could be colonial investors who had financial partners elsewhere. Capital investment in improving pastoral runs in this period was much less than in the older, mixed-use estates. Partly because of the insecurity of land tenure for squatters, the buildings and infrastructure they erected were often regarded as temporary or makeshift, put together from local materials. This in turn encouraged squatters to claim more land than they needed, and, rather than improving pastures, finding fresh ones as they needed them. These factors encouraged a speculative attitude towards pastoralism, including an emphasis on quick financial returns. Labour availability was a complicated issue for pastoralists, especially workers to use as shepherds. Up until the late 1840s and early 1850s in the convict colonies, convicts on assignment provided much of the labour. In the non-convict colonies of the southern mainland, procuring sufficient labourers was a nagging problem. Workers were often mobile, and squatters in districts at a remove from the settled areas often exercised a good deal of freedom in their management of labourers.[5]

It was in this economic context that pastoralists augmented the available labourers through systems of importing indentured labour if they could. From the 1820s, indentured British labourers were brought to the Australian colonies in groups. German labourers were also imported to a few parts. In addition to European indentured workers, various indentured labour schemes brought Indian, Chinese, Pacific Islander, and Māori workers to the Australian colonies in the first half of the nineteenth century. A few Indians arrived as convicts and as servants brought directly by masters and mistresses, while groups of indentured labourers were brought from India in a range of schemes from the 1810s. Chinese workers were brought to the Australian colonies from the 1820s.[6] And it was also in this context that settlers turned to requesting, cajoling, and compelling Aboriginal people to perform labour; sometimes for nothing, sometimes for supplies, and, especially up to the mid-century, very rarely for anything like real wages.

While the specificities of Australian settler pastoralism are salient, it is also worth thinking for a moment about its commonalities with older plantation societies such as in the Caribbean. Undoubtedly there were crucial legal and cultural differences between plantation colonies based on the labour of the enslaved, and settler colonialism. Yet there may be similarities that help us to see some connections between economy, violence, and morality. As David Lambert points out in his study of the British colony of Barbados during the period of abolition, Barbadian plantation owners forged a white creole identity that hinged in part on committing and witnessing acts of terror perpetrated as planters and others put down acts of revolt.[7] Witnessing and complicity forged a shared identity unifying the planter class against those on whose labour they depended.

It may be useful to consider whether early-mid nineteenth century settlers in Australia, in their preparedness to use violence against Indigenous people, shared a moral economy not unlike that forged by planters in Barbados. Perhaps it is confusing to introduce the term 'moral economy' into the same discussion as morality—because they are different, albeit related. When E.P. Thompson described his notion of a moral economy amongst eighteenth-century workers protesting economic and social change, he referred to the 'legitimising notion' shared by those who participated in food riots and the 'belief that they were defending traditional rights or customs' and 'were supported by the wider consensus of the community'. Workers, according to Thompson, acted within a consensus grounded on 'a consistent traditional view of social norms and obligations, of the proper economic functions of several parties within the community'.[8]

Does some of Thompson's definition of a moral economy help us to see how Australian settlers were forging their own unified identity at least partly through complicity in violence, as Lambert has suggested for planters in Barbados? Recently arrived settlers in the Australian colonies did not draw on a venerable sense of shared traditional rights, customs, or social norms, like eighteenth-century labourers. Their pastoral districts were only just being carved out, not entrenched even as long as Barbadian plantations. Settlers lived in loosely connected communities that were often beyond the active reach of the law. But to some extent they depended on each other for assistance and community, and together they developed a shared sense of communal values, including methods of labour management that could involve moral judgements. Like the witnessing and complicity in acts of terror by planters in Barbados, managing Aboriginal labourers on whom squatters relied at times involved violence—in the form of reprisals or sometimes threats. This violence could be directed at controlling and sustaining a local economy in which the labour of Aboriginal workers was necessary; a coexistence rather than elimination. As Amanda Nettelbeck put it recently, in her article 'Proximate Strangers and Familiar Antagonists', 'privatised settler violence' occurred 'on remote frontiers where a culture of secrecy kept settler acts of so-called "rough justice" outside the law's line of sight'.[9] It is in the precarious functioning of a pastoralism dependent on Aboriginal cooperation and labour that we can see the linkages between intimacy, violence, and colonial economies. Pastoral runs supported modest settler homesteads, with Aboriginal labourers camped nearby in a proximity that could be at once quotidian and tense.

As we know, settlers in the southern and eastern Australian colonies in the 1830s–1850s quickly learnt to improvise and to adapt. Europeans negotiated unfamiliar geographies and climate, and learnt bush skills such as hut-building. People from various parts of the British Isles learnt to recognise Australian trees, birds, and animals, how to fight bushfires, and how to substitute local fauna in familiar recipes. Britons with diverse backgrounds became farmers, pastoralists, and gold-seekers. Desperate for labour, especially in the non-convict colonies of Western Australia (until the 1850s), South Australia, and Victoria, they assessed the possibilities of Aboriginal workers. Turning to Indigenous people for help with hut-building, shepherding, and tracking lost animals, among other forms of labour, settlers soon adapted to living close to Aborigines.

In 1841, a key proponent of Edward Gibbon Wakefield's scheme of systematic colonisation, Henry Chapman, even went so far as to propose that Aborigines could be turned into a peasant class to supply labour for settlers. A lawyer who would go on to a judicial career in New Zealand and a political career in Tasmania and Victoria, Chapman expounded his vision of Aboriginal people's role in a treatise advocating the Western Australian Company's then-incipient settlement at Australind, initially planned for a location north of Perth near what is now Geraldton. Confident of Western Australia's agricultural potential, imagining crops from olives, wine, and fruit, to nuts, cotton, rice, and tobacco, Chapman acknowledged that labour supply would be a problem. He mentioned the possibility that free labourers could be brought from India or 'the Malay archipelago'. In a whole chapter of his treatise devoted to 'The Natives and their Civilization', Chapman noted that Aboriginal people in Western Australia 'exhibited considerable aptitude for European habits' and had already been employed by some settlers. He expressed the view that there were 'ample proofs' that Aboriginal people could be employed in 'various occupations ... if adequate inducements were held out'. Aboriginal people's skills at crafts, their engagement in trade, and inclination towards cultivation of the land showed that 'the civilization and settlement of the native population' was a possible goal. If they were paid the same as white labourers, rather than receiving only meagre food, they might indeed be brought 'into the state of an industrious peasantry'.[10] While Chapman's conception of a feudal society recreated in Western Australia was not to be, his imagining reflects the contemporary reality that Aboriginal people were working for settlers—even as they were not properly compensated.

In settler accounts of daily life on pastoral properties, we can see systemic links between economic reliance on Aboriginal labour and ubiquitous violence. Settlers needed Aboriginal labour, yet their even more fundamental demand for the land allowed them to accept moral ambiguities. Within what Nettelbeck has termed the 'localised frontier and its everyday proximities',[11] it was possible for settlers to know Aboriginal clans and individuals well enough to name them, and to observe their ways of life—and yet to accept the use of violence against them.

We know from the work of multiple historians about the ubiquity of Aboriginal employment across the southern mainland colonies. We know too that Aborigines were employed not only as shepherds, jackaroos, and trackers for pastoralists, but as agricultural labourers, domestic servants (including child-nurses and laundresses), grooms, and handymen, bullock drivers, guides, interpreters, and native police, to collect wood and build huts, for fetching and delivering, in shearing, fishing, whaling and sealing, and other jobs besides. Aboriginal labour was especially valuable beyond areas where convicts were assigned to settlers. Further, we know that Aboriginal workers were often not properly compensated, expected to work for tea, sugar, tobacco, and other meagre rations, and that Aboriginal children were often kidnapped and forced into service.[12] In many areas, a mutual if unequal interdependence developed between settlers and displaced Aboriginal people who were desperate to stay on or near their country and for whom casual employment became part of their livelihood. This daily coexistence within specific localities led to moral ambiguity for many settlers, including the moral juggling act of bonding with Aboriginal workers while seeing non-domesticated Aborigines as requiring punitive violence.

In Western Australia, we know a little about the use of Aboriginal labour in the settlement at Australind which, despite initial intentions, was founded by the Western Australian Company in 1840 south of Perth at Port Leschenault, near what is now Bunbury. Australind (the name intended to connect Australia and India) was established as one of the two Wakefieldian systematic colonies in Australia, along with those later set up in New Zealand. Imagined as a sizable town with a full complement of urban amenities, it would not fulfill its founders' dreams. It survived, but only on a small scale. The chief commissioner Marshall Waller Clifton and his eldest daughter Louisa Clifton both kept diaries, which allow us to piece together something of settlers' dependence on and familiarity with Aboriginal people (probably the Pinjarup)—as well as defining and punishing them as criminals.

As soon as he arrived in March 1841, Waller Clifton began to rely on Aboriginal guides, including immediately taking 'a Native Guide' along 'on Horse back with Us' when he rode up to Perth to meet with the governor.[13] For the local Aboriginal people, working for these new arrivals was a survival strategy in a world where, since around 1830, coastal groups of the southwest had suffered deaths from frontier conflicts, dispossession, and loss of their food sources.[14] Language must have been an issue between settlers and Aborigines, yet they managed to communicate. On 27 April 1841, Clifton noted in his journal that the 'Natives forboded Rain', recording also his own scepticism; the rain arrived two days later.[15] It is possible that one reason Australind did not prosper to the degree its founders had hoped was Clifton's own temperament; in June 1843 the directors of the Western Australian Company would dismiss Waller Clifton as chief commissioner. Certainly we can see in his journal the vehemence with which he expressed his dislike of Aborigines. When he took the Aboriginal man Jugan and his wife as guides on a short exploratory trip of the region, he wrote in his diary:

> I was entirely disgusted with the savage brutality of this Native. In fact they are all Murderers & fellows who are a disgrace to human Nature and have not one redeeming quality. The selfishness of the Man & his brutal unkindness to his Wife & refusing her almost anything we offered her made me detest this Race more than ever.[16]

Despite Clifton's low opinion of Aboriginal people, the Australind settlers' dependence included using them for labour such as clearing land for roads, for which they were paid in flour. Trouble erupted when Aboriginal people helped themselves to food from the community's storehouses—perhaps not surprisingly, given that they were paid in rations. That settlers knew Aboriginal people as individuals is reflected in the fact that Clifton and other regional officials soon had warrants for the arrest of eight Aborigines. The warrants for men including Ninda, Yourga, and 'Morechap called Troublehouse' shows the cultural mix settlers used in applying names. Clifton sent a party to arrest these men, who initially escaped; the pursuers instead seized several women and broke about fifty spears. Soon, one of those under warrant surrendered, and two were captured. These three Aboriginal men were remanded and committed for punishment, though one escaped. The unlucky two were sent by ship to Fremantle. This incident at Australind in 1841 was one small part of the historical process, continuing into the twentieth century, by which Western Australian Aborigines were criminalised and turned into convicts.[17]

It was not only the chief commissioner himself who interacted with local Aboriginal people. It is evident that they lived in and around the settlers, assisting them in various ways. His eldest daughter Louisa, who would later marry the resident magistrate at Bunbury, referred repeatedly to Indigenous people in her diary. At first, when they had just arrived and were sleeping in tents, she and her sister Mary were fearful of noises at night in case it was 'a native' coming in. When a servant woman wandered off and was lost, 'natives and other people' went in search. Two diary entries discuss the matter of the stolen flour and the pursuit of the men held responsible. Louisa expressed pity for the men arrested:

> Some of them will be sent, I fear, to [the prison on] Rottnest [Island]; a dreadful punishment it is; their heads are shaved and they become convicts in fact; but being deprived of liberty and independence so dear to wild man, they soon die of broken hearts. ... When will justice appear upon earth? Not I fear while white man who professes Christianity falls so far short of acting up to its first principles. I cannot help liking these poor people, especially the children.[18]

Part of the moral complexity, at least for some settlers, was understanding that criminalising Aboriginal people and imprisoning them was itself a form of violence.

Australind settlers and Aborigines continued to live in close proximity, in a relationship of economic interdependency that occasionally flourished as social amicability. In September 1841, Aboriginal people held a corroboree 'at Tea Time by the store', which the settlers 'all attended'.[19] Yet Waller Clifton described the event in demeaning terms, recording in his diary that it was 'degrading to Human Nature to see Men in such a state of Monkeish action'.[20] Clifton's racist language and determination to severely punish Aboriginal workers, whom he knew personally, provide us with some insight into the ways in which, in contrast to those like his daughter, other settlers were able to justify harsh treatment to themselves in moral terms—including criticizing gender relations within Aboriginal society (see Fig. 3.1).

In South Australia too we have much evidence of close and conflicted relations from the first settler landing at the end of 1836. Contemporary observers recorded the ubiquitous presence of Aborigines, and the relations of mutual curiosity and codependence that quickly evolved. Settlers in specific areas developed arrangements with local Aborigines about work such as hut-building. G.B. Earp, who around 1850 established a small pastoral run in the eastern part of South Australia, recorded that when he arrived at his lease he 'was told that there were in the neighbourhood some *tame blacks* who could run up a couple of bark huts, weather tight and quite large enough for our purpose in three or four days, and that a messenger should be sent off at once ... to bring up a couple or three to set to work on our stockyard'.[21] Even in the town of Adelaide itself, settlers continued to employ Aboriginal people for household chores:

Fig. 3.1 S.T. Gill (1818–1880), *Captain Davison's house 'Blakiston' near Mount Barker*, 1848, Adelaide, watercolour on paper, 21.3 × 33.8 cm; South Australian Government Grant 1979, Art Gallery of South Australia, Adelaide

> Long after wood was carted to town for sale the natives proffered their services to cut it up for a small consideration and to obtain this employment they presented themselves at the doors and windows of the early settlers with some such application as this ... 'me cut wood; you give me ... bit of baccy'.[22]

While such intimate and quotidian interdependence must have engendered familiarity, there is ample evidence in early settler accounts of violence. Settler memoirs reveal familiarity with Aboriginal skills, their practices of using Aboriginal labour, and the pervasive violence. Simpson Newland, who grew up in the 1840s and 1850s in the Encounter Bay area of South Australia, recalled that his father 'encouraged the blacks to come to the settlement, and in time they became very useful ... at Harvest time'. His retrospective view was that it was a mistake to try to 'make the blacks into agriculturalists and farmers, when by nature and habits they were essentially hunters'. His father managed them successfully by employing them but not using pressure with them, such that 'they were still able to catch fish or hunt opossums and other small animals whenever they chose.' Later, when the younger Newland joined in a pastoral venture in the River

Darling area of New South Wales which involved droving sheep overland, he would learn first-hand that the 'blacks were wonderful swimmers, and proved invaluable allies in many of my journeys with sheep, as they could always save them from drowning'. Despite these close working relationships and appreciation of Aboriginal labour, Newland's memoir refers to bloody clashes between Aborigines and settlers, especially along the droving routes of the upper Murray River. He recites that one droving party 'had an encounter with the natives, which gave the latter the strong reason to avoid attacks on white travellers in future'. Moreover, 'other parties at a later date had also serious losses from the fierce tribes of the Lower Murray'.[23] The stock-droving inherent to the spread of pastoralism thus directly sparked some of the bloodshed between settlers and Aborigines.

Some accounts reveal sustained and cooperative interactions. In early 1840, the Sanders family, for example, took up a selection of land at Echunga Creek southeast of Adelaide, where they engaged in small-scale pastoralism as well as mixed farming. Jane Sanders, a child when they first arrived, later recorded that 'the natives had their camp close to our garden in which were growing vegetables and melons … but they never meddled with them'. She described them as 'a tribe of natives, not numerous, twenty or thirty perhaps', and called them 'a kindly race' who 'until they were spoilt by the Europeans, [were] honest'. These Aborigines (who would have been either Kaurna or Peramangk people) interacted with other settlers too, sometimes asking for food. The Sanderses sometimes employed one of the Aboriginal women to sweep outside their house. It may be pertinent that the father, George Sanders, was a Quaker. Particularly telling of just how familiar relations became is Jane's recollection that her 'brothers often visited the natives in their wurlies'. Her 'younger brothers copied their weapons, spears, waddies etc. And they became quite expert in using the weapons, accompanying the native men and boys on their hunting expeditions.'[24] Yet it is clear that this intimate proximity was a temporary stage of accommodation, albeit one that may have lasted for several decades. As we know from Amanda Nettelbeck's work with Rob Foster and Rick Hosking, what they call 'an undeclared war' would unfold across the colony.[25]

And of course sexual violence was woven into colonisation, with interracial sexuality a key way in which intimacy and violence were intertwined. The close daily relations of settlers and Aboriginal people on pastoral frontiers facilitated cross-racial sexuality, mostly though not wholly between white men and Aboriginal women. As Hannah Robert has argued, sex between white men and Aboriginal women in the nineteenth century was commonplace, running the gamut from rape and sexual slavery, through prostitution, to cohabitation and marriage. Settlers normalised it by viewing it as shameful and with horror, to be seen in the same kind of ubiquitous category of vice and immorality as drinking and gambling. One effect of such categorising was that, with such relationships to be hidden and considered illicit, they were separated from acceptable marriages and families.[26] Yet here too ambiguities abounded. Settler women often suspected or knew of settler men's abuse of Aboriginal women. Occasionally, white women on the frontier sought to persuade men to desist from sexually assaulting Aboriginal women. At other times, it was easier to turn a blind eye or to pretend ignorance, just as it could be easier to be oblivious to violence or reprisals against Aboriginal people. Through one case study from Western Australia at the end of the nineteenth century, Victoria Haskins has demonstrated 'the significance for the colonial project of a particular construction of white womanhood as chaste, morally irreproachable and above all innocent of any knowledge of interracial sex'.[27] Women's own interactions with Aboriginal people could be fraught, and in some we can see the ways in which fear played into moral ambiguities through specific interactions. From one particular incident when a large group of Aborigines visited a settler hut, we can apprehend the tense intimacy of frontier life, when violence was always possible—but did not always erupt.

My final narrative episode centres on a moment in which violence did not escalate, yet is a vignette replete with the complexities of intimacy and frontier violence during the expansion of settler pastoralism. It comes from the published memoir of settler Katherine Kirkland of the years 1839–1841 when she, her husband, and infants lived (with her brother and some employees) on their sheep station at Trawalla, now between Ballarat and Ararat in the state of Victoria, but at that time considered the far up-country, numerous days' travel northwest of Melbourne (see Fig. 3.2). Kirkland's memoir is full of descriptive detail of the country, their journeyings, their and other settlers' humble huts, the monotonous diet of mutton and damper, and the bush itself, which she finds both beautiful and challenging. Interwoven in all of this are details of her observations of the local Aboriginal people, the Moner balug clan of the Wathaurong people, and her interactions with them.[28] Despite finding them at first 'very ugly and dirty', she becomes less afraid and even curious

Fig. 3.2 Katherine Kirkland, 'Life in the Bush: By a Lady,' *Chambers's Miscellany of Useful and Entertaining Tracts* 1, no. 8 (Edinburgh: William and Robert Chambers, 1845), 1

about them. She proudly notes that she 'was the first white woman who had ever been so far up the country', an honour she seems to claim only for herself and not for her servant Mary. Her interactions with Wathaurong people, both in her neighbourhood and en route from Geelong and Melbourne, include moments of mutual curiosity and friendly interaction, that seem to indicate the Wathaurong had established a *modus vivendi* with the settlers, at least for the time being.[29]

While criticising Aboriginal people as cannibals and for their gender relations (the unfair treatment she thought women received from men), she also consciously learns from them, describing some of their food-gathering practices, and learning to carry her baby in a basket like the 'native' women do. Kirkland evidently spent time alongside Aboriginal women, gathering food and learning from them how to cook particular plants:

> Maranong is a root found in the ground: it is white, and shaped like a carrot, but the taste is more like a turnip. The leubras dig for it with long pointed sticks, which they always carry in their hands. I have often eaten maranong; it is very good; and I have put it in soup for want of better vegetables, before we had a garden.[30]

From detailed observations in her memoir, Kirkland must have closely watched the Aboriginal women in the neighbourhood diving for mussels in the freshwater ponds, and collecting grubs from cherry and honeysuckle trees: 'they can tell, by knocking the tree with a stick, if any grubs are in it. When they knock the tree, they put their ear close to listen, and they open it with a tomahawk at the very spot the grubs are to be found. It is a large white grub, with a black head.' While Kirkland seems not to have tasted the grubs herself, she was willing to try the 'manna' from gum trees: 'Manna falls very abundantly from the gum-trees at certain seasons of the year. I think it was in March I gathered some. It is very good, and tastes like almond biscuits. It is only to be procured early in the morning, as it disappears soon after sunrise.' Ongoing practical exchanges between the Kirklands and the local Aborigines seemed to become a source of some pleasure as well as material benefit for both sides: 'We sometimes got some skins of the opossum and flying-squirrel, or tuan, from the natives. It was a good excuse for them to come to the station. I paid them with a piece of dress, and they were very fond of getting a red pocket handkerchief to tie round their necks.'[31]

The scene which I wish to focus on, which mixed intimacy with the threat of violence, occurred following an incident when a group of Aborigines took ninety of the Kirklands' sheep, which they finally found them with about 140 miles away—retrieving the live ones they could (along with taking the Aborigines' spears, tomahawks, waddies, and baskets), although Kirkland does not recount just what, if any, further reprisals the settlers inflicted. This taking of sheep reflects how tensions could play out through attacks on stock and property that culminated in violence.

One day when Kirkland was alone in the hut, she was visited by a large group of Aboriginal people, a group she estimated as being about a hundred. It is possible that this unusual mass visit was intended as a response to whatever reprisals the Kirklands had inflicted on those who took their sheep. She described the encounter thus:

> Some of the men came into [the hut], and examined all they saw very attentively, especially the pictures we had hanging on the walls. They were much

taken with a likeness of my mother, and laughed heartily at some black profiles; they said they were 'black leubras'. [I assume she means here the silhouette portraits that were popular from the mid-eighteenth century.] I told them to leave the hut, but they would not; and one, a very tall fellow, took the liberty of sitting down beside me on the sofa. I did not much like being alone with these gentry, so I rose to go to the door to call some one, but my tall friend took hold of my arm and made me sit down again; on which I cried out sufficiently loud to alarm my husband, who was building a hut behind. He came in and turned them all out; but they still kept hanging about the station for some time.[32]

This cameo of an intimate incident is intriguing, because of its dynamics—the Aboriginal men closely inspecting the pictures on the wall and laughing at them, and the incongruity of the Aboriginal man sitting with her on the sofa. Clearly, there is an implication of possible violence—violence that might have escalated if Kirkland's husband had not been close by. But she does not dwell on it, nor does she say specifically what she feared might happen. Moreover, the narrative goes on to say that in the further year or so that they remained on the station, they had a good and happy life. Nor does Kirkland suggest that when they moved, to take up a dairy farm closer to Melbourne, it was because of fear of the Aborigines.

Yet this incident is located in the narrative not long after Kirkland notes that they were receiving 'a good many visits from the natives' and that they had begun 'not to turn them away so quickly as we used to do'. It seems that the interactions between settlers and Indigenous people were increasing, perhaps as a result of the escalation of Indigenous displacement. But they never allowed the Moner balug to sleep at the station, other than a 'big boy' they called Tom, whom they sought to keep around to help them track stray cattle and sheep, and to chop wood.[33] Moreover, the account of this incident is quickly followed by her critical comments on their neighbouring squatter Mr. Baillie's attitude towards the Aborigines: he always allowed them to remain as long as they chose, and 'was too kind to them, and gave them great encouragement in his own hut'. This was mistaken, in the Kirklands' view, because: 'In many instances the undue severities of the settlers lead to reprisals from the natives, who are apt to inflict vengeance in a very indiscriminate manner.'[34] They were not surprised, she notes, when a groom at Mr. Baillie's was injured, by an Aborigine throwing a spear which stuck in his arm.

In the narrative at least, Kirkland seems to have sublimated any fear she felt—during both the visit from the hundred or so Aborigines, and the

Aboriginal man grabbing her arm and intimidating her in her hut—through criticising her neighbour Mr. Baillie. This small picture of intimate violence, circumscribed as it is, is useful as a window into evolving relations between the settlers and the local Aboriginal people. It would seem that the Aborigines who visited her hut en masse wanted to threaten or intimidate the Kirklands. But she does not record any larger incident occurring. It is as though this was a moment when things could have gone either way. There could have been an escalation of violence, but there was not. This vignette is arresting as well because of the possibility of interracial sexual violence that it seems to imply. Kirkland's memoir not only does not exaggerate the possibility of sexual violence; she does not even name it. It seems to be a story about what did NOT happen.

Kirkland's encounter with Aboriginal men inside her own hut is a relatively contained incident, but one which may allow us to glimpse something of Aboriginal people's dilemmas and decisions about when to escalate violence and when to eschew it. Kirkland's narrative does not tell us about what her husband, her brother, and the other British men were or were not doing beyond her observation. There was widespread warfare in this region around this time. Kirkland repeatedly comments on the men in the area wearing pistols, and refers to having one herself; yet, as Barbara Dawson notes, she is silent on specific details of any violence in which her husband or brother may have engaged.[35] Perhaps what this anecdote gives us is a picture of a moment of mutual restraint—a moment when the Kirklands chose not to use violence, and when this group of Aborigines used their own agency to maintain what was then the status quo. As for Aboriginal people elsewhere, accommodating settler pastoralism and living in its interstices was at least a way of staying on their own land.

We cannot, of course, know what the intentions of the Aboriginal men were, if indeed they had any fixed intention at all; but it is important to remember that the Kirklands cannot have known either. Nor can we know what Mr. Kirkland might have done had the group not left the hut. But then neither did the Aborigines. We are left to ponder an instant when what might have happened did not, and by that very fact reveals the indeterminacy of some frontier moments. Fraught interactions that did not result in assault or bloodshed, and were not sensationalised, can, perhaps, help us to apprehend the frontier as it was inhabited at once by settlers and Indigenous people, using our knowledge of the imbalance of power, Aborigines' ongoing loss of their lands and livelihoods, and the pervasive violence against them.

Conclusion

As settler territorial control expanded, interracial relations were at once immediate and fraught: the economic requirements of pastoralism made moral ambiguity a staple of settler life. If Australian pastoralism was both economically and morally distinguishable from Barbadian plantation society, it was an economic form whose imperatives made settler intimacy with Aborigines inevitable. Pastoralists wanted land—plenty of it, for their cattle and sheep to graze—which meant that they were often the first invaders in any area. They were at once at a distance from the centres of law and politics, and in close proximity to Aboriginal people. Moreover, Aboriginal tracking skills and familiarity with their own country were highly useful for pastoralists.

Perhaps the most telling line in Katherine Kirkland's narrative is when she criticises their neighbour Mr. Baillie for being too kind and encouraging to the Aboriginal people, an attitude she blames for the incident when his groom receives a spear in his arm. She commented: 'In many instances the undue severities of the settlers lead to reprisals from the natives, who are apt to inflict vengeance in a very indiscriminate manner.'[36] This suggests that there was a working understanding among at least some settlers about how to minimise violence, by treating the Aboriginal people without 'undue severity'. She blames Baillie for putting his workers at risk of violence by encouraging too close an arrangement with the Aborigines, who she thinks do not distinguish when it comes to directing vengeance. Kirkland's comments and her criticism of Baillie suggest that some settlers shared a sense of how much violence was acceptable; just how close by to keep the Aboriginal people on whose presence they depended to some extent; and how to moderate their interactions with them.

The 1835–1836 British Parliamentary Select Committee on Aborigines' worry that Australian settlers were 'peculiarly corrupt and immoral' perhaps reflected a more general sense that the convict system, on which the Australian colonies had been founded, had corroded settlers' morals. The Kirklands seem not to have been particularly sinful, immoral, or corrupt; indeed, Christianity probably underlay their views of Aboriginal people. But this willingness to make judgments about what was or was not unduly severe, in meting out violence to local Aboriginal people, reflected settlers' adaptability to their new environment. At least to some extent, it was a product of the exigencies of pastoralism. Living in isolated circumstances far from concentrated settlement, settlers depended in various ways on their neighbours, including for a social life, even if they did not always especially like them. They may not always have approved of the ways their neighbours treated either their paid labourers or the Aborigines they employed in less regular arrangements. But, at least to some extent, the level of interracial warfare was a circumstance settlers in any locale shared. Even if they blamed a particular neighbour for inciting or provoking violence, to some degree they were complicit in the fact of its existence unless they sought official intervention.

Focusing on the practical exigencies of pastoralism as an economic activity does not absolve settlers morally, nor does it justify frontier violence. But it may provide some insight into how and why they engaged in the moral juggling act of cultivating a 'big boy' like Tom to live at close range and be available for various tasks, while turning a blind eye to instances of violence in their local area. This moral juggling act may have enabled settlers who were not 'peculiarly corrupt and immoral' to find an emotional *modus vivendi*, even as it served to allow instances of violence against Aboriginal people to continue without official intervention. It also resembles a 'legitimising notion' of the sort that E.P. Thompson saw as part of a moral economy, one that could serve to forge a community consensus. What intrigues me most about the incident inside the Kirklands' hut, which could so easily have become violent but did not, is that it suggests that at least at moments settlers and Aborigines negotiated a consensus about violence not being necessary.

The economic demands of pastoralism in the bush led settlers to accept moral ambiguities and to develop their own particular moral economy, perhaps not very different from that of the Barbadian plantation owners in being based on complicity and shared knowledge. In Kirkland's narrative, as well as in the diaries kept by the Cliftons at Australind, and the memoir of Jane Sanders at Echunga Creek, we can see how the economic imperatives of pastoralism, in this early period of settler territorial conquest, led to a way of life in which intimacy and violence were closely intertwined, and were juggled on both sides.

Notes

1. James Belich, *Replenishing the Earth: The Settler Revolution and the Rise of the Anglo-World 1783–1939* (Oxford: Oxford University Press, 2009); Robert Aldrich and Kirsten McKenzie, eds. *The Routledge History of Western Empires* (London: Routledge, 2014), chapters 6 and 8.

2. On the broader historical connections between gender and warfare, see Karen Hagemann, Stefan Dudink, and Sonya O. Rose, eds. *Oxford Handbook on Gender, War and the Western World since 1650* (New York: Oxford University Press, forthcoming 2018).
3. Elizabeth Elbourne, 'The Sin of the Settler: The 1835–36 Select Committee on Aborigines and Debates Over Virtue and Conquest in the Early Nineteenth-Century British White Settler Empire', *Journal of Colonialism and Colonial History* 4, no. 3 (Winter 2003).
4. Patrick Wolfe, 'Settler Colonialism and the Elimination of the Native', *Journal of Genocide Research* 8, no. 4 (2006), 387–409. On the importance of recognising coexistence of settlers and Indigenous people, see Penelope Edmonds, *Urbanizing Frontiers: Indigenous Peoples and Settlers in 19th-Century Pacific Rim Cities* (Vancouver: UBC Press, 2010).
5. Philip McMichael, *Settlers and the Agrarian Question: Capitalism in Colonial Australia* (Cambridge: Cambridge University Press, 1984), 123–133.
6. On the variety, mixing and crossing of labour categories, see Angela Woollacott, *Settler Society in the Australian Colonies: Self-Government and Imperial Culture* (Oxford: Oxford University Press, 2015), chapter 3, 'Settler Men as Masters of Labour: Convicts and Non-white Workers'.
7. David Lambert, *White Creole Culture: Politics and Identity During the Age of Abolition* (Cambridge: Cambridge University Press, 2005), 126–127.
8. E.P. Thompson, *Customs in Common: Studies in Traditional Popular Culture* (New York: The New Press, 1991), 188.
9. Amanda Nettelbeck, 'Proximate Strangers and Familiar Antagonists: Violence on an Intimate Frontier', *Australian Historical Studies* 47, no. 2 (June 2016), 212.
10. Henry S. Chapman, *The New Settlement of Australind* (London: Harvey and Darton, 1841), esp. 95–103.
11. Nettelbeck, 'Proximate Strangers', 211.
12. On employment of and conditions for Aboriginal children in Western Australia, see Penelope Hetherington, *Settlers, Servants and Slaves: Aboriginal and European Children in the Nineteenth-Century in Western Australia* (Perth: University of Western Australia Press, 2002); for Queensland, see Shirleene Robinson, *Something like Slavery? Queensland's Aboriginal Child Workers 1842–1945* (Melbourne: Australian Scholarly Publishing, 2008).
13. Phyllis Barnes, J.M.R. Cameron, and H.A. Willis with Ian Berryman and Andrew Gill, eds. *The Australind Journals of Marshall Waller Clifton 1840–1861* (Perth: Hesperian Press, 2010), 26.
14. E.S. Ilbery, 'The Battle of Pinjarra, 1834: I. The Passing of the Bibulmun', *The Western Australian Historical Society: Journal and Proceedings* 1, no. 1 (1927), 24–30.

15. Barnes, *The Australind Journals*, 32.
16. Barnes, *The Australind Journals*, 35.
17. Barnes, *The Australind Journals*, 46–50.
18. Louisa Clifton, 'Fatigue and Bustle at Australind, 1841', in *No Place for a Nervous Lady: Voices from the Australian Bush*, ed. Lucy Frost (Melbourne: McPhee Gribble/Penguin Books, 1984), 74–82.
19. Barnes, *The Australind Journals*, 71.
20. Barnes, *The Australind Journals*, 71.
21. G.B. Earp, ed. *What We Did in Australia: Being the Practical Experiences of Three Clerks* (London: George Routledge and Co., 1853), 81.
22. H. Hussey, *More than Half a Century of Colonial Life and Christian Experience* (Adelaide: Hussey and Gillingham, 1897), 29.
23. *Memoirs of Simpson Newland CMG* (Adelaide: F.W. Preece and Sons, 1926), 34–58.
24. C.S. Sanders, ed. *The Settlement of George Sanders and his Family at Echunga Creek from the Journal of Jane Sanders* (Adelaide: Pioneers Association of South Australia, 1955; edited from an original manuscript), 9, 15–16.
25. Robert Foster, Rick Hosking, and Amanda Nettelbeck, *Fatal Collisions: The South Australian Frontier and the Violence of Memory* (Adelaide: Wakefield Press, 2001), 8.
26. Hannah Robert, 'Disciplining the Female Aboriginal Body: Inter-racial Sex and the Pretence of Separation', *Australian Feminist Studies* 16, no. 34 (2001), 71–72. On this topic, also see Bobbi Sykes, 'Black Women in Australia: A History', in *The Other Half: Women in Australian Society*, ed. Jan Mercer (Melbourne: Penguin Books Australia, 1975); Raymond Evans, '"Don't You Remember Black Alice, Sam Holt?": Aboriginal Women in Queensland History', *Hecate* 7 (1982); Kay Saunders and Raymond Evans, eds. *Gender Relations in Australia: Domination and Negotiation* (Sydney: Harcourt, Brace Jovanovich, 1992).
27. Victoria Haskins, '"Down in the Gully & Just Outside the Garden Walk": White Women and the Sexual Abuse of Aboriginal Women on a Colonial Australian Frontier', *History Australia* 10, no. 1 (2013), 13.
28. Barbara Dawson, *In the Eye of the Beholder: What Six Nineteenth-century Women Tell Us about Indigenous Authority and Identity* (Canberra: ANU Press, 2014), chapter 5, 'An Early, Short-term Settler—Katherine Kirkland: Valuable Insights Through the Silences', 83.
29. Katherine Kirkland, 'Life in the Bush: By a Lady', *Chambers's Miscellany of Useful and Entertaining Tracts* 1, no. 8 (Edinburgh: William and Robert Chambers, 1845), 13–14.
30. Kirkland, 'Life in the Bush', 14.
31. Kirkland, 'Life in the Bush', 19–20.

32. Kirkland, 'Life in the Bush', 20.
33. Kirkland, 'Life in the Bush', 19.
34. Kirkland, 'Life in the Bush', 20–21.
35. Dawson, *In the Eye of the Beholder*, 93.
36. Kirkland, 'Life in the Bush', 20–21.

CHAPTER 4

Intimate Violence in the Pastoral Economy: Aboriginal Women's Labour and Protective Governance

Amanda Nettelbeck

THE ABDUCTION OF 'JENNY LIND'

On 22 August 1898, Western Australia's recently appointed Chief Protector of Aborigines received a letter from Frank Wittenoom, one of the most established pastoralists of the north-west. The letter's subject was the abduction of 'Jenny Lind', a young Indigenous woman employed as the cook on Wittenoom's Boolardy station in the northern region of the Murchison River. Jenny and her Indigenous husband 'Dan' worked together at the station, and Wittenoom considered her 'a most useful servant'. Jenny and her three-year-old son had been taken from Boolardy at gunpoint by its former bookkeeper, a man named Braddock, and the pastoralist was now eliciting the Chief Protector's assistance to bring about her return to the station 'where she is under employment, and to the native who owns her'.[1]

Wittenoom's letter triggered a long trail of correspondence that continued over the next two months between the Chief Protector of

A. Nettelbeck (✉)
University of Adelaide, Adelaide, SA, Australia

© The Author(s) 2018
P. Edmonds, A. Nettelbeck (eds.), *Intimacies of Violence in the Settler Colony*, Cambridge Imperial and Post-Colonial Studies Series, https://doi.org/10.1007/978-3-319-76231-9_4

Aborigines, the pastoralist employer, the Law Department, and the police about how to legally achieve Jenny Lind's retrieval. Far from being limited to the immediate crisis of her abduction, this body of correspondence speaks eloquently to a much broader set of issues about the vulnerability of Indigenous women workers in colonial industries, and about the uncertain place they occupied at the intersection of raced and gendered forms of colonial labour relations. This chapter will consider the threads of Jenny Lind's case in order to explore the law's limited capacity to provide protection to Indigenous women employed in colonial economies, even during a late colonial age when statutory powers of 'Aboriginal protection' were becoming normative across the Australian colonies.[2]

As scholars have shown, the place of colonised peoples in institutions of colonial service was ambivalently intimate, grounded in conditions of uneven power but also erosive of a colonial hierarchy built upon the separation of racial boundaries.[3] A key agenda of the protection policies that became incrementally applied to Indigenous people through the later nineteenth century was to reinforce the boundaries of racial separation, although in reality this governmental objective was frequently subverted.[4] Instead, intimate relations between Indigenous women and white men on Australia's pastoral frontiers were common. As feminist historians have argued, they were also highly complex, unfolding on a sliding scale between agency and disempowerment, consent and coercion. Sometimes consensual and mutually beneficial as part of a wider colonial culture of exchange and adaptation, such intimacies were also grounded in the violence and exploitation of colonial conquest.[5] But as a structural problem for the law that played out beyond individual degrees of choice or its absence, the 'detaining' of Indigenous women was a common practice within colonial frontier economies, as authorities were well aware. This practice was embedded in the pastoral sector and other frontier economies like the pearling and mining industries, and sometimes the representatives of law and government were themselves part of the problem.[6]

In a transparent way, Jenny Lind's abduction reflected the reality that legal and other policy measures were inadequate in fully policing the borders of interracial contact. But beyond the familiar question of the legal system's limited reach over colonial frontiers and over the interracial encounters that underpinned their developing economies, her case illuminated a more profound set of limitations in the gendered politics of protective governance itself. The extensive official correspondence that followed her abduction reveals the way that existing legal provisions—established to protect Indigenous workers from exploitation—actually helped reinforce the paternalistic economic norms of a late colonial culture, which assumed that Indigenous women were already placed under the protection of their husbands and employers. In effect, protective legislation was not only inadequate in upholding the rights of Indigenous women to the law's protections; more subtly, it tolerated a culture of intimate violence against Indigenous women who worked in colonial industries by privileging the rights of the men and masters who 'owned' them.

The letter to the Chief Protector, Henry Prinsep, outlined all known facts about Jenny Lind's disappearance from the station. Her abductor, Braddock, had left behind a letter for the station manager, George Thompson, which Wittenoom also forwarded to the Chief Protector. In it, Braddock attempted to explain his actions and to dissuade Thompson from a pursuit. He was 'so deeply attached to Jenny Lind', he declared, that he would defend his flight with her even to the point of an armed struggle. He stated his plan to marry her, and asked Thompson to 'let the matter drop'. A pursuit resulting in a scandal would 'ruin two lives', he wrote: his own and that of his mother, who would be heartbroken if he came to trouble; even so, for Jenny Lind he was prepared 'to run the risk of all this'. Braddock promised to send Thompson a copy of the marriage certificate when the wedding had taken place, and a cheque for £8 to cover his 'indebtedness' to the station for the loss of its cook.[7]

Along with Braddock's letter, Wittenoom provided more detail about Jenny Lind's background. Firstly, of course, she already had a husband, Dan. She and Dan had both been raised from childhood on the Boolardy station and were now contracted under signed agreements to work there as part of its Indigenous labour force. Wittenoom observed that the abduction of an Indigenous wife and mother by a white man was exactly the kind of case 'which has so frequently caused the murder of whites by blacks' in the past, and if Dan had chosen to pursue Braddock and kill him, it would 'only have been according to aboriginal custom'. In addition to upsetting the balance of racial and labour relationships on the station, Wittenoom wrote, Braddock's action had also removed Jenny from its sphere of protection, since he was likely at some point to 'leave her to the mercy of more unhealthy surroundings' in one of the towns. Prinsep would have understood his implication. At this late point in the nineteenth century, settlers were increasingly complaining about the visibility of Indigenous destitution, unemployment, and prostitution in urban areas, and the Aborigines Department was becoming absorbed with policing strategies that would prevent dispossessed Indigenous people from gathering in the colony's northern towns and goldfields.[8]

As a station owner and employer, Wittenoom concluded, he had intervened himself 'many times' over the years to settle similar cases where white men had interfered with Indigenous women, but the establishment of the Aborigines Department now put such matters into the Chief Protector's hands. He urged Prinsep to use his powers 'to protect the native Dan from the loss of his woman, the station from the loss of a valuable servant, and to … restrain the man Braddock from further interference'.[9] Elided from this dialogue, and from the official correspondence that followed it, was any reference to Jenny Lind's rights of protection from abduction and probable sexual servitude.

Intimate Colonial Violence and Legislative Interventions

Whether coercive, consensual, or a mixture of both, a sexual economy between settler men and Indigenous women was a commonplace reality across Australia's colonies. In Western Australia's northwest, its everyday occurrence was enhanced by the fact that Indigenous people had been deeply entwined in colonial economies from the earliest phases of settlement, creating an especially permeable frontier culture.[10] Born as she was into this permeable frontier culture, Jenny's background reflected a broader picture of interracial relations in the region. It is likely that she belonged to the country where she was now employed in service, like many other Indigenous workers in Australia's colonial pastoral sector.[11] But even at this late stage of the nineteenth century, the northwest pastoral industry was scarcely a generation old. The Wittenoom family had been central to its development, building a pastoral empire in the Murchison River region that absorbed more than two million acres of land.[12] Pastoralism, as well as mining and pearling as the other valuable industries in the north, had been dependent since their inception upon Indigenous labour, producing frontier economies threaded through with equal degrees of intimacy and violence.[13]

As both a pastoralist and a major employer of Indigenous labour, Wittenoom embodied these tensions. In the early 1880s, he told a visiting magistrate sent north to investigate the state of relations between settlers and Indigenous people that pastoralists should be left 'to deal with the natives in their own way'. Indigenous stock theft was rife, he said, and if 'half-a-dozen' of the worst ringleaders were shot, it would 'put an end' to the pastoralists' difficulties.[14] At the same time, Wittenoom's stations were heavily dependent upon Indigenous labour, as were those of his neighbours, and he employed many of the Yamatji people who remained on their land as pastoral workers after the onslaught of colonisation. Effectively, while pastoralists like Wittenoom believed in the power of brute force to keep Indigenous 'outsiders' at bay, they equally believed in what Tim Rowse has called an 'ideology of paternal responsibility' towards the Indigenous 'insiders' who grew up on pastoral stations and became part of the industry's permanent labour force. Among pastoralists, Rowse notes, this paternal responsibility was considered more enduring than changable government policies of Indigenous governance.[15] Pastoral stations like Boolardy, then, operated partly as the visible expression of violent Indigenous dispossession, and partly as sites where an Indigenous cultural world continued to function under the umbrella of the colonial regime, intersecting with it in everyday life and labour relations.

As indicated by Wittenoom's decision to delegate this case to the Chief Protector, however, Jenny Lind's abduction occurred at a moment of the colony's history when matters relating to Indigenous people were becoming more subject to centralised management, under the auspices of the new Aborigines Department. The previous year, the passing of the *Aborigines Act* (1897) authorised the establishment of this department as a new branch of government empowered to 'exercise general supervision and care over all matters' relating to Indigenous people in the colony. At the time he received Wittenoom's letter, Prinsep had been installed for five months as the department's inaugural head.[16] But while it signalled an institutional shift of energy towards centralised Indigenous governance, the Act was just the latest in a series of recent statutes introduced to regulate labour relations between Indigenous people and settler employers, particularly in the northern pastoral economies, and to improve government oversight of Indigenous affairs. This shift towards legislative management of Indigenous affairs began in the 1870s as the economic value of the northern pastoral and fisheries industries began to boom.

Beyond a sexual economy involving Indigenous women, 'blackbirding' or kidnapping of Indigenous men was known to be endemic on the northwest frontier, as it was in Queensland, as a means of securing an indentured labour force for the pearling industry that flourished from the late 1860s.[17] The *Pearl Shell Fishery Act* (1871) was introduced with the two-fold purpose of deterring the trade in kidnapped labour and repressing the abduction of Indigenous women. From the inception of the industry, women were employed as divers who worked from the shoreline. As colonial officials were aware, pearlers also kept women as sexual servants on board their luggers, where authorities had little oversight or capacity to intervene. Under the provisions of the Act, then, written agreements were required that would confirm Indigenous labourers' consent, and Indigenous women's presence was prohibited on pearling boats.[18] In 1873, an amended *Pearl Shell Fishery Regulation Act* sought to strengthen the original Act with additional provisions that limited written contracts of employment to twelve months, imposed a daily fine on anyone deemed to have detained an Indigenous labourer against his will, and upheld the prohibition of Indigenous women on luggers.[19]

This early protectionist legislation had a parallel in Queensland, where the notorious trade in kidnapped Aboriginal and Pacific Island labour led to the enactment of the *Pearl Shell and Bêche-de-mer Fishery Act* (1881) and *Native Labourers Protection Act* (1884).[20] As Noel Loos has argued, however, protective provisions in the Queensland legislation were rendered toothless by the government's priority on collecting revenue from valuable industries.[21] Likewise, there was little sign that Western Australia's protective legislation worked in the interests of Indigenous workers when revenue from valuable colonial industries was at stake. In northern Roebourne, the heartland of the pearling industry, the Resident Magistrate confessed his reluctance to issue more than cautions or minor fines for abuses against Indigenous employees, for fear that more pronounced penalties would set back the pearling industry; indeed, virtually all the local officials had investments in it.[22] Other local authorities advised that legal prohibition could have little meaningful benefit even when Indigenous women were known to be forcibly held on pearling luggers, because it was virtually impossible to secure sufficient evidence to prosecute such cases.[23]

But in 1886, the enactment of Western Australia's *Aborigines Protection Act* appeared to strengthen legal provisions for regulating the conditions of Indigenous employment. The system of written agreements, first introduced into the pearling industry, was extended across the pastoral sector and all other industries where Indigenous people were employed. These so-called 'native agreements' had a duration of up to one year and required a magistrate or similar 'responsible officer' to assign Indigenous workers to an employer on written condition of their own consent, free of 'fear, coercion or constraint'. While rarely including actual wages, these contracts required that employers provide suitable working conditions, capacity for leave, and board and rations. The Act also allowed for the appointment of Protectors of Aborigines who, in theory, would monitor the conditions under which Indigenous workers were employed and could release them from their agreements if employers failed in their obligations.[24]

The *Aborigines Protection Act* was passed in a climate of widely circulating accounts that a normative culture of abuse prevailed against Indigenous people in the pastoral and pearling industries of the northwest. Such accounts were not new: through the 1870s and early 1880s, a series of government inquiries were held to investigate rumours of widespread violence in the colony's north.[25] In the mid-1880s these concerns were particularly fuelled by the Reverend John Brown Gribble's highly publicised accusations that a system akin to slavery operated inside the Indigenous labour sectors.[26] His claims that the assignment system was a 'thinly veiled form of slavery', and that Indigenous women were 'the victims of compulsory servitude' and 'systematically used for immoral purposes', brought the colony under the scrutiny of the Colonial Office and London's Aborigines' Protection Society.[27]

In principle, the *Aborigines Protection Act* and the Aborigines Protection Board it gave rise to were intended to regulate the treatment of Indigenous people and appease demands for humanitarian intervention, although there is little sign that the Board achieved much more than maintaining rations distributions to the sick, elderly, or destitute.[28] With the enactment of the *Aborigines Act* a decade later, the Protection Board was replaced by the more managerial Aborigines Department, headed by a Chief Protector. When Braddock abducted Jenny Lind from Boolardy station the following year, then, protective statutes were already in place to regulate the treatment of Indigenous workers, and a Chief Protector was in place as the most senior government officer in the colony to put them into effect.

Protecting the Indigenous Woman Servant: The Limits of the Law

On receiving Wittenoom's letter, Prinsep sought counsel from the Law Department about what legal options were available to achieve Jenny Lind's quick restoration to Boolardy station.[29] Perhaps to his surprise, the Law Department Secretary, William Sayer, advised that there was nothing in existing protective legislation that would allow authorities to prosecute Braddock and thereby prompt Jenny's return. Within a few years, the amended *Aborigines Act* (1905) would harden prohibitions on interracial contact, making it an offence for a white man to travel with or marry an Indigenous woman without the protector's written consent.[30] But at the time of Jenny's abduction, these state powers of surveillance over the movements and relations of Indigenous women and white men were still several years away. Existing legislation dating back to 1844 prohibited anyone from 'enticing' Indigenous girls under sixteen years of age away from schools or service, but this statute could not be leveraged in Jenny's case because she was a grown woman who, as Prinsep put it, already 'belongs to a native named Dan'.[31] Wittenoom's reports from Indigenous eyewitnesses indicated that Braddock had wielded a gun and threatened to shoot Jenny unless she left with him, but nonetheless Sayer offered the rather lame possibility that she might have eloped with Braddock of her own volition.[32]

While authorities debated the limitations on available legal options, the pastoralist and the Chief Protector engaged in some tense exchange about where responsibility lay for retrieving Jenny from her abductor. As Jenny's rightful employer, Wittenoom had the option of taking civil action against Braddock for damages, on grounds that he had caused economic loss to the station by removing a contracted servant. However, suing for civil damages would be slow, and would only yield monetary compensation for Jenny's labour; it would not necessarily bring her back. Nonetheless, Prinsep urged this path on Wittenoom as the best step, given the lack of options for proceeding under existing protective legislation. 'There seems to be no act by which I can specifically, by my office, prosecute Braddock', Prinsep told him, '& I think perhaps it would be better for you as owner of the premises' to 'make him pay the cost of her return to her husband'. In turn, Wittenoom argued that 'it would have a much more wholesome effect if done thro' your department, not only in this case, but as a deterrent in future'. Surely, he wrote, 'it is in your power to put a stop to this', or was Prinsep Protector of Aborigines 'only [in] name?'[33]

As it turned out, the provisions of the *Aborigines Act* offered another way forward, and this was to prosecute Jenny herself as an absconded servant. In advising this route as a means of achieving Jenny's return to Boolardy, the Law Department was following a well-trodden path. On the northern frontiers in particular, absconding from service prevailed as one of the most consistently prosecuted Indigenous offences, with a frequency perhaps second only to stock theft.[34] The regulation of Indigenous labour through the prosecution of deserting workers had a long tradition in colonial Australia, dating back to earlier nineteenth-century measures designed to rein in escaped convict labourers.[35] In this case, the legal avenue that allowed Jenny to be prosecuted as an absconding servant was a provision of Masters and Servants law embedded within legislation designed for 'Aboriginal protection'.

In theory, Indigenous servants had legal protection from ill treatment by their employers because the *Masters and Servants Act* included capacity to impose penalties on abusive masters, and its provisions were carried over into the *Aborigines Protection Act* and subsequently into the *Aborigines Act*.[36] Chinese workers, who like Indigenous people were deeply embedded in northern colonial industries, proved to be regular users of the protective provisions available in Masters and Servants law, drawing upon the courts to pursue legal redress for wrongs such as non-payment of wages and bodily assault.[37] In contrast, Indigenous people were rarely sufficiently empowered to enlist the colonial legal system in prosecuting abusive masters, and local magistrates—themselves regular employers of Indigenous servants—showed little appetite for prosecuting their settler neighbours on Indigenous workers' behalf.[38]

Instead of being enlisted in the protection of Indigenous workers' rights, the Masters and Servants provisions embedded in the *Aborigines Protection Act* and *Aborigines Act* were most commonly used to prosecute Indigenous servants for breaches of contract against their settler masters, particularly for absconding from their employment. Under the terms of the *Aborigines Protection Act*, absconding from one's employer was subject to the summary punishment of one month's imprisonment with hard labour.[39] Even so, pastoralist employers considered their rights inadequately protected. In 1887, a pastoralist body petitioned the government to increase the penalties for breach of contract, arguing that the existing *Aborigines Protection Act*'s provisions to prosecute absconding servants did not go far enough in remedying the problem. Those provisions authorised police to arrest runaway workers up to thirty miles away from the place where a warrant was issued; but pursuits were not generally continued beyond that distance, since they absorbed unreasonable policing time and resources. Pastoralists complained that this geographical limit too often allowed escaped Indigenous servants to elude punishment, since they knew that as long as they travelled beyond a thirty-mile radius, police would not arrest them.[40] Such lobbying was effective. Under amendments to the *Aborigines Protection Act* in 1892, the law's capacity to punish runaway Indigenous servants was expanded: the radius of police pursuit was increased to fifty miles, and the term of imprisonment was increased to three months with hard labour.[41]

Similarly, the written agreement system that became colony-wide policy after the passing of the *Aborigines Protection Act* quickly came to serve employer interests rather than to check illegal practices surrounding indentured Indigenous labour. When the *Aborigines Protection Act* was first introduced, the government initiated inquiries among local magistrates in the north to see whether the system of written agreements might be modified to better accommodate the particular conditions of an Indigenous labour force.[42] These inquiries generated a picture of pastoralists who enlisted the agreement system to establish their own 'monopolies' on Indigenous labour, each station holding a list of workers who were recurringly contracted for a year but whose 'real term' of service was presumed to be for life.[43] However, no steps were taken to fundamentally change the agreement system, and a later government review held at the turn of the century suggested little alteration in it. Indeed, settlers offered feedback on the benefits of having a guaranteed supply of Indigenous workers who risked prosecution as absconders if they walked away from station work, or were enticed away by more competitive offers.[44]

The flip side of this system of indentured labour, as Tim Rowse has argued, was that Indigenous workers could be subject to guaranteed protections of station life, and oftentimes to a continuing attachment to their own traditional country, under the pastoralist's code of 'paternal responsibility'. But to a significant degree, such a system placed the treatment of Indigenous workers at the discretion of station owners or managers and their individual temperaments. Frank Wittenoom was sufficiently invested in Jenny Lind's case to maintain pressure on the Aborigines Department for her safe return. His stated motivations, of course, were to protect both the rights of her husband Dan to his wife and the rights of the station to its valued servant. His lobbying also indicated the value he placed on maintaining the delicate balance of cross-cultural relations on the station, and on not allowing that balance to be undermined by the recklessness of an outsider. 'You may think I am inclined to make too much of this case', he wrote to Prinsep during their protracted correspondence, 'but if no restraint is put on this man, I should not be surprised to hear of a tragedy at any time.'[45]

However, Indigenous workers on other stations could not necessarily be presumed to have the protection of their pastoralist employers in the same way. Just a year before Jenny Lind's case, the colony's north again became the focus of controversy when three Indigenous servants—two women and an elderly man—ran away from the Bendhu station and on being brought back were flogged to death by their employers, brothers Ernest and Alexander Anderson.[46] This case received extensive press attention, but it was not the colony's only instance of Indigenous servants being flogged to death by settler masters.[47] The Bendhu case represented an extreme, but it also highlighted the quotidian dangers that faced Indigenous servants in the pastoral sector, where corporal punishment was normative practice and breach-of-contract laws constrained their rights to leave. Indigenous women who worked as domestic servants inside pastoral homesteads also faced a particular risk of sexual servitude to the settler masters in whose proximate space they lived and worked.[48]

In recommending the arrest of Jenny Lind as an absconded servant, the Secretary of the Law Department suggested that this action would enable the police to take her into custody and, if her statement proved 'that she was forcibly abducted', it would then be possible to seek prosecution of Braddock.[49] A warrant was duly taken out for Jenny's arrest. She was found and taken into police custody, together with her young son. She and her son were in police custody for six days, producing some official correspondence about the 'excessive' cost of extra rations incurred to feed her little boy.[50] She was tried before a local Justice of the Peace on the charge of absconding from her employer, and acquitted on the order that she be returned to the station to complete her agreement of service.[51]

Two weeks later, with Jenny back at Boolardy station, Wittenoom pursued the possibility of securing Braddock's prosecution by arranging for another Justice of the Peace to take her statement, along with that of Billelia, another servant who witnessed her abduction. Jenny Lind's deposition comprises the one trace of her voice in the extensive official file on her case. In it, she describes Braddock's violent coercion and her attempt to resist it. She told him, she said, that she was under a written agreement of employment, and that if she left the station without consent she 'would be taken to jail'. Knowing that the loss of her employment agreement would delay a police pursuit, Braddock told her he had taken it and hidden it 'where no one would find it'. He threatened to shoot her unless she went with him, she said, an account corroborated by Billelia.[52] By the time the Justice of the Peace took this statement from her, Jenny had been absent from Boolardy station for more than three months, during which she had spent approximately a week in police custody with her young child, and had been tried before a local court on a charge of breach of contract.

With the depositions recorded, Wittenoom continued to pressure the Aborigines Department to 'make an example of Braddock'.[53] The Chief Protector asked police to inquire into his whereabouts; but learning that he had left the neighbourhood, Prinsep and the government agreed it would be best to 'let the matter rest'.[54] Braddock's disappearance was officially accepted as a natural point of closure to this case, but it left blatantly unaddressed the larger limitations of the law in providing protection to Indigenous servants in general and to Indigenous women in particular.

Another notable aspect of Jenny Lind's case is that Wittenoom's letter requesting the Protector's intervention was written in August, months after her kidnapping on 10 May. Perhaps her husband Dan was initially reluctant to complain to his white employers; perhaps the station owner and manager first attempted to settle the matter without assistance from the Aborigines Department; perhaps they initially predicted that Braddock would return her when he realised 'his folly', as Wittenoom put it. Regardless of the reasons for the delay between Jenny's abduction in May and Wittenoom's approach to the Aborigines Department in August, it cast the shadow of an assumed sexual economy in which the detaining of Indigenous women by white men was known to be part of the familiar repertoire of colonial relations.

In 1887, the government had made efforts to regulate this sexual economy by issuing a circular to all magistrates cautioning them against signing employment agreements for Indigenous women except with 'respectable' employers and in cases of 'bona fide' domestic service.[55] But as numerous cases testified, the status of respectability was no obstacle against station owners or their managers from employing Indigenous women in domestic service and then keeping them at the homestead as sexual partners, even when the women had Indigenous husbands who pressed for their return.[56] More widely, both within and beyond the pastoral sector, authorities were aware of practices whereby would-be employers of Indigenous men kept Indigenous women as a form of currency to secure a surety of men's labour. A policeman tasked with investigating practices of Indigenous labour in the northern pastoral sector reported that Indigenous women were 'given' to station hands as a means to broker their loyalty.[57] Another report referred to police constables who allowed Indigenous women to be 'turned over' to their 'native assistants' in order to gain their ongoing service.[58] One Justice of the Peace reported that on the goldfields, it was assumed practice for miners to keep Indigenous women at their mining camps in order to keep the women's husbands nearby as available workers.[59]

Beyond the partial interventions of policy measures, individual officials periodically tried to intervene in regulating the exploitation or abduction of Indigenous women in this tacitly understood economy. Three years after Jenny Lind's case, Aborigines Department Travelling Inspector George Olivey attempted to have miner Jack Stewart prosecuted, after Stewart stole 'Wanda' away from her Indigenous husband 'General' and then shot and wounded General when he attempted to retrieve his wife. Two local Justices of the Peace had already dismissed the case on grounds of insufficient evidence, encouraging Stewart to publicly declare that he would get Wanda back by having her assigned to him as a servant. In order to prevent this, Olivey arranged for her to be assigned instead as a domestic servant to the local constable's household.[60] In this instance, Stewart remained unpunished by the law, both for abducting Wanda and for assaulting her husband when he intervened, and Wanda's protection from Stewart was only achieved by arranging her indenture to a more 'respectable' employer.

Of course, cases such as Wanda's or Jenny Lind's did not preclude the possibility that in the intimate domain of cross-cultural economies, Indigenous women could exercise agency as willing participants in interracial relationships. As well as recording cases of women's abduction, the colonial archive suggests that violence could also erupt when an Indigenous woman preferred to remain with a white man against her husband's wishes.[61] However, even if Indigenous women might have chosen or accepted a sexual contract with a settler man in some circumstances, the point remains that when they were drawn without choice into sexual servitude, they received little by way of legal protection from the settler state. In 1901, pastoralist Henry LeFroy wrote to the Chief Protector to protest a culture whereby white men 'forc[ed] the women against their will' and asked 'if nothing could be done' to prevent it. The Chief Protector's only available response was that he was looking for ways to amend the 'laws relating to the Aborigines'.[62]

Conclusion: Increasing Powers of Protective Governance

Jenny Lind's abduction from Boolardy station in 1898 came at a moment of transition in late-colonial Western Australia, as the colony sought to implement a manageable and economic model of Indigenous governance in a new climate of self-government.[63] Prompted by the Chief Protector's efforts, the decade ahead would usher in new legislative changes that significantly increased the Aborigines Department's range of surveillance. In 1905, anticipating the passing of an amended *Aborigines Act* that would grant him greater legal powers over his Indigenous charges, Prinsep wrote about the limitations he had faced when he became head of the Aborigines Department in 1897. At that time, he wrote, he had been obliged to grapple with an 'exceedingly imperfect' legal culture that was inadequate in coping with 'the irregularities and improprieties [of] intercourse between natives and whites'. Despite his hopes to monitor 'unreliable employers', to 'prevent abduction' and to repress the 'prostitution of the black women', he stated, he enjoyed no real legal powers that enabled him to interfere.[64]

In contrast, the terms of the amended *Aborigines Act* (1905) gave him extensive legal powers of intervention, not only over employers of Indigenous people but also over Indigenous people themselves. Under the 1905 Act, the Chief Protector was empowered to take custody of Indigenous children, to send Indigenous people to and from reserves, and to control most aspects of their personal resources and movements. The Act also gave him specific legal powers to monitor the employment, mobility, and marriage of Indigenous women, and to control their interactions with white men.[65] From this time forward, protective policies both in this jurisdiction and around the nation became more legally robust in supporting a paternalistic supervisory regime.[66]

Jenny Lind's case prefigured this legal moment, but it already mirrored the ways in which protective governance implicitly sustained the racial and gendered orthodoxies of the colonial establishment. In finding resolution to Jenny's abduction by prosecuting her as an absconded servant, officials mobilised her rights to protection not in terms of her own rights to liberty from an abductor, but in terms of her place as the wife of an existing husband and as the contracted servant of a settler master. Meanwhile, her white abductor escaped prosecution altogether simply by exercising his rights of mobility to leave the district.

Victoria Haskins and Claire Lowie have asked how we might view histories of colonial service in ways that open onto larger, connected histories of colonial dispossession, expropriation, and social upheaval.[67] The case of Jenny Lind is not exceptional in the way that it reflects back a much wider colonial history of Indigenous women's formally unpaid labour, constrained mobility, and often assumed sexual servitude on the pastoral frontiers where they lived and worked in the aftermaths of dispossession. Indeed, the persistent lobbying of the station owner to whom she was contracted might be read as granting her more advocacy than some other women who worked under similar circumstances. But as an illuminating example of the point where race and gender came together to mark the limits of the law in protecting Indigenous women employed in colonial economies, her case reflects the extent to which government provisions designed to safeguard Indigenous people's rights from exploitation were shaped and limited by conventional assumptions of economic paternalism. Jenny Lind's case reveals just how much the rights of an Indigenous woman servant were constrained by the very legislation that was supposed to protect her.

Notes

1. Frank Wittenoom to Chief Protector Henry Prinsep, 22 August 1898: Acc 255, 1898/1175, State Records Office of Western Australia, Perth (hereafter SROWA).
2. The statutory age of Aboriginal protection began in Australia with Victoria's *Aborigines Protection Act* of 1869. In New South Wales, an Aborigines Protection Board was established in 1883 under the auspices of the Department of Police, and gained statutory authority with the *Aborigines Protection Act* of 1909. Equivalent Acts for the 'protection' and management of Indigenous people were passed in Western Australia in 1886, in Queensland in 1897, in the Northern Territory in 1910, in South Australia in 1911, and in Tasmania in 1912.
3. For instance, Laura Ann Stoler, *Capitalism and Confrontation in Sumatra's Plantation Belt, 1870–1979* (Ann Arbor: University of Michigan Press, 1985); Ian Keen, ed. *Indigenous Participation in Australian Economies: Historical and Anthropological Perspectives* (Canberra: Australian National University Press, 2010); Victoria Haskins, *Matron and Maids: Regulating Indian Domestic Service in Tucson, 1914–1935* (Tucson: University of Arizona Press, 2012); Victoria Haskins and Claire Lowrie, eds. *Colonization and Domestic Service: Historical and Contemporary Perspectives* (London: Routledge, 2015); Claire Lowrie, *Masters and Servants: Cultures of Empire in the Tropics* (Manchester: Manchester University Press, 2016).
4. For instance, Regina Ganter, *Mixed Relations: Asian-Aboriginal Contact in North Australia* (Perth: University of Western Australia Press, 2006); Katherine Ellinghaus, 'Absorbing the Aboriginal Problem: Controlling Marriage in Australia in the Late Nineteenth and Early Twentieth Century', *Aboriginal History* 27 (2003), 185–209.

5. On questions of agency and consent in Australia's histories of colonial conquest, see for instance Lyndall Ryan, 'The Struggle for Recognition: Part-Aborigines in Tasmania in the Nineteenth Century', *Aboriginal History* 1, no. 1 (1977), 27–52; Ann McGrath, 'Black Velvet: Aboriginal Women and Their Relations with White Men in the NT, 1910–40' in Kay Daniels, ed. *So Much Hard Work: Women and Prostitution in Australia* (Sydney: Fontana, 1984); Kay Merry, 'The Cross-cultural Relationships Between the Sealers and the Tasmanian Aboriginal Women at Bass Strait and Kangaroo Island in the Early 19th Century', *Counterpoints* 3, no. 1 (2003), 80–88; Ann McGrath, 'Consent, Marriage and Colonialism: Indigenous Australian Women and Coloniser Marriages', *Journal of Colonialism & Colonial History* 6, no. 3 (2005); Victoria Haskins and John Maynard, 'Sex, Race and Power: Aboriginal Men and White Women in Australian History', *Australian Historical Studies* 126 (2005), 191–216; Ruth Balint, 'Aboriginal Women and Asian Men: A Maritime History of Color in White Australia', *Signs* 37, no. 3 (2012), 544–554; Karen Hughes, 'Micro-Histories and Things that Matter: Opening Spaces of Possibility in Ngarrindjeri Country', *Australian Feminist Studies* 27, no. 73 (2012); Liz Conor, '"Black Velvet" and "Purple Indignation": Print Responses to Japanese "Poaching" of Aboriginal Women', *Aboriginal History* 37 (2013); Victoria Haskins, '"Down in the Gully and Just Outside the Garden Walk": White Women and the Sexual Abuse of Aboriginal Women on a Colonial Australian Frontier', *History Australia* 10, no. 1 (2013), 11–33. Larissa Behrendt makes the point that even when colonial interracial relationships were consensual, they occurred within a wider context of 'frontier and sexual violence'. Larissa Behrendt, 'Consent in a (Neo)Colonial Society: Aboriginal Women as Sexual and Legal "Other"', *Australian Feminist Studies* 15, no. 33 (2000), 355.

6. Ann McGrath points out that across colonial Australia, many frontier policemen cohabited with Indigenous women under the radar of official sightlines (McGrath, 'Black Velvet', 269). In a case from the northwest in the late 1860s, Police Constable Albert Francisco was investigated after he and his Indigenous tracker 'Johnny' forcibly took two Indigenous women for sex, and Francisco subsequently shot and wounded the husband of one of the women, Toonamarra, when he came to retrieve his wife. The local resident magistrate, Robert Scholl, overlooked Francisco's actions in this instance, but acknowledged to the Colonial Secretary that 'interference' with Indigenous women constituted a major cause of local conflict between white men and Indigenous people. Scholl to Colonial Secretary, 25 January 1869: Acc. 36, vol. 646 (1868–1869), SROWA. On the legal difficulty of

prosecuting such abuses, see for instance 'Memorandum of Attorney General H.H. Hocking', Part V of *Despatches and Other Papers Relating to Transactions Arising out of the Homicide and Other Alleged Outrages on Aboriginal Natives* (Perth: Government Printer, 1873). On colonial humanitarian interventions into settler men's relationship to Indigenous women, see Penelope Edmonds, 'Collecting Loorerryminer's "Testimony": Aboriginal Women, Sealers and Quaker Humanitarian Anti-Slavery Thought and Action in the Bass Strait Islands', *Australian Historical Studies* 45, no. 1 (2014), 13–33.
7. A.E. Raddock to George Thompson, 10 May 1898: Acc 255, 1898/1175, SROWA.
8. For instance, letter to the Travelling Inspector of Aborigines George Olivey, 4 January 1901: Acc 255, 1900/51, SROWA; report of Corporal W. Feely, 15 March 1903, Acc 430, 1903/123; letter to Prinsep, 30 March 1905: Acc 255, 1905/177, SROWA.
9. Wittenoom to Prinsep, 22 August 1898: Acc 255, 1898/1175, SROWA. On the politics of Indigenous people 'inside' and 'outside' the pastoral sector, see Tim Rowse, 'Were You Ever Savages?; Aboriginal Insiders and Pastoralists' Patronage', *Oceania* 58, no. 2 (1987).
10. On the position of Indigenous people in Western Australian colonial economies see, for instance, Paul Hasluck, *Black Australians: A Survey of Native Policy in Western Australia 1829–1897*, 2nd ed. (Melbourne: Melbourne University Press, 1970); Peter Biskup, *Not Slaves, Not Citizens: The Aboriginal Problem in Western Australia 1898–1954* (Brisbane: University of Queensland Press, 1973); R.H.W. Reece and Tom Stannage, eds. *European–Aboriginal Relations in Western Australian History* (Perth: Studies in Western Australian History, 1984); Penelope Hetherington, *Settlers, Servants and Slaves: Aboriginal and European Children in Nineteenth-Century Western Australia* (Perth: University of Western Australia Press, 2002).
11. This likelihood is suggested by Wittenoom's confirmation that Jenny was raised on Boolardy station, although it is also possible that she was the child of an Indigenous worker who came or was brought to the station from elsewhere. On the longer trajectory of Indigenous people's central place in the pastoral economy in other parts of Australia, see Ann McGrath, *Born in the Cattle: Aborigines in Cattle Country* (Sydney: Allen and Unwin, 1987); Dawn May, *Aboriginal Labour and the Cattle Industry: Queensland from White Settlement to the Present* (Cambridge: Cambridge University Press, 2009).
12. Wendy Birman and G.C. Bolton, 'Frederick Francis Wittenoom (1855–1939)', *Dictionary of Australian Biography*, http://adb.anu.edu.au/biography/wittenoom-frederick-francis-frank-9292

13. On the relationship between intimacy and violence on colonial frontiers see, for instance, Henry Reynolds, *With the White People* (Melbourne: Penguin, 1990); Lynette Russell, ed. *Colonial Frontiers: Indigenous–European Encounters in Settler Societies* (Manchester: Manchester University Press, 2001); Penelope Edmonds, *Urbanizing Frontiers: Indigenous Peoples and Settlers in Nineteenth Century Pacific Rim Cities* (Vancouver: UBC Press, 2010).
14. Comments of Frank Wittenoom reported by Magistrate Robert Fairbairn in *Despatches and Other Papers Relating to Transactions Arising Out of the Homicide and Other Alleged Outrages on Aboriginal Natives* (Perth: Government Printer, 1873); *Instructions to and Reports from the Resident Magistrate Despatched by Direction of His Excellency on Special Duty to the Murchison and Gascoyne Districts* (the 'Fairbairn Report') (Perth: Government Printer, 1882), 8 July 1882.
15. Rowse, 'Were You Ever Savages?', 97.
16. *Aborigines Act* (61 Vict no 5) 1897 (WA). This Act abolished the short-lived Aborigines Protection Board that had been established on the authority of the colony's earlier *Aborigines Protection Act* (50 Vict no 25) 1886 (WA).
17. Noel Olive, *Enough is Enough: A History of the Pilbara Mob* (Fremantle: Fremantle Arts Centre Press), 73–4.
18. *Pearl Shell Fishery Act* (34 Vic. No 13) 1871 (WA).
19. *Pearl Shell Fishery Regulation Act* (37 Vic. No 11) 1873 (WA).
20. *Pearl Shell and Bêche-de-mer Fishery Act* (45 Vic. No 2) 1881 (Qld) and *Native Labourers Protection Act* (48 Vic. No. 20) 1884 (Qld).
21. N.A. Loos, 'Queensland's Kidnapping Act: The Native Labourers Protection Act of 1884', *Aboriginal History* 4 (1989), 150.
22. Resident Magistrate Laurence to the Colonial Secretary, 3 July 1884: Acc 388, 2815/84, SROWA; report of Constable Payne, Acc 430, 1887/26, SROWA.
23. Resident Magistrate Scholl (Roebourne) to the Colonial Secretary, 1 June 1871: Acc 36, vol. 646 (1871), SROWA.
24. Sections 18 to 31, *Aborigines Protection Act* (50 Vict no 25) 1886 (WA).
25. The 'Fairbairn Report' (1873); *Instructions to and Reports from the Resident Magistrate Despatched by Direction of His Excellency on Special Duty to the Murchison and Gascoyne Districts* (the 'Fairbairn Report') (Perth: Government Printer, 1882); *Legislative Council Papers Respecting the Treatment of Aboriginal Natives in WA* (Perth: Government Printer, 1886).
26. Reverend J.B. Gribble, *Dark Deeds in a Sunny Land; or Blacks and Whites in North-West Australia* (Perth: Stirling Bros., 1886); 'Investigations into the allegations of Reverend Gribble': Acc 388, items 6–32, SROWA.

27. 'Mr Gribble Again', *Eastern Districts Chronicle*, 6 November 1886, 4; correspondence of Reverend Gribble to Frederick Chesson: Aborigines' Protection Society correspondence files, March 1886–January 1887, MSS British Empire S22 G97, Weston Library (former Rhodes House collection), Oxford.
28. The colony's Legislative Council was particularly vocal in arguing that the Aborigines Protection Board was largely ineffective; but this was unsurprising, given that its members were heavily represented by the wealthy pastoral industry. See *Western Australian Parliamentary Debates* (Perth: Government Printer, 1888), 343–346.
29. Prinsep to Secretary of the Law Department William Sayer, 23 August 1898, 255, 1898/1175, SROWA.
30. *Aborigines Act* (5 Edw. VII No 1) 1905 (WA).
31. *Act to Prevent the Enticing Away of Aboriginal Girls from School or Service* (8 Vic. No 6) 1844 (WA); Prinsep to Sayer, 23 August 1898, 255, 1898/1175, SROWA.
32. Sayer to Prinsep, 25 August 1898, Acc 255, 1898/1175, SROWA.
33. Prinsep to Wittenoom, 29 August 1898, and Wittenoom to Prinsep, 31 August 1898, Acc 255, 1898/1175, SROWA.
34. The historical record suggests that the prosecution of Indigenous absconders was pursued even in cases where the workers were the wronged parties. In an example from the pearling sector, where forcible indentured labour was a known problem, Dugalgarry was 'sold' for £10 to a pearler and ran away because he refused to dive. He was sentenced by three local justices of the peace to two months' imprisonment with hard labour. Acc 527, 1886/4569, SROWA. In another case, 'Henry' left his employment to seek the return of his wife, who had been stolen by a white man. He was sentenced to one month's hard labour. Acc 527, 1888/236, SROWA.
35. David Roberts, 'A "Change of Place": Illegal Movement on the Bathurst Frontier, 1822–1825', *Journal of Australian Colonial History*, 7 (2005), 97–122.
36. Section 44, *Aborigines Protection Act* (50 Vic. No 25) 1886 (WA).
37. In an early and unusual instance of an Indigenous servant using Masters and Servants legislation in Western Australia, a case was successfully brought by Mooyan against his employer for non-payment of wages in 1843. *The Inquirer*, 5 April 1843. On the regular use of the courts by Chinese to prosecute abuses of settler employers in the late colonial northwest, see for instance the Wyndham Courthouse Deposition Book, 1888–1895: Acc 742/1, and Roebourne Police Court Proceedings, 1893, Acc 913/15, SROWA.
38. Sometimes Justices of the Peace, the very officials who adjudicated Indigenous cases, were themselves the worst offenders of abuses against

their own Indigenous servants. 'Ill-treating a Native: A Magistrate Fined', *Western Mail*, 10 February 1899; 'Ill-treatment of Natives', *Western Mail*, 3 March 1899.
39. Successive iterations of Masters and Servants legislation in Western Australia were *An Act to provide a summary remedy in certain cases of Breach of Contract* (6 Vic. No 5) 1842; *Masters & Servants Act* (Amended) (46 Vic. No 11) 1882; *Masters & Servants Act* (Amended) (50 Vic. No 20) 1886; *Masters & Servants Act* (Amended) (55 Vic. No 28) 1892.
40. Minute Paper on 'Arrest of Natives under Sec 44 of the Aboriginal Protection Act', 17 May 1887, Acc 527, 1887/1967.
41. *Aborigines Protection Act* (Amended) (55 Vic. No 25) 1892 (WA).
42. Attorney General Alfred Hensman to the Colonial Secretary, 9 February 1886: Acc 527, 1886/542, SROWA.
43. Resident Magistrate Edward Angelo to the Colonial Secretary, 6 April 1886: Acc 527, 1886/542 SROWA.
44. Reports of Olivey to Prinsep, 28 December 1899–4 March 1900: Acc 255, 51/1900, SROWA.
45. Wittenoom to Prinsep, 8 September 1898, Acc 255, 1898/1175, SROWA.
46. Aborigines Department annual report of 1897, Acc 255, 1889/28, SROWA.
47. In 1889, charges were brought against brothers Arthur and Gordon Shaw for beating Indigenous servant Bungordy to death, but the case was dismissed. *Western Mail*, 12 October 1889.
48. On the more complex dimensions of Indigenous women's role as workers for white settlers, see for instance Ann McGrath, '"Spinifex Fairies": Aboriginal Workers in the Northern Territory, 1911–1939', in *Women, Class and History: Feminist Perspectives on Australia, 1788–1978*, ed. Elizabeth Windschuttle (Sydney: Fontana Collins, 1980), 237–267.
49. Sayer to Prinsep, 25 August 1898: Acc 255, 1898/1175, SROWA.
50. Inspector Lawrence to Constable Donovan, 6 September 1898, and Constable Donovan to Inspector Lawrence, 13 September 1898: Acc 255, 1898/1175, SROWA.
51. Telegram from George Thompson to Frank Wittenoom, 28 August 1892: Acc 255, 1898/1175, SROWA.
52. Depositions of Jenny Lind and Billelia, alias 'Nellie', to H.M. Maloney JP, 14 September 1898: Acc 255, 1898/1175, SROWA.
53. Wittenoom to Prinsep, 20 September 1898: Acc 255, 1898/1175, SROWA.
54. Premier John Forrest to Prinsep, 5 November 1898: Acc 255, 1898/1175, SROWA.
55. Governor's Circular to Magistrates and Justices of the Peace, 12 September 1887: Acc 527, 1887/3128, SROWA.
56. See for instance the case of J. Bailey, manager of Namatharra station, who in 1906 was investigated for 'cohabiting' with his domestic servant, refus-

ing the claims of her Indigenous husband 'Cable' for her return. Acc 255, 1099/1906, SROWA. In the same year, George Burrows, manager of Minderoo station, was charged with 'cohabiting' with his domestic servant 'Nellie', again in spite of the demands of her Indigenous husband 'Dicky Dad' that she be allowed to return to his camp. Despite Nellie's own statement that she asked 'Mr Burrows to let me go camp, he no let me go', the case against Burrows was discharged for want of sufficient evidence. Acc 255, 690/1906, SROWA. Respectable pastoralist Walter Nairn, co-owner of Byro station, was also investigated for 'cohabiting' with his domestic servants during the 1890s and was considered to be 'one of the worst offenders against the [Aborigines] Act'. Report of Constable Doody, 12 January 1907: Acc 255, 1099/1906, SROWA. After the *Aborigines Act* (1905) set limits on interracial marriage, some men in the pastoral sector sought Indigenous women as wives in order to have access to a housekeeper or cook. See James le Chung to the Chief Protector, 10 July 1906: Acc 255, 690/1906, SROWA.
57. Report of Sub Inspector Patrick Troy, 11 February 1889: Acc 430, 1889/471, SROWA.
58. 'A Drastic Indictment of the Police—By a Resident of the West Kimberley', *Sunday Times*, 7 February 1909, 1.
59. Stewart McGill, J.P. to Prinsep, 25 May 1901: Acc 255, 486/1901, SROWA.
60. Olivey to Prinsep, 24 November 1901, Acc 255, 1901/975, SROWA.
61. For instance, also in Western Australia, Francis Whitfield was acquitted in 1852 of grievous bodily harm after he shot and wounded Mordecai, who was attempting to retrieve his wife 'Annie'. Annie allegedly wanted to stay with Whitfield against Mordecai's wishes, leading to the confrontation. Acc 3472, item 93, case 535, SROWA.
62. Henry LeFroy to Prinsep, 12 April 1901, Attorney General George Leake to Prinsep, 11 May 1901, Prinsep to the Law Department, 11 May 1901: Acc 255, 1901/406, SROWA.
63. Whereas self-government was granted to Australia's other colonies during the 1850s, it was achieved much later in Western Australia in 1890.
64. Prinsep's notes on the drafted Aborigines Act of 1905 (undated), Acc 255, 1905/97.
65. Section 40–44, *Aborigines Act* (5 Edw. VII No 14) 1905 (WA).
66. On the nationwide impact of protectionist policies see, for instance, Anna Haebich, *Broken Circles: Fragmenting Indigenous Families, 1800–2000* (Fremantle: Fremantle Arts Centre Press, 2000).
67. Victoria Haskins and Claire Lowrie, 'Decolonising Domestic Service: Introducing a New Agenda', in Victoria Haskins and Claire Lowrie, eds. *Colonization and Domestic Service*, 1.

CHAPTER 5

The 'Proper Settler' and the 'Native Mind': Flogging Scandals in the Northern Territory, 1919 and 1932

Ben Silverstein

In 1921, Prime Minister of the United Kingdom David Lloyd George proudly declared that the British Empire was distinguished by being 'based not on force but on goodwill and a common understanding'.[1] This mythic imperial imagination took hold in the interwar years, rendering public exposures of colonial violence both anomalous and embarrassing. For this reason, when in 1932 the Australian overlander Francis Birtles provided disturbingly detailed allegations of the 'inhuman treatment of natives in the North', he sparked one of several scandals regarding violence perpetrated against Aboriginal workers in the Northern Territory. Two such episodes—one incited by Birtles' claims, the other by accusations against

I am grateful to the participants at the 'Colonial Economies: Violence and Intimacy' workshop at the University of Tasmania in November 2016 for their comments on an earlier version of this chapter, and to Warwick Anderson for his helpful advice and suggestions. This research was supported by a grant from the Australian Research Council (FL110100243).

B. Silverstein (✉)
School of History, Australian National University, Canberra, ACT, Australia

© The Author(s) 2018
P. Edmonds, A. Nettelbeck (eds.), *Intimacies of Violence in the Settler Colony*, Cambridge Imperial and Post-Colonial Studies Series, https://doi.org/10.1007/978-3-319-76231-9_5

Paddy Cahill in 1919—are the subject of this chapter, which explores arguments about the propriety, or sometimes the utility, of such violence. These disputes, I argue, centred on the nature of the proper male settler, and were transacted through the question of his relationships with Aboriginal people.

In the course of these Australian scandals, many settlers argued, on the basis of their knowledge of the 'native mind', that violence was a privileged element of the proper relationship between settlers and Aboriginal people. They rationalised this violence through two claims which, despite their seeming contradiction, could coexist within the same analysis: the 'native mind' as equivalent to that of a white child, for whom beating was a necessary pedagogical tool; and the 'native mind' as structured by an ordered and sophisticated normative system within which violence was an essential and appropriate response to transgression. This ambivalent knowledge structured the everyday, framing life for Aboriginal workers in the Northern Territory.

Scholars of colonial violence have recently turned to study these everyday experiences, looking beyond the violence of conquest, rebellion, and counter-insurgency to examine the intimate violence 'central to the workings of empire'.[2] Such studies locate colonial violence as more than merely transitional, punctuating the birth of a new order. Instead, an orientation towards the everyday brings to light the insidious shifting modalities of violence that Tracey Banivanua-Mar suggests were 'essentially structural' to colonialism.[3] Histories of Australian colonial violence have tended to continue to focus on the frontier, tracing the massacres and 'dispersals' that remained central to Indigenous dispossession until at least the interwar period.[4] And even when looking beyond colonial wars, many of these works have located the daily violence that, in part, constituted relationships between white settlers and Aboriginal people as the product of a frontier era. Some of this scholarship has reimagined the frontier concept in productively malleable and transgressive terms, describing sites of cross-cultural exchange and mobility.[5] And the continued deployment of the 'frontier' to characterise spaces of violence both echoes a recurrent motif present in formal discussions of the Northern Territory until well into the twentieth century and registers the continuing massacres perpetrated there in the interwar period.[6]

In describing a frontier, though, the historian risks reproducing its logic. The frontier, as Deborah Bird Rose has pointed out, can be understood as a 'Rolling Year Zero', a time of conflict which is to be resolved by the emergence of a nation through the erasure or marginalisation of legible Aboriginal political life. The historical frontier was thus purposeful; its naming actively authorised an asymmetrical violence which inscribed a settler colonial teleology on bodies and on land.[7] As Patrick Wolfe noted in his discussion of dispossessing frontier violence in North America, relegating violence 'behind the screen of the frontier' locates it as the subject of regretful disavowal.[8] Naming a frontier has an insulating effect, distancing its effects from the ongoing everyday. This is, to some extent, a problem avoided by descriptions of the frontier as a site of both war and cross-cultural exchange.[9] But retaining the citation of the frontier sets extra-legal violence temporally apart from and prior to the nation, bracketing its manifestations and consigning them to a past now surpassed. Writing this history in 2017—as once again a Royal Commission sits in the Northern Territory to hear evidence of the abuse of Aboriginal children by 'rogue' correctional officers in youth detention centres—to relegate extrajudicial violence against Aboriginal people in the Northern Territory to a pre-national past, to the status of exception, appears unsustainable.[10]

How, then, might we study the everyday violence to which Aboriginal people are, and have been, subject in Australia? How can we frame the mundane, the quotidian, the recurring and enduring distributions of force that are transformed but not concluded by assertions of sovereign completion? It has become almost a truism in histories of colonial violence to argue, like Jock McCulloch, that such a 'history of violence is difficult to recover' as the 'people who used violence denied they did so and those who were subject to violence are often invisible in the archival record'.[11] Similarly, Florence Bernault and Jan-Georg Deutsch have attributed the disproportionate historical focus on subaltern uprisings and state practices of counter-insurgency to the 'nature of historical sources', which, in Africa at least, provide only 'tenuous or isolated ... traces of individual acts and temporary outbursts'.[12] But this does not render the study of everyday violence completely opaque. As Brett Shadle writes of Kenya, settlers in fact 'rarely hesitated, in private or in public, to discuss their violence against Africans'. In Australia's Northern Territory we do not find the same 'outpouring of books, newspapers, and personal reminiscences' that Shadle relies upon as his 'entre into the contexts and meanings of violence'.[13] But nor is there a paucity of traces. Written and oral historians have documented the milieu of violence that suffused life on Northern Territory cattle stations in the first half of the twentieth century.[14] And settlers spoke regularly of their violence, in both critical and exculpatory forms, in newspapers and Royal Commissions, in letters and memoirs. In this chapter I explore the contours of their explication of violence by turning to scandal.

Studying scandals, Kirsten McKenzie has argued, 'allows us to trace the connection between the large politics of the state and the small politics of private life that made up the relations of colonial power'. Scandals are sites for the articulation of moralities, for discussions of norms and their transgression.[15] Here we find scandals as occasions for debating the proper behaviour of the settler at a time when such norms were being reconfigured around the British Empire. Responses to scandal provide us with a revealing glimpse into vernacular understandings of violence and its unexceptional place in performing and maintaining social order. They render visible the ordinarily obscured undercurrents that ran through settler society; obscured not necessarily because they were objects of shame or guilt, but because they were so typical as to be unworthy of comment. Violence was, to so many settlers, unremarkable. It was only when forced to account for their practice that they ventured forth with discourses on the 'native mind', on Aboriginal people's comprehension and reception of physical force. But that the accusations against Cahill and by Birtles were sensationally republished, that they provoked widespread condemnation and debate, and that they were subject to official disavowal, suggests a wider disapproval for such violence. In this context, encapsulating settler violence as scandalous emphasised the singularity of abuse, instantiating distinctions between proper and transgressive settlers that distorted the colonial formation to insulate respectability from impropriety.[16] A distinction emerges between white men in the Northern Territory and those in the south, as the latter scrambled to distance themselves from the 'outsiders' up north.

Settlers disagreed about the utility and propriety of colonial violence, articulating justifications that countered the alleged imperial norm. This chapter traces this story through accusations made against Cahill in 1919–1920, examining theories of the 'native mind' produced in the wake of his defence, and tracing responses to Birtles' allegations in 1932. I argue that in settlers' arguments about whether force could or should be deployed against Aboriginal workers, we find contests over the proper behaviour of the (usually) male settler. And we see in these debates two main positions: one that the settler should engage Aboriginal workers using his powers of persuasion only, that violence should be prohibited as unlawful or unjust; and the other that the settler should know how to practice violence, that he should understand the utility of an economy of force based on his intimate knowledge of what was termed the 'native mind'. We find here an articulation of white manliness as muscular but also knowing, demonstrated through expertise in the proper regime of governing black labour.[17] The vernacular knowledge of white men who drew authority from living with or alongside Aboriginal people uncannily resembled scientific conceptions then being produced by anthropologists and psychologists. Theirs was official knowledge, a recognition that troubled efforts to distance colonial violence from everyday life in the modern nation.

Flogging in Paradise

Paddy Cahill had first made his way to the Northern Territory as a young man in 1883 when he was among the first to drive cattle in from Queensland. He spent much of the remainder of his life there, sometimes working as a stockman and station manager, but best known as one of the most successful buffalo hunters of the Top End. Shooting buffalo was a trade romanticised and celebrated for its wildness and masculinity—its performance of white mastery—and Cahill became an iconic settler of the Northern Territory.[18] In 1909, he took up a lease at Oenpelli near the East Alligator River in Western Arnhem Land, an area to which he was no stranger. He knew the terrain and people well from his time shooting buffalo, and was possibly already incorporated into kin networks by virtue of his Yolngu son Paddy Cahill Jr. (Neyingkul).[19] He built a homestead where he lived with his wife, Maria Pickford, and their son, Thomas Cahill, and they were joined for some years by his niece Ruby Mudford. Carl Warburton, a traveller who visited in 1921, described the homestead as a 'large, rambling place covered with bright, flowering creepers, and surrounded by wonderful mango and other tropical fruit-trees', and including a substantial library. To the *Northern Territory Times*, it was a 'veritable paradise'.[20]

At Oenpelli, Cahill was a part—albeit an intruding part—of the Gunwinjgu community, employing a number of senior men and providing food, tobacco, and medical assistance. Together they planted gardens of fruits and vegetables and sowed a range of cash crops, none of which turned out to be commercially sustainable at such a distance from markets. His one potentially commercially successful endeavour was in dairying, but the station more realistically was only able to produce for sustenance, an endeavour that itself was only financially sustainable so long as Cahill had access to unpaid and intensive Aboriginal labour.[21] Between June and August of 1912, he hosted an extended visit from the anthropologist and then Chief Protector of Aboriginals Baldwin Spencer, with whom he was to become a frequent correspondent. Spencer was sufficiently impressed to recommend that Oenpelli be made an Aboriginal Reserve and Cahill a Protector of Aboriginals with the responsibility of training Aboriginal people in pastoralism and agriculture.[22]

Though he was implicated in a number of massacres or incidents of violence in his earlier years in the Territory, Cahill, by the time he stopped at Oenpelli, was celebrated by other white settlers for his treatment of Aboriginal people.[23] Elsie Masson, a friend of Spencer's and an *au pair* in the Administrator of the Northern Territory John Gilruth's house in Darwin in 1913–1914, described him as 'beginning in the right way ... the secret of Paddy Cahill's success lies in his unbounded influence over the natives and in his wonderful sympathy with their customs and beliefs'. And 'there is never a tinge of insolence on the part of the blacks. You feel that here they have found a true friend and protector'.[24] Gilruth agreed that at Oenpelli he had witnessed Aboriginal people 'becoming gradually acquainted with the best side of the white man's supremacy and discipline' and noted that 'no one knows the native more thoroughly ... nor views him more sympathetically' than Cahill.[25] This was also a popular view. An article in the Adelaide *Observer* claimed in 1919 that '[n]o one is better qualified to dilate upon the subject of the native than is Mr Cahill', and when he died in 1923 he was remembered in the *Northern Territory Times* as having 'understood the abos. probably as well as any man who ever set foot in the Northern Territory'. Cahill was, for settlers, a man whose approach to Aboriginal people should be emulated.[26]

It therefore marked a spectacular, albeit fleeting, fall when at the Royal Commission he was called to account for the practice of punitive flogging at Oenpelli. The Royal Commission, presided over by Justice Norman Ewing, had been called to inquire into the administration of the Territory after the so-called 'Darwin Rebellion' of 1918 had prompted Gilruth's retreat to Melbourne.[27] Identifying Cahill as an ally of Gilruth, the Commission examined three incidents at Oenpelli, two perpetrated by Paddy and one by his son Thomas, questioning Cahill repeatedly as to whether his flogging constituted 'proper treatment' of Aboriginal people, taking an interest in violence as a sign of maladministration.[28]

Flogging had been characterised as distasteful and degrading, at least in the case of white adult subjects, across the British Empire since the 1830s.[29] A century later, the turn against flogging had become even more strident. Martin Weiner has argued that, in the early twentieth century, the Colonial Office increasingly practiced an interventionist approach to the Empire and the Dominions in the interests of 'justice between the races', an approach influenced by colonial labour standards instituted by the newly founded International Labour Organisation and the League of Nations.[30] Reports of flogging tended to be the subject of scandal. The Oenpelli incidents, reported in newspapers around Australia, were no exception.[31]

The first had taken place around 1912, when two fourteen-year-old Aboriginal workers, Butcher and Jimmy Ah You, escaped from the station. They were recaptured and brought back, at which point Cahill ordered one to tie up the other and thrash him with either a riding whip or a chain. When he finished, the boy who had been flogged was ordered to tie up his comrade and flog him in turn.[32] This was effective, Cahill declared, in preventing any further absconders. Questioned at the Royal Commission as to whether this punishment was an act of hardship or cruelty, Baldwin Spencer declared: 'I think it shows great knowledge of native customs. It would appeal to the natives, and to the natives concerned. I would not object to that at all. ... That particular case showed Cahill's knowledge of native customs, and probably it was the best thing he could have done.'[33] Violence, in other words, was a form of communication consonant with Aboriginal understanding, a way of conveying a message of white mastery. Asked at the Royal Commission if he wanted 'to be Pooh Bah of Oenpelli', Cahill responded, 'Yes; that was quite right. I wished to have power over the natives.'[34] That power, he argued, must be capable of physical demonstration. As he wrote to Spencer in 1915: 'If I had power to imprison these chaps, for a little time, it would soon make them look foolish and take all the flashness out of them.'[35] This was physical force that performed and reconstituted a social order.

It was a moment of Aboriginal resistance to this order that provoked the other incident that occupied much of the Royal Commission's time with Cahill. One evening in 1917, an Aboriginal man named Romula— who had worked for Cahill for some twenty-five years and who Masson had described as a 'faithful black henchman'—laced butter in the homestead with strychnine.[36] The following morning, after breakfast, Mrs. Cahill, the two Aboriginal kitchen-staff Marealmark and Topsy, a non-

Aboriginal assistant Tom O'Brien, and the Cahills' dog were all stricken, though emetics saved the human sufferers. Cahill described setting off in a righteous rage to arrest Nulwoyo and Nipper, who he immediately blamed for the poison. Nulwoyo blamed Romula for putting the strychnine in the butter, so Cahill 'at once got a chain and padlock and arrested Romula'. In his official correspondence, Cahill wrote, 'I was almost mad at the time, and I do not rightly know what I did to Romula while putting the chain on him. You can imagine my feelings.' In a private letter to Spencer, Cahill wrote that he 'doubled up the chain and struck him on the head very hard; knocking him down. I at once fastened the chain on his neck and tied him up.'[37] Cahill then called to Ah You to come for treatment, as he too had been given bread and butter for breakfast. On being told that Ah You had buried the food rather than eating it, Cahill gave him 'two or three good hits on the head and back, and chained him up', before freeing him the next day after finding that while he might have been aware of the poisoning in advance, Ah You was not himself involved as a perpetrator.[38]

This poisoning incident suggests that while Cahill had been celebrated by Northern Territory whites, for some Aboriginal people he was a less likable figure. Nipper, who Cahill identified as the ringleader, was an owner of the land on which Oenpelli was located, and carried himself as a Gunwinjgu leader. Cahill complained to Spencer: 'Nipper done as he liked among the other natives ... there was no disputing his authority ... I blame this man for all the trouble.' The poisoning took place, Cahill wrote, after a meeting where the Aboriginal men had all agreed on the injustice of Cahill's rules and decided collectively to poison him.[39] His narration suggests that an Aboriginal moral economy had been transgressed, that his authority had, for many Gunwinjgu men at least, become intolerably unlawful. The ever-fluctuating relationship between settler and Indigenous authorities constituted a fluid station environment in which struggles to impress meaning were enmeshed in a complex dialectic of force and interpretation.

Having identified the individuals personally responsible, Cahill gathered the men of Oenpelli together and asked them what had caused the unrest. They claimed, he reported, the problem stemmed from his 'order that no fighting was allowed on the Station, and no man was to beat his [wife]. Any rows at the camp were to be refered [sic] to me and I would fix up matters.' Romula's personal disaffection stemmed from Cahill's having given him 'a good talking too' [sic] after he beat his wife a week before the poisoning, telling 'him that I would send him to gaol if he ever did such a thing again'. As Cahill told the Royal Commission, 'I had stopped the natives hammering their wives. That is the whole of the trouble at Oenpelli.'[40] Violence, in Cahill's account, was an essential part of Aboriginal life, a privileged mode of instituting gendered authority and subordination, of producing and maintaining order. It was normalised and naturalised: it may be unlawful under settler law, but its abolition could not be countenanced.

Cahill wrote in his annual report for 1919, also published in the *Northern Territory Times*, that the problem had been one of interpretation. His prohibition of 'hammering' wives had led men to 'the impression that their women were to be their bosses', a conclusion of which Cahill quickly disabused them. To resolve the situation he reinstated the right of Aboriginal men to beat their wives but asserted his own dominion: when Aboriginal husbands found that their wives had become 'sulky or jealous', they were to bring them to Cahill who would arbitrate the dispute, either settling the matter with words of admonishment or authorising the 'husband [to] take a piece of leather, and give her a few strokes'. This, Cahill wrote, had settled the matter, sacrificing Aboriginal women's bodies in the interests of colonial order.[41] Cahill's reasoned assertion of knowledge, obscuring the heightened emotions that attended his anguished attack on Romula, inscribed his violence as orderly and authoritative. He entrenched a hierarchy of force, articulating and naturalising violence inflicted by Aboriginal husbands on their wives, but insinuating himself into an Aboriginal order by positioning himself at the apex of sovereign violence and arrogating the power to command beatings.

The gender order Cahill described was his model for a customary economy of violence that he insisted he understood as a result of long and intimate relationships with Aboriginal people. Just as husbands possessed dominion over wives, white men possessed dominion over 'natives'. And this dominion could best be manifested through performative violence that was naturalised as a part of Aboriginal life. As Paddy's son Tom declared in 1921, 'I have associated with men we would term murderers … and found them apparently fine fellows. … But why judge them from our standards?'[42] According to Aboriginal standards as he described them, violence was a part of the everyday, a functional way of regulating relationships and maintaining order. As Bernault has argued in a different context, in constituting the native customary as a space of violence, this 'doctrine naturalised, traditionalised, and, to a large extent, patronised physical violence as a marker of racial difference'.[43] And it effected a diffuse distribution of sovereignty, empowering settlers to mete out force summarily, governing their labour according to their own commonsense calculations based on intimate knowledge of the 'native mind'.

Arrested Development

In operationalising Aboriginal thought as his rationalisation for violence, Cahill participated in a debate on the distinction between the 'primitive' and the 'civilised' that embroiled settlers and travellers alongside anthropologists and psychologists. The line between scientific and vernacular knowledge at this time was blurred and porous. The early twentieth century marked the last years of an era in which 'the accounts of travellers, sailors, [and] missionaries', alongside pastoralists, police, and other men on the spot were authoritative not as a result of their professional training, but instead by virtue of their extended periods in intimate contact with people they named 'primitive'.[44] As Baldwin Spencer's career demonstrates, scientific knowledge drew much of its authority from its proximity to the vernacular: his key collaborator was the central Australian telegraph station master Frank Gillen.[45] In their anthropological texts, Spencer and Gillen referred regularly to the 'native mind', noting that '[i]n many respects the mind of the Australian native is like that of a child amongst ourselves'. Cahill understood the 'mentality of the Australian black' through a similar analogy. 'They have', Cahill told Warburton, 'the minds of children.'[46] Others in the Northern Territory shared this view, and it was becoming the norm across much of Australia. When the Melbourne newspaper *The Argus* editorialised in 1929 on the problem of 'people who have never dealt with natives' being 'thoroughly incompetent to deal with native problems', they located this incompetence in such individuals' persistence 'in regarding the native mind as adult instead of hopelessly infantile'.[47]

By the late 1920s, the 'native mind' had become a major subject of investigation in the Northern Territory. Warwick Anderson has described the extraordinary scenes at Hermannsburg in central Australia, when in 1929 no fewer than three anthropological expeditions visited the Lutheran mission to assess 'primitive' psychology. The Arrernte people, on whose land the mission sat, had been subjects of Spencer and Gillen's research in the late nineteenth century and had continued to be subjects of intensive research since.[48] The neurologist Henry Kenneth Fry, a member of the

Adelaide University anthropological expedition, performed a series of psychological tests on mostly listless and starving research subjects and concluded that 'their minds in spite of their primitive state of culture are cast in the same mould as our own'. In his conception, Aboriginal people had an underdeveloped mentality akin to an adolescent white man.[49] The University of Hawai'i psychologist and former Melbourne schoolteacher Stanley Porteus, funded by a grant from the Australian National Research Council, also likened the Aboriginal mentality to that of a white youth.[50] Based on his research at Hermannsburg and in the course of another expedition to northwest Australia, he concluded that the physical brain capacity of an Aboriginal person was roughly equivalent to that of a thirteen-year-old white schoolboy, noting that other tests revealed that Aboriginal adults possessed a lower 'average mental age' of approximately twelve years (in the case of the Porteus maze test), or under six (in an 'auditory rote memory' test).[51]

Considering the 'native mind' as equivalent to that of a white child was to have implications for the institution of corporal punishment. Paul Ocobock has argued that in Kenya at this time, white settlers argued that Africans were 'mentally underdeveloped and therefore must be punished like children'; since corporal punishment was deployed against the young in British juvenile justice and schooling, it became an essential pedagogical tool available to settlers seeking to discipline black workers.[52] But in Australia, both amateurs and professionals conceived of the 'native mind' as more than simply 'childlike', understanding it also as conditioned by what they came to consider a normative system of laws and customs within which violence was an active and essential social institution.

Following Porteus' central Australian research, the University of Hawai'i offered a fellowship to enable an Australian fieldworker to train under him in methods of racial psychological research. Nominated by A.R. Radcliffe-Brown, Ralph Piddington took up this position and, in Hawai'i, collected some of the comparative data that informed Porteus' book.[53] In 1931, he and his wife Marjorie followed in Porteus' footsteps and visited missions in northwest Australia to perform similar tests of mental capacity. Despite their conclusion that 'such tests ... are not suitable for application to aborigines who have had no schooling' and produced 'quantitative results ... of little value', Porteus used their data to conclude that while Aboriginal children developed much like white children, their mental development slowed, or ceased, around the age of ten.[54]

The Reverend Theodore Webb, a Methodist missionary at Milingimbi in Arnhem Land, was to clarify this position in 1944. While it is 'true', he wrote, that the 'race mind of the aboriginal is childlike', it was distinct from the 'mind of a normal child [which] is ever expanding, developing, and absorbing fresh truth'. The Aboriginal 'race mind', by contrast, 'up to the point of its arrested development is simply crammed with a mass of beliefs and conceptions which are extremely difficult to eradicate or go beyond because of mental stagnation'. It was both full and 'static', and would remain neither developed nor developing.[55] Though 'childlike', this was not the mind of a child. Instead, it was the mind of a person who had emerged in what white thinkers understood as a fundamentally different Aboriginal community. It was for this reason that Cahill believed Aboriginal adults could become modern thinkers if 'only' he could 'Get 'em young.' Malcolm Ellis, the journalist who drove with Birtles from Sydney to Darwin in 1924, wrote that 'generations of experience … have tended to lead native thought … out of the realm which most white people understand'.[56] Their 'mass of beliefs and conceptions' could only be comprehended by describing the native mind in a register of presence rather than absence, outlining a system of laws and customs within which physical violence was crucial.

The French anthropologist Lucien Lévy-Bruhl described what he termed 'ordeals', in which an Aboriginal man who had injured another in some form of transgression must himself in turn submit to injury, as central to Aboriginal culture. The offender here was not so much punished as he was compelled to subject himself to an 'ordeal according to rule'. This ceremonial ritual, in which a restoration of lawful order followed as response to a transgression, was 'indispensable'; it was an 'expiation'.[57] Spencer agreed that corporeal violence must follow the transgression of custom to restore order and repair the well-being of the group.[58] Violence, in other words, was positioned by scientists as an essential element of the social institutions of Aboriginal society. It was a form of communication, of subjectivation and of social order; its function could not be denied.[59] For both amateurs and professionals, this violence was interpreted through a conception of the 'native mind' that was contradictorily both 'undeveloped' and in a state of 'arrested development'. As Claire Lowrie and Julia Martínez have demonstrated, for white women in Darwin at this time to treat Aboriginal men as childlike was to defuse their sexuality and power, rendering them appropriate domestic servants.[60] For the white men who supervised their pastoral or agricultural work, as well as for anthropologists and psychologists, it emphasised Aboriginal men as both agents and recipients of violence. This manner of objectifying the 'native mind' as a product of 'native culture' articulated racialised difference, naturalising the 'native' body as both subject and object of violence.

On the Need for Unnecessary Force

On 30 December 1931, Francis Birtles announced to the press that he was preparing a dossier of complaints regarding the brutal treatment of Aboriginal people in the Northern Territory, alleging '[w]holesale trafficking' of women, 'brutal assaults and murders by police and other white people, … prominent men mixed up in an opium ring, which supplies the drug to natives, [and] black labour enslaved by means of methylated spirits, overproof rum and opium'.[61] Details of these would be provided, he declared, in a statement he was preparing for the Racial Hygiene Association of New South Wales to be passed on to the Federal Government.[62] The Minister declared he would investigate if further details were provided, and over the following weeks Birtles' claims were repeated in newspapers across the country.[63]

Birtles was a self-styled overlander and explorer, a celebrity best known for cycling around Australia several times, then crossing the continent in multiple directions in a motor car, before becoming the first person to drive from London to Melbourne in 1928.[64] Publicising his exploits through syndicated newspaper reports, books, and films, Birtles enacted what Georgine Clarsen has described as a peculiarly settler colonial form of travel and mobility.[65] He was described in the Melbourne newspaper *The Argus* as a model white settler, a 'typical Saxon, fair-skinned, fair-haired, blue-eyed, and emotionless. He is the personification of the spirit of adventure'. And he was not always renowned for his care for Aboriginal people, declaring in 1910 that 'I had several brushes with them. … I had two repeating rifles. Oh yes, I used them often.' As *The Argus* put it: 'The blacks and Birtles are not friends.'[66] Whether true or not, such stories illustrated both the harshness and Birtles' hard-fought domination of the country over which he moved. His shift after 1912 to the characteristic twentieth-century performance of driving a car—a symbol of modern technological mastery—through a Northern Territory populated by allegedly pre-modern Aboriginal people, further entrenched his representation as an archetype of knowing and capable whiteness, winning the land through feats of exploration.[67]

His accusations were given particular prominence by the Labor-affiliated papers, including *The Railroad*, the official newspaper of the Australian Railways Union. In a well-illustrated double-page spread, Birtles presented moving stories of abuse. He wrote of Aboriginal children who had accidentally knocked over a pail of milk being 'thrashed unmercifully with a pailing' and of their mother being thrashed with chain and padlock. When that woman escaped the station with her children overnight, he wrote, she was chased and caught, thrashed, and then tied to a horse, forcing her to run or be dragged back to the homestead. There she was beaten once more, manacled with government-issued handcuffs and chained around the ankles, and fastened to a post in the harness room. Birtles also wrote of driving a police constable to a cattle station, where they found an Aboriginal man handcuffed around a veranda post at the homestead. At 'the nearby kitchen door ... a white man [was] maliciously grinning at the captive. Without saying a word, the constable walked up, punched and kicked the helpless aboriginal, maltreated him until the victim, saying "Please boss," slid down, a huddled-up mass to the earthen floor.' Another man was 'thrashed to endurance point' for 'cheeking the boss'.[68] The article detailed several other stories of brutality, each portraying the horrors of station life and many alluding to the officially sanctioned nature of that violence, whether perpetrated by a police constable or abetted by the use of police handcuffs.

These affecting stories—presenting the abuse of Aboriginal bodies in detailed accounts that indicate precisely who was at fault—spoke authoritatively for the sufferings of the wronged, engendering moral concern and action for those in need of aid.[69] There were obvious villains in Birtles' stories, and in clearly portraying the injustice of violence suffered by innocent children, protective mothers, and persecuted men, he invited readers to identify Aboriginal victims as objects of both sympathy and pity. His humanitarian narrative drew on the specific repertoire of antislavery that Fiona Paisley has argued was accruing intensifying force across the British Empire in the years preceding the 1933 Centenary of Emancipation.[70] And Birtles' accusations of slavery were supported in a widely circulated article published in *The World* titled 'Aborigines On Cattle Stations are in Slavery', which detailed an interview with Ralph Piddington. Piddington, whose mother Marion had been a founding member of the Racial Hygiene Association—to whom Birtles had submitted his allegations—and remained a correspondent with the group, backed Birtles' claims of slavery, trafficking, and flogging. He demanded that an inquiry be 'conducted by persons who understand the native mentality and are known and trusted by the natives'. And, 'knowing something of the native mind', he described this system of violence as 'evil in Northern Australia'.[71]

Some northern settlers denied the veracity of Birtles' and Piddington's claims, ridiculing Birtles' capacity as an overlander while the Minister for Home Affairs declared his accusations unsubstantiated.[72] But many others instead accepted their veracity but refused to condemn such practices as 'evil' or 'atrocity'. Instead, they wrote letters or articles for newspapers around the country, claiming authority based on their intimate knowledge of Aboriginal people to explain the utility, or perhaps the necessity, of this violence. One former resident of the Northern Territory who had since moved to New South Wales, C. Graham, wrote in March:

> I have been up till recently for several years a resident of the Northern Territory and can certify that a lot of unnecessary ill-treatment and cruelty is meted out to the natives and immoral use is made of the native women by white men. But I also maintain that natives need rather harsh and drastic treatment to keep them under control, otherwise the Northern Territory would not be safe for the white race, white women especially.[73]

Beatings and sexual violence, Graham thus argued, were necessary to maintain social order, articulating a racialised logic of gendered sacrifice and security. This was violence that functioned as both communicative and performative, constituting the white male settler as sovereign, possessing and practicing a right to decide when and how to enact force on others. And that force was justified by reference to what the 'natives need'. This was a view articulated by a number of letter-writers on a similar basis. Charles Gaunt, an old stockman who in earlier years had travelled extensively across the British Empire, wrote to the *Northern Standard* to note that the 'general run of Territorians' would respond to Birtles by cautioning him of the 'weakness of being too lenient'. A settler would, by treating an Aboriginal person 'as an equal', betray 'his ignorance in native matters'.[74]

Similarly, the pastoralist Robert Macintyre wrote to the *Sydney Morning Herald* to complain about reports of 'harsh treatment' that 'emanate from people who are non-residents in the north, and have never worked amongst the natives for any length of time'. It was not, he declared, harsh treatment that caused problems, but rather those non-residents and their defective understanding of the proper relations between white and black. 'In my experience', he went on, those:

> sorts of people are the main cause of the troubles amongst the natives in the north, and I think station managers and Northern Territory police will bear me out in this. As a rule they treat the native as if he were a white man, and proceed to spoil them in every way possible. The native really considers them a joke, and proceeds to play them for all he can get. If these well-meaning people only worked amongst the natives, for, say, twelve months, they might wake up and find that the permanent resident after all does understand the native mind.[75]

Just as anthropologists of the same era would argue, the 'native mind' was knowable only by those who spent extended periods of time among Aboriginal people. But for the manly settler, this knowledge was represented as inciting a violence that was necessary in creating a society in which Aboriginal people would work. Permanent residents of the Territory, Macintyre wrote, 'are considerably more respected by the aborigines than the casual visitors, most of whom the natives sum up as "plurry fools"'. Aboriginal people on stations 'live quite contentedly under the supervision of the police and station managers. These men know their jobs, and, left alone, do it well.'[76]

These letters do not detail violence explicitly but instead disclose a constellation of euphemisms which were understood by a northern settler community 'on the basis of a fund of assumed knowledge'.[77] Their letters detail their iteration of settler common sense, articulating an economy of force based on knowledge of a 'native mind' that emerges here as an alibi for violence, a way of both legitimising force and displacing responsibility for it onto the nature of 'native' peoples.[78] For these protagonists, to become a proper settler was to acquire knowledge and thus to know when, and how, to perform violence. This force was articulated as necessary to order, to subjugate Aboriginal people and to make them work. While a paucity of violence would disturb this order, too much force would have similar effect. As the explorer and writer Charles Conigrave declared, the 'northern blackfellow is a pretty sophisticated individual these days, and it is wrong to suggest that a native would remain working for a buffalo hunter or any other employer who did not ... [treat him as] he was entitled to'.[79] These apologists for colonial violence argued that the white men of most Northern Territory stations had found the right balance. They had created a situation where, as Macintyre argued, on 'practically all stations peace and contentment remains'.[80]

Northern settler myths of peace and contentment were a counterpoint to southern and metropolitan fantasies of normalised goodwill that framed allegations of abuse as scandalous, transgressive, and anomalous. But these moments instead disrupt the boundaries drawn between force and benevolent agreement. The violence that was the stuff of scandal on the national stage was less evidence of aberrant breaches than it was a window into ingrained and endemic habits of rule.[81] In these everyday instances we find functional violence that would discipline labour; though contingent and often rash or disorderly, it was purposeful and justified by a conception of the 'native mind' that licensed, or beseeched, violence against the 'native' body. This was the official and scientific knowledge that underpinned the Australian national project of performing social order and claiming the Northern Territory for White Australia, a project from which southern and metropolitan critics would not resile. Though violence itself was scandalous, the knowledge its apologists produced retained legitimacy, even as mention of its implications was resisted by those who articulated their desire for a nation based on goodwill through a web of disavowal and self-justification.

Notes

1. David Lloyd George, 'Opening Speech', in *Conference of Prime Ministers and Representatives of the United Kingdom, the Dominions, and India: Summary of Proceedings and Documents* (London: Cmd. 1474, 1921), 15.
2. Matthew Carotenuto and Brett Shadle, 'Introduction: Toward a History of Violence in Colonial Kenya', *International Journal of African Historical Studies* 45, no. 1 (2012), 4; Elizabeth Kolsky, *Colonial Justice in British India: White Violence and the Rule of Law* (Cambridge: Cambridge University Press, 2010), 2.
3. Tracey Banivanua-Mar, *Violence and Colonial Dialogue: The Australian–Pacific Indentured Labour Trade* (Honolulu: University of Hawai'i Press, 2007), 11.
4. See, for example, Henry Reynolds, *Forgotten War* (Sydney: New South, 2013).
5. See, for example, Penelope Edmonds, *Urbanizing Frontiers: Indigenous People and Settlers in 19th-Century Pacific Rim Cities* (Vancouver: UBC Press, 2010).

6. See, for example, C.L.A. Abbott, *Australia's Frontier Province* (Sydney: Angus and Robertson, 1950).
7. Deborah Bird Rose, 'Hard Times: An Australian Study', in *Quicksands: Foundational Histories in Australia and Aotearoa New Zealand*, ed. Klaus Neumann, Nicholas Thomas, and Hilary Ericksen (Sydney: UNSW Press, 1999), 6; Julie Evans, 'Where Lawlessness is Law: The Settler-Colonial Frontier as a Legal Space of Violence', *Australian Feminist Law Review* 30 (2009).
8. Patrick Wolfe, 'Settler Colonialism and the Elimination of the Native', *Journal of Genocide Research* 8, no. 4 (2006), 391–392.
9. Amanda Nettelbeck, 'Proximate Strangers and Familiar Antagonists: Violence on an Intimate Frontier', *Australian Historical Studies* 47 (2016), 210.
10. Some instances of this violence were scandalously screened on national television in July 2016. Caro Meldrum-Hanna, Mary Fallon, Elise Worthington, 'Australia's Shame', *Four Corners*, ABC TV, 25 July 2016, <http://www.abc.net.au/4corners/stories/2016/07/25/4504895.htm>. A Royal Commission into the Protection and Detention of Children in the Northern Territory was announced the morning after the report was screened, and it enacted hearings between October 2016 and June 2017. Its final report, tabled in Parliament in November 2017, is exemplary in its scathing criticism of abuses and its simultaneous refusal to reject the necessity of the incarceration of, and use of force against, Indigenous children. *Report of the Royal Commission and Board of Inquiry into the Protection and Detention of Children in the Northern Territory* (Canberra: Royal Commission into the Protection and Detention of Children in the Northern Territory, 2017).
11. Jock McCulloch, 'Empire and Violence, 1900–1939', in *Gender and Empire*, ed. Philippa Levine (Oxford: Oxford University Press, 2004), 224.
12. Florence Bernault and Jan-Georg Deutsch, 'Control and Excess: Histories of Violence in Africa', *Africa* 85, no. 3 (2015), 385.
13. Brett Shadle, 'Settlers, Africans, and Inter-Personal Violence in Kenya, ca.1900–1920s', *International Journal of African Historical Studies* 45, no. 1 (2012), 63.
14. Ann McGrath, *Born in the Cattle: Aborigines in Cattle Country* (Sydney: Allen & Unwin, 1987), 106–115; Deborah Bird Rose, *Hidden Histories: Black Stories from Victoria River Downs, Humbert River and Wave Hill Stations* (Canberra: Aboriginal Studies Press, 1991), 24; Transcript of Interview with Rosalie Kunoth-Monks, April 1988, 4–5: NTRS 226, TS 501, Northern Territory Archives Service, Alice Springs (hereafter NTAS).
15. Kirsten McKenzie, *Scandal in the Colonies* (Melbourne: Melbourne University Press, 2004), 5, 9.

16. James Epstein, *Scandal of Colonial Rule: Power and Subversion in the British Atlantic during the Age of Revolution* (Cambridge: Cambridge University Press, 2012), 16; Nicholas Dirks, *The Scandal of Empire: India and the Creation of Imperial Britain* (Cambridge: Harvard University Press, 2006), 29–30. On other interwar scandals relating to violence against Aboriginal people in the Northern Territory, see Fiona Paisley, 'Race Hysteria, Darwin 1938', *Australian Feminist Studies* 16 (2001); Mark Finnane and Fiona Paisley, 'Police Violence and the Limits of Law on a Late Colonial Frontier: The "Borroloola Case" in 1930s Australia', *Law and History Review* 28, no. 1 (2010).
17. See generally Mrinalini Sinha, *Colonial Masculinity: The 'Manly Englishman' and the 'Effeminate Bengali' in the Late Nineteenth Century* (Manchester: Manchester University Press, 1995).
18. A.B. (Banjo) Paterson, 'The Cycloon, Paddy Cahill and the G.R.', in *North of the Ten Commandments: A Collection of Northern Territory Literature*, ed. David Heaton (Sydney: Hodder & Stoughton, 1991), 214. See John M. MacKenzie, *The Empire of Nature: Hunting, Conservation and British Imperialism* (Manchester: Manchester University Press, 1988).
19. John Mulvaney, *Paddy Cahill of Oenpelli* (Canberra: Aboriginal Studies Press, 2004), 37.
20. Carl Warburton, *Buffaloes* (Sydney: Consolidated Press, 1944), 119–120; 'Oenpelli: A Promising Country', *Northern Territory Times*, 30 March 1916, 15.
21. 'News & Notes', *Northern Territory Times*, 25 March 1915, 16; 'News & Notes', *Northern Territory Times*, 1 July 1915, 8.
22. Cahill was appointed as Protector in August 1912, but the Reserve was not formally proclaimed until 1922, a few months before he departed Oenpelli. Patrick Cahill to the Acting Chief Protector of Aboriginals, Report by the Protector of Aboriginals, Aboriginal Station Oenpelli, 16 January 1920: A1, 1930/979, National Archives of Australia, Canberra (hereafter NAA); Baldwin Spencer, *Wanderings in Wild Australia* (London: Macmillan and Co., 1928), vol. 2, 741–858.
23. Mulvaney, *Paddy Cahill of Oenpelli*, 7–9.
24. Elsie R. Masson, *Untamed Territory: The Northern Territory of Australia* (London: Macmillan, 1915), 102–103.
25. *Northern Territory of Australia: Report of the Administrator for the Years 1915–16 and 1916–17* (Melbourne: Government Printer, Cmd Paper No 31 of 1918), 14.
26. 'The Natives of the North', *Observer*, 22 March 1919, 2; 'The Bushman's Gazette', *Northern Territory Times*, 28 April 1925, 2. For later praise for Cahill, see Ernestine Hill, *The Territory: The Classic Saga of Australia's Far North* (Sydney: Angus and Robertson, 1951), 372; Tony Austin, '"Get 'em young": Paddy Cahill and the Oenpelli "Industrial" Reserve', *Journal of Northern Territory History* 1 (1990), 16.

27. Alan Powell, *Far Country: A Short History of the Northern Territory* (Darwin: Charles Darwin University Press, 5th ed., 2009), 115–116.
28. *Royal Commission on the Northern Territory: Minutes of Evidence* (Melbourne: Government Printer, 1920), 212.
29. Penelope Edmonds and Hamish Maxwell-Stewart, '"The Whip is a very Contagious Kind of Thing": Flogging and Humanitarian Reform in Penal Australia', *Journal of Colonialism and Colonial History* 17, no. 1 (2016).
30. Martin Weiner, *An Empire on Trial: Race, Murder and Justice under British Rule, 1870–1935* (Cambridge: Cambridge University Press, 2009), 18; David M. Anderson, 'Punishment, Race and "The Raw Native": Settler Society and Kenya's Flogging Scandals, 1895–1930', *Journal of Southern African Studies* 37, no. 3 (2011); Steven Pierce, 'Punishment and the Political Body: Flogging and Colonialism in Northern Nigeria', in *Discipline and the Other Body: Correction, Corporeality, Colonialism*, ed. Steven Pierce and Anupama Rao (Durham: Duke University Press, 2006).
31. See, for example, 'The Territory Inquiry. Further Revelations', *Age*, 20 December 1919, 13; 'Darwin Inquiry. Aborigines Sometimes Flogged', *Daily Standard*, 20 December 1919, 4; 'Darwin Scandals. The Flogging Episode', *Advertiser*, 21 February 1920, 9.
32. *Royal Commission on the Northern Territory*, 135, 152.
33. *Royal Commission on the Northern Territory*, 350.
34. *Royal Commission on the Northern Territory*, 145.
35. Cahill to Spencer, 11 March 1915 in Mulvaney, *Paddy Cahill of Oenpelli*, 106.
36. Masson, *Untamed Territory*, 104.
37. Cahill to H.E. Carey, 25 January 1917: A3, NT1917/427, NAA. Cahill to Spencer, 10 October 1917, in Mulvaney, *Paddy Cahill of Oenpelli*, 119.
38. *Royal Commission on the Northern Territory*, 135.
39. Cahill to Spencer, 10 October 1917 in Mulvaney, *Paddy Cahill of Oenpelli*, 120. See Sally K. May, *Collecting Cultures: Myth, Politics, and Collaboration in the 1948 Arnhem Land Expedition* (Lanham, MD: AltaMira Press, 2010), 170–174.
40. Cahill to Spencer, 10 October 1917 in Mulvaney, *Paddy Cahill of Oenpelli*, 120–121; *Royal Commission on the Northern Territory*, 145.
41. 'Oenpelli Blacks. Gins Get a Few Strokes', *Northern Territory Times*, 3 January 1920, 8.
42. 'Land of Promise', *Observer*, 19 March 1921, 38.
43. Florence Bernault, 'The Shadow of Rule: Colonial Power and Modern Punishment in Africa', in *Cultures of Confinement: A History of the Prison in Africa, Asia and Latin America*, ed. Frank Dikötter and Ian Brown (Ithaca: Cornell University Press, 2007), 81.
44. Lucien Lévy-Bruhl, *How Natives Think (Les Fonctions Mentales dans les Sociétés Inférieures)* (London: George Allen and Unwin, 1926), 30; George

W. Stocking, *After Tylor: British Social Anthropology, 1888–1951* (Madison: University of Wisconsin Press, 1995), 122–123.
45. See John Mulvaney, Howard Morphy, and Alison Petch, eds. *'My Dear Spencer': The Letters of F.J. Gillen to Baldwin Spencer* (Melbourne: Hyland House, 1997); John Mulvaney with Alison Petch and Howard Morphy, eds. *From the Frontier: Outback Letters to Baldwin Spencer* (Sydney: Allen and Unwin, 2000). Compare with Martin Nakata, who argues that quasi-scientific research at the turn of the twentieth century was authoritative for being found 'in the vicinity of science'. Martin Nakata, *Disciplining the Savages, Savaging the Disciplines* (Canberra: Aboriginal Studies Press, 2007), 195.
46. Baldwin Spencer and F.J. Gillen, *Native Tribes of Central Australia* (London: Macmillan & Co, 1899), 510; Warburton, *Buffaloes*, 122.
47. 'The Aborigine', *Argus*, 21 January 1929, 6. For similar comments made in the Northern Territory see C. Price Conigrave, *North Australia* (London: Jonathan Cape, 1936), 214. Masson argued that the 'blackfellow's mind is that of an absolutely uneducated intelligent child', implicitly rejecting Lévy-Bruhl's argument that primitive minds were not undeveloped or childlike but were instead utterly different to European ones. Bronislaw Malinowski, who Masson met in 1916 and married in 1919, and who praised her book as 'synthetic', concurred with her position in his sharp critique of Lévy-Bruhl, arguing that primitive thought ought to be understood as akin to a 'rudimentary stage' in the development of 'modern' European thought. Masson, *An Untamed Territory*, 154; Lévy-Bruhl, *How Natives Think*, 43–44, 105–138; Masson to Malinowski, 11 June 1916, in *The Story of a Marriage: The Letters of Bronislaw Malinowski and Elsie Masson, Volume I, 1916–20*, ed. Helena Wayne (London: Routledge, 1995), 2; Bronislaw Malinowski, *Magic, Science and Religion, and Other Essays* (Glencoe: Free Press, 1948), 8–9, 17.
48. Warwick Anderson, 'Hermannsburg, 1929: Turning Aboriginal "Primitives" into Modern Psychological Subjects', *Journal of the History of the Behavioural Sciences* 50, no. 2 (2014), 133. The 'native mind' was also an object of contested scientific knowledge elsewhere in the British Empire. See Diana Jeater, *Law, Language, and Science: The Invention of the 'Native Mind' in Southern Rhodesia, 1890–1930* (Portsmouth: Heinemann, 2006), 215–232.
49. Anderson, 'Hermannsburg', 134–135.
50. Anderson, 'Hermannsburg', 137. The third expedition to Hermannsburg in 1929 was that of the Hungarian psychoanalyst Géza Róheim, who sought to test Sigmund Freud's theories of totem and taboo (Anderson, 'Hermannsburg', 139–142).
51. Stanley D. Porteus, *The Psychology of a Primitive People: A Study of the Australian Aborigine* (London: Edward Arnold & Co, 1931), 333, 362, 384.

52. Paul Ocobock, *An Uncertain Age: The Politics of Manhood in Kenya* (Athens: Ohio University Press, 2017), 120; Mark Finnane, *Punishment in Australian Society* (Melbourne: Oxford University Press), 113.
53. Porteus, *The Psychology of a Primitive People*, x, 400–401.
54. Marjorie Piddington and Ralph Piddington, 'Report of Field Work in North-Western Australia', *Oceania* 2, no. 3 (1932), 355–356, 358; S.D. Porteus, 'Mentality of Australian Aborigines', *Oceania* 3, no. 3 (1933), 31–32. See also Erik Linstrum, *Ruling Minds: Psychology in the British Empire* (Cambridge: Harvard University Press, 2016), 99–109.
55. T.T. Webb, *From Spears to Spades* (Melbourne: The Book Depot, 1944), 53.
56. Warburton, *Buffaloes*, 125; M.H. Ellis, *The Long Lead: Across Australia by Motor-Car* (London: T. Fisher Unwin, 1927), 241.
57. Lucien Lévy-Bruhl, *Primitive Mentality* (London: George Allen & Unwin, 1923), 254, 256–257.
58. Spencer and Gillen, *Native Tribes of Central Australia*, 15, 68, 100, 128.
59. For Ted Strehlow, an anthropologist and patrol officer in the Northern Territory Native Affairs Branch who had grown up at Hermannsburg, such force was privileged as an 'effective … show of … authority'. But this was a 'show' that could only be effectively performed by those who had made a 'careful study … of the customs and rules of the ancient native code and of their ideas of morality'. Strehlow, 17 October 1936, quoted in Tim Rowse, 'Strehlow's Strap: Functionalism and Historicism in a Colonial Ethnography', in *Power, Knowledge and Aborigines*, ed. Bain Attwood and John Arnold (Melbourne: La Trobe University Press, 1992), 91–92.
60. See Julia Martínez and Claire Lowrie, 'Colonial Constructions of Masculinity: Transforming Aboriginal Australian Men into "Houseboys"', *Gender and History* 21, no. 2 (2009).
61. 'Birtles' Charges', *Northern Standard*, 15 January 1932, 3.
62. The Racial Hygiene Association resolved to encourage members to attend the annual meeting of the Association for the Protection of Native Races. See Racial Hygiene Association, Minutes of Meeting, 18 January, 29 February, 29 March 1932: MLMSS 3838/Box 01/Item 7, State Library of New South Wales, Sydney (hereafter SLNSW); Annual Report of the Association for the Protection of Native Races Presented at the Twenty-first Annual Meeting held on 21 April 1932: Papers of the Association for the Protection of Native Races, S55/2, University of Sydney Archives, Sydney (hereafter USA).
63. See, for example, 'Condition of Natives', *West Australian*, 1 January 1932, 6; 'Northern Territory. Treatment of Blacks', *Age*, 5 January 1932, 8; 'Aborigines in Northern Territory', *Daily Standard*, 5 January 1932, 9. Birtles also conveyed his allegations directly to Parkhill, to whom a deputation of the Association for the Protection of Native Races put similar criti-

cisms. Birtles to Archdale Parkhill, 7 March 1932: A1, 1937/3013, NAA; 'Aborigines. Federal Responsibility. Mr. Parkhill Sympathetic', *Sydney Morning Herald*, 1 March 1932, 10.
64. See generally Warren Brown, *Francis Birtles: Australian Adventurer* (Sydney: Hachette Australia, 2012).
65. Georgine Clarsen, 'Pedaling Power: Bicycles, Subjectivities and Landscapes in a Settler Colonial Society', *Mobilities* 10, no. 5 (2015), 709.
66. 'From West to East', *Argus*, 15 December 1910, 6.
67. Victoria Haskins, 'The Smoking Buggy', in *Off the Beaten Track: A Journey Across the Nation* (Adelaide: History Trust of South Australia, 2008); Georgine Clarsen, 'The 1928 MacRobertson Round Australia Expedition: Colonial Adventuring in the Twentieth Century', in *Expedition into Empire: Exploratory Journeys and the Making of the Modern World*, ed. Martin Thomas (London: Routledge, 2014), 194.
68. Francis Birtles, 'Black Slave Labor in Australia. Scathing Indictment of Police Methods', *Railroad*, 10 February 1932, 12–13.
69. Thomas W. Laqueur, 'Bodies, Details, and the Humanitarian Narrative', in *The New Cultural History*, ed. Lynn Hunt (Berkeley: University of California Press, 1989), 179–180.
70. Fiona Paisley, 'An Echo of Black Slavery: Emancipation, Forced Labour and Australia in 1933', *Australian Historical Studies* 45 (2014). The illustration accompanying Birtles' claims in *The Railroad* recalled images earlier published in both Arthur Vogan's Queensland antislavery text *The Black Police: A Story of Modern Australia*, and Harriet Beecher Stowe's classic novel *Uncle Tom's Cabin*. Birtles' stories were enveloped in the 'canonical' antislavery narrative through references to men who flogged Aboriginal people as 'Simon Legrees', and to a beaten Aboriginal man as 'Uncle Tom'. Jane Lydon, *Photography, Humanitarianism, Empire* (London: Bloomsbury, 2016), 59, 63–66.
71. 'Aborigines On Cattle Stations are in Slavery: Anthropologist Piddington Backs World's Probe Demand', *World*, 14 January 1932, 7; 'Sensational Abo. Slavery Story', *Daily Standard*, 15 January 1932, 15.
72. The Organiser, 'The Bagman's Gazette', *Northern Standard*, 26 February 1932, 3; C. Price Conigrave, Letter to the Editor, *Sydney Morning Herald*, 8 March 1932, 5; 'Prospector Michael', Letter to the Editor, *Northern Standard*, 12 September 1933, 8; 'No Outrages on Blacks, Says Parkhill', *Northern Standard*, 5 April 1932, 6.
73. C. Graham to *Sydney Morning Herald*, 4 March 1932: A1, 1937/3013, NAA.
74. C.E. Gaunt, 'The Territory's Defence', *Northern Standard*, 16 February 1932, 3.
75. R. Macintyre, Letter to the Editor, *Sydney Morning Herald*, 4 March 1932, 5.

76. Macintyre, Letter.
77. McKenzie, *Scandal in the Colonies*, 28.
78. Karuna Mantena, *Alibis of Empire: Henry Maine and the Ends of Liberal Imperialism* (Princeton: Princeton University Press, 2010).
79. 'Birtles Prejudiced, says C.P. Conigrave', *Northern Standard*, 5 February 1932, 7. Birtles' moment of sympathy was brief. In his 1935 memoir he wrote that 'if the white rulers govern the black people with a slack hand, big trouble will certainly come'. Francis Birtles, *Battle Fronts of the Outback* (Sydney: Angus and Robertson, 1935), 17.
80. Macintyre, Letter.
81. Epstein, *Scandal of Colonial Rule*, 12.

PART II

Emotional Economies and Cultural Hybridities

CHAPTER 6

Eliza Batman's House: Unhomely Frontiers and Intimate Overstraiters in Van Diemen's Land and Port Phillip

Penelope Edmonds and Michelle Berry

In 1845 in early colonial Melbourne, Port Phillip, a group of Aboriginal men dived into the treacherous rapids of the Yarra River over many hours through the night to retrieve the body of drowned John Charles Batman, the seven-year-old son of Eliza and John Batman. Young Charles was well known to the group of men, often referred to as the 'Sydney Natives', as many of them had lived with the Batman family for at least fourteen years in Van Diemen's Land (now Tasmania) and Port Phillip. Diving for the body of Charles was an intimate act on behalf of the Aboriginal men, who were attached to and in the service of the Batman family and associated with its fate across violent southeastern frontiers.[1] From Melbourne distraught mother Eliza Batman penned an emotional and religious letter describing the funeral to her daughter Elizabeth, who had remained in Van Diemen's Land. As Eliza recounted, at the funeral 150 children followed the hearse to mourn the loss of the only son born to the so-called

P. Edmonds (✉) • M. Berry
University of Tasmania, Hobart, TAS, Australia

© The Author(s) 2018
P. Edmonds, A. Nettelbeck (eds.), *Intimacies of Violence in the Settler Colony*, Cambridge Imperial and Post-Colonial Studies Series, https://doi.org/10.1007/978-3-319-76231-9_6

founding father of Melbourne, John Batman.[2] Charles Batman had seven older sisters. But Charles was not the Batmans' only 'son', for along with the seven Sydney Natives, the Batmans had brought with them at least two adopted Tasmanian Aboriginal boys to Melbourne: Rolepana, known as 'Ben Lomond' or 'Benny', and another called Lurnerminner, known as 'John Allen' or 'Jacky'.[3] In Van Diemen's Land they had also taken possession of a third small Aboriginal boy for a time, who was christened 'John Batman'.

At the time of her son's death, Eliza was in difficult straits. John Batman Senior had been dead for nearly seven years, and he had written Eliza out of his will. Yet in 1838, the year before his unseemly death from syphilis, the Batmans were a wealthy lower-middle-class landholding family, possessing twenty acres of land on Batman's Hill, Melbourne, and five allotments in the Port Phillip area. They were in charge of around thirty 'servants', a number which included convicts and Aboriginal people, owned thirty to forty thousand head of sheep and cattle, and orchards, and held a major government contract to supply meat to the new settlement in Port Phillip.[4] When their weatherboard house on the eponymous Batman's Hill was robbed in February 1838, nearly three years after their arrival, Eliza reported that the thieves had taken items including 'a silver pencil case, two gold earrings, silver clasps, a neck chain … seven silk handkerchiefs, one silver and two plated spoons, 3 drinking horns silver mounted, 3 striped sheets, 2 decanters', as well as tablecloths, fine pieces of linen, 'lace and network, 6 pairs of stockings … and glass and crockery'.[5] This domestic taxonomy reveals a list of expensive middle-class objects, both personal and for the table, belonging to a pastoral family with large land and agricultural holdings. Eliza Batman, an Irish former convict, had become the mistress of a major entrepreneurial 'overstraiter' household, a business with extensive landholdings and servants, generated from the wealth of two colonial frontiers.

The Batmans had taken part in and profited from the 'Black War' between Aboriginal people and settlers in Van Diemen's Land (1828–1834), as their household became a depot and service point in the execution of orchestrated attacks against Aboriginal peoples.[6] Nevertheless, they sought more land. In May 1835, Batman sailed across the Bass Strait to Port Phillip to appropriate the Aboriginal lands of the Kulin Nation through an attempted treaty with Kulin chiefs.[7] By April 1836, Eliza and their seven daughters had joined him at Port Phillip to live in the house on Batman's Hill. Within a year, Port Phillip was also beset by frontier violence as pastoral holdings expanded and Aboriginal groups resisted such incursions, which would continue until the late 1840s. In 1882, in the old cemetery at West Melbourne, a memorial stone was erected by 'public subscription to perpetuate the memory of John Batman, the adventurous settler who first selected the site of Melbourne'. John Batman's historiographical apogee as intrepid settler and founding father reached its peak in the 1930s centenary celebrations of his landing, but his ignominious and early death in 1839 was politely glossed over at that time.

This chapter does not seek to rehearse the popular notion of Batman as the founding father of Melbourne, or of a triumphal crossing of a founding family from Van Diemen's Land to Port Phillip.[8] Rather, it reveals other crossings in its examination of the overstraiter household and large enterprise of Eliza and John Batman. This chapter locates the Batman family's intimate and violent colonial entanglements with Aboriginal people both in Van Diemen's Land and in Port Phillip, and it also examines the cross-cultural affective economy of the Batman frontier household amid the daily economic workings of pastoralism and labour on the frontier. It examines the Batman household to explore the uncertain domestic borderlands of both extreme violence and sometimes forced intimacy, and argues that it was through the vectors of imperial power—where land, homes, and children were taken from Aboriginal people—that these prosaic domestic 'unhomely', and gendered relationships were forged. Freud describes the 'unhomely' (*unheimlich*), or 'uncanny', as the becoming alien of the familiar through the process of repression.[9] It refers to the 'estranged sense of encountering something familiar yet threatening which lies within the bounds of the intimate'.[10] The 'unhomely' is that which 'ought to have remained secret and hidden but has come to light'; the uneasy feeling arises when that which is concealed disrupts what is 'familiar and agreeable'.[11] In this chapter, we draw on this concept to think through the affective processes of white settler homemaking amid an aggressive and tumultuous land war and tense Port Phillip frontiers. We suggest that the settler home was a colonial economy in miniature, constructed upon the unstable and shifting foundations of convict and Aboriginal labour, and domination and resistance in the context of frontier warfare. It was also a space of denial, where danger and threat leaked into the home, a place too often imagined as offering safety and security. In this ambivalent space, the 'homely' is at once 'unhomely', revealed in those feelings of familiarity and safety that simultaneously rely on the repression of the violent means by which settlers confiscated and remade

Aboriginal land as their own. Aboriginal children like Rolepana and Lurnerminner were taken from their own families to become reincorporated into the colonial family home as both dependents and sources of labour. Here, we argue that intimate affective economies recast acts of aggression as acts of kindness, and dispersal of Aboriginal families as care. In the intimate sphere of the colonial homestead, built on the violent dispossession of Aboriginal land, Aboriginal people were often reintegrated into such new 'homes', where their loss could be erased and resignified as gain through the affective economies of care and gratitude.

Intimacy and Violence on Domestic Southeastern Colonial Frontiers

Violence, proximity, and intimacy between colonised Indigenous peoples and Europeans were fundamental to the formation of settler colonial societies, yet still we know surprisingly little of how they were connected.[12] Too often, traditional studies of settler colonialism have conceptualised violence as largely martial, top-down, situated in—and inflicted by and upon—male bodies sited on remote borderlands or frontiers, as clashes between strangers, and narrowly framed within nineteenth-century masculinist understandings of warfare. Gratifyingly, for more than three decades now, and post the cultural turn, new feminist, poststructural, and postcolonial work has amply demonstrated that violence is a continuum stretching from martial acts, harsh physical punishment, and terror to the bureaucratic, everyday, linguistic and discursive, the local and the domestic. Crucially, colonial violence is not only raced, but gendered and intimate, and it all too often occurs between those known to each other.[13] Such bonds, as Ann Laura Stoler instructively observed in her reflections on North American history, could be both 'tense and tender ties', where the powerful yet 'intimate domains—sex, sentiment, domestic arrangement, and child rearing—figure in the making of racial categories and in the management of imperial rule'.[14] There is also an established and growing scholarship on the home and colonial domesticity, cross-cultural intimacy, and violence in spaces of colonisation, which foregrounds women, both colonised and European, in the understandings of intimacy and proximity, and child-rearing on the colonial frontier. Building on an important body of scholarship that has sought to interrogate white women, in particular, within the machinations of colonial rule and their imbrication with frontier violence, historians Victoria Haskins and Claire Lowrie have observed that in the nexus between domesticity and colonisation we must see the 'significance of the home and household work for the construction and maintenance of the power relations that underpinned colonial rule'.[15] As they recount, with the emergence of the new imperial history informed by postcolonial theory in the 1990s, domestic work, and domesticity more generally, came to be seen as critical to understanding the mechanisms of colonial power. As Stoler shows, the colonial home, and domestic labour attached to it, could be described, in the Foucauldian sense, as a 'dense transfer point of power' between coloniser and colonised.[16] And further, as Antoinette Burton has observed suggestively, in the interdependence between 'history' and 'home' we may find a space where 'contests over colonial dominion can be discerned and historicized'.[17]

Despite these crucial shifts in understanding, which are due largely to feminist scholars of empire, there is still little work that closely considers the colonies of southeastern Australia, especially Van Diemen's Land and the early Port Phillip district, through such lenses, and, indeed, in the period of the Batman family, which was not Victorian but the earlier Regency period of the 1820s. Some scholars have turned their attention to questions of domesticity, colonialism, and the experiences of white, affluent, and free settler women who were 'making home' in the 1850s as their families took up pastoral land in Van Diemen's Land, after the period of intense conflict with Aboriginal peoples. Patricia Grimshaw and Ann Standish have reflected on genteel English woman Louisa Meredith's published writing on 'making home' in the new colony in the 1840s, in the decade after Aboriginal women had lost their homes.[18] Penny Russell has scrutinised the elite colonial home as a cross-cultural site and the ways in which the 'home' has gained a powerful hold in history, particularly in postcolonial scholarship, and has sought to explore the tensions of love, pain, and disruption of the home in colonial Australia, where the 'colonising, civilising agenda' of home 'disturbed the very illusion of refuge on which it crucially depended'.[19] In her work on the life of Tasmanian Aboriginal girl Mathinna, who was taken into the home of Lady Jane Franklin and Governor of Van Diemen's Land John Franklin as an experiment in civilisation and then abandoned, Russell draws on Homi Bhabha's concept of the 'unhomely' to foreground the discomforting tensions of the civilising domestic world of colonial Australia. Bhabha explains the 'unhomely moment' as that which 'creeps up on you stealthily as your own shadow' until suddenly you find yourself 'taking the measure of your dwelling in a state of "incredulous terror"'.[20]

The story of Eliza Batman, a woman of quite another station from the English Lady Jane Franklin and Louisa Meredith, has not been examined. Eliza was an Irish convict woman who became the mistress of a pastoral holding more than a decade earlier, in the very midst of the violent Black War. In this chapter, we respond to Julie Gough's call for more research into cross-cultural and mixed contact on frontier farms and households by examining flows of intimacy and dominion in the colonial economy and in the context of Eliza's daily relations with the Aboriginal women, men, and children who were part of the Batman pastoral enterprise.[21]

Eliza Batman can no longer be dismissed as a mere footnote to the enduring 'founding father' story of John Batman and the Port Phillip Association in early Melbourne. She has been routinely characterised by historians as a convict doxy, and as a broken Irish woman who later lived under an alias and was murdered in a rooming house in Geelong in 1852.[22] Traditional and even recent scholarship has persisted in portraying Eliza as a drunk who 'drifted back into the habits of her earlier existence to die a sordid death'.[23] Eliza's murder was never solved, testament to her problematic status as the ignominious 'founding mother' of Melbourne among the Port Phillip elite.[24] Rather, it is clear from the colonial records that she was literate, religious, and an intriguing woman who lived well beyond the cliché of fallen 'convict'.[25] Nevertheless, we do not seek to rehabilitate Eliza as such. In line with Joan Scott's important insights, we argue that a gendered analytic can show how Eliza's record goes beyond achieving her 'recovery' to instead shed light on how she was constituted as a colonial figure within a field of gendered power relations built on dispossession, pastoralism, the homestead, and the violence of the frontier wars in Van Diemen's Land in the 1820s and 1830s and in Port Phillip—a history too often recounted as overwhelmingly martial and male.[26] Likewise, in settler colonies such as these, the theft or removal and 'adoption' of dispossessed Aboriginal children into European homes as labourers and servants during periods of frontier aggression only added to the destruction of Aboriginal families. Such actions gave rise to intimate affective economies threaded with terror, gratitude, care, and cruelty—tense and tender ties—which circulated in pastoral households that were both home and unhomely.

Life at Kingston: Making Home on Plangermaireener Land

John Batman arrived in Van Diemen's Land in December 1821 from Sydney. In early April 1823, he received from the colonial government an initial grant of six hundred acres of land in the foothills of Ben Lomond in the north of the island, sited in the Buffalo Plains in the valley of the Ben Lomond rivulet, a tributary of the South Esk river.[27] His farm, which came to be known as 'Kingston', was based on a land grant situated on the expropriated land of the Plangermaireener nation. The Plangermaireener consisted of three and possibly four bands, with numbers totalling 150 to 200 people, who occupied around 260 square kilometres of country surrounding the Ben Lomond plateau.[28] With meat in short supply, especially for convict rations, by June 1823 Batman, always the entrepreneur, was tendering to supply three thousand pounds of meat to His Majesties Stores in George Town in the north of Van Diemen's Land.[29]

Elizabeth Callaghan (Eliza) arrived in the penal colony of Van Diemen's Land in December 1821. As a young Irish woman living in London, she was convicted and transported for fourteen years for 'uttering', or passing, a forged banknote.[30] Eliza arrived in Hobart on the convict ship *Providence* in December 1821 and was assigned to Hobart Gaoler John Petchey. She remained with him until early 1823 when she was reassigned to P.A. Mulgrave, Superintendent of Police in Launceston. Within a few months, Eliza had absconded from Mulgrave and formed a relationship with Batman, living secretly at Kingston for years, and there she gave birth to three of their seven daughters.[31]

In January 1828, Batman applied to Lieutenant-Governor Arthur for permission to marry Eliza, noting 'your memorialist is possessed of upwards of Two thousand acres of land and a large flock of both sheep and cattle at Ben Lomond'. A supporting letter from G.W. Barnard, a fellow settler, praised Batman's 'zealous efforts against the bushrangers and as being the fortunate capturer of Brady'.[32] Batman's request for permission to marry Eliza was granted, and in March 1828 they were married in St Johns Church, Launceston.[33] While Arthur's permission might be seen as a reward for capturing Brady, it also supported Arthur's idea of an ordered colonial domesticity as well as reflecting the longstanding encouragement by London for colonial governors in New South Wales to 'promote marriage as a means of moralising the settlements'.[34] As historian Kirsty Reid has argued, control of settlers and convicts was achieved through the extension and withdrawal of a range of state privileges on the basis of moral conduct and by the broader construction of a gendered morality and domestic respectability.[35] Arthur was not about to unravel the family group, as this model was an economic and moral success.

Kingston was a significant pastoral holding and home to a large community of assigned convicts, free labourers, children, and Aboriginal people. According to Batman's May 1828 application for more land, the Kingston farm then consisted of 5300 acres of leased, granted, and purchased land, 250 cattle, 2900 sheep, three horses, a weatherboard house, a kitchen, a stable, and outbuildings (including a barn) and five miles of fence, along with five convict servants, ten free mechanics, and a number of labourers.[36] In 1828, Eliza was mother to three daughters, Maria, Lucy, and Eliza, and lived in the weatherboard house. As mistress, Eliza's role in the pastoral enterprise can be partially followed in the records. In August 1829, she successfully applied for an assigned servant in her own name, a nineteen-year-old farm labourer from Nottingham, and in the same month Eliza is recorded as selling rum and alcohol for Batman.[37] The Kingston enterprise was materially advantaged by the unpaid labour and economic management provided by Eliza in her role as John Batman's wife at Kingston.

While the colonial archive is replete with information on the capital and value of pastoral homesteads such as Kingston, it is rare to find first-hand accounts of the intimate and proximate experiences of those who lived there. An 1833 account of a visit to Kingston by an English tourist, five years after the 1828 land application, reveals much about the homestead that Eliza and John Batman created, the relations they formed, and, importantly, something of Eliza herself. While on a tour of Van Diemen's Land in February 1833, Peregrine Massingberd spent several days in the company of Eliza, John, their daughters, 'six [Aborigines] from Sydney', and two Aboriginal boys who lived at the Kingston farm. Massingberd noted in his diary that the two boys—Ben Lomond (Rolepana), who was five years old, and John Allen (Lurnerminner), who was twelve—had been 'taken from a tribe of this Island', by the six Aboriginal men in Batman's employ.[38] Massingberd's diary recorded his impressions of the intimate daily life of Eliza's home and enterprise, and detailed Eliza and John's background and their relations with the Aboriginal men and children who were living there. Massingberd, a male member of the English landed gentry, is the author of one of the few first-hand accounts of Eliza to be found in the archival record. In his diary, he spoke admiringly of the convict wife who was nevertheless Batman's 'greatest blessing'. He wrote:

> [it is not] possible to form an idea of a more mild, gentle obliging creature than is Mrs Batman; exceedingly respected by all that know her—beloved by all the persons on the property, who would sacrifice anything to serve. She appears to be of the lower rank, probably the daughter of some little farmer to have improved her mind with more reading than such persons generally have an opportunity of doing, and is always cheerful, attentive and kind. The best of wives, of mothers and of mistresses.[39]

Although Massingberd identified Eliza as being of lower rank, he suggested that her literacy served to elevate her position, and he clearly approved of those qualities that he felt were a virtue of her sex. Mild, gentle, obliging, kind, cheerful, and attentive as well as religious, Eliza was characterised as the epitome of colonial womanhood and domesticity. In Massingberd's eyes, Eliza Batman embodied a compassionate model of civilising female colonial benevolence. Of the two Aboriginal boys in Eliza's care, Massingberd wrote that 'they speak English very well', and he praised Eliza's efforts in teaching them to read: 'Mrs Batman is very kind to them and told me that she was having them instructed in reading and taught how to say the Lord's Prayer.'[40] As mistress of the household, Eliza Batman performed the 'gendered work of familial socialisation', as described by Fitzpatrick and Protschky, under the guise of civilising white benevolence.[41]

The Ben Lomond Massacre: Stolen Children and the Affective Redescriptions of Family

The two children to whom Massingberd refers—Ben Lomond (Rolepana) and John Allen (Lurnerminner)—had in fact been abducted from their parents by John Batman three years earlier. Rolepana was taken from his mother, Luggenemenener, after one of Batman's 'roving parties' attacked their camp near Ben Lomond in what is now known as the 'Ben Lomond massacre'. These roving parties were groups of men who, often with Aboriginal decoys, scoured the bush to track and capture or kill Aboriginal people. The Kingston farm was a key strategic settler site for planning, supplying, and executing the activities of these parties as part of the Black War, acting as a depot for Batman's roving parties as well as the Danvers roving party in the Ben Lomond area.[42] Rather than viewing the homestead as separate from the 'frontier'—somewhere out in the bush and out of sight, far from the roving parties that sought to kill and capture Aboriginal people—we consider Kingston farm as a frontier space thoroughly embedded and constituted through the violent relations of settler homemaking and Aboriginal dispossession. As Edmonds has observed elsewhere on space, intimacy, and colonial violence, settler aggression against Indigenous peoples operated across multiple sites, such as colonial towns, 'native' camps, the homestead, and the pastoral frontier.[43] Eliza was not detached from either the daily activities of frontier violence or those of Batman as a leader of roving parties. The pastoral 'home' or station was a site of colonial domesticity, but it was at once home and unhomely; a 'contact zone' in which Eliza as the 'mistress' of the household taught dispossessed Aboriginal boys to read, served captured Aboriginal people food, and had daily contact with the white men and New South Wales Aboriginal men who participated in violent sorties. It was also the place where she gave birth to her daughters.

Commonly used concepts of shared space and mutual accommodation, or 'middle ground', must therefore be carefully reviewed. The notion of the pastoral station as a 'contact zone' and a 'shared landscape' has been productive.[44] Yet the very term 'shared landscape', though it came into fashion in the late 1990s (and has taken on particular meaning in the field of landscape heritage), must always be subject to interrogation, especially around relations of power in the frontier settler-colonial context. To argue that the pastoral landscape was 'shared' denies the reality that settlers took land and moved men, women, and children by force and harnessed their labour. Colonial authorities and settlers such as Batman coerced Aboriginal people, including children, to occupy sites such as the homestead that some scholars now describe as 'shared', and such dominance was frequently maintained through terror and harsh physical punishment.[45]

The first newspaper account of Batman and his response to Aboriginal incursions dates from April 1828, when a Ben Lomond Aboriginal group chased one of Batman's shepherds right to the house at Kingston.[46] Batman, however, had prior experience of raids and attacks on Aboriginal camps, conducted with other European settlers before 1828, and he quickly became embroiled in a battle for land with the Ben Lomond Aborigines who were fighting a war of resistance.[47] In 1828, Batman began to initiate a 'new type of roving party', supported by convicts and supplied with rations and equipment, in order to stay out in the bush for longer.[48] Batman, with a band of nine selected convicts, was to pursue Aboriginal people in a series of such roving parties and was nominally under the direction of Police Magistrate of Oatlands Thomas Anstey.[49] In return for their services, the convicts were to be 'offered conditional pardons'.[50] And as reward, Batman received grants of land up to two thousand acres. Batman also used the New South Wales Aboriginal men in his roving parties, as well as some local Aboriginal men. The first two New South Wales Aboriginal men Batman employed were Pigeon and Johnny Crook, who were later sent to Sydney to bring back five more Aboriginal men.[51] The deployment of Indigenous peoples in all the British colonies against others in the processes of violence colonisation has been explored by historian Kristyn Harman. She notes that Pigeon and Johnny Crook were brought in first and 'clothed by the government store'.[52] Pigeon, probably as a whaler or sealer, had spent time in the Bass Strait islands and knew something of the Tasmanian Aboriginal languages. For their services, Pigeon and Johnny Crook were granted one hundred acres of land each near Batman's estate in the Ben Lomond area, although it is unlikely that they ever took them up.[53]

Eliza's knowledge and contact with Aboriginal people would have been scarce compared to those of Batman. As an Irish girl living in London, then transported to the colony of Van Diemen's Land in 1821 at around the age of seventeen, her knowledge of Aboriginal people would have been initially limited, and then wholly shaped by her time in the colony, in the midst of growing violence. Batman's experience with Aboriginal people had originated in his childhood in Parramatta, New South Wales. Alastair Campbell notes the influence of Wesleyan liberalism in Batman's early life in Sunday school and the Aboriginal people he knew there. John Batman likely became acquainted with several Aboriginal youths at this school, which, Campbell writes, was 'attended by at least 120 children, nineteen of whom were Aborigines'. According to Campbell, in 1829, when Batman was assembling his roving parties, he would write to Thomas Hassell, son of Wesleyan missionary Rowland Hassell, to request that he send several of his Aboriginal acquaintances over to Tasmania.[54] Batman had therefore used his New South Wales connections to hire the Aboriginal men, and they were procured specifically to assist him in the capture of the Tasmanian Aborigines.

As is well established, Batman was the leader and instigator of the roving party that committed the Ben Lomond massacre; evinced, in part, by his own letters to Anstey. In the early days, Batman would frequently couch his roving-party letters to Anstey in the language of 'reconciliation' and humanitarianism; but, as Campbell has noted, 'underlying attitudes of racism and violence were to strongly influence John Batman's future actions, whatever the influence of a Wesleyan liberalism'.[55] On 3 September 1829, Batman, along with the assistance of several of the New South Wales Aboriginal men, planned and led an attack on an Aboriginal family group together numbering sixty to seventy men, women, and children in the Ben Lomond district of northeast Tasmania. He recorded, in his letter to Anstey, on 'Tuesday 1st [September] I started again in pursuit of the Aborigines who have been committing so many outrages in this district'. The next day, he 'fell in with their tracks ... We considered there must have been upwards of 100 in this tribe'. Later, Batman ordered his men to 'lay down [as] we could hear the Natives conversing distinctly [and] we then crept into a thick forest and remained there until after sun set'.[56] After 11 o'clock at night, the men left their 'knapsacks and blankets' and 'crept up on them'. Batman had intended that his party would:

> rush upon them before they arise from the ground, hoping that I should not be under the necessity of firing at them. But unfortunately as the last man was coming up he struck his musket against that of another of the party which immediately alarmed the dogs (in number about 40). They came directly at us. The Natives arose from the ground and were in the act of running away into a thick forest when I ordered the men to fire upon them, which was done and a rush by the party immediately followed. We only captured that night one woman and a male child about Two Years old. The party was in search of them the remainder of the night but without success.[57]

The party had killed an estimated fifteen people, but many more were wounded. The next morning, Batman left for his farm with two badly wounded Tasmanian men, a woman, and her two-year-old boy, all of whom he had captured. However, he 'found it impossible that the two former could walk, and after trying them by every means in my power, for some time, found I could not get them on I was obliged to shoot them'. The captured woman was Luggenemenener, who was later sent to Campbell Town Gaol and separated from her two-year-old 'son', Rolepana ('she was his father's sister'). It is these two children, taken from their families, whom Eliza taught to read at the Kingston farm.

The Aboriginal child survivors of roving parties, such as Rolepana, became discursively reconstituted as *like* family, through affective languages of emotional attachment and gratitude that functioned to conceal the 'home' as a violent frontier space and 'home-making' as a mechanism of aggressive colonisation—part of the process that we term 'affective redescription'. The settler home so often configured as a place of safety and respite becomes both the site of labour and a site where the intense contests over colonial dominion occur, and where, under the guise of family and home, Indigenous attachments to land and community are obliterated.

The government official John Helder Wedge, who was a regular visitor to Kingston farm, also kept Aboriginal children at his homestead; he would use the affective language of family and home in his letter to the settler Mr. Leake on the death of one Aboriginal boy: 'Whetee Coolere [Teetoreric] also known as May Day, I miss him very much and feel his loss'. He continued: 'Since that event *my family has had a great increase* I now have *three* native boys with me one of them a brother of poor Whetee.'[58] The precarious and anomalous position of Aboriginal children is exemplified in such accounts of affection by aggressors who had participated in killing or separating families from children who they saw themselves as 'benevolently' taking in. The affective redescription of family and home, such as that used by Wedge, served to obfuscate the violence that brought these new Aboriginal members into the family.

Historian Shirleene Robinson has shown that the removal of Aboriginal children from their families has been a long-term practice conducted across Australia since the beginning of European arrival. As she notes, Aboriginal children were 'forcibly incorporated into European families on an unofficial basis that was not governed by the state', often during the process of violent frontier conflict. Such 'unofficial removal' and the role of private families 'has received considerably less scrutiny', she suggests, than the role of state-based missions and reserves in separating Aboriginal families. Robinson has examined this 'private incorporation' of Aboriginal children into European families in the colonial era as a type of moral regulation, where the family 'operated as a mechanism for "civilising" Indigenous children by regulating their "reform"'.[59] Jan Kociumbas states that many Aboriginal children became 'available for "rescue"'—a euphemistic term—in the late eighteenth and early nineteenth centuries in New South Wales, while in their work on the colonial contexts of Australia and the United States, Victoria Haskins and Margaret Jacobs argue that child removal was conducted as a method of warfare.[60]

In her landmark book, *Broken Circles*, Anna Haebich examines Aboriginal child removal in Australia from 1800, and considers the early history of unofficial child removal in Van Diemen's Land. As Haebich notes, Aboriginal children across the settler colonies were 'swept up in the tragic processes of dispossession as Indigenous land and resources were taken', and 'snatched from their parents' arms during raids and confrontations'.[61] The practice became widespread in early colonial Van Diemen's Land, such that in 1817, as Lyndall Ryan has reckoned, 'over fifty children were living with settlers'.[62] In Van Diemen's Land, several proclamations made by governors made it clear that removal of children was unlawful; but, as Haebich notes, this had little impact. Most settlers kept children in defiance of the law, without consequence, as no 'official action was taken during the escalation of hostilities in the 1820s'. The declaration of martial law in 1828 only served to legitimise these atrocities.[63] By 1830, throughout the settled areas, an unknown number of Aboriginal children were 'living in the homes of prominent land owners and officials, publicans, shopkeepers and farmers'. Haebich writes that possibly 'as many as eighty-nine children may have been taken in between 1810 and 1836', although 'this clearly underestimates the number of abductions'.[64]

Likewise, baptism of these children could also serve as both an affective and religious redescription. On 2 June 1830, John Batman rode home to Kingston for the baptism of his four daughters and Rolepana, the survivor of the Ben Lomond massacre, who would then have been about three years old.[65] Batman recorded the event in his diary: 'Maria, Lucy, Eliza, Elizabeth Mary, and Ben Lomond are baptised together in Launceston at St. Johns.' Eliza was a religious woman, an Irish Protestant, and St Johns was an Anglican church. The baptism is an act of renaming, and the individual is initiated into the Christian faith. Rolepana became known formally as 'Ben Lomond', losing his Plangermaireener name. Just as Wedge's phrase 'my family has had a great increase' was an affective redescription, so too Batman's baptism of Rolepana brought him into the Batman family within a Christian, civilising covenant of the 'home'. In this space, Rolepana was brought into personal kinship relations—with the Batmans and their children—that were at once protective and deeply colonising.

Colonial Economies: Boys as Labourers

The unofficial means of acquiring Aboriginal children served the Batman family's farm economy well, as both Rolepana and Lurnerminner were taken to be used as domestic farmworkers.[66] At the Batmans' pastoral home, they drove the plough, milked the cows, and tended the swine. As Massingberd had recorded from his visit to Kingston in 1833, the boys were 'useful on the farm; tho very idle if not strictly watched'.[67]

At the close of the Black War in 1834, Aboriginal 'conciliator' George Augustus Robinson and Lieutenant-Governor Arthur urged that the two boys at Kingston be taken to Flinders Island to the Aboriginal establishment because their mothers, Luggenemenener and Karnebucher, wanted them back. Karnebucher, who was Lurnerminner's mother, had been in Anthony Cottrell's roving party, and also attached to Robinson's party. She had been 'separated from her son Lurnerminner for some time and requested his return'. Robinson wrote to Cottrell, asking '[as] Karnerbunga [Karnerbutcher] is most anxious to see her son will you have the goodness to mention this to Mr Batman so that the lad may be forwarded to Hobart Town by the first conveyance'.[68] Although the Governor gave his approval for both the boys to be returned, Batman refused. Batman and Robinson would have a long-running struggle over the boys, prompting the latter to send his own son 'with the black women and two men' to Batman's property at Kingston to retrieve them. But, he wrote, 'Batman refused to give up either of the lads and said they were as much his property as his farm and that he had as much right to keep them as the government'.[69]

In March 1834, Batman's friend and associate J.W. Darling, Commandant of Flinders Island, afforded Batman the following testimonial to support retaining the boys:

> I have seen Jacky [Lurnerminner, then ten years old] driving the plough at your farm, and have expressed to you my admiration of his shrewdness and intelligence, and my hope that under the care and kindness with which both he and little Benny [Rolepana] are evidently treated by your family, they would one day become useful members of society.[70]

Yet while Darling's testimony had observed that Batman treated the boys with 'care and kindness', Robinson claimed that he had received information from Batman's neighbour that the boys were 'flogged with a whip'.[71] In the end, Darling and Batman both agreed that in general

Fig. 6.1 'Pellonymyna' (Pellenominer) as recorded in Walker's unpublished journal. George Washington Walker diaries, Flinders Island, 1832, Mitchell Library, SLNSW

Aboriginal boys should be sent from Flinders Island to the orphan school or into the services of 'kind' masters to be educated. Batman retained the two Aboriginal boys, probably assisted by Darling's advocacy, and eventually took them to Port Phillip.[72]

Four months after Darling's testimony, in July 1834, Eliza gave birth to her seventh daughter, who was named Pellenominer Frances Darling Batman. The Batmans had named their child after Pellenominer, an Aboriginal woman from Ben Lomond, who was also incarcerated at Flinders Island Aboriginal Station, and placed under the direct guardianship of Commandant Darling.[73] Travelling Quakers Backhouse and Walker also met Pellenominer on Flinders Island, and her name appears in Walker's unpublished journal in a list of Aboriginal names (see Fig. 6.1).[74]

The transference of the name Pellenominer Frances Darling Batman to Eliza's seventh daughter appears as a reciprocal, if disquieting, gesture to the Ben Lomond or Plangermaireener people, and possibly to the associations that the young Aboriginal woman Pellenominer may have had with surviving members of her tribe, or perhaps to the boys held at their home. This exchange of names cannot be easily read as cross-cultural affection, but sits as an uncanny accompaniment to the small Aboriginal boy who was christened 'John Batman' along with the Batmans' girls, although it is unclear what became of him. The naming of his daughter 'Frances Darling' appears also as an honorific gesture to Darling as the supporter for the boys to be kept with Batman. While Rolepana lost his Plangermaireener identity to become Benny or Ben Lomond, the Batmans' seventh daughter claimed a Plangermaireener name. This practice of redescription points once again to the parallel ways colonial brutality and affect are imbricated under the seemingly benevolent signs of family and home, and it shows how forced kinships were made through the exchange of names. It is both poignant and disquieting, for the act of naming a child is surely one of the most intimate gestures that can be made. Was this act of naming a gesture from Darling to the Batmans, the 'gift' of an incarcerated Aboriginal woman's name, conveyed between men? Such affective redescriptions served to mask the violent displacements of settler colonialism.

Once in Melbourne, and after John Batman's death in May 1839, Eliza eventually lost her home and much of the family's land holdings. She was ultimately left destitute, and most of her children were boarded out to Nicola Cooke, who had established Roxburgh Ladies Seminary at one of Batman's properties. Though the children were separated and sent to the households of friends, they were largely spared the fate of having to work to support themselves and their siblings. Their educations continued and they were cared for by a network of overstraiter friends of their parents, friendships which were established on the frontier of Van Diemen's Land and which survived the collapse of Eliza's household. Later, Pellenominer Frances Darling Batman would go on to marry Daniel Bunce, the botanist who accompanied Ludwig Leichhardt on his expedition, and who later became the director of the Geelong Botanic Gardens.[75]

By contrast, John Batman's death left the two young Aboriginal boys, Lurnerminner and Rolepana, without access to the network of support that was available to the Batman children. Rather than seeking help from the other Aboriginal men such as Pigeon and Johnny Crook (after all, these men from New South Wales had participated in the roving parties against their own peoples), they both turned to G.A. Robinson, who was now the Chief Protector of Aborigines in Port Phillip, for help. Robinson also assumed responsibility for the New South Wales Aborigines that had been in Batman's employ. He arranged for Rolepana (Ben Lomond) to be employed by George Ware, and Rolepana later died in Port Phillip in 1842.[76] Robinson organised for Lurnerminner (Jacky Allen) to be employed by Walter Coates; but after a horse died in his care, he fled back to Hobart, where he signed on to a whaling ship. Lurnerminner later returned to Hobart and joined other members of the Ben Lomond tribe at Oyster Cove Aboriginal Station, where he died in 1862. The differing fates of these children are stark. While the Batman children continued their childhood and education, the Aboriginal boys, who were 'like' family, were never to be equal members of the Batman family, and became labourers for the emerging colony.

Conclusion

When the Aboriginal men from New South Wales dived for the body of young Charles Batman at the Yarra Falls, it was an intimate act by a group of men who were bound to Eliza Batman through years of experience, across frontiers marked by both intimacy and violence. The large, entrepreneurial overstraiter household of John and Eliza Batman was built on and embedded in such relations, tense and tender ties indeed. This chapter has explored how the affective economy, or emotional exchanges, of the Batman frontier household supported the pastoral economy on the frontier, across the uncertain and gendered domestic borderlands of both extreme violence and forced intimacy. The home was at once a dense transfer point of power and an unhomely site of both repose and exploitation. It was a frontier depot for roving parties and a place of incarceration and civilisation, and also an economic unit that operated on the labour of dispossessed Aboriginal children, the men from New South Wales and convicts, all bound by various degrees of unfreedom. As Kingston's exconvict mistress, Eliza would live with, raise, and tutor Aboriginal children taken from their groups and parents, at a time of frontier warfare instigated by her husband, John Batman. She would take the namesake of an Aboriginal woman for her seventh daughter. In turn, upon Batman's death, Rolepana would be separated from Eliza, his adoptive mother and the woman who had taught him to read, who was also the widow of the man responsible for the murder of his family.

These strange entanglements take us to the tense borderlands of violence, intimacy, and affect on southeastern colonial frontiers from Van Diemen's Land, where cross-cultural relationships of force and submission are suffused with familial affections and glosses within the economy of the household. Attention to the homestead—and the brutal vectors between Eliza, John, the Sydney Aborigines, and the two Aboriginal boys—shows how the domestic realm works as a dense and poignant site of importance for the shaping of the boundaries between coloniser and colonised.[77] While violence is destructive, it is also productive of the precarious intimacies that take shape throughs the cross-cultural 'affective economy' of early settler households like Kingston, built on Aboriginal land.

Notes

1. Letter from Eliza Batman to Elizabeth Batman, 30 January 1845, John Batman Documents collection, National Museum of Australia, Canberra, http://collectionsearch.nma.gov.au/object/113416

2. Letter from Eliza Batman to Elizabeth Batman, 30 January 1845, John Batman Documents collection, National Museum of Australia, Canberra, http://collectionsearch.nma.gov.au/object/113416
3. Lurnerminner or Jacky Allen may also be known as Meelerleeter, Karnebutcher's son. The census taken in early Melbourne notes that present at the Batman's house on 12 September 1838 were the Aboriginal men 'Mr Pigeon, Mr. Sam, Mr. Steward, Mr. Allan, Mr. Bull, Mr. Bullett, Mr. Bunget', who were the men from New South Wales, and the two boys. Also Mrs. Pigeon, and 'Mr Jackey' (probably Jacky Allen) and 'Mr Benlomond' (probably Rolepana). See Michael Cannon and Ian MacFarlane, eds. *Historical Records of Victoria*, vol. 3 (Melbourne: Victorian Government Printing Office, 1984), 440.
4. Cannon and MacFarlane, *Historical Records of Victoria*, vol. 3.
5. See Eliza Batman, 'Property Stolen', Deposition in Melbourne Court Register, 23 February 1838, in Pauline Jones, ed. *Historical Records of Victoria*, vol. 1 (Melbourne: Victorian Government Printing Office, 1981), 431.
6. See, for example, Lyndall Ryan, *Tasmanian Aborigines: A History Since 1803* (Sydney: Allen and Unwin, 2012); Henry Reynolds, *Fate of a Free People: A Radical Re-examination of the Tasmanian Wars* (Melbourne: Penguin, 1995); and Nick Brodie, *The Vandemonian War* (Melbourne: Hardie Grant, 2017).
7. Bain Attwood, *Possession: Batman's Treaty and the Matter of History* (Melbourne: Miegunyah Press, 2009).
8. See Penelope Edmonds, 'Batman's Hill', eMelbourne, 2008, http://www.emelbourne.net.au/biogs/EM00164b.htm; Penelope Edmonds, 'Founding Myths', eMelbourne, 2008, http://www.emelbourne.net.au/biogs/EM00603b.htm; see also James Bonwick, *John Batman, the Founder of Victoria* (Melbourne: Fergusson and Moore, 1868); James Bonwick, *John Batman: Founder of a City* (Hobart: Education Department, 1971); Agnes Paton Bell, *Melbourne: John Batman's Village* (Melbourne: Cassell, 1965); P.L. Brown, 'Batman, John (1801–1839)', *Australian Dictionary of Biography*, National Centre of Biography, Australian National University, 2006–2017, http://adb.anu.edu.au/biography/batman-john-1752/text1947
9. Sigmund Freud, 'The "Uncanny"', in *The Standard Edition of the Complete Psychological Works of Sigmund Freud*, vol. 17, trans. James Strachey (London: Vintage, 1958 [1919]), 241.
10. 'The Uncanny/Unhomely in Bhabha's "The World and the Home"', *The Cultural Reader*, 27 March 2014, http://culturalstudiesnow.blogspot.com.au/2014/03/the-uncannyunhomely-in-bhabhas-home-and.html
11. Freud, 'The "Uncanny"', 224–225.
12. This chapter is drawn from the Australian Research Council Discovery Project 'Intimacy and Violence on the Pacific Rim', DP150100914.
13. Penelope Edmonds, *Urbanizing Frontiers: Indigenous Peoples and Settlers in 19th-Century Pacific Rim Cities* (Vancouver: University of British

Columbia, 2010); Penelope Edmonds, 'The Intimate, Urbanising Frontier: "Native Camps", Gender Relations and Settler Colonialism's Violent Array of Spaces around Early Melbourne', in *Making Settler Colonial Space: Perspectives on Race, Place and Identity*, ed. Tracey Banivanua Mar and Penelope Edmonds (Basingstoke: Palgrave, 2010), 129–154.
14. Ann Laura Stoler, 'Tense and Tender Ties: The Politics of Comparison in North American History and (Post) Colonial Studies', *Journal of American History* 88, no. 3 (2001), 829–865.
15. Victoria Haskins and Claire Lowrie, 'Introduction: Decolonizing Domestic Service: Introducing a New Agenda', in *Colonization and Domestic Service: Historical and Contemporary Perspectives*, ed. Victoria Haskins and Claire Lowrie (UK: Routledge, 2015), 7.
16. Haskins and Lowrie, 7.
17. Antoinette Burton, *Dwelling in the Archive: Women Writing House, Home and History in Late Colonial India* (Oxford: Oxford University Press, 2003), 5–6.
18. Patricia Grimshaw and Ann Standish, 'Making Tasmania Home: Louisa Meredith's "Colonizing Prose"', *Frontiers: A Journal of Women Studies* 28, no. 1/2 (2007), 1–17; Ann Standish, 'The Fabrication of White Home Making: Louisa Meredith in Colonial Tasmania', in *Re-Orienting Whiteness*, ed. Katherine Ellinghaus, Jane Carey, and Leigh Boucher (New York: Palgrave, 2009).
19. Penny Russell, '"Unhomely Moments": Civilising Domestic Worlds in Colonial Australia', *The History of the Family* 14, no. 4 (2009), 329.
20. Russell, 'Unhomely Moments', 329; Homi K. Bhabha, *The Location of Culture* (London and New York: Routledge, 1994), 10, cited in Russell, 329. See also Homi Bhabha, 'The World and the Home', *Social Text* 31/32 (1992), 141–153.
21. Julie Gough, 'Were We Not There Together?', paper presented at 'Conciliation Narratives in Settler Societies: Objects and Performances in Historical Perspective' conference, 18–19 November 2010, National Museum of Australia, Canberra.
22. E.F. Fitzsymonds, *Callaghan and Batman, Van Diemen's Land 1825* (Adelaide: Sullivan's Cove, 1978), 31.
23. Max Cameron, 'The Rise and Fall of Eliza Batman', in *Double Time: Women in Victoria, 150 Years*, ed. Marilyn Lake and Farley Kelly (Melbourne: Penguin, 1984), 11.
24. The men responsible for Eliza Batman's death were quickly apprehended but later released and never brought to trial.
25. See also Michelle Berry, 'Seeking Eliza', Masters thesis in progress, University of Tasmania (2016–), which considers Eliza Batman's life and the intersections of her experiences as a female convict, mistress of a pastoral household, and colonial widow.

26. Joan Scott, 'The Evidence of Experience', *Critical Inquiry* 17, no. 4 (1991), 773–797.
27. Alistair Campbell, *John Batman and the Aborigines* (Malmsbury: Kibble Books, 1987), 16.
28. Ryan, *Tasmanian Aborigines*, 32.
29. *Van Diemen's Land Advertiser*, 28 June 1823; see also Campbell, *John Batman and the Aborigines*, 16.
30. Trial of Eliza Callaghan, John Newnham, John Madden (t18200918-57), September 1820, *Old Bailey Proceedings Online*, 2015, www.oldbaileyonline.org
31. Fitzsymonds, *Callaghan and Batman*, 17.
32. Fitzsymonds, *Callaghan and Batman*, 25.
33. Marriage register of St Johns, Launceston, NS748/1-5, Tasmanian Archive and Heritage Office, Hobart (hereafter TAHO).
34. Kirsty Reid, *Gender, Crime and Empire* (Manchester: Manchester University Press, 2007), 94.
35. Reid, *Gender, Crime and Empire*, 75.
36. Fitzsymonds, *Callaghan and Batman*, 24.
37. *Appropriation List for the Lady Harwood*, Appropriation Lists of Convicts, 1 January 1822–31 December 1846, CON 27/1/4, TAHO; *Launceston Advertiser*, Police Intelligence, 24 August 1829, 2.
38. Peregrine Massingberd, diary, 1832–1833, MLMSS 1644, State Library of New South Wales.
39. Peregrine Massingberd, diary, 29 June 1832–22 September 1833, 160, MM111 /1/1, Z3307, TAHO.
40. Peregrine Massingberd, diary, 29 June 1832–22 September 1833, 165, MM111 /1/1, Z3307, TAHO.
41. Matthew P. Fitzpatrick and S. Protschky, 'Families, Frontier and the New Imperial History', *The History of the Family* 14, no. 4 (2009), 326.
42. Brodie, *The Vandemonian War*.
43. Edmonds, 'The Intimate, Urbanising Frontier', 148–149.
44. On the 'contact zone', see Mary Louise Pratt, *Imperial Eyes: Travel Writing and Transculturation* (New York and London: Routledge, 1992). On the idea of the 'shared landscape', see Rodney Harrison, *Shared Landscapes: Archaeologies of Attachment and the Pastoral Industry in New South Wales* (Sydney: UNSW Press, 2004).
45. As Ian McNiven and Lynette Russell point out, the idea of a 'shared' space during the contact period is to be contested on both terminological and conceptual grounds. Ian McNiven and Lynette Russell, *Appropriated Pasts: Indigenous Peoples and the Colonial Culture of Archaeology* (Lanham: Alta Mira Press, 2005), 226.
46. 'The Country Post. Esto es otro que palabras', *Hobart Town Courier*, 12 April 1828, 3.

47. Campbell, *John Batman and the Aborigines*, 26.
48. Campbell, *John Batman and the Aborigines*, 31.
49. Campbell, *John Batman and the Aborigines*, 40.
50. Colonial Secretary to John Batman, 14 August 1929, CSO1/321/7578, TAHO, cited in Kristyn Harman, '"Send in the Sydney Natives!" Deploying Mainlanders Against Tasmanian Aborigines', *Tasmanian Historical Studies*, vol. 14 (2009), 10.
51. Campbell, *John Batman and the Aborigines*, 57.
52. Harman, 'Send in the Sydney Natives!', 19.
53. Campbell, *John Batman and the Aborigines*, 30. Maps show that Batman, Wedge, and Fawkner all had land grants around each other. Pigeon and Johnny Crook's land grants of 100 acres each were contiguous with each other, and alongside the Lord family, but away from Batman's land grants.
54. Campbell, *John Batman and the Aborigines*, 10. Thomas Hassell was the son of Wesleyan missionary Rowland Hassell, who had established a Sunday School in Parramatta which Batman attended as a child.
55. Campbell, *John Batman and the Aborigines*, 11.
56. John Batman, report to Thomas Anstey Esq, 7 September 1829, TAHO.
57. John Batman, report to Thomas Anstey Esq, 7 September 1829, TAHO.
58. Letter from John Wedge to Leake, 3 September 1831, Leake Family Papers, B545, University of Tasmania Library Archives, Hobart. Emphasis added.
59. Shirleene Robinson, 'Regulating the Race: Aboriginal Children in Private European Homes in Colonial Australia', *Journal of Australian Studies* 37, no. 3 (2013), 303; Victoria Haskins and Margaret Jacobs, 'Stolen Generations and Vanishing Indians: The Removal of Indigenous Children as a Weapon of War in the United States and Australia, 1870–1940', in *Children and War: An Anthology*, ed. James Marten (New York: New York University Press, 2002), 227, 41.
60. Kociumbas is cited in Robinson, 'Regulating the Race', 308; Haskins and Jacobs, 'Stolen Generations and Vanishing Indians', 227, 41.
61. Anna Haebich, *Broken Circles: Fragmenting Indigenous Families 1800–2000* (Fremantle: Fremantle Arts Centre Press, 2000), 69.
62. Lyndall Ryan, *The Aboriginal Tasmanians*, 2nd ed. (Sydney: Allen and Unwin, 1996), cited in Haebich, *Broken Circles*, 81.
63. Haebich, *Broken Circles*, 81–83.
64. Haebich, *Broken Circles*, 85.
65. Baptism 2 June 1830, St Johns Baptism records. Microfilm ref # Z2360, TAHO.
66. On frontier violence in Tasmania, see Benjamin Madley, 'Tactics of Nineteenth Century Colonial Massacres: Tasmania, California and Beyond', in *Theatres of Violence: Massacre, Mass Killing and Atrocity*

Throughout History, ed. Philip G. Dwyer and Lyndall Ryan (Berghahn: New York and Oxford, 2012), 110–125.
67. Peregrine Massingberd, diary, 29 June 1832–22 September 1833, p. 165, MM111, Z3307, TAHO.
68. Plomley, *Friendly Mission*, 2 November 1833, 2008 ed., 945, fn 4. See also Campbell, *John Batman and the Aborigines*, 61.
69. Plomley, *Friendly Mission*, 2 November 1833, 2008 ed., 945, fn 4, 946. Campbell, *John Batman and the Aborigines*, 61.
70. Campbell, *John Batman and the Aborigines*, 63, fn 28.
71. Plomley, *Friendly Mission*, 868.
72. Campbell, *John Batman and the Aborigines*, 231.
73. From Robinson's journals, Plomley lists 'PEL.LONE.NE.MIN. NER = PLOW.NE.ME (PANGUM). Age 22 Nt of Ben Lomond. Abducted by Thomas Moore, a sealer, when a girl. He sold her to Brown (since drowned). Plomley, *Friendly Mission*, Appendices, 1026.
74. Pellenominer later died at Oyster Cove Aboriginal Station, south of Hobart. She was also known as Flora; see also Julie Gough, 'Photographs of Tasmanian Aboriginal People', *Calling the Shots: Indigenous Photographies*, ed. Jane Lydon (Canberra: Aboriginal Studies Press, 2014), 37, 38.
75. Marriage certificate of Pelonamena Frances Darling Batman and Daniel Bunce, 24 March 1851, http://archival.sl.nsw.gov.au/Details/archive/110363431 accessed online September 20, 2017. See also Roy H. Holden, 'Bunce, Daniel (1813–1872)', *Australian Dictionary of Biography*, National Centre of Biography, Australian National University, http://adb.anu.edu.au/biography/bunce-daniel-1847/text2139, published first in hardcopy 1966, accessed online 20 November 2017.
76. *Journals of George Augustus Robinson*, vol. 1, 16 editor's comment. Rolepana worked for 'George Ware Esq., at 12 pounds per annum with board and lodging'. See Michael Cannon and Ian MacFarlane, eds. *Historical Records of Victoria*, Volume 2B: *Aborigines and Protectors, 1838–1839* (Melbourne: Melbourne University Press, 1978), 744. Campbell notes: 'sadly, the two Tasmanian Aboriginal boys brought up as servants by the Batmans, and held against the wishes of their parents were also destitute. John Allen or Lernerminner, was reasonably mature and he worked firstly with E.T. Newtown and then with David Hill and Walter Coates at 26 pounds per annum with board and lodging. He was still with them in 1840 when he was unjustly blamed for the death of a horse and escaped to Hobart. Little Ben Lomond, Rolepaner, who survived the massacre of September 1829 had been taken from his mother at the age of two. When his master died he was only 12 and without support, Robinson arrange for him to be taken in by George Ware.' Campbell, *John Batman and the Aborigines*, 231.
77. Stoler, cited in Haskins and Lowrie, 7.

CHAPTER 7

Women's Work and Cross-Cultural Relationships on Two Female Frontiers: Eliza Fraser and Barbara Thompson in Colonial Queensland, 1836–1849

Victoria K. Haskins

In October 1849, walking along a remote beach at the very northernmost tip of the Australian continent on the Cape York peninsula, the crew of a colonial surveying ship were startled to hear a voice calling out to them in English: 'I am a white woman—why do you leave me?'[1] The astonished sailors turned and went back to her and, in that moment, the hitherto-unknown Barbara Thompson entered Australian history.

The sole survivor of a shipwreck in the Torres Strait, Thompson had been pulled from the sea and taken in by the Kaurareg people of Muralag (Prince of Wales Island) some five years earlier. She had, by all accounts, been treated with the greatest kindness and care by the Kaurareg, and she spoke of them in turn as her brothers and sisters. But both in her own time and since, her story was submerged beneath the much more sensational story of her predecessor Eliza Fraser, whose horrifying 'ordeals' a decade

V. K. Haskins (✉)
University of Newcastle, Callaghan, NSW, Australia

© The Author(s) 2018
P. Edmonds, A. Nettelbeck (eds.), *Intimacies of Violence in the Settler Colony*, Cambridge Imperial and Post-Colonial Studies Series, https://doi.org/10.1007/978-3-319-76231-9_7

earlier among the Butchulla and Kabi-Kabi people of Queensland's southern coast have reverberated throughout Australian culture and society.

The two women's stories came to my attention in the process of researching the experiences of non-Indigenous people who lived with Aboriginal or Torres Strait Islander communities in the earliest days of colonisation. Such people were, if they left a record of their experiences of any substance at all, nearly always male. Indeed, Fraser and Thompson are the only non-Indigenous women, among those various individuals who are known to have lived with Indigenous people on the other side of Australia's early colonial frontiers, for whom any detailed historical account can be reconstructed.[2]

As such, their experiences can offer a rare and valuable glimpse into the lives and interactions of women in the 'contact zone'. Feminist historians have shifted the terrains of imperial and colonial historiography to those more homely domains we tend to associate with women: the micro-scale and often embodied worlds of intimacy and affective personal relations in the home and family.[3] Thompson and Fraser's stories can certainly be located within the framework of intimacies and labour, yet they played out in very early frontier spaces indeed. Their Indigenous hosts did not live under colonial control, nor were they yet surrounded by the invading culture; and it is true that Thompson and Fraser certainly looked more like refugees in Indigenous country than agents of conquest and empire. The cross-cultural relationships that were created out of this kind of colonial crucible must therefore look quite different from the familiar model of women's cross-cultural relations in settler colonial societies.

A summary of the two stories is in order at this point. Fraser's iconic status belies the relatively short time she spent living with Aboriginal people—a mere six weeks at the most, between July and August 1836. In late May 1836, the merchant ship that she was on, captained by her husband, was wrecked on a reef off northern Queensland. At the end of June, a group of survivors in the ship's longboat (including the Frasers) made landfall on the northern shore of the island K'gari (later Fraser Island). There, the ravenous survivors were met by Aboriginal people who brought them fish to eat. After a week or two, having set out to walk south towards what they hoped would be white settlement, straggling and squabbling, the survivors were eventually rounded up together sometime in July by the Butchulla and distributed between different groups, in what would seem to have been a formalised gathering of the clans in the area. Following the death of her husband, Fraser and another man, the ship's first mate, were taken together over to the mainland, where the seaman too perished. Three of the other survivors, who had also been rowed over to the mainland, continued to press on and eventually found the camp of a British Lieutenant Charles Otter on present-day Bribie Island, some fifty miles north of the Moreton Bay settlement. A formal search party was immediately sent to retrieve the rest of them, and Fraser was recovered in mid-August (along with three more survivors) and returned to Moreton Bay.

Thompson was a shipwreck survivor too, but unlike Fraser she was apparently the only survivor when the small cutter she was on with her husband and another man (on a wreck-salvaging expedition) was smashed apart on a reef just off the island of Ngurapai (Horn Island) during a midday storm, towards the end of 1844. When the storm subsided, some Indigenous men out hunting turtle on the reef collected her in a sea canoe and took her back to their island, Muralag. Over the next five years, she remained with the Kaurareg. Ships came and went through the area during that time, but without sighting her. In October 1849, news of the arrival of a European ship, HMS *Rattlesnake,* on the northern shore of Cape York reached the Kaurareg, and Thompson was canoed across to the mainland to meet it. With one of her original rescuers beside her, Thompson caught the attention of the men of the crew and was taken by them back to the ship. The *Rattlesnake* finished its survey mission and returned with her to Sydney in late February 1850.

These are the bare bones of the two narratives. Both were framed as captivity narratives virtually from their first retelling, and a substantial body of scholarship on the Eliza Fraser story (and much less on Barbara Thompson's) has addressed the two women's (mis)representation since. Such studies have delineated their function as allegorical rather than historical figures and their gendered symbolic significance to the colonising project, as precursor and generator of violence. At a time when the ideals of bourgeois white womanhood—fragility, vulnerability, and submissiveness—were in formation, their narratives intersected with contemporary anxieties around sex and race that animated and inflamed white male settler violence in their conflicts with Indigenous people over land.[4] In attempting to recover a historical account of women's cross-cultural experiences from the stories of Thompson and Fraser, I am in a sense writing back against these very powerful mythical representations.

The limitations for such a project are obvious. Recovering an Indigenous perspective when there is no surviving contemporary Indigenous voice in the records is the clearest challenge. We have, fortunately, a Butchulla oral history to draw upon for Fraser, reported in the 1990s by Olga Miller (who heard it from her mother, a non-Butchulla Aboriginal woman of Fraser Island),[5] but there is nothing comparable for Thompson.[6] From Fraser herself there is also very little direct voice; we are limited to a six-page statement that she gave at the time of her return, recorded by a clerk, and her highly charged and unreliable testimony before a Committee of Enquiry held by the Lord Mayor of London over two days in August 1837.[7] These sources are confused by the multiple published versions of her story, including an 1838 book by English journalist John Curtis purportedly based on his personal interviews with Fraser, as well as an excessively exaggerated North American version attributed to Fraser herself.[8] For the illiterate Thompson, however, we do have a substantial account in her own spoken words of her five years with the Kaurareg, as recorded in detail at the time of her return by the *Rattlesnake*'s artist Oswald Brierly, and published many, many decades later, in 1978. Yet even here we need to read the white woman's voice cautiously and critically, mediated as it was, as Kate Darian-Smith reminds us, 'through the middle-class, male, and scientific preoccupations of Brierly'.[9]

Such a reading requires a deliberate decentring of the white male perspective. That perspective dominates the sources and has inevitably framed the kinds of questions that have been asked. Of these, the most pressing and shameful question was—and remains—whether the white woman had had any sexual relations with Indigenous men. An awful possibility alluded to in some of the published Fraser accounts,[10] the question of whether the nubile and attractive Thompson had been taken 'possession of' by a Kaurareg man exercised the imaginations of the officers of the *Rattlesnake* and has continued to excite argument between white male authors.[11] For as Kate Darian-Smith has observed, 'the pivotal meaning' of the female captivity narrative was interracial sex.[12]

This white male perspective and focus has resulted in the marginalisation of the question of women's relationships with each other, typically reduced to sexual rivalry over the attentions of Indigenous men. Certainly it can be argued that heterosexual relations are of fundamental significance to women's interactions with each other and impact upon race relations;[13] but in order to explore a more fuller understanding of the interactions between Thompson and Fraser, and the Indigenous women who hosted them, we are going to need to tear our own eyes away from men and their preoccupations for a time.

Let us turn then to a different kind of history, a history that centralises women's relationships with each other, and where men's activities and doings are peripheral, of contingent interest only in terms of how they impact women's lives. Let us consider how these two lost individuals negotiated the female Indigenous world they entered, and how they were negotiated in turn by the women whose world it was.

One of the striking aspects of Fraser's story is the way in which her entry into Aboriginal society was managed by women. In July 1836, when the survivors were first distributed among separate groups of people on K'gari, Fraser, the only female, was simply left behind on the beach. The Curtis account had her remaining there on her own all night, waiting for her husband to return, until late the following afternoon 'a great number' of Aboriginal women came to see her and, surrounding her on the sand, began teasing and ridiculing her and pelting her with wet sand, until she was 'stuccoed' all over.[14] In her testimony during the 1837 enquiry, Fraser said she was following the path of the group that had taken her husband, when 'a crowd of black women' from that group approached her, compelled her 'to rub herself over with gums and herbs', and also, at some point, 'tattooed her all over' and stuck parrot feathers to her head.[15] The Butchulla oral history recounts that the women had found 'a white lubra' on the beach, hysterical with the pain of sunburn, and that they rubbed her 'with ointments and things that were their own medicines'. They then further marked her with 'ochre signs' that read 'let this woman through' and 'do not harm this woman'.[16] Where all accounts agree is that Fraser was received into the charge of the Aboriginal women.

It has been conjectured that Fraser was left by the men because she had recently been delivered of a child, and was therefore taboo, although Fraser's rather belated claim to have given birth at sea (to a child that lived only a few moments) is viewed with scepticism by many scholars, and flatly denied in the Butchulla oral history.[17] However, the Butchulla history does emphasise that the sexes were traditionally segregated from the age of ten, and so it makes sense that, postpartum or otherwise, Fraser should have been assigned to the care of the women. The women's actions may have had a ceremonial ritual significance tied to the healing and protective purpose pointed to in the Butchulla account. Elsewhere and in the present day, Australian Indigenous women's ceremonies that are aimed at attaching their bodies to place, and thus securing their physical and spiritual safety, do so through establishing an intimate, corporeal connection between substances of the earth and of the body. As anthropologist Elizabeth Povinelli has documented, such women's rites as practiced today are preceded by socially inversive acts of teasing and play between women, as a way of forging social connections; perhaps something like this was going on.[18]

Thompson's account of her introduction into the Kaurareg community, framed through Brierly's eyes, does not foreground the role of women at all, and yet they were undoubtedly involved. 'My principal friends on the island were Pequi's three wives, all sisters of one another,' Thompson told Brierly, by way of introducing the story.[19] She went on to explain how, as soon as the men who had rescued her brought her into the camp, a senior man called Pequi and his wives 'all jumped out and caught hold of me, calling me after his daughter'. Pequi claimed to recognise the spirit of his deceased daughter Giom in Thompson's chin and eyes. Giom had been his first child by his first wife, Gibow, who had herself just died, tragically and by accident, at Pequi's own hands. 'They asked why I did not bring my mother back with me.'[20] We might surmise that Pequi's wives as Giom's close female relations—her maternal aunts and affiliate mothers—played a major role in Thompson's acceptance. *Their* mother— 'she called herself my grandmother'—may have been even more critical.[21] Second master George Inskip was under the impression that Thompson had been taken under the 'special charge of an Old Woman' who imagined Thompson to be the spirit of her recently deceased daughter; presumably referring to Giom's grandmother.[22] The Kaurareg observed strict regulations between sons- and mothers-in-law, and so Pequi could not speak with Gibow's mother directly, but we might imagine that in embracing Thompson as her late daughter's daughter, there was some kind of resolution of the unhappy recent events.

Thompson's 'adoption' fit a pattern that was common across the experience of non-Indigenous people who took refuge with Aboriginal or Torres Strait Islander communities from the earliest days. Often regarded as an example of native credulity or superstition by the British, recognising the strangers as returned relatives might alternatively be seen as a culturally appropriate way of allocating a place for the newcomers within the tightly woven kinship networks of rights and responsibilities.[23] In Thompson's case, as a Kaurareg girl—and a girl she was, being no older than thirteen when she entered their world—it provided her with both a social position in the Kaurareg community and a physical place.[24] She was provided a home with the late Giom's sister, a married woman named

Urdzanna, and Urdzanna's mother-in-law Aburda, both of whom Brierly noted had taken particularly good care of her over the years.[25] The Kaurareg would also, in time, show her a small island, well stocked with yams, which they explained was 'my island and that it was named after me'.[26]

Thompson's position was complex, however. At the time that Thompson's contact with the white men of the *Rattlesnake* was being planned by the Kaurareg, she was also spoken of as his *gassimigir* by one of the men who initially rescued her, Tomagagu, apparently placing her in the position of honorary sister to her rescuers and their wives.[27] Thompson explained to Brierly that there were numbers of older individuals who lived with the Kaurareg who were *gassimigie* or 'caught people'. They had been taken as children in the course of fighting with a particular Aboriginal group that lived in the western area of Cape York, 'a long time ago'. All of them had grown up and married, and most had adult children on Muralag. Tomagagu's argument was, because he and another man, Alika, had 'saved her life' and she therefore 'belonged' to them, they had preceding rights over others in sending her to negotiate with the white people for various items they desired. Thus it appears that the *gassimigie* might have been intended as intermediaries in difficult or conflict-prone trading relations, although the practice, unlike the fighting, hadn't been continued.[28] Presumably on the basis of his claim to her, it was Tomagagu who took the lead in assisting Thompson to make contact with the white people and, indeed, supported her in her desires to return to white society; he was standing by her side when the white men first approached them, and his first imperative was to make them understand his role in her original rescue. 'Tomagagu began to talk to them before I could speak,' Thompson told Brierly, 'telling them in his own talk how I had been wrecked and how he had taken me up out of the water. I stopped him and said, *komi arragi arragi atzir nathya krongipa*—"Friend, hold your tongue. I know what they are saying".'[29]

In addition, Thompson was recognised as a white person, or *marki*.[30] Tomagagu might have been opportunistic or strategic in claiming her as his *gassimigir* on the point of her return, but there is no doubt that she was understood to be a white person from the outset. The Kaurareg had some passing familiarity with white men prior to Thompson's arrival. They knew the man 'Weenie', a non-Indigenous man of uncertain ethnicity who lived with the Badu and 'belonged' to two men. Weenie was apparently quite useful and the Kaurareg were envious. 'Our people say they would like to get a white man who could mend their canoes in the same way as Weenie does for the Badoos,' reported Thompson.[31] The word *marki* literally meant 'ghost' and was oppositional to the word the Kaurareg used for themselves, meaning 'human', *garki*,[32] and, as Thompson explained, the Kaurareg believed 'white men are the spirits of blacks come again in a new form'.[33] But the Kaurareg also recognised the *markibat* as constituting a distinct society, complete with its own exotic and mystifying ways. Thompson explained that her people 'think that white fellows in ships live on sharks and whales, porpoises, etc. and are always sailing about in ships'.[34] She also described a new 'ghost ship dance' that had recently been brought to the Kaurareg by the Kulkulaga people of Nagir (Mount Ernest), which involved performers imitating white men 'holding up and shaking their hands'.[35]

Thompson learned much—or rather, was taught much—about Kaurareg women's lives and practices during her stay. She had, coincidentally, arrived on the island at the age when girls of the Torres Strait underwent an initiation process, involving a period of public seclusion and immobilisation, during which time she received instruction from 'an elderly female' called *Ipika Maway*, her aunt, in the ways of adult women's lives, including childbirth and care.[36] If Thompson actually went through the process herself, it wasn't explicated in her conversations with Brierly, but she did proffer considerable information on intimate topics such as childbirth and child-rearing practices, norms surrounding pregnancy in and out of marriage, relationships between wives, and courtship and extramarital affairs. She told him of the various food taboos (*adzarr*) that applied to Kaurareg women,[37] and talked of the hard work done by Kaurareg women collecting yams and the seasonal visits of women from the mainland to gather mangrove oysters, women who could spear fish 'as well as the men'.[38] There were no gender differences when it came to land inheritances (the gardens or *pods* that were handed on from parents to children): 'Girls get as much land as boys.'[39] Kaurareg women were assertive; they fought with 'poles' between themselves,[40] and older women, widows, courted younger men with gifts of food.[41] Aggressive husbands were contrite, and sexual violence was frowned upon: the Badu men had a very bad reputation among the Kaurareg for doing 'what they pleased' with their women (though an older Badu woman insisted to Thompson that 'this was all *lakipai*—lies').[42] At the same time, the Kaurareg women found Thompson a source of information about the curious ways of *marki* women and gender relations. 'The women used to ask me if it was so in my country,' she told Brierly (that women made gifts to men they were interested in). 'I said no, the women had more attention than the men.'[43] They asked her if white mothers put their babies into bags when they were born. 'They thought something of this kind must be done to make them grow up white' and wondered how often they washed their babies.[44] Clearly, the Kaurareg women saw Thompson as being not just a woman, but a woman from a different culture, and one that was in key ways morally inferior. They were particularly astonished and shocked to discover from her that white people always spoke with their in-laws[45]—and, when Thompson refused to cry at the death of a respected elder, they admonished her, saying, 'Your people are like ghosts. They don't cry, they have no feeling. We are people, *garkigi*, we cry.'[46]

But if Thompson did not quite fit in with the Kaurareg women, Fraser's inability to adapt was on another level altogether. Among the Aboriginal people who encountered her and her fellow survivors, there had evidently been some unpleasant previous encounters that did not predispose them to trust the strangers from the sea. Fraser's fellow survivors attested to the dislike the Aboriginal people bore them, one observing that, from having been shot at by British soldiers, some of the Aboriginal men on the mainland 'could not bear the sight of a white man at all',[47] with another noticing that the survivor Joseph Corallis, as a 'black' man, was regarded somewhat more easily.[48] A third survivor recorded that on K'gari it was, in fact, 'the aged women' who at first seemed 'most eager' to drive the white people on, by pelting them with stones.[49] Although Fraser herself denied receiving virtually any concession on the grounds of her sex, it is possible that as a woman—one of the few, possibly only, white women the Aboriginal people would have seen up close—she might have received less animosity than the white men.[50]

The Butchulla oral history recounts that the women of K'gari who found Fraser were not hostile to her but rather unsure about what to do with her, although the tone suggests they found her presence disturbing. They decided to take her with them down to the place of 'the Clever Man', on the southwestern coast of the island. 'The men were not at all pleased with the arrival of the women with the stranger. However, the women insisted that they did not want the stranger to stay with them.'[51] There, the decision was made that messengers be sent to locate Duramboi, the escaped convict James Davis who had been living with the Kabi-Kabi people around the Moreton Bay region since 1829, with instructions to meet at a certain point on the mainland opposite the island.[52] Duramboi 'and his party' then duly collected Fraser and took her further south, towards the British settlement. Learning of the official rescue party, Duramboi got Fraser to the vicinity of Otter's camp and directed Fraser to go forward alone, while he and his people 'hurried away' back to where they lived.[53]

The implication in this account is that the Aboriginal men only reluctantly took on some of the responsibility for managing Fraser, and then only at the women's insistence. Further, the oral history tells of a Kabi-Kabi man with Duramboi being speared by the Butchulla for ignoring the signs the women had marked on Fraser's body to protect her, and for shoving her; and that Duramboi was later called to account by a formal meeting of the Butchulla for a complaint, made by Fraser to the official rescue party, that Duramboi had raped her, which he denied altogether.[54] It appears then that while the women of K'gari had passed Fraser along, they had not entirely abdicated responsibility for her care.

Historical anthropological research carried out in the 1930s by anthropologist Caroline Kelly, working with older Butchulla women, provides tantalising glimpses into the matrilineal Butchulla society. Kelly recorded, for instance, the important position allotted to paternal aunts, the use of food taboos by women to mark social status, and the existence of female initiation, marriage, and mourning ceremonies that involved the participants being 'decked' in feathers. Women were highly contributing members of the economy, the more senior holding restricted knowledge of how to prepare toxic seed plants to make flour for bread. They used digging sticks to fight as well as to gather food, and certain women considered to be 'lucky' went along with the men on hunting trips, to ensure success in the hunt. Women were active participants in the very important trading culture with the Kabi-Kabi people from the mainland, and 'frequently' paddled the canoes over (thus Fraser and the others who were brought over to the mainland by canoe may well have been rowed over by women rather than men). There was intermarriage with men from the mainland, but the 'invariable' rule was that the husband joined the wife's group and came to live on the island (Kelly didn't mention if women ever married off the island). Kelly referred to the mystical figure of 'the Clever Little Man' who lived in a cave on Fraser Island and was said to have 'a power over all relating to the sea', including the capacity to cause shipwrecks. Kelly believed his existence was known only to the men, but perhaps she was mistaken on that count; we might surmise, rather, that the site was considered a locus for masculine responsibilities pertaining to the sea.[55] Given the female-centred culture of the island, we might also surmise that the initial appearance of Fraser in 1837 could have been of quite some interest to the Butchulla women.

At some point, Fraser may have attached herself to, or was allotted to the charge of, one particular woman. In her London testimony, Fraser stated that after her husband's death, there was a woman 'whom I thought it was the safest way to follow and depend upon', and whose child Fraser helped look after. 'While her child used to sit on my shoulders, with its legs around my neck, I used to perform offices for her personal comfort, for one of her sides was in a state of apparent mortification.' In return, Fraser indicated, 'she treated me better than all the rest'. It appears that this woman took on the responsibility for Fraser's survival and education. She not only taught Fraser how to catch and kill snakes 'which frequently formed our meals', but also 'how to use the spear and shield'. This woman also set her to work digging at the roots of trees for a 'wood or bark, which they call bungara', which they used for bread—possibly the toxic plant referred to by Kelly, suggesting that Fraser was being placed at the very start of her education as a Butchulla woman.[56]

An outrageous depiction of the woman appeared in the North American version of the story. Described as Fraser's 'squaw-mistress', this was a monstrous caricature of Aboriginal motherhood, compelling Fraser to nurse her 'disgusting and ill-humoured brat' and beating her when it cried. 'Great was the abuse that I received from this savage monster,' Fraser told her readers, 'who, in her fits of rage, would, beast-like, gnash her teeth, and sometimes seize me by the throat until I became nearly strangled!'[57] In complete contrast, the Curtis version depicted the woman as a weakened invalid, with Fraser taking on the more noble role as the woman's nurse. Here, Curtis offered an anecdote purportedly provided by Fraser, describing how, as she carefully covered the woman's ulcerous sores with leaves and bark to protect them from insects, she was reminded of the mawkish English nursery story of the two lost children in the woods being covered with leaves by the red robin bird, and so called the woman 'Robina'. (The cosiness of the image was, however, considerably jarred by Curtis's concluding description of a rather excessive bodily intimacy between the two, with Robina prevailing upon 'her nurse' to eat the vermin that preyed upon her flesh as she did, '[s]uch was the scarcity of provision'.) The Curtis version had Robina as Fraser's sole if ineffectual ally amongst the jealous women.[58] But whether there was ever an actual individual woman among the Butchulla (or Kabi-Kabi) whom Fraser was close to in any sense, or any woman she might have had the opportunity to learn from, it is impossible to know.

Thompson, however, had ample opportunity over five years to develop relationships with individual Kaurareg women, and the *Rattlesnake*'s officers could hardly fail to observe the affection that existed between her and various women, as Thompson waited on board for the work of the surveying expedition to be completed. (It is rather ironic that the five to six weeks Thompson waited with the white men, while the ship lay at anchor in Evans Bay, was about the same length of time that Fraser had spent with the Aboriginal people.) Almost every day, her 'friends from the shore' came to visit her, and many of them were women.[59] Aburda, the mother-in-law of Giom's sister, came to see Brierly to tell him 'she had been crying for Giom, the white woman, and talking a great deal, which I could not understand, about her'.[60] On another occasion, a party of seven women, three of them with children, came to visit Thompson, bringing mats for sitting on while they talked and made baskets together. One of them, again an older woman, Gameema:

> showed the greatest joy at seeing Mrs T. at the port and stood up in the canoe till she might take hold of her hand, which she kissed with great affection, at the same time showing a shell which had belonged to Mrs T. while on the land, saying *Giom meeno no* [meaning not known] and in which she had bored a hole and now wore round her neck as a remembrance, saying *Giom, ye noosa eena*—'Giom, this is yours', and at the same time kissing it.[61]

The bemused officers eagerly seized upon hints that, in the beginning at least, the women had not treated her so warmly.[62] The conjectured cause of this supposed enmity was, of course, their jealousy of the 'attentions' shown to her by the men.[63] Yet one incident alone in Thompson's account points to any conflict between Thompson and the women she lived with, and it was possibly this one account—admittedly compelling— that gave the white men the evidence they sought.

Thompson told Brierly how a violent confrontation between herself and an older woman transpired. The women prepared their own individual ground ovens of heated stones (*ami*) to cook in, she explained, but as these typically accommodated more food than one woman required for her own family, it was customary to call to the others, 'the *ipili*—wives— to each come and bring their portion of *buyu* or *koti* and put it in with hers'.[64] Thompson unwittingly offended Yuri, a widow, by neglecting to invite her to share her *ami*, and Yuri, being 'vexed', hurled a large shell at the younger woman. Thompson responded immediately, taking up the shell, filling it with water, and throwing it over her:

> She was a big woman, much taller than I am. She ran to get a stick. I ran after her and, as she stooped down to pick up a stick, I caught her by the hair behind and struck her about the face. She could not do anything at all with her hands, only cried out *Giom, warmera* [let go], *Giom, warmera*. None of the people took her part, but they called out to me *Giom perkee*, etc—'Strike, Giom, strike'.[65]

Crucially, Thompson had the support of the others. They 'said I was a stranger amongst them and that the woman should not hurt me', and even Yuri's daughter, 'a woman, stood by and did not say anything' as Thompson beat her mother.[66]

In fighting back as she did, Thompson possibly won some respect among the women, and she probably learned a lesson herself in the process. 'Yuri never said anything to me after this', Thompson reflected; but afterwards the older woman became Thompson's 'friend' and would take Thompson with her 'to dig the *koti* [yam]'.[67]

The last point is significant. Perhaps sexual jealousy was at the root of Thompson's clash with Yuri, as has been suggested.[68] Yet there is a more obvious implication in this account of a fight over a cooking space and a truce forged in shared harvesting: that Thompson needed to show that she could work with and for the collective, and not just for herself. Perhaps to that point, Thompson's contribution to the collective had been rather less than the other women judged her lot to be. The women of Muralag were impressively hard workers in pre-colonial times: 'women had all the chores, looked after the baby, went hunting for food … fished, got wild yams or fruits, they did all the work … They were strong and they did the lot.'[69] Undoubtedly, a capacity to work and contribute was a marker of womanly value for the Kaurareg.

Such female economic independence and autonomy was not, however, at all valorised in the white men's eyes. In the colonial construction of bourgeois white femininity, female toil was the marker of blackness and primitivism, as well as low class status.[70] Thus one of the first questions Thompson was asked by the men of the *Rattlesnake* was whether the Indigenous people 'make you work'. Thompson, a working-class girl herself, might not quite have understood what they were getting at. 'At first they made me fetch water', she replied, 'but when they made me work too hard some of them say brother take my part.'[71] In Kaurareg society, as Thompson later told Brierly, from the time a child was old enough to dig for their own yams and roots they were expected to feed themselves, while married men could expect that their wives would provide for them from their garden plots.[72] As an unattached young woman, Thompson would have been expected to fend for herself, but the men who rescued her may have had to be responsible for ensuring that she did not starve, or, indeed, fail to meet her contribution to the collective.

The *Rattlesnake* officers, however, were curiously insistent upon the point that Thompson did not perform the kind of female physical labour of food foraging and harvesting that they found so affronting. 'The natives appear to have treated her quite as a pet', Thomas Huxley asserted; she 'never shared in the labours of women but stayed in the camp to look after the children while they went out on "hospitable cares intent"'.[73] This was in direct denial of Thompson's own account, and can only represent the wilful imagination of the white men, for Thompson was unequivocal about how hard she worked. 'I know it well—my body used to be quite sore all over with the heavy rain beating upon me when I was out in the scrub with all the other women looking for *buyu*', she told Brierly.[74] She seemed to want to impress upon Brierly the work that all the women did. 'The poor women must get the *buyu*', she told Brierly. 'You see the women coming home with a bit of tea-bark over their heads, stooping down under the great dilly bags full of *buyu*, all shivering with the cold. I could manage very well in the *ibu* [dry season] when there was plenty of turtle, but the *kuki* [wet] was very bad. ... [t]he *kuki* frazzled me...'.[75]

It is work, and the representation of their work, in fact, that so divides the accounts of the two white women. If Thompson was regarded as the 'pet' of the Kaurareg people, in disregard of her own report, the dominant representation of Fraser was that of a slave—or, rather, 'a slave to slaves', since in the white male view 'all the [Aboriginal] women were in a sense slaves'.[76] So different from the Thompson story in tone, Fraser's story yet has curious echoes when read back against the other. Our 'masters ... employed us in carrying Wood, water and bark, and treated us with the greatest cruelty', Fraser declared in the statement she dictated at the time of her return. 'With the exception of a small portion of Fish which we but very seldom got, all we had to subsist on was a kind of Fern root which we were obliged to procure ourselves in the swamps.' Compare, with Thompson's description of working in the heavy rain alongside the

Kaurareg women, the aggrieved conclusion to Fraser's statement. 'During the whole of my detention among the Natives I was treated with the greatest cruelty', she reiterated:

> being obliged to fetch wood and water for them and constantly beaten when incapable of carrying the heavy loads they put upon me; exposed during the night to the inclemency of the weather, being hardly ever allowed to enter their huts, even during the heaviest rain.[77]

Fraser's class background surely had something to do with her belief that she had been treated unjustly. Perhaps the calculated 'tormenting' she supposedly endured at the hands of Aboriginal women was just their steadfast insistence that she help them, in some basic way. If the Butchulla and Kabi-Kabi women she encountered did indeed despise and dislike her, even to the point of being 'cruel', it appears that this was not, as the Curtis account would have it, 'because attentions of a diabolical nature were paid to her by the men'.[78] Rather, we have to acknowledge that Fraser's uncooperative and self-pitying attitude would have profoundly alienated the Aboriginal women and meant that for Fraser, unlike Thompson, there was—quite literally—no place for her among them.

Using these two stories to tease out what we can about women's relationships beyond the frontier, insights emerge into the nature of those relationships that are more nuanced and complex than the sexual-jealousy thesis. In both cases, the entry of the women into Indigenous society was negotiated by the Indigenous women, in the first instance, and acceptance and assistance from women was critical to the experience the white woman would have. Labour, affection, and status were intimately entwined. For Fraser, it was the height of cruelty that she should be expected to contribute her share; for Thompson, work was fundamental to her integration. While Fraser learned almost nothing of a vibrant Butchulla women's culture on the K'gari island, Thompson was received as a young woman in need of an education by the Kaurareg women of Muralag, and received affection and care in addition. In this, the work of women was central.

It is a very great shame that Fraser's story has exerted such a hold over the Australian imagination, while Thompson's alternative account that stressed mutual affection and integration rather than alienation and fear has barely struck a chord. My intention in revisiting the two accounts alongside each other is driven not by any idealistic hope that Thompson's recuperated story—a reconciliation story, surely, if there ever was one—

might yet dislodge Fraser's toxic parable from its position of prominence in Australian culture. The time for that might not yet be here; but coming to a greater understanding of this history of women's cross-cultural relationships, and to a respect for the Indigenous women who took these white women into their society and for the work they did, must surely be a step in the right direction.

Notes

1. John MacGillivray, *Narrative of the Voyage of the H.M.S. Rattlesnake, Commanded by the Late Captain Owen Stanley during the Years 1846–1850*, vol. 1 (London: T. & W. Boone, 1852), 305.
2. See John Maynard and Victoria Haskins, *Living with the Locals: Early Europeans' Experience of Indigenous Life* (Canberra: National Library of Australia, 2016).
3. Amanda Nettelbeck, 'Proximate Strangers and Familiar Antagonists: Violence on an Intimate Frontier', *Australian Historical Studies* 47, no. 2 (2016), 209–224, 211.
4. The scholarship on the Fraser story is far too extensive to cite comprehensively. Kay Schaffer's work has led a field which includes the following key works: Kay Schaffer, *In the Wake of First Contact: The Eliza Fraser Stories* (Cambridge: Cambridge University Press, 1995); Ian J. McNiven, Lynette Russell, and Kay Schaffer, eds. *Constructions of Colonialism: Perspectives on Eliza Fraser's Shipwreck* (London: Leicester University Press, 1998), 51–62; Larissa Berendt, *Finding Eliza: Power and Colonial Storytelling* (Brisbane: University of Queensland Press, 2016). There has been comparatively little sustained study of Thompson's narrative, however: see Kate Darian-Smith, '"Rescuing" Barbara Thompson and Other White Women: Captivity Narratives on Australian Frontiers', in *Text, Theory, Space: Land, Literature and History in South Africa and Australia*, ed. Kate Darian-Smith, Liz Gunner, and Sarah Nuttall (London: Routledge, 1996), 99–114, 102–105; Kate Darian-Smith, 'Material Culture and the "Signs" of Captive White Women', in *Body Trade: Captivity, Cannibalism and Colonialism in the Pacific*, ed. Barbara Creed and Jeanette Hoorn (London: Routledge, 2001), 180–191, 187–188.
5. Olga Miller, 'K'gari, Mrs. Fraser and Butchulla Oral Tradition', in McNiven, *Constructions of Colonialism*, 28–36.
6. When missionaries visited the Prince of Wales group of islands in 1867, they found that some of the people mentioned by Thompson were still living and remembered her. See 'The Kennett Report, February 1867–June 1868', in David R. Moore, *Islanders and Aborigines at Cape York: An*

Ethnographic Reconstruction Based on the 1848–1850 'Rattlesnake' Journals of O.W. Brierly and Information he Obtained from Barbara Thomson [sic] (Canberra: Australian Institute of Aboriginal Studies, 1979), 237–251, 244. Ion L. Idriess claimed in his novel about Thompson that he had spoken with an 'old islander' about an incident in her life, but this seems unlikely, especially as the episode in question was one where Thompson was in danger of drowning in quicksand, and communicated telepathically with her Kaurareg lover, beseeching him to rescue her. See Ion L. Idriess in *Isles of Despair* (Sydney: Angus & Robertson, 1947), 216. I would like to acknowledge the generous advice and feedback I received from my colleague John Doolah, a scholar of Torres Strait Islander cultures and histories, who read an early draft of this chapter: any errors of course remain my own.

7. Statement by Eliza Ann Fraser and Statement by John Baxter: Corroborated by Joseph Corralis, 6 September 1836: SZ976 Misc. 2 Colonial Secretary's Correspondence COD 183, 1836, Archives Office of New South Wales, Sydney; 'Police', *The Times*, Thursday 24 August 1837, 4. See also Yolanda Drummond, 'Progress of Eliza Fraser', *Journal of the Royal Historical Society of Queensland* 15, no. 1 (1993), 15–25, 21; Captain Foster Fyans, who was the commandant at Moreton Bay when Eliza Fraser returned, recorded his recollections of a conversation with Fraser at the time in his memoirs, written some years later, but these are notably flawed. See P.L. Brown, ed. *Memoirs Recorded at Geelong, Victoria, Australia, by Captain Foster Fyans (1790–1870): Transcribed from his Holograph Manuscript Given by Descendants to the State Library, Melbourne, 1962* (Geelong, VIC: Geelong Advertiser, 1986), 163–171.

8. John Curtis, *Shipwreck of the Stirling Castle: Containing a Faithful Narrative of the Dreadful Sufferings of the Crew, and the Cruel Murder of Captain Fraser by the Savages: also, the Horrible Barbarity of the Cannibals Inflicted upon the Captain's Widow, Whose Unparalleled Sufferings are Stated by Herself, and Corroborated by the Other Survivors: To Which is Added the Narrative of the Wreck of the Charles Eaton, in the Same Latitude* (London: George Virtue, 1838); Eliza Fraser, *Narrative of the Capture, Sufferings, and Miraculous Escape of Mrs. Eliza Fraser, Wife of the Late Captain Samuel Fraser, Commander of the Ship Sterling* [sic] *Castle, which was wrecked on 25th May* (New York: Charles S. Webb, 1837). For an overview of the many different published versions see Schaffer, *In the Wake of First Contact*, 29–65.

9. O.W. Brierly, 'Journals of HMS *Rattlesnake*', in Moore, *Islanders and Aborigines at Cape York*, 223–233; Darian-Smith, '"Rescuing" Barbara Thompson', 104–105.

10. Fraser, *Narrative*, 17; Curtis, *Shipwreck of the Stirling Castle*, 149.

11. MacGillivray, *Narrative*, 302. See Moore, *Islanders and Aborigines at Cape York*, 8–9; Raymond J. Warren, *Wildflower: The Barbara Crawford Thompson Story* (Brisbane: R.J. Warren, 2007), 152, 218–219; Iain McCalman, *The Reef: A Passionate History* (Melbourne: Penguin, 2013), 134–138. Notably, Idriess built his whole novel around the theme of Barbara and Boroto's romance.
12. Darian-Smith, '"Rescuing" Barbara Thompson', 105.
13. Cf. Miriam Dixson, *The Real Matilda: Women and Identity in Australia, 1788 to 1975* (Harmondsworth: Penguin, 1976), 197–198.
14. Curtis, *Shipwreck*, 143–144.
15. 'Police', *The Times*, 19 August 1837.
16. Miller, 'K'gari', 34–35.
17. Kay Schaffer, 'Colonizing Gender in Colonial Australia: The Eliza Fraser Story', in *Writing Women and Space: Colonial and Postcolonial Geographies*, ed. Alison Blunt and Gillian Rose, 101–120 (New York: Guildford Press, 1994), 111–112; Drummond, 'Progress of Eliza Fraser', 20–21; Miller, 'K'gari', 33–34.
18. Elizabeth A. Povinelli, 'Native Sex: Sex Rites, Land Rights and the Making of Aboriginal Civic Culture', in *Gender Ironies of Nationalism: Sexing the Nation*, ed. Tamar Mayer (London: Routledge, 2000), 162–184, 176, 179.
19. Brierly, 'Journals', 177.
20. Brierly, 'Journals', 178, 198.
21. Brierly, 'Journals', 178, 198.
22. G.H. Inskip diary entry, 19 October 1849: G.H. Inskip, Manuscript of Diary, 1849–1850, NLA MS 3784, National Library of Australia, Canberra.
23. See Maynard and Haskins, *Living with the Locals*, 2, 5–6. I am indebted to Larissa Berendt for her suggestion to consider this point.
24. See Maynard and Haskins, *Living with the Locals*, 149–159.
25. Brierly, 'Journals', 154, 96.
26. Brierly, 'Journals', 162.
27. Brierly, 'Journals', 192, 109.
28. Brierly, 'Journals', 197–198.
29. Brierly, 'Journals', 195.
30. Brierly, 'Journals', 172, 213.
31. Brierly, 'Journals', 177.
32. Brierly, 'Journals', 327.
33. Brierly, 'Journals', 143.
34. Sharks and dolphins were protected by the Islanders, who would not harm them, so this was a significant marker of difference. Brierly, 'Journals', 143, 151.

35. Brierly, 'Journals', 199–200.
36. As outlined by Ephraim Bani, a male elder who acknowledged that he purposefully avoided discussion of restricted knowledge. Ephraim Bani, 'Initiation', *Torres News*, in *Woven Histories Dancing Lives: Torres Strait Islander Identity, Culture and History*, Richard Davis (Canberra: Aboriginal Studies Press, 2004), 230–231, 230.
37. Brierly, 'Journals', 150.
38. Brierly, 'Journals', 151.
39. Brierly, 'Journals', 171–172.
40. Brierly, 'Journals', 151.
41. Brierly, 'Journals', 154–155.
42. Brierly, 'Journals', 170, 206.
43. Brierly, 'Journals', 151.
44. Brierly, 'Journals', 184.
45. Brierly, 'Journals', 172.
46. Brierly, 'Journals', 213.
47. 'Police', *The Times*, 26 August 1837, 6.
48. 'Police', *The Times*, 26 August 1837, 6.
49. Harry Youlden, 'Shipwreck in Australia', *The Knickerbocker* 16, no. 4 (1853), 291–330, 294.
50. 'Police', *The Times*, 26 August 1837, 6. See also 'Darge's Testimony' (which appears to be a fuller account) in Michael Alexander, *Mrs. Fraser on the Fatal Shore* (New York: Simon & Schuster, 1971), 137, and Fraser's testimony in 'Police', *The Times*, August 24, 1837, 4.
51. Miller, 'K'gari', 35.
52. For Duramboi, see Maynard and Haskins, *Living with the Locals*, 83–99.
53. Miller, 'K'gari', 35.
54. Miller, 'K'gari', 35. For a summary of the different versions of her rescue and the competing white contenders for the role of hero, see Maynard and Haskins, *Living with the Locals*, 141–145; Alexander, *Mrs. Fraser*, 108–123.
55. Caroline Kelly, unpublished manuscript, 'Fraser's, or Great Sandy Island, Island Queensland', c.1932, 6: Folder 1, Box 7, Series 5 Anthropological Papers, Caroline Kelly collection, UQFL489, Fryer Library, Brisbane.
56. 'Police', *The Times*, 24 August 1837, 4.
57. Fraser, *Narrative*, 12.
58. Curtis, *Shipwreck*, 143–144, 157. For discussions of this representation of Aboriginal womanhood, see Schaffer, *In the Wake of First Contact*, 89–90, and Lynette Russell, '"Mere Trifles and Faint Representations": The Representations of Savage Life Offered by Eliza Fraser', in McNiven et al., ed. *Constructions of Colonialism*: 51–62, 55.
59. MacGillivray, *Narrative*, 306.

60. Brierly, 'Journals', 83.
61. Brierly, 'Journals', 121.
62. Huxley, *Diary*, 243.
63. MacGillivray, *Narrative*, 302.
64. Brierly, 'Journals', 169–170.
65. Brierly, 'Journals', 170.
66. Brierly, 'Journals', 170.
67. Brierly, 'Journals', 170.
68. Warren, *Wildflower*, 128–130.
69. An unnamed 'old woman', quoted in Elizabeth Osbourne, *Torres Strait Islander Women and the Pacific War* (Canberra: Aboriginal Studies Press, 1997), 4.
70. See Anne McClintock, *Imperial Leather: Race, Gender and Sexuality in the Colonial Context* (London: Routledge, 1995), 160–162, 253–256.
71. Brierly, 'Journals', 80.
72. Brierly, 'Journals', 146.
73. Huxley, *Diary*, 243; Inskip diary entry, 19 October 1849.
74. Brierly, 'Journals', 205.
75. Brierly, 'Journals', 206.
76. Alexander, *Mrs. Fraser*, 62.
77. Statement by Eliza Ann Fraser.
78. Curtis, *Shipwreck*, 157.

CHAPTER 8

'Murder Will Out': Intimacy, Violence, and the Snow Family in Early Colonial New Zealand

Kristyn Harman

The 'murder mystery' genre relies on the relationships that evolve between a death or deaths, the evidence left by the killer(s), the investigators, and the field of prospective suspects. For the historian of intimacy and violence, murder is instructive of community relationships, not only through the facts of the case, but also through the suspicions and circumstances that play out following cases involving violent deaths. In this chapter, I use the murder of a settler colonial family as a focal point through which to explore the intimate, complex, and changing cross-cultural relationships between Māori and Pākehā in mid-nineteenth century Aotearoa New Zealand. Revealing issues of class, race, politics, gender, and identity, the wider set of circumstances within which this family was murdered speaks directly to the ambiguities of a frontier society at once both socioeconomically and physically intimate and yet inherently unstable and sometimes violent. In the private domain and public sphere, in the doctoring of evidence and the rumours of newspapermen, in the community of the

K. Harman (✉)
University of Tasmania, Hobart, TAS, Australia

© The Author(s) 2018
P. Edmonds, A. Nettelbeck (eds.), *Intimacies of Violence in the Settler Colony*, Cambridge Imperial and Post-Colonial Studies Series, https://doi.org/10.1007/978-3-319-76231-9_8

innocent and the catching of the perpetrator, and in other circumstances and suspicions surrounding this case, one of Auckland's most notorious violent crimes reveals interwoven layers of intimacy and violence.

The initial facts seemed straightforward. When three mutilated corpses were removed from the ashes of Lieutenant Robert Snow's incinerated raupō (bulrush) house on Auckland's North Shore on 23 October 1847, it was immediately apparent that the Snows had been murdered. The late lieutenant's body exhibited 'marks of blows and incisions or deep cuts in the forepart of the face and chin sufficiently deep to have caused death'. Another wound seemed to have been caused by a spear. Snow's wife, Hannah, died from 'a large wound ... which had fractured a portion of the skull, and the jaw, and severed the arteries', while their daughter Mary suffered a fractured skull from which 'small quantities of the brain [were] protruding'.[1] While suspicion initially fell on nearby Māori, it took the colonial authorities many months to bring the perpetrators to justice.

The Snow family murders are still recalled as 'one of New Zealand's most sensational crimes', and the facts of the case have been studied in some detail.[2] Ultimately, a colonial sailor, Joseph Burns, was hanged for the murders, and his common-law wife Margaret Reardon was transported to Van Diemen's Land.[3] The notoriety of the event has largely remained in the sphere of colonial criminal history. A particularly brutal crime that resulted in Auckland's first public hanging, it serves as a touchstone for the dark history of early colonial society. While present, Māori largely serve as side characters, tangential to the main story of the Snows, Burns, and Reardon. Specifically concentrating on Māori within the story, however, helps reorient the case to connect micro- and macro-relations within frontier Aotearoa New Zealand.

From the outset, Māori suspected and accused Māori. One report noted that because of mutilation to the bodies, 'our native police pronounced the wounds to be Maorie handiwork at once'. The *New Zealander* described how 'from all three ... large pieces of flesh had been cut with knives'. The parts of the bodies from which flesh was removed apparently provided 'conclusive evidence' of Māori culpability. 'What was done with that flesh', opined the newspaper, 'we leave our readers to suppose'. Rumours persisted that two Māori canoes left the scene under the cover of darkness, and that the late Lieutenant Snow was involved in several altercations with local Māori.[4] Such rumours are characterised by 'the intensity with which they spread'. The more they spread, the greater the need that such speculations 'conform to the laws of plausibility'.[5] Intimate connections forged between Burns, Reardon, and local Māori facilitated at least one, if not both, of the former to emulate modes of violence practiced by the latter with sufficient authenticity to misdirect Māori and Pākehā investigators for months following the event.

Colonial Auckland: Physical and Economic Intimacy

In many ways the Snow murders reveal aspects of what Vincent O'Malley has characterised as a 'middle ground' in Aotearoa New Zealand. Through increased contact between Māori hosts and a growing number of Europeans, there was a balance of power between the tangata whenua (people of the land) and the newcomers that is more complex and equal than the older models of colonisers and colonised.[6] While these 'middle ground' conditions gradually diminished, they were still evident in Auckland at the time of the Snow family murders.

For instance, at the time of the murders, seven years after the Treaty of Waitangi was signed, Auckland remained a frontier settlement numbering around four thousand colonists. Since Auckland's founding, commercial buildings such as a courthouse, gaol, military barracks, and a government house had been built. Public houses were plentiful. Domestically, the original tents and raupō houses were gradually being replaced by more substantial wooden structures.[7] The North Shore, where the Snow family lived and Lieutenant Snow oversaw the naval stores and magazine, remained sparsely populated. An 1845 census reveals seven wooden dwellings and fifteen raupō huts there. The Snows were among those living in a raupō house, a physical manifestation of O'Malley's 'middle ground'.

Despite a steady increase in Auckland's colonial population, which was significantly boosted between 1847 and 1852 by the arrival of Fencibles (retired British soldiers) and their families, the colonists were far from self-sufficient, another defining element of O'Malley's 'middle ground'.[8] They relied heavily on Māori for their daily necessities, including food. Within Māori society, food was 'the fundamental measure of wealth', as it 'represented economic control, reputation, and social power'. Food, and the capacity to supply ample quantities of it, was 'essential to chiefly mana [power and prestige]', with recipients being drawn into relationships of reciprocity with the suppliers.[9] For Māori, regularly supplying food to the newcomers accrued sociopolitical and economic benefits. Ben Schrader has explained how in early Auckland, 'Māori dominated the fresh produce trade, and without it townspeople would have gone hungry. ... By 1847, the year Auckland was declared the new capital, Māori were the "very lifeblood" of the town.'[10] Some of the townsfolk's food was cultivated at Ōkahu, a nearby Māori settlement. However, Māori from further afield at the Coromandel sailed to Auckland with waka (canoes) piled high with 'pigs, potatoes, wheat, maize, melons, grapes, pumpkins, onions, flax, turkeys, geese, ducks, chickens and firewood' to trade. Colonial shopkeepers benefitted as Māori traders purchased gardening implements and some homewares while in town.[11] According to Hazel Petrie, 'until at least 1855 ... [t]here is considerable evidence that ... Māori production was the mainstay of the colonial economy and, in particular, of the largest population centre, Auckland'.[12] Māori would not, therefore, have been an unexpected sight near the scene of the crime.

In fact, Māori canoes passing by the vicinity of the murders would have seemed mundane in their ordinariness, as even larger Māori watercraft were a common enough sight. Before the implementation of road—and later rail—networks, waterways (oceans, seas, and rivers) were significant in facilitating trade and communications. As Aotearoa New Zealand's hungry European population continued to increase, coastal-dwelling Māori invested in schooners to facilitate trading relationships with the newcomers. Petrie has pointed out, for example, how in the 1840s and early 1850s Māori at Whakatāne at the North Island's Bay of Plenty accumulated twenty schooners to engage in the northern trade with Auckland and the Bay of Islands.[13] With missionary encouragement, Māori cultivated wheat (a biblically sound crop) and utilised their schooners to export wheat to the Australian colonies.[14] Ultimately, though, the increasingly large numbers of British immigrants arriving saw Māori turn away from inter-colonial trade in favour of the growing domestic market.[15] Domestic trade saw 'large numbers of Māori sojourning in big towns such as Auckland'.[16] However, Māori traders experienced difficulties finding overnight accommodation as 'hotels and boarding houses largely refused to accept them', so even their departure into the darkness may not have been out of the ordinary on the night the Snows' house burned to the ground.[17]

In fact, at the time of the Snow murders, Māori visiting Auckland slept on its beaches. In their study of the British, Ottoman, and Japanese empires, Tony Ballantyne and Antoinette Burton explained how '[i]mperial officials seeking to manage indigenous populations utilized a variety of mechanisms for reterritorializing extant spatial relations', but this sort of colonial management had yet to develop at Auckland.[18] Only in 1849 did the government decide to build a hostel on a 'native reserve' at Mechanics Bay for visiting Māori, which, again illustrative of the 'middle ground', was also made available to impoverished Pākehā.

Auckland and Political Intimacy

A Māori determination, in the early investigation of the Snow murders, that the perpetrators were also Māori reveals a type of intimacy that goes beyond physical proximity and economic interdependence. While generally seen only through the lens of colonial sources and perspectives, Europeans often forged alliances with key Indigenous stakeholders, and utilised their allies as intermediaries during times of peace and war. Indigenous people had their own motivations for entering into intimate relationships with colonists, such as gathering intelligence about the newcomers, (mis)directing colonial endeavours, and safeguarding or improving their standing.[19] The 'native police' who aided the Snow murder investigation are part of this international phenomenon, and lend the Snow murders a resonance that criss-crossed the British Empire.

Other exemplars, however, offer better-documented cases. One such figure in early colonial Auckland was Patuone, whose engagements with the British helped explain the very situation of the Snows' residence. Governor George Grey 'valued [rangatira/chief] Patuone's presence … [as] it gave some assurance of safety to the unprotected town', meaning that the political alliance offered military security.[20] The colonists were also aware that 'Auckland's security [from potential Māori-led attacks] depended on Waikato friendship', an observation that stemmed in part from colonial observations of a 'huge banquet for a great intertribal gathering' hosted by Waikato rangatira Te Wherowhero, another significant figure, at Remuera in May 1844. On 11 May, Governor FitzRoy visited the gathering where he observed sixteen hundred Māori armed with a mix of traditional and European weaponry dance a haka [war dance]. Because of his obvious influence, Te Wherowhero was frequently consulted by a succession of colonial governors about matters relating to Māori.[21] At the time of the Snow family murders, both Patuone and Te Wherowhero were significant interlocutors between Māori and the colonists.

Patuone's role as an intermediary between Māori and Pākehā was possibly influenced by his father, Ngāti Hao rangatira and tohunga (priest) Tapua, who traded fish in 1769 at the Bay of Islands with the crew of the

Endeavour. Tapua met the 'leader of the goblins' (presumably James Cook) who gave him gifts including a garment made from red fabric.[22] This would have been highly prized, as the material closely resembled the colour of ochre, a substance used by Māori for decorative and ceremonial purposes. By the time of the Snow murders, therefore, there were generations of cross-cultural encounter at work that help explain Māori co-operation in the investigation.

Yet the 'native police' also point to a shifting balance of power, and a more structured subordination. Visits such as Cook's were fleeting and, as Tony Ballantyne has explained, prior to the arrival of Protestant missionaries in the far north of New Zealand in 1814, European visitors were generally 'sailors and sealers' who 'had no intention of settling in New Zealand'. Those who stayed briefly among Māori 'had no choice but to accept the power of Māori leaders and the authority of local lore and law'; but by 1847, this had shifted considerably.[23] Certainly Patuone exerted considerable political authority, but it was increasingly inflected by colonial symbols and structures. In the 1820s he had extended his patronage and protection to Europeans at Hokianga, and made several diplomatic visits to Sydney between 1826 and the early 1830s.[24] In 1833, following the loss of his first wife, Patuone married Takarangi, a high-ranking Ngāti Paoa woman from the Hauraki Gulf (the body of water between Auckland and the Coromandel Peninsula). Because of his ongoing role in ensuring that British naval vessels were resupplied in New Zealand, in 1837 Patuone received 'a gift of armour and a suit of green clothes' from the Crown. He was also a signatory to the 1831 petition to King William IV to request the British sovereign's protection from the French, and He Whakaputanga, the Declaration of the Independence of New Zealand formally acknowledged by the Crown in 1836. He was at Waitangi when the treaty was signed on 6 February 1840. Less than a fortnight earlier, Patuone had been baptised by the Church of England missionary Henry Williams, taking Williams family names Eruera Maihi (Edward Marsh) as his own, further cementing his relationship with them. Takarangi took Riria (from the Williams family name Lydia) as her baptismal name.[25] By the 1840s Patuone was living and trading at several sites around Auckland. The parcel of land that later became the North Shore, the site of the Snow family murders, fell into colonial hands as a result of a transaction between Riria and the Crown in 1841 through which the latter gained 9500 acres.[26]

Yet while the Snows' occupation of a particular plot of land flowed from intercultural activity, it also helped mark a turning point. 'Land', as

Lachy Paterson and Angela Wanhalla have explained, 'was the defining issue of New Zealand race relations in the nineteenth century', as 'Māori had the land that Pākehā wanted, not just for the economic aspects of settlement, but also as a means to realise Crown sovereignty and to gain effective control'.[27] Processes of British land acquisition in Aotearoa New Zealand particularly saw Māori women's authority and agency diminish over time. Miranda Johnson has described how prior to the 1870s, some Māori women exercised significant authority as rights-holders over land and were also influential agents in the socio-political sphere. For example, at least thirteen high-ranking Māori women are known to have signed the Treaty of Waitangi. Over time, amendments to colonial land laws saw their authority increasingly usurped by their Māori or Pākehā husbands. Despite petitioning parliament at least forty times in the late nineteenth century in relation to their diminishing standing under these land laws, the colonists' determination to assimilate Māori to European sociocultural mores and economic practices meant Māori women's status declined.[28] A 'new conceptualisation of masculine identity' across Britain's nineteenth-century empire saw 'a broadening of the masculine franchise' that benefitted white middle-class men. Economic, political, and social shifts saw 'a new bourgeois style' emerge as these men embraced 'values that were anathema to the traditional elite'.[29] Such structural changes were particularly disadvantageous for Māori women. Lieutenant Snow's raupō house thus sites a complex thread of land history, not solely a murder.

Nonetheless, it is through the murder investigation and Māori police that the frontier intimacies most clearly emerge from the Snow family murders, and again Patuone is instructive. Angela Ballara has highlighted Patuone's status in colonial Auckland, noting that when Auckland's police magistrate Thomas Beckham arrested Patuone to question him about a matter, Grey was furious and demoted Beckham. The rangatira's value as an ally was also evidenced through Grey giving him 110 acres of land at Takapuna Beach in Auckland to persuade Patuone to remain in town following the death in 1840 of Riria. Patuone lived out his remaining years between this block and on Ngāti Paoa land at Devonport and in his old age he 'was a familiar sight on the Auckland streets, his tall frame bent with age and dressed in a military uniform'.[30] Writing in the context of Aboriginal warriors wearing colonial jackets in early New South Wales, Grace Karskens has pointed out how the men favoured military coats, presumably because of their 'symbolic prestige and power'.[31] Patuone's adoption of British military dress in his later years can be read as denoting his high status traditionally and in the rapidly changing colonial world in which he was an interlocutor. Similarly, the 'native police' investigating the murder should be seen as exercising an agency of power and identity that goes beyond the passing and demeaning press characterisation of them as 'our native police'.

Māori Auckland: Proximity, Suspicion, Intimacy, and Violence

Underplayed in the history of an event usually framed by murder, investigation, and trial, is the story of the immediate military response. In the aftermath of the conflagration, twenty-two Māori people sleeping at the nearby beach were taken prisoner and their canoes confiscated, because of their proximity to the scene of the crime and the mutilated condition of the Snow family's corpses, as well as of sightings of canoes leaving the area following the murders. An armed party from the HMS *Dido*, a naval vessel anchored nearby, and from which help was sent when the Snows' home was seen to be ablaze, effected the capture.[32] That one of the deceased was a lieutenant was not the only militaristic element to the story. The colonial response to this murder reveals, as well as a rich cross-cultural context, a highly militarised frontier where the cooperation and overlap of civil and military authorities was an important element in the power structure of empire.

Yet while there was a swift raid on the first-suspected Māori, from the outset several Europeans also provided dissenting voices, revealing tensions of prejudice and the strength of intimacies within colonial society. For instance, a friend of Patuone's who later became the latter's biographer, Charles Davis, observed how 'knowing the natives had no motives to induce them to perpetrate these outrages, I assured the authorities the guilty parties were almost beyond doubt, of our own race'.[33] A local clergyman had sufficient faith in these Indigenous members of his flock to pledge 'his word for their re-appearance on the day of the inquest' and secured their release from colonial custody. '[A]s good as his word', the unnamed gentleman of the cloth later arrived at the coronial inquest into the Snows' deaths accompanied by all twenty-two suspects. This demonstration of good faith, however, did not dissuade the *New Zealander* newspaper from railing against what it saw as the clergyman's unwarranted interference in the matter, and from stating emphatically: 'There can be no doubt but that natives were the perpetrators of the foul deed.'[34] When the coronial inquest drew to a close, the jury returned a verdict of '"Wilful Murder" against some person, or persons unknown', although most people continued to believe that the as-yet-unknown perpetrators of the crime were Māori.[35]

This widespread prejudice partly derived from the key evidence in the case, but also points to the role of the colonial newspapers as recorders and formers of opinion. The Snows' murders were widely reported throughout the colony, and so the event as read at the time related to wider concerns and narratives about conflict between colonists and Māori. Despite the signing of the Treaty of Waitangi, intermittent conflict occurred from the 1840s onwards as Māori endeavoured to curb the Europeans' apparent lust for land. In Auckland at the time of the Snow family murders, there were some fears that instructions issued from London by the Secretary for War and the Colonies, Earl Grey, directing Aotearoa New Zealand's Governor George Grey to recognise Māori ownership only over those lands occupied or cultivated by them, would be incendiary. This directive provided for all remaining 'waste lands' to be sold by the Crown to colonists. Governor Grey prudently ignored these instructions, yet Māori felt sufficiently antagonised for Te Wherowhero to petition Queen Victoria.[36] Colonists, too, were unsettled, and some were worried that Earl Grey's instructions could spark intercultural conflict. This context, as well as the apparent barbarity of the crime itself, is crucial for properly understanding the sensational reporting of the case.

This bigger context was made explicitly clear. While the notion of Māori culpability largely went unquestioned, local newspapers debated whether the Snows' murders were politically motivated or an act of personal vengeance. When the sensational news initially broke in October 1847, the *New Zealander* was quick to liken the incident to high-profile intercultural conflicts that had taken place elsewhere in New Zealand. In particular, it drew comparisons with the Wairau 'massacre … a conflict, open and hand to hand' that occurred near the top of the South Island on 17 June 1843 between a surveying party from the nearby New Zealand Company settlement of Nelson and a group of Ngāti Toa led by Te Rauparaha and his nephew Te Rangihaeata. The North Island 'murders of the Gillespies, in the Hutt, and of the Gilfallans, at Wanganui', involving particular colonial families were also mentioned, yet the newspaper pointed out how both incidents took place 'at a period of high excitement, and in a time of war'. An incident in Northland in which Māori youth Wiremu Kingi Maketu killed members of the Roberton family and their employee was also aired, although the newspaper supposed that the tragic event had 'been prompted by the mere appetite of blood in the savage who committed it', rather than being triggered by more widespread political unrest.[37] Nonetheless, the point was clear, that the Snows' murders were being read as a potential portent for renewed frontier violence between Māori and colonists.

However, the murders' place in recent history was also contested in a way that reflects and hints towards the colonial tendency within Australasia to criminalise frontier warfare. The *Daily Southern Cross* took issue with the *New Zealander*'s reportage, refuting broader suppositions about the mood of local Māori towards Auckland's settlers, and arguing that it was not 'strictly correct' to discuss the Snow family murders 'in connexion with the murders committed on the Hutt, and at Wanganui', distancing the Snows from the wartime comparisons made by the *New Zealander*. 'This case', the *Daily Southern Cross* claimed, 'may exceed those in barbarity … but it is entirely distinct from them in character.' For the *Daily Southern Cross*, 'the murder of Lieutenant Snow is not the result of any political animosity, but a deadly display of individual revenge'. After all, the *Daily Southern Cross* asserted confidently, if local Māori were 'ripe for immediate action' against the colonists, a 'single family would not be the only victims'.[38] The alleged Māori violence, at this stage untested at law, was already being discussed as primarily a matter of criminal proceedings.

Suspecting Māori was one thing; but in the 1840s, imposing colonial justice on Māori accused of transgressions was another matter entirely, and this again highlights the way that the Snows' murders affirm a microhistorical 'middle ground' while at the same time pointing to its waning. In the colony's first decade, there had been 'doubts … about the extent to which the new governor could claim to be in control of the country'. While some Māori were 'willing to participate in Pākehā justice to settle disputes with Pākehā … they were less willing to allow British justice to intervene in their own communities'. According to Jennifer Ashton, Patuone represented the views of a number of rangatira when he claimed that Māori preferred to adhere to their own traditions to resolve matters solely involving Māori. In cases concerning Māori and Pākehā, the colonists relied heavily on Māori cooperation when aiming to rectify matters in accordance with colonial law.[39] This reliance was demonstrated in the aftermath of the Snow family murders when, in light of suspicions over Māori involvement, colonists found it 'satisfactory to know that the head chief of Waikato, Te Wherowhero, is, with other influential chiefs in the neighbourhood, exerting himself for the discovery of the murderers of the lamented Lieutenant Snow and family'. In reporting this, the *New Zealander* observed how 'the natives around us have determined … to find out the true guilty parties, and deliver them up to justice'.[40] Māori cooperation was essential to locating the murderers. Colonial reliance on their support highlights the limits of empire while also blurring its edges.

While Māori and Pākehā sought the culprits, 'various rumours [were] flying about' as to likely perpetrators, and the micro-details of these rumours highlight a great spectrum of intimacies. Early in November 1847, the *New Zealander* reported how an informant had provided 'an accurate account … worthy of attention' in which two Māori men were seemingly implicated in the murders through observations of their demeanour. They had paddled their canoe up the Piako River on 26 October and boarded a European vessel 'lying off the pa of Mowkero [Maukoro]'. The two were 'very uncommunicative, contrary to the usual habits of the natives', an interesting revelation of intimacy via reticence. The men said they were travelling from 'Houraki' [Hauraki] to the Waikato to deliver a letter. One of the two was observed unpacking 'some European clothes from his bundle', following which he 'dressed himself in a grey linen blouse, a white shirt, and a pair of new trousers of drab woollen stuff, and put on a straw hat, with narrow turned up brim, and a black ribbon tied round it'. According to the *New Zealander*, 'the hat … is said to have borne a striking similarity to one which Lieut. Snow used to wear'. The hat 'had evidently not been bought' by its Māori wearer as it was 'too small for him', and was simply 'stuck on the top of his bushy head'. The man completed his wardrobe with the addition of a 'watch guard of hair or silk fastened by gold clasps' worn around his neck. European observers swore they would be able to identify these men, if later required to do so, 'particularly he who dressed in European clothes, from his peculiar appearance'.[41]

In an episode that further underlines suspicions of Māori involvement and highlights the tenuous imposition of colonial law over matters concerning Māori and Pākehā, newspaper reports circulated about several Māori being interviewed on 17 December 1847 in Auckland in relation to the murders. The main suspect was 'a native of the Ngatiruru tribe of Waikato, named Ngamuka', with some 'accomplices, of the Ngatitematera tribe, of which Taraia is chief'. Taraia 'and a number of other natives' accompanied Ngamuka to Auckland, perhaps with Māori, as Terry Carson has suggested, offering the latter as a 'sacrificial lamb' to shore up Māori–

Pākehā relations. Rather than Ngamuka being examined before the Magistrate's Court, 'a mixed assemblage was gathered together in the front of Government house, and the affair conducted in regular maori style in the presence of the Governor, and some of his officials', including Beckham, on the veranda before a huge crowd gathered on the lawns. The lengthy discussions included oratory from Te Wherowhero, following which the principal suspect was allowed to go free. Journalists concluded that Ngamuka 'has sufficiently exculpated himself in the eyes of his Excellency', but lamented the lack of adherence to the colonists' legal processes. The suspect, they thought, ought to have been examined before the magistrate's court.[42] On the road to the truth, the colonial investigation had taken some decidedly Māori turns, to the annoyance of some reporters, but further situating the Snows' murders at the heart of an intimate 'middle ground'.

This 'middle ground' was, however, gradually giving way to colonial norms. As Angela Wanhalla has explained, Grey's strategy to ensure that English law was gradually extended into '"native districts" with the aim of eventually supplanting indigenous customs' informed his dismantling of Aotearoa New Zealand's Aborigines Protectorate Department in 1846. He replaced it with a system of resident magistrates' courts. Magistrates 'had the power of civil and criminal jurisdiction over European colonists'. Grey intended that Māori would be drawn into the colonial legal system as the 'justice of English law' was demonstrated, through their being co-opted 'into the system as native assessors and interpreters when Māori brought cases before the court'.[43] Grey's appointments of Māori as 'native police' served a similar function, and also formed part of his strategy to supplant Māori beliefs and traditions with English-derived cultural norms and practices. At the time of Ngamuka's examination, the resident magistrates' courts were still in their infancy, with his Māori-style interrogation at Government House demonstrating that the 'middle ground' continued to function in colonial Auckland in the quest for justice in relation to the Snow family murders, a case of historical events not quite following colonial plans.

As 1847 drew to a close, the police were no closer to identifying a murder suspect or suspects. In March 1848, the Inspector of the Armed Police wrote to Grey for permission to offer a reward for information leading to the apprehension of the Snow family murderer(s). Late in the preceding year, he had had a draft reward notice translated into te reo Māori. However, as the governor did not consider a reward 'advisable', the notice was not circulated.[44] The likelihood of the police identifying the culprit(s), whether Māori or Pākehā, was diminishing over time, and with it the historiographical usefulness of the reports and rumour also diminish. But with the false lead of Māori culpability fading, the Snow murders reveal a very different set of information, pointing to a different spectrum of intimacy and violence in the intercolonial world and the domestic sphere.

Domestic Auckland: Intimate Violence

On 28 December 1847, an episode of domestic violence that seemed unrelated to the Snow family murders unfolded at the Aldwell family's home at Smale's Point, Auckland. The protagonist was the sailor Joseph Burns, who arrived in Aotearoa New Zealand in 1840 on HMS *Victory*. The woman whose throat he slashed was Margaret Reardon, his former common-law wife of half a decade and mother of his two children. Reardon, previously known as Margaret Lackey, had in 1836 relocated from Ireland to New South Wales with other family members on the *Duchess of Northumberland* where, aged twenty-three, she married the sixty-six-year-old Daniel Reardon (or Riordan). The marriage did not last long, and in 1843 she moved to Auckland where her sister Sophia lived with her husband William Aldwell.[45] The domestic details of their lives were, it turned out, of crucial importance in resolving the mystery of the Snows' murders.

Kirsten McKenzie has explored how nineteenth-century port cities, while regarded as 'dubious', were transient spaces within which people could reinvent themselves, and Burns and Reardon typify the phenomenon. 'Fortunes could be made', as McKenzie has observed, 'and new identities forged in these liminal zones between land and sea.' Ever present, though, was the 'danger of slipping back from a position of respectability and status'.[46] Such backsliding characterised Burns's and Reardon's lives together at the colonial port of Auckland. Sometime after disembarking from the HMS *Victory*, Burns was employed as a stock man on Auckland's North Shore. Unfortunately, in early 1847, he was dismissed from his job on suspicion of having stolen and butchered some of his employer's livestock. At the time, he was living with Reardon, with whom he had had two sons. The couple, with 'a well-deserved reputation as heavy drinkers', had fallen on hard times as the loss of Burns's job also meant the loss of the roof over their heads.[47]

As McKenzie has elaborated, 'whether in material culture, housing style, gender relations or politics, the colonial middle class was aware that adherence to a British model held out the best hopes of social acceptability'.[48]

Burns and Reardon, whose lives were already being played out at the margins of colonial society, became increasingly socially unacceptable in colonial Auckland as their changing circumstances resulted in a marked deterioration in their standard of living. The family essentially became fringe-dwellers, living in a rough hut constructed by Burns on the outskirts of a Māori settlement on the North Shore. To ensure his and his family's survival, Burns relied 'largely on the charity of Māori', labouring for Patuone.[49] Reardon engaged in the heavy labour that characterised daily life for most colonial women at the time, although her changed domestic circumstances worsened not only her living but also her working conditions. Barbara Brookes has pointed out how 'the quality of housing, be it a tent near a work site, a raupo whare, a cob hut or a gabled weatherboard house, had a direct effect on the nature of women's work experience. ... Tents or thatched rush huts were chilly and damp, and the risk of fire meant that all cooking must be done outside.'[50] The 'primitive dwelling' built by Burns would have lacked basic comforts and conveniences, consigning Burns to a daily life of drudgery. Whether solely to feed her family, or also to obtain surplus produce for barter, as well as tending to her rough hut and outdoor cooking fire, Reardon cultivated vegetables while living with Burns.[51] Like the Snows, albeit in a diminished social status, Burns and Reardon lived not just proximate to, but were socially intimate with and economically reliant on, Māori people around Auckland.

Yet it was a broader intercolonial judicial network that ultimately elicited the connection between Burns, Reardon, and the Snows. For reasons that were not immediately apparent, Burns signed on to the crew of the HMS *Inflexible* and sailed for New South Wales on 6 November 1847. It was during this absence that Reardon and their sons moved in with her sister's family. Burns returned to Auckland on 6 December, a month after his departure and several weeks before assaulting Reardon on 28 December.[52] Following his arrest, Burns was tried for the assault at the Supreme Court in Auckland on 1 March 1848 before Chief Justice William Martin. After hearing the evidence, it took the jury just twelve minutes to find the man guilty of 'intent to do grievous bodily harm', but not guilty of attempted murder. Burns was remanded in custody, and the following day Martin sentenced him to be 'transported beyond the seas, to such place as His Excellency the Governor shall appoint, for the term of your natural life'. Burns was gaoled so arrangements could be made to transport him to Van Diemen's Land, the site to which at least 110 convicts were transported from Aotearoa New Zealand in the nineteenth century.[53] Only in the aftermath of Burns's trial did the salient detail appear, revealed in an article printed in the *New Zealander*, that mentioned that Reardon had been 'detained in custody' as she was thought to be someone who could 'throw further light upon the melancholy fact of the late murder of Lieutenant and Mrs Snow and child'.[54]

Initially, Burns falsely accused two other men of the Snows' murders; but after attempting suicide, he retracted this accusation. Eventually, and sensationally, Burns admitted his own involvement in the murders, following which the *New Zealander* published its regret at having suspected Māori involvement and stated that it would be 'among the first to offer reparation for the stain that we ourselves have innocently contributed to fix upon them'.[55] Burns appeared before the Supreme Court on 1 April 1848. Reardon became the prosecution's key witness, telling the court that she had seen Burns leave their home on the evening of the murders, armed with a tomahawk. A forensic examination revealed blood on the weapon, which had been retrieved from Burns's tool chest. Reardon said that Burns returned home in the early hours of the morning, boasting of murdering the Snows and showing her some silver coins that he had stolen from them.

Auckland: Intimacy, Violence, and Execution

After hearing evidence from several witnesses, the jury took forty-five minutes to find Burns guilty of the murder of Robert Snow. Despite responding 'My God, I'm as innocent as the child unborn!', Burns was sentenced to be hanged at midday the following Saturday. The execution was slated to take place at the scene of the murder, a punishment reserved for the most heinous of crimes. Just before midnight on the eve of his execution, Burns provided a full and frank confession to Reverend Churton, who had been ministering to him. He told the churchman how Reardon claimed to have seen the Snows shopping in Auckland and suggested that she and Burns ought to rob the family. According to Burns, he and Reardon had both gone to the Snows' home, armed with weapons. His version of the night's events saw Reardon cutting Lieutenant Snow's throat and murdering the child, while he admitted to killing Mrs. Snow. Despite the man's admission of guilt and incrimination of Reardon, the latter never faced criminal charges in relation to the Snow murders.[56] In the aftermath of Burns's execution, however, Reardon was charged with perjury for her part in falsely accusing two others of the Snow murders, found guilty, and sentenced to transportation to Van Diemen's Land for seven years, becoming the sole female convict shipped from New Zealand across the Tasman Sea.[57]

In the lead-up to Burns's public hanging, and in a curious echo of the former intensity of the suspicion against Māori, 'official notice of the execution' was 'sent to the natives for ten miles around Auckland'.[58] It is not clear whether the colonists' intention was simply to encourage a good turnout, to ensure that Māori were mollified for having been wrongly implicated, or to demonstrate the full force of colonial law. Perhaps all these factors came into play. In the end, however, the multilayered colonial intimacy that the murders revealed was reaffirmed. A large flotilla of watercraft, including numerous Māori waka (canoes) whose crews were plying for passenger fares, accompanied the *Ann* as she transported Burns from Official Bay, Auckland, across to the North Shore, where he was hanged on a temporary scaffold.

Following Burns's death and Reardon's sentencing to transportation, the *Anglo-Maori Warder* took an opportunity to do 'justice to [Governor] Captain Grey's shrewdness of perception in never having yielded to the notion' of the Snow murders 'having been Maori handiwork'. The newspaper still managed to scapegoat Māori by observing how its suspicion of Māori involvement, shared by many others, stemmed in large part not only from the mutilated condition of the bodies but also 'the unhesitating assertion of Natives belonging to the Police force … that their own countrymen had been the actors in it'. Nevertheless, to play its part in shoring up racial harmony, the newspaper apologised to 'the Native Race', and to the missionaries who had refuted claims of Māori involvement.[59]

Conclusion

Through a sequence of murder, investigation, allegation, trial, and execution, the Snow murders highlight the ways that intimacies and violence can serve as useful lenses for the macro- and micro-historical investigation of colonial relationships. At a macro level, complex interactions between Māori and colonists are evident in the provision of land, food, and security by the former in return for trade goods and prestige by association provided by the latter. At a micro level, significant if fluctuating relationships were forged at the highest levels of society, with successive colonial governors liaising with key rangatira. The complexities of these relationships are reflected in the diversity of leaders with whom the governor sought to work, ranging from signatories to the Treaty of Waitangi such as Patuone who later became a Christian and dressed in military garb, to men such as Te Wherowhero who refused to sign the Treaty, never converted to Christianity, and was eventually installed as the first Māori king. It was these relationships, and the commissioning of 'native' police as part of a policy to gradually assimilate Māori to colonial law, that helped facilitate police investigations into the Snow murders. The hybrid nature of the legal system was illustrated through the style of interrogation to which Māori suspects were subjected on the veranda of Government House in Auckland.

Intimate encounters between Pākehā protagonists Burns and Reardon and local Māori enabled the newcomers to survive when cast out from their own society. Yet at the same time, such intimacies of encounter provided sufficient local knowledge for Burns to feign Māori culpability in the commission of the Snow murders. First-hand knowledge of Māori weapons and their effect enabled the corpses of the deceased to be presented as though their deaths resulted from such an assault. If nothing else, the case proved that a Pākehā criminal could fool some Māori police, leaving perhaps the most vivid artefact of both intimacy and violence in the bodies that were discovered, as well as the sequence of suspicion and confusion that followed.

Notes

1. 'Horrible Murder', *Daily Southern Cross*, 30 October 1847, 2.
2. Terry Carson, *The Axeman's Accomplice: The True Story of Margaret Reardon and the Snow Family Murders* (Auckland: Alibi Press, 2016), 9.
3. Kristyn Harman, *Cleansing the Colony: Transporting Convicts from New Zealand to Van Diemen's Land* (Dunedin: Otago University Press, 2017).
4. *New Zealander*, 27 October 1847, 2.
5. Luise White, *Speaking with Vampires: Rumor and History in Colonial Africa* (Berkeley: University of California Press, 2000), 56.
6. Vincent O'Malley, *The Meeting Place: Māori and Pākehā Encounters, 1642–1840* (Auckland: Auckland University Press, 2012), 8.
7. Carson, *The Axeman's Accomplice*, 15.
8. Carson, *The Axeman's Accomplice*, 15.
9. Hazel Petrie, *Chiefs of Industry: Māori Tribal Enterprise in Early Colonial New Zealand* (Auckland: Auckland University Press, 2006), 22.
10. Ben Schrader, *The Big Smoke: New Zealand Cities 1840–1920* (Wellington: Bridget Williams Books, 2016), 173.
11. Schrader, *The Big Smoke*, 173.

12. Petrie, *Chiefs of Industry*, 227.
13. Petrie, *Chiefs of Industry*, 186.
14. Petrie, *Chiefs of Industry*, 164.
15. Petrie, *Chiefs of Industry*, 226.
16. Petrie, *Chiefs of Industry*, 189.
17. Schrader, *The Big Smoke*, 190.
18. Tony Ballantyne and Antoinette Burton, *Empires and the Reach of the Global: 1870–1945* (Cambridge, MA: The Belknap Press of Harvard University Press, 2014), 71.
19. See, for example, Shino Konishi, Maria Nugent, and Tiffany Shellam, eds. *Indigenous Intermediaries: New Perspectives on Exploration Archives* (Canberra: Australian National University Press, 2015); Tiffany Shellam, Maria Nugent, Shino Konishi, and Allison Cadzow, eds. *Brokers and Boundaries: Colonial Exploration in Indigenous Territory* (Canberra: Australian National University Press, 2016).
20. Angela Ballara, 'Patuone, Eruera Maihi', first published in the *Dictionary of New Zealand Biography*, vol. 1, 1990, and updated online in November 2010. *Te Ara: The Encyclopedia of New Zealand*, accessed 25 June 2017, http://www.TeAra.govt.nz/en/biographies/1p12/patuone-eruera-maihi
21. Steven Oliver, 'Te Wherowhero, Potatau', first published in the *Dictionary of New Zealand Biography*, vol. 1, 1990. *Te Ara—The Encyclopedia of New Zealand*, accessed 25 June 2017, http://www.TeAra.govt.nz/en/biographies/1t88/te-wherowhero-potatau
22. Petrie, *Chiefs of Industry*, 30.
23. Tony Ballantyne, *Entanglements of Empire: Missionaries, Māori, and the Question of the Body* (Auckland: Auckland University Press, 2014), 3–4.
24. Ballara, 'Patuone, Eruera Maihi'.
25. Ballara, 'Patuone, Eruera Maihi'.
26. Ballara, 'Patuone, Eruera Maihi'.
27. Lachy Paterson and Angela Wanhalla, *He Reo Wahine: Māori Women's Voices from the Nineteenth Century* (Auckland: Auckland University Press, 2017), 3.
28. Miranda Johnson, 'Chiefly Women: Queen Victoria, Meri Mangakahia, and the Maori Parliament', in *Mistress of Everything: Queen Victoria in Indigenous Worlds*, ed. Sarah Carter and Maria Nugent (Manchester: Manchester University Press, 2016), 239.
29. Kirsten McKenzie, *Scandal in the Colonies* (Melbourne: Melbourne University Press, 2014), 86.
30. Ballara, 'Patuone, Eruera Maihi'.
31. Grace Karskens, 'Red Coat, Blue Jacket, Black Skin: Aboriginal Men and Clothing in Early New South Wales', *Aboriginal History* 35 (2011), 22.

32. *New Zealander*, 27 October 1847, 2.
33. Carson, *The Axeman's Accomplice*, 28.
34. *New Zealander*, 27 October 1847, 2.
35. 'Horrible Murder', *Daily Southern Cross*, 30 October 1847, 2.
36. Carson, *The Axeman's Accomplice*, 29.
37. *New Zealander*, 27 October 1847, 2.
38. *Daily Southern Cross*, 30 October 1847, 2.
39. Jennifer Ashton, *At the Margin of Empire: John Webster and Hokianga, 1841–1900* (Auckland: Auckland University Press, 2015), 58.
40. *New Zealander*, 3 November 1847, 2.
41. *New Zealander*, 6 November 1847, 2.
42. *Daily Southern Cross*, 11 December 1847, 2; *Daily Southern Cross*, 25 December 1847, 2; 'Auckland', *New Zealand Spectator and Cook's Strait Guardian*, 15 January 1848, 3; Carson, *The Axeman's Accomplice*, 31.
43. Angela Wanhalla, *Matters of the Heart: A History of Inter-racial Marriage in New Zealand* (Auckland: Auckland University Press, 2013), 49.
44. Carson, *The Axeman's Accomplice*, 32.
45. Kristyn Harman, *Cleansing the Colony: Transporting Convicts from New Zealand to Van Diemen's Land* (Dunedin: Otago University Press, 2017), 164, 174–175.
46. Kirsten McKenzie, *Scandal in the Colonies* (Melbourne: Melbourne University Press, 2004), 1.
47. Carson, *The Axeman's Accomplice*, 34.
48. McKenzie, *Scandal in the Colonies*, 13.
49. Carson, *The Axeman's Accomplice*, 34.
50. Barbara Brookes, *A History of New Zealand Women* (Wellington: Bridget Williams Books, 2016), 60.
51. Carson, *The Axeman's Accomplice*, 34.
52. Carson, *The Axeman's Accomplice*, 33.
53. Harman, *Cleansing the Colony*, 164–165.
54. *New Zealander*, 11 March 1848, 2.
55. *New Zealander*, 4 March 1848, 2.
56. Harman, *Cleansing the Colony*, 167–169.
57. Harman, *Cleansing the Colony*, 169–171.
58. 'A Murder by Law', *Daily Southern Cross*, 17 June 1848, 2.
59. *Anglo-Maori Warder*, 6 June 1848, 2.

CHAPTER 9

'Tangled Up': Intimacy, Emotion, and Dispossession in Colonial New Zealand

Angela Wanhalla and Lachy Paterson

Many Indigenous peoples encountered the colonial state through its representatives who worked and lived among them, yet the resident officials who interacted with colonised subjects on a daily basis and who were employed to effect government policy in those communities have generally been marginal subjects of historical investigation.[1] Depending on location, such officials often had long careers in the public service, and that continuity was an important factor in the functioning of the state in a region. Encouraged to build close working relationships with local elites, resident officials, such as native agents and interpreters, actively engaged in the work of colonialism on an intimate and personal level; but cultivating close bonds could also lead to complicated and entangled lives. This chapter examines the activities of one such figure, George Thomas Wilkinson (1846–1906), employed in the Land Purchase Branch of the

---

Initial research for this chapter was enabled by a Royal Society Te Āparangi Marsden Fast-Start Grant and completed with the assistance of a New Zealand Government-funded Rutherford Discovery Fellowship.

A. Wanhalla (✉) • L. Paterson
University of Otago, Dunedin, Otago, New Zealand

© The Author(s) 2018
P. Edmonds, A. Nettelbeck (eds.), *Intimacies of Violence in the Settler Colony*, Cambridge Imperial and Post-Colonial Studies Series, https://doi.org/10.1007/978-3-319-76231-9_9

New Zealand Native Department, a government entity that was responsible for the purchase of Māori land.

A soldier and surveyor turned public servant, Wilkinson resided at Parawai, in the mining town of Shortland (now known as Thames) in the Hauraki region where he was deployed by the state to negotiate the opening of new fields for gold prospecting, empowered to obtain signatories to cession deeds, collect revenues, and pay a portion of miners' rights fees, rents, and timber licenses to local Māori. Individuals like Wilkinson figure in studies of state-making, colonial policy, and race relations in New Zealand, where their reports are used to give texture and detail to how dispossession was enacted, but they are often cast as two-dimensional figures. This work has called attention to the fact that in the mid-nineteenth century, those professions crucial to advancing colonialism in New Zealand often employed men with established connections to Māori with the cultural knowledge and language skills to advance the interests of the state. Out of these situations, intimate cross-cultural relationships sometimes arose.[2] The affective dimensions of these personal associations are often asserted, but, as Christopher Hilliard has noted, how they informed governance in concrete ways is very rarely specified.[3] This is partially due to the limits of the colonial archive; for, as Amanda Nettelbeck notes, the lack of personal records created by protagonists who appear in the official record restricts the extent to which one can 'gain detailed insight into the private dimensions of such cross-cultural relationships'.[4]

Wilkinson has been identified as an example of how 'close connections between influential persons were not uncommon in nineteenth-century New Zealand', especially in land purchasing.[5] It is possible to evaluate such an assertion because he made a daily record of his work at Shortland and in the wider region in his surviving 1881 diary, which also recorded his social networks and personal relationships. By the end of that year, he had simultaneously cohabited with two Māori partners, Eliza and Raurau, at Parawai, while fathering a child with a third Māori woman, Merea. From 1882, he operated two households, one his Shortland home, the other located at Alexandra (now Pirongia) on confiscated land at the border of the King Country. Following the Waikato War (1863–1864), the Kīngitanga (the Māori King Movement, established to prevent land sales and protect Māori autonomy) had closed this region to Pākehā (European) settlement; in the early 1880s, they were in the first stages of allowing it to be 'opened up'.

Wilkinson's diary and his personal correspondence offer detailed evidence of how affective worlds were laced into the practice of dispossession on one New Zealand frontier. In this chapter, we use his 1881 diary, supplemented by twenty-three letters in te reo Māori (the Māori language) to his Māori wives written during 1882 and 1883, as a means of addressing the relationship between affective practices, structural violence, and dispossession.[6] His daily diary entries are concerned with the everyday: the weather, what he ate, what time he rose and went to bed, and how much time he spent in the field or writing reports. Such mundane information has value, for it brings us close to the quotidian tasks that underpinned colonialism and 'the real-time interactions between officials and their subjects that make up colonial practice', constituted by a set of relationships that cultural anthropologist Danilyn Rutherford has described as 'strange forms of sympathy'.[7] Notwithstanding the complicity of officials in the structural violence that underpinned colonialism, this chapter attempts to show that their relationships with Indigenous people were as often affective as they were strategic; that useful knowledge gained was a by-product, as much as a goal, of such relationships; and that officials were sometimes as open to manipulation as they were able to control those whom they administered.

Colonial Violence and Extractive Economies

George Thomas Wilkinson's early life was shaped by empire. He was born in Berhampore, India, in 1846 to Henry and Catherine, who served with the General Baptist Mission at Odisha. By 1861 the family had returned to England. Apart from the fact that he grew up in a non-conformist household, little is known about Wilkinson before he arrived in New Zealand in 1864 and was sent to survey the confiscated lands in Waikato.[8] While there, Wilkinson volunteered for the final stage of the Waikato Campaign at the Battle of Ōrākau in April 1864, after which he helped survey the town of Alexandra, including farm lots for military settlers, before moving to the Bay of Plenty to assist in the survey of Te Papa, now a suburb of Tauranga. His time there also involved armed skirmishes with local Māori. In 1867, after serving on the east coast in an engineering company, he established a farm near Ōpōtiki.[9] Wilkinson thus spent his twenties engaged in key activities of colonisation: war, surveying, and farming.

In 1881, Wilkinson was in his mid-thirties and had been in government service since at least 1870 as a licensed interpreter to the Thames courts, before being appointed an interpreter for the Thames region under the Native Land Act 1873.[10] In 1875, Native Minister Sir Donald McLean appointed him an assistant land purchase agent with a salary of £500. His first task was to go to the Bay of Plenty and negotiate the purchase of a 6000-acre block of land and 'ascertain what other lands may be offered for sale or lease'.[11] He acted as a Land Purchase Officer for Thames District and Patatere from 1878, in addition to the district north of Auckland already in his charge, at a salary of £800.[12] Two years later, he was a Land Purchase Officer and Native Agent for Hauraki.[13]

The Hauraki district presented an unsettled frontier, particularly as the primary Pākehā interest was in the gold-bearing lands, with the nearby Coromandel fields first opened in 1852, the inland fields on the Hauraki plain at Ōhinemuri in 1875, and Te Aroha in 1880. Based on quartz mining, which required long-term capital investment, the region attracted mainly 'wage labourers working on company mining leases and then settling in the district', effectively swamping the local Māori population.[14] However, although Thames was still a bustling mining town in 1881, gold mining had effectively peaked, and its economic influence was in decline.

A number of iwi (tribes) comprised the Māori population of Hauraki, with Ngāti Maru, Ngāti Tamaterā and Ngāti Paoa dominant iwi, alongside former vassal iwi such as Ngāti Koe and Ngāti Hako. Many Hauraki chiefs had supported the notion of the Kīngitanga, but the subsequent war and land confiscation in Waikato effectively cut them off from King Tāwhiao's remaining base in the King Country. The government was thus able to assert its power, although some chiefs remained obstructive to colonial projects, such as Tukukino of Ngāti Tamaterā, over 'the cession of the Ohinemuri Block to the Government for gold-mining purposes, the telegraph, the road, and the railway'.[15] In his 1881 report, Wilkinson described Ngāti Maru and Ngāti Paoa and parts of Ngāti Tamaterā as 'loyal', although he lamented that Ngāti Hako 'have fully adopted all the laws and doctrines (religious or otherwise) of king Tawhiao', opposing land alienation and invasive infrastructure.[16] The following year, Wilkinson compared his position to a ship compromised by multiple small leaks constantly needing his attention.[17]

Wilkinson's ship sometimes sprang large leaks, too. In 1879, Ngāti Hako shot and wounded a member of a surveying party on the border of their lands. Wilkinson was part of the resultant 'council of war', and designated to accompany the arresting party, although this plan was abandoned once the element of surprise had been lost.[18] The government determined that a Māori-run enquiry might have a better chance of inducing the wanted men to being given up; Wilkinson gave evidence at this enquiry to which Ngāti Hako arrived 'in fighting costume' armed with double-barrelled guns.[19] The men were not handed over and remained at large for three years until captured in dramatic circumstances.[20]

Much of Wilkinson's own work in Hauraki was more mundane, but with significant effects on Māori communities. In particular, he worked on Māori landowners to sell or lease their land to the Crown; once he had a sufficient amount under his control, he would then apply to the Native Land Court—the principal mechanism for extinguishing native title from the 1860s—for a subdivision. Going before the court was an expensive exercise and, as the remaining owners were required to participate in its processes, his tactics often mopped up those still holding out. For example, the Crown had paid advances (including in some cases rations) to many of the owners of the Ōhinemuri Block, but it was unclear whether these were for mining royalties or for the land. In 1880, Wilkinson took the block to court in the face of Māori objections, unethically discussed the case with the judge, and deliberately slowed the process down for several years in order to get more signatures.[21]

With the Te Aroha gold field, Wilkinson used Māori allies to break down the resistance of other owners. As the government became interested in the land, these owners requested a £1000 bonus to ease the sale. He garnered support from several influential chiefs who 'had already tasted the sweets' of revenues from goldfields already opened. Their signing resulted in 'a decided split in the opposition camp, who now reduced their demand for a bonus to £500'. The government decided that 'the bold but necessary stroke of opening the field, whether some of the Natives were willing or not, could be carried out without any real danger'. Māori 'seemed quite taken aback' but having 'found that the opening was accomplished, and their opposition fruitless, they accepted the position, and the following day most of them came in and signed the agreement'.[22]

Wilkinson's many labours are noted in his diary. Telegrams, report and letter writing, maintaining miners'-rights accounts, and paying revenue to Māori were part of his daily work. In addition, he undertook census work for the Native Department, interpreted for visiting officials, and worked with local doctors to arrange smallpox vaccinations in willing Māori communities. While particularly alert to any Māori resistance or obstruction, he also managed cases of European incursions onto Māori reserves and interpreted in court cases where Māori witnesses and defendants were involved.

Wilkinson's diary gives the appearance of a man just 'doing his job' without any personal malice. He seems to have been scrupulous when paying out money to Māori, but the bureaucratic nature of the job, governed by the limits set by his superiors, shaped his relationships with local Māori. For example, he notes in his diary: 'Got telegram from Mr Gill saying that he would not sanction my paying Te Momotu Rangimiria any thing on a/c of her share in Waiharakeke but must get the deed back from Brabant at Tauranga and then get signature.'[23] He also advocated on behalf of Māori. This included writing letters to the government to ensure that earlier promises were kept;[24] but also on personal matters, such as money for a Māori man to purchase a coffin for his wife;[25] and he later protested to the government when legislative changes resulted in a large drop in miners'-right payments to Māori.[26]

Diaries play many roles in people's lives. Wilkinson, though, did not explain why he kept a diary. It was not designed as a form of self-memorial because there is no 'you' or imagined audience, nor was it a companion or friend, for he did not address it as 'my dear diary'.[27] Having worked as a surveyor, where keeping a journal of activities was a routine part of fieldwork, he likely carried this practice into his government career, which is reflected in his writing style. A focus on daily routine written in plain language suggests that he used it as a source for writing monthly progress reports to his superiors. In managing a large district, Wilkinson travelled extensively, covering communities situated along the Waihou River (Waitoki, Hikutaia, Paeroa, Kōmata, and Ōhinemuri) and further afield to Tauranga, Katikati, Te Aroha, Waihī, Coromandel, and Auckland: thus, the diary was an aide to memory. He accounted for days spent in the field (these entries were always marked with a cross), with an emphasis on modes of transport, time taken to get somewhere and at meetings, to ensure that he was fully remunerated for his travelling and other allowances.

In keeping track of time and personal finances, Wilkinson conforms to a 'tradition of self-accounting diarists'.[28] This practice of measuring daily activity and conduct has a long history and was undertaken initially 'within a religious framework of values'.[29] Despite a childhood immersed in religion and missionary service, Wilkinson made few references to God or faith. Although Eliza occasionally attended the nearby Anglican Māori Church,[30] and he paid a subscription to a Wesleyan Church,[31] he does not mention any church attendance on his part. Wilkinson's faith is private, but his diary reveals an intellectual interest in religion: he was open to discussion and debate about spiritualism; one Sunday he read 'Goulbourn's thoughts on personal religion in the afternoon by the parlour fire'; and in December he lent his friend a book on 'Modern Christianity and civilised heathenism and civilised Christianity'.[32] However, he never used the diary to reflect on personal improvement or self-sacrifice in keeping with evangelical requirements of 'introspection, self-control, and self-denial'.[33] Instead, Wilkinson's self-accounting is more secular and practical in approach, providing details of how, in the words of Hilliard, 'Colonisation depended on workers'.[34]

Although rarely introspective or reflective, Wilkinson's diary is full of drama and emotional expression and provided him with an important outlet for coming to terms with job-related and personal stress.[35] Wilkinson was appointed to the Native Department at a time when the state had expanded to cope with a growing settler population in need of land, and, as such, the department focused its efforts on land purchasing. It was reorganised in 1879 to increase efforts in this area, with the land-purchase branch made into a separate sub-department under the control of Richard T. Gill.[36] Over the next decade, the size of the department was further reduced during a period of economic recession. In an environment of retrenchment, the department cut back the numbers of native officers resident in districts, and also reduced the numbers of clerks and interpreters, which substantially increased the workload of those individuals retained.[37] At a distance from the centre of government, resident officials worried about their economic future and were alert to rumours of restructuring or termination, as Wilkinson noted in his diary when 'Mr J. Chase told me privately that he had been requested by John King in a letter to inform me that it was the intention of the Gvt shortly to give my district to Mr Chas. Nelson and I should either be dispensed with or work under him.'[38] Job insecurity and the stresses of an ever-increasing workload are reflected in comments about bodily fragility: illness, fatigue, and headaches were a regular occurrence requiring doses of Holloway's pills. Another source of anxiety was his domestic life, which underwent significant change from May 1881, and these shifts are candidly recorded in his diary. That he used his diary to make a record not only of his work but to also document his relationships offers evidence of the entangled nature of these worlds.[39]

'TANGLED UP': WILKINSON'S CROSS-CULTURAL HOUSEHOLD IN SHORTLAND

In the opening pages of his *Lett's Australasian Diary and Almanac*, the annotated monthly calendar immediately locates Wilkinson within a set of economic and affective relationships, as does the memoranda page on which a few Māori words are listed that all broadly refer to entanglements.[40] While the word list speaks to his interest in the Māori language, an area of expertise by which he gained employment, it also evokes not only his state of mind but also his domestic arrangements: he began the year living with one Māori woman at Shortland, and was later joined by another. At the same time, he was in a relationship with Merea, who resided at Waitoki; and in December 1881, she gave birth to his first child.

Wilkinson's primary relationship was with Eliza (Raiha, also known as Piki). Together since 1868, their partnership appears to have been tender and affectionate.[41] Concerns for Eliza's health and welfare pepper the diary in the first few months of the year, with items purchased for the household to improve the material conditions of domestic labour, including the installation of a colonial oven.[42] Domestic comfort was enhanced by the presence of a live-in Pākehā domestic servant, as well as a woman to do the laundry.[43] They kept an open home, also looking after a number of children in keeping with the principles of *atawhai* (kindness) and *manaakitanga* (generosity), including Hemaima Meremanu's son Makiwi, as well as six-year-old Wairingiringi, the daughter of Eliza's relation Te Okowai.[44] Many others spent time at their home, including Hariata, Raiha Ngāonewhero, and Ngakiore, often staying for days or weeks at a time. The presence of children may have helped Eliza recover from the loss of her daughter, who had died in 1878 at just ten years of age, and whom Wilkinson had adopted and raised as his own. Together they tended her grave at the Parawai Māori Cemetery, where 'Eliza and I pulled some weeds up and I trimmed the willow tree'.[45] They also shared a love of the garden. During the year, they established an orchard and vegetable and flower gardens, and they regularly walked the property together to discuss areas for improvement.[46] This picture of mutual affection and domestic comfort was not to last.

A significant transition in Wilkinson's personal situation was initiated when Eliza left Shortland for Ōhinemuri on 21 May with Wairingiringi and Raiha Ngāonewhero.[47] Three days later, they returned, 'bringing with them Tahipapa and Raurau also two other native women. They stayed at my place.'[48] On 27 May, 'Raurau came into the office in the afternoon and had a confidential talk to me about herself', and while it is not known what they discussed, that night Raurau and Wilkinson shared a bed.[49] From this point, Wilkinson started to regularly note the sleeping arrangements in the household, particularly his own. These were important enough to merit inclusion in his daily entries; it was a key pivot in his life around which public and private worlds were built, and a source of anxiety for him.

It is rare for historians interested in cross-cultural relationships to have access to evidence, however partial, to the terms on which they were entered. From Wilkinson's perspective, it appears Raurau's entry into the household was by mutual agreement between Eliza, Raurau, and their female relations. Invited to Ōhinemuri by Tahipapa and Raurau, Eliza was accompanied by Raiha Ngāonewhero who may have negotiated between the parties. This assertion is supported by the fact that the women stayed with Raurau till the end of the month, leaving only when satisfied that her future was secure. Yet, not all Raurau's relatives were happy, for 'Kingi a relative of Raurau's rode in from Ohinemuri and wanted to take Raurau away by force' on 8 June. Kingi stayed at the house that night, but in the morning 'Raurau got up early and went and hid herself as Kingi had threatened to drag her away'.[50] A week later, Wilkinson heard that 'Kingi and his relations from here have gone to Police Court and laid a complaint about Eliza and I keeping Raurau from being taken by him'.[51]

Raurau's presence in the household was a source of tension. Even if Eliza had given her consent, she was clearly unhappy with the arrangement, something Wilkinson noted: 'Eliza and I do not get on comfortably together now that Raurau is here although she would have her stay.'[52] It is unclear what Eliza had agreed to, but it seems she did not expect it to include sharing Wilkinson's bed, because nearly two months after Raurau arrived, Wilkinson finally gained Eliza's approval, noting in his diary: 'Slept with Raurau last night with Eliza's consent.'[53] Eliza continued to express her disapproval by withdrawing her affections, for which Wilkinson rebuked her. On his arrival in Thames after having spent some time in the field, he was 'cross with Eliza because she did not come to greet me on my arrival and see if I wanted anything'.[54]

Throughout August and September, Eliza and Wilkinson's shared anxiety over Wairingiringi's increasingly fragile health brought them together. They both spent many evenings caring for her, although much of the responsibility fell on Eliza. All attention was focused on the little girl's health, and as she got worse, 'Eliza, Te Okowai, and Raurau all slept in [the] parlour to be with Wairingiringi as we thought from her appearance that she might go off during the night'. Wilkinson wrote often of her discomfort, which he found 'painful to witness', and of the efforts he and Eliza expended in seeking to alleviate her suffering.[55] These sleeping arrangements were a source of frustration for Ngāonewhero who, in early October, 'came home drunk and commenced quarrelling with Eliza outside [the] kitchen window about my not sleeping with Raurau. Eliza got vexed and commenced striking me. I had afterwards to turn Ngaonewhero away from the window and off the verandah several times on account of the row she made shouting and talking.'[56] That night, he comforted Eliza, as 'she was very unsettled'. On the following morning, he 'gave Ngaonewhero a good talking to saying that she had better take Raurau away from my place altogether'. After Wairingiringi's death, Raurau's presence became a touchstone for recrimination, emotional possessiveness, and jealousy on both sides.[57]

During the year, Wilkinson was also engaged in a relationship with Merea, who lived at the settlement of Waitoki. The nature of his work afforded him opportunities to meet women with whom he might cultivate a sexual relationship. But Merea was more than a sexual companion; theirs was a bond built upon mutual affection. They sought each other out: when working near Waitoki, he arranged to meet her at her home, often staying several days at a time, while Merea also took opportunities to join him while he was in the field.[58] When apart, they maintained their relationship through correspondence, their letters to each other carried by mutual friends and associates. On 22 May, he sent her a large package of paper to replenish her supplies. They also engaged in an emotional economy, exchanging tokens of affection. He bought her clothes and food, and sent her money. Merea replied in kind, sending him apples and cherries, as well as a 'new kiekie hat made by herself, also a little fancy flax bag'.[59] Eliza was aware of the relationship. On one occasion, she was 'vexed' by Merea's presence in Thames, wrote Wilkinson, and the couple were 'on bad terms' on account of it.[60] Reflecting his lack of introspection, Wilkinson perceived Merea as the source of Eliza's unhappiness, rather than his own behaviour.

The following month, Wilkinson received a message heralding further domestic upheaval. Merea wrote to him on 20 June, 'in which she informs me she is in the family way'.[61] Although he was attentive to her needs, sending her food and other goods and visiting regularly, the pregnancy caused him anxiety. He sought advice from his friends Henry Dunbar Johnson and Nepean Kenny.[62] At the end of October, he went 'over to Kenny's house after tea and had a long private talk with him relative to my approaching trouble through Merea being in the family way. He offered to write to Mr. Lewis about getting me appointed to some other district.'[63] Two weeks later, Kenny called by his office 'and read his letter to Mr Lewis in which he refers to me'; and not long after this, Wilkinson 'drafted a private letter to US [Under Secretary] Lewis asking for removal from Thames'.[64]

Affective Economies

In 1881, Wilkinson was engaged in relationships that have been categorised in a range of ways by scholars interested in delineating the connections between intimacy and governance, such as Ann Laura Stoler's 'tense and tender ties', and Damon Salesa's 'strategic intimacies', a phrase that has been expanded and further developed by Tony Ballantyne and Amanda Nettelbeck.[65] Much of this scholarly intervention focuses on periods when governance was fragile. Writing specifically of Samoa, Salesa's 'strategic intimacies' refer to moments of uncertain jurisdiction when 'the frontier' was made manifest through individuals and their personal associations, creating a 'domain that was at once tactical and strategic, imperial and intimately local'.[66] Nettelbeck has applied Salesa's notion of strategic intimacies to the work of protectors of Aborigines in South Australia, where she argues that such relationships underpinned 'protection as an early mode of colonial governance'.[67] Ballantyne has considered 1850s southern New Zealand, then distant from the centre of power, and the role of personal associations between colonial officials and elite Māori men in shaping the production of colonial knowledge.[68]

Thames was certainly on the frontier and had competing jurisdictions. Situated between two confiscation zones (Waikato and Bay of Plenty) whose Māori inhabitants were largely anti-government, it was personal associations that extended and consolidated state presence in the region, initially through the efforts of James Mackay. As Civil Commissioner, Mackay was heavily involved in negotiating the opening of Māori land for prospecting and worked closely with local elite, particularly Chief Taipari. Wilkinson followed Mackay's lead, taking care to cultivate a close relationship with Taipari's son, W.H. Taipari.

Were Eliza, Raurau, and Merea simply sources of strategic information?[69] Cross-cultural relationships and marriages were not unusual in colonial New Zealand. Wilkinson, for instance, socialised with a number of cross-cultural couples, including David Stewart and his wife Miriama Te Kiritahanga Rapana, while his close friend Henry Dunbar Johnson, of the Native Department at Wellington, was married to Rawinia Manakau. His plural relationships were unusual, though. It was not unknown for European men to engage in relationships with Māori women for opportunistic reasons and then abandon their Māori family, or to operate two households within Māori and settler worlds simultaneously.[70] Wilkinson differs from both of these situations in that he did not seek to strategically use his relationships to gain access to land, and nor were his relationships a secret, from either the women or the wider community.[71]

Anger and shame, as well as love, circulate between people within affective economies of exchange and obligation.[72] In particular, this cross-cultural household operated within a world of emotional exchange informed and shaped by Māori cultural principles that generated adhesiveness. Certain *tikanga* (protocols) guided the formation and maintenance of relationships, including sharing of goods, money, and food. For instance, Eliza's brother Te Kotuku returned Wilkinson's horse on 5 January 'that I gave him when he returned to his home at Te Matata some time ago'[73]; and 'Hoera Te Mimiha came up to borrow some money off me [and he] promises to pay me with a pig. Walked into town with him. Gave him £1.'[74] Hemaima Meremana presented a 'kit of peaches and large eel for Eliza' on 4 February and Wilkinson gave melons from their garden to Taipari on 13 March, and in each instance an obligation was nurtured. An open home, or showing *manaakitanga* demonstrated care and heightened the status of family and that of wider kin, as did Eliza and Wilkinson's financial and emotional support for the children of Māori family and friends.

Did this Māori affective economy inform Wilkinson's sympathies and public work? In cross-cultural situations, it is vital to take seriously the extent to which the economic and affective world of colonised subjects shaped the terms of engagement, because doing so adds nuance to what Danilyn Rutherford identifies as 'strange sympathies'. The Tribunal's Hauraki Report notes 'that the close and intimate relations developed by James Mackay, George Wilkinson, and Charles Dearle with Hauraki Maori [meaning they all had local Māori wives or partners] were "essential to the success of the Crown's purchasing activity in Hauraki"', although there is nothing to suggest that any knowledge born out of such relationships was used for underhanded purposes.[75] Indeed, the report offers no actual evidence of how Wilkinson's relationships were 'essential' to his work, although of course an archival lacuna does not preclude the possibility. Merea, Wilkinson's lover, was a local Māori, but she lived at Waitoki and they met only occasionally, sometimes for Wilkinson to pass over money due from the government.[76] Although they exchanged gifts, Merea appears to have been relatively independent, holding shares in land blocks and investing in mining operations.[77] Wilkinson was likely of as much advantage to her as she was to him.

Raurau and Eliza belonged to Ngāti Maniapoto, a tribe whose lands were many miles distant, and there is nothing to suggest that they possessed any land interests in Hauraki. The sort of knowledge Wilkinson gleaned from these women was more likely indirectly useful: a continual re-grounding in te reo Māori through daily use; exposure to Māori custom and opinion; and political news on the Kīngitanga and King Country from the women and their many visiting relatives.

Continuing Entanglements: The Shift to Alexandra

In 1882, Wilkinson shifted to Alexandra to take on an expanded role in the Waikato district.[78] His base sat on the Kīngitanga *aukati*, the border between the confiscated Waikato lands and the King Country formally imposed in 1866.[79] From the end of the Waikato War in 1864, the border was a site of tension; the King Country remained outside government control, and unwelcome Pākehā intruders were likely to be killed. In 1881, after sporadic negotiations over many years, King Tāwhiao crossed the border at Alexandra and made peace with W.G. Mair, the Resident Magistrate; this in turn initiated further negotiations between the government and Kīngitanga leaders that saw the 'opening up' of the King Country.[80] Wilkinson's expanded role included encouraging Waikato exiles whose lands had been confiscated to accept small reserves of land, a process historian Vincent O'Malley describes as cynical,[81] and to purchase what land he could in the King Country. In 1882 he had more direct contact with the Native Minister, John Bryce, who needed to negotiate with the principal Ngāti Maniapoto chiefs with rights in the King Country, such as Rewi Maniapoto and Te Wahanui. Wilkinson's personal relationships were now, perhaps, more valuable to the government, and the Native Department had certainly been aware of them. One of the few examples in the archives where use was made of them is an 1879 telegram marked STRICTLY CONFIDENTIAL, from Lewis:

> You will remember when at Cambridge Rewi Maniapoto brought you to my room and told me you were a relative of his for whom he had a great regard, it is desired to obtain in an informal sort of way information as to the present state of the old man's mind as the recent changes of Govt which he will not clearly understand may have had the effect of unsettling him and rendering him somewhat liable to be influenced by interested parties, I have therefore suggested you as one who could pay him friendly visit, ascertain the state of his feelings and assure him of the friendship of the Government and its desire to work cordially with him in promoting the welfare of both races.[82]

Wilkinson's superiors thus recognised the value of these connections when opening up land for settlement, eventually appointing him in August 1882 to a position in the Waikato where he might use his influence with the Ngāti Maniapoto leaders to negotiate the opening of the King Country. Intimate relationships could act as binding forces, but they were also disruptive and troubling. In 1888, Lewis advised Wilkinson that 'if you cannot stay in Alexandra without having to entertain natives it will be necessary to shift your quarters'.[83] That he was asked not to have so many Māori living in his house, when this was not an issue at Shortland, shows the benefits and risks of his links with Ngāti Maniapoto, which were more significant now that he was living in their own district.

It is possible that Wilkinson derived little practical information from his two Ngāti Maniapoto wives, but they gave him a connection to the iwi nevertheless. Wilkinson maintained a flow of letters and telegrams in te reo Māori from Auckland and Alexandra to Eliza and Raurau, then to Eliza after Raurau joined him at Alexandra. The women, particularly Eliza, also corresponded, although these letters are not part of the archive. It was often Eliza and Raurau who gained strategic knowledge from Wilkinson's letters. For example, in November 1882 he wrote:

> Bryce and Tāwhiao have talked but their discussion didn't end well. The reason why their talk wasn't resolved was because Tāwhiao and Wahanui wouldn't agree to Bryce's insistence that Tāwhiao's mana be shifted aside, and for the Queen's mana to be above that of Tāwhiao, but Wahanui was the most obstinate. Their discussions ended yesterday. I was the interpreter. Yesterday Bryce and the others returned to Auckland so it's just me staying to listen and talk, but Bryce may be returning here on Wednesday.[84]

Similarly, in July 1883 he told Eliza about Māori disrupting road-building at Kāwhia, and that 'perhaps Bryce will send me to Kawhia to ask Tāwhiao what he's up to that his people are acting in such a way'.[85] Wilkinson also wanted to be kept informed on news from Hauraki. On 11 March 1883, he wrote enquiring about the *uhunga* for Paraone, saying that they could update him when he got back to see them.[86] Such a ceremony, to remove tapu from the bones of a deceased person, was also an opportunity for people to meet. He possibly wanted to know who was there, who was talking to whom, and what they were discussing.

Despite the political discussion, Wilkinson's letters speak mainly to emotional ties. Signing as Whakatangi, meaning 'to cause to cry', Wilkinson evoked a metaphor for the distress and upheaval caused by his leaving Hauraki; and from his responses to their letters, it is clear that both women are quite open in their feelings. Wilkinson was forced to engage in emotional management, to empathise with the women's anxieties and physical ailments, to oversee domestic crises at a distance, and to provide continued financial support. Often he was responding to issues at home. On 11 March 1883, he said 'I am greatly pleased to hear that you are on good terms with each other now. If you were still having your quarrel, I wouldn't want to return there.'[87]

Wilkinson had no intention of abandoning Eliza, Raurau, or Merea, visiting when he could, but this could also raise concerns.[88] In a letter sent on 4 June, he was waiting for the tribe to assemble and, as it was too far to return, 'I thought I would go and stay at Waitoki which wasn't far away so that I could see my child, so I went there on the Saturday night'.[89] This must have hit a nerve, because in a letter to Eliza a week later, he felt the need to state 'Now hear this, I won't be bringing Merea here to Alexandra.'[90]

When Raurau moved to Alexandra with their daughter in July, this in turn caused tensions. Wilkinson regularly assured Eliza that he was thinking only of her, and 'although I lie on my bed at night, my thoughts still fly out to you, Piki, and to our home'.[91] Raurau's move also annoyed Merea, who 'is angry at me for bringing Raurau here to Alexandra'.[92] Merea was perhaps seeking to ally herself to Eliza, writing a short note asking that they meet,[93] and Wilkinson soon after told Eliza that Merea would be in Shortland, and 'perhaps she will go to your place to see you'.[94] Later in the month, he revealed that he and Raurau were no longer on good terms; 'I think that our living together will be over soon, and maybe Raurau will go back to her people, the Tekau-ma-rua'. His concern was for their daughter, as 'I don't know what will happen with her, Te Wairingiringi, because Raurau and I aren't talking to each other'.[95] In his role as a colonial official, Wilkinson may have gained some advantage in having his three concurrent relationships, but the emotional toll was high.

Conclusion

Disentangling how intimate bonds played a direct role in the practice of statecraft is a difficult task. To date, the strategic elements of these relationships have been stressed over their intimate dimensions, largely because of a reliance on official archives. Turning to private sources, such as we have here, brings intimacy more completely into the picture, even if these are fragmentary and partial perspectives. Wilkinson's diary and letters, for instance, materialise the grounds upon which relationships were forged, cultivated, and maintained, and bring attention to the range and nature of those personal associations. Employment as the state's resident official required building close working relationships with local elites, but he also used the opportunities it provided to develop more intimate bonds with Māori women. In such cross-cultural situations, these personal records are valuable because they illuminate Māori emotional and affective practices that gave shape to his personal and public life. As such, the archival record brings emotion to the fore in assessing the extent to which relationships can be measured as 'strategic'. In Wilkinson's case, his private life and public world of work were deeply entangled, both emotionally and financially, and this is registered in his daily diary entries where public and domestic life are integrated.

Nonetheless, Wilkinson was an agent of the state, and as such he was complicit in the structural violence of colonisation. He was responsible for obtaining thousands of acres of land for the government during his long career, manipulating situations to gain the best deal for his political masters. But he was scrupulous in his financial dealings with Māori, and at times he would advocate on their behalf. Notwithstanding this, he was one of many resident officials active in mid-nineteenth-century New Zealand who cultivated personal associations with local Indigenous leaders and communities that were used to influence Māori, although direct evidence of the use of such strategic relationships is sparse. Clearly, he was able to rationalise the dissonances of his public and private worlds.

While his relationships may be seen as 'strategic' at certain moments, they were also genuinely affectionate and long-lasting. Eliza eventually moved to Alexandra, residing with Raurau and Wilkinson. He and Raurau had four children together. They legally married in 1905. Although never cohabiting with Merea, he maintained a relationship with her, fathering four children in total, all of whom came to live with him and Raurau in later years.[96] To acknowledge the depth and intensity of these intimate and familial bonds over a lifetime, as well as their 'strategic' potential, not only registers the significance of these relationships to those involved, but also generates an account of the colonial past that encompasses its messy and complicated entanglements.

Notes

1. Surveyors in New Zealand have been explored in more depth, but they were mobile colonial agents. We are interested in government employees with responsibility for carrying out state policies and who lived in close proximity to Indigenous communities. For an example, see Cathleen Cahill, *Federal Fathers and Mothers: A Social History of the United States Indian Service, 1869–1933* (Chapel Hill: University of North Carolina Press, 2011).
2. Judith Binney, '"In-Between Lives": Studies From Within a Colonial Society', in *Disputed Histories: Imagining New Zealand's Pasts*, ed. Tony Ballantyne and Brian Moloughney (Dunedin: Otago University Press, 2006), 93–118; Damon I. Salesa, *Racial Crossings: Race, Intermarriage and the Victorian British Empire* (Oxford: Oxford University Press, 2011); Angela Wanhalla, *Matters of the Heart: A History of Interracial Intimacy in New Zealand* (Auckland: Auckland University Press, 2013).
3. Christopher Hilliard, 'Licensed Native Interpreter: The Land Purchaser as Ethnographer in Early-20th-Century New Zealand', *Journal of Pacific History* 45, no. 2 (2010), 230.
4. Amanda Nettelbeck, 'Colonial Protection and the Intimacies of Governance', *History Australia* 14, no. 1 (2017), 34.
5. Waitangi Tribunal, *The Hauraki Report*, vol. 2 (Wellington: Waitangi Tribunal, 2006), 441.
6. G.T. Wilkinson Diary, 1881: G.T. Wilkinson Papers, 98-026, Hocken Collections, Dunedin (hereafter HCD); Letters to Te Piki from Whakatangi, 13 September 1882–16 December 1883: MS-2512, HCD. All translations of the letters are by Lachy Paterson.
7. Danilyn Rutherford, 'Sympathy, State Building and the Experience of Empire', *Cultural Anthropology* 24, no. 1 (2009), 4.
8. 'The Late Mr. G.T. Wilkinson', *Taranaki Herald*, 8 February 1906, 6.

9. Thomas W. Gudgeon, *Reminiscences of the War in New Zealand* (London: Samson Low, Marston and Company, 1879), 145–148; Thomas W. Gudgeon, *The Defenders of New Zealand: Being a Short Biography of Colonists who Distinguished Themselves in Upholding Her Majesty's Supremacy in these Islands* (Auckland: H. Brett, 1887), 197–198.
10. *New Zealand Gazette*, 5 March 1874, 179.
11. Donald McLean to G.T. Wilkinson, 24 February 1875, Folder 1, MS 613, Wilkinson Papers, Auckland Museum, Auckland (hereafter AM).
12. T.W. Lewis to G.T. Wilkinson, 4 June 1878: Folder 1, MS 613, Wilkinson Papers, AM.
13. See Maori Affairs Department, Register of Service, 1863–1885: MA 25/1 Archives New Zealand, Wellington (hereafter ANZW).
14. Waitangi Tribunal, *The Hauraki Report*, vol. 1 (Wellington: Waitangi Tribunal, 2006), xxix.
15. 'Native Disturbance at Ohinemuri', *Appendix to the Journals of the House of Representatives* (hereafter AJHR), G-6, 1879, 5.
16. 'Reports from Officers in Native Districts', AJHR, G-8, 1881, 8.
17. 'Reports from Officers in Native Districts', AJHR, G-1, 1882, 3.
18. *Thames Star*, 2 September 1879, 2.
19. *Thames Advertiser*, 8 September 1879, 3.
20. *Thames Star*, 14 February 1883, 2. For an official account of the 1879 events, see 'Native Disturbance', AJHR, G-6, 1879. For a narrative of the affair, see Philip Hart, *The Daldy McWilliams 'Outrage' of 1879*, Te Aroha Mining District Working papers, No. 16 (Hamilton: University of Waikato, Historical Research Unit, 2016).
21. Tribunal, *Hauraki Report*, vol. 2, 433–435, 464.
22. 'Reports from Officers in Native Districts', AJHR, G-8, 1881, 9–10.
23. 19 January 1881.
24. For example, 5 February 1881.
25. Tribunal, *Hauraki Report*, vol. 2, 424.
26. Tribunal, *Hauraki Report*, vol. 2, 476.
27. Miles Fairburn, *Nearly Out of Heart and Hope: The Puzzle of a Colonial Labourer's Diary* (Auckland: Auckland University Press, 1995), 3.
28. Fairburn, *Nearly Out of Heart and Hope*, 4
29. Fairburn, *Nearly Out of Heart and Hope*, 4.
30. 8 May and 15 May 1881.
31. 11 August 1881.
32. 20 February 1881; 22 May 1881; 18 December 1881.
33. Anna Clark, 'James Hinton and Victorian Individuality: Polygamy and the Sacrifice of the Self', *Victorian Studies* 45, no. 1 (2011), 35–36.
34. Hilliard, 'Licensed Native Interpreter', 229.
35. Fairburn, *Nearly Out of Heart and Hope*, 5.

36. G.V. Butterworth and H.R. Young, *Maori Affairs: Nga Take Maori* (Wellington: GP Books, 1990), 45.
37. Bryce was Native Minister from October 1879 to January 1881; Rolleston served from January 1881 to October 1881, with Bryce reappointed from October 1881 to August 1884.
38. 24 January 1881.
39. His private papers held at Auckland Museum include reference to a private letterbook, but it no longer appears to exist and may have been lost in a fire at his Pirongia office in 1888: Morpeth to Wilkinson, 8 October 1888: Folder 1, MS613, AM.
40. These words were, as recorded by Wilkinson: 'Pa-ti-ti, to splinter; reo tiwarawara, shrill voice; pukikikiki, tangled up; hutetetete, tangled up, curled up; hungenengene (similar).'
41. G.T. Wilkinson to P. Sheridan, Land Purchase Department, 25 September 1896: J1 596 1898/674, ANZW.
42. See, for instance, entries for 15 January; 5 February; 4 April; 1 May 1881. The colonial oven was installed on 15 March 1881.
43. 7 February; 9 February, 10 February, 15 February, 1881.
44. Makiwi and Wairingiringi were remembered by Wilkinson and Raurau in the naming of their children.
45. 15 May 1881; *Thames Advertiser*, 16 January 1878, 2.
46. See, for example, the entries for 16 January; 5 February; and 23 February 1881.
47. 21 May 1881.
48. 24 May 1881.
49. 28 May 1881.
50. 8 and 9 June 1881.
51. 15 June 1881.
52. 18 June 1881.
53. 11 August 1881.
54. 28 October 1881.
55. 30 September 1881.
56. 6 October 1881.
57. See, for example, the entries for 24–31 December 1881.
58. For instance, she joined him at Ōhinemuri on 4 March 1881, and they stayed at Bennett's hotel.
59. See 28 February 1881; 11 April 1881; 13 May 1881; 20 December 1881. He 'Bought 2 silk handkerchiefs for Merea' on 28 January; sent Merea £1 on 2 April 1881, oysters on 20 May, two bundles of fish on 11 July, and many other items, including flour, sugar, soap, a tent, and candles.
60. See entries for 26 and 27 April 1881.
61. 20 June 1881.

62. On 10 September, he posted a 'private letter' to Johnson, and another on 20 October 1881.
63. 31 October 1881.
64. See entries for 14 and 27 November 1881.
65. Ann Laura Stoler, 'Tense and Tender Ties: The Politics of Comparison in North American History and Post (Colonial) Studies', *Journal of American History* 88, no. 3 (2001), 829–865; Damon Salesa, 'Samoa's Half-Castes and Some Frontiers of Comparison', in *Haunted By Empire: Geographies of Intimacy in North American History*, ed. A.L. Stoler (Durham: Duke University Press, 2006), 71–93.
66. Salesa, 'Samoa's Half-Castes', 72.
67. Nettelbeck, 'Colonial Protection', 32.
68. Tony Ballantyne, 'Strategic Intimacies: Knowledge and Colonization in Southern New Zealand', *Journal of New Zealand Studies* 14 (2013), 4–18.
69. Lynn Zastoupil, 'Intimacy and Colonial Knowledge', *Journal of Colonialism and Colonial History* 3, no. 2 (2002), paragraph 11.
70. For a discussion of cases in the Bay of Plenty, see Binney, '"In-Between Lives"'.
71. See discussion of the family in Wanhalla, *Matters of the Heart*.
72. As Sara Ahmed argues, emotions 'do things': 'Affective Economies', *Social Text* 22, no. 4 (2004), 117.
73. 5 January 1881.
74. 28 February 1881.
75. Tribunal, *Hauraki Report*, vol. 2, 837.
76. 25 April 1881.
77. Tribunal, *Hauraki Report*, vol. 2, 441, 476.
78. T.W. Lewis to G.T. Wilkinson, 21 August 1882: Folder 1, MS 613, AM.
79. Vincent O'Malley, *The Great War for New Zealand: Waikato 1800–2000* (Wellington: Bridget Williams Books, 2016), 353.
80. See Carmen Kirkwood, *Tawhiao: King or Prophet?* (Huntly: MAI Systems, 2000), 133–137; Michael Belgrave, *Dancing with the King: The Rise and Fall of the King Country, 1864–1885* (Auckland: Auckland University Press, 2017).
81. O'Malley, *The Great War for New Zealand*, 508.
82. Telegram, T.W. Lewis to Wilkinson, 20 November 1879: Folder 1, MS 613, AM.
83. Telegram, Lewis to Wilkinson, 5 May 1884: Folder 1, MS 613, AM.
84. Wilkinson to Piki and Raurau, 5 November 1882: MS-2512, HCD.
85. Wilkinson to Piki, 5 July 1883: MS-2512, HCD.
86. Wilkinson to Piki and Raurau, 11 March 1883: MS-2152, HCD.
87. Wilkinson to Piki and Raurau, 11 March 1883: MS-2152, HCD.
88. T.W. Lewis to Wilkinson, 21 August 1882: Folder 1, MS 613, AM.

89. Wilkinson to Piki and Raurau, 4 June 1883: MS-2512, HCD.
90. Wilkinson to Piki, 11 June 1883: MS-2152, HCD.
91. Wilkinson to Piki, 29 July 1883: MS-2152, HCD.
92. Wilkinson to Piki, 4 November 1883: MS-2152, HCD.
93. Merea to Piki, 27 October [1883], MS-2512: MS-2152, HCD.
94. Wilkinson to Piki, 18 November 1883: MS-2152, HCD.
95. Wilkinson to Piki, 25 November 1883: MS-2152, HCD.
96. His 1904 and 1906 diaries attest to these relationships. These form part of the G.T. Wilkinson Papers at the Hocken Collections, Dunedin. Although there were eight children in total, Raurau and Merea each lost a child in infancy.

PART III

Economies of Colonial Knowledge

CHAPTER 10

Arctic Circles: Circuits of Sociability, Intimacy, and Imperial Knowledge in Britain and North America, 1818–1828

Annaliese Jacobs

In 1827, a 36-year-old spinster named Jane Griffin was pulled aside by her brother-in-law in a London drawing room. As she noted in her diary, Mr. Simpkinson 'asked if I had succeeded in meeting Captain F. [Franklin] in arctic circles, that being the report, & whether some cape or bay was not

---

Support for this research was generously provided by the Social Sciences Research Council International Dissertation Research Fund, the American Council of Learned Societies, and the Graduate College of the University of Illinois. I am indebted to the archivists and volunteers at the Scott Polar Research Institute, Cambridge; the Derbyshire Record Office, Matlock; the National Maritime Museum, Greenwich, London; the Royal Geographical Society, London; the Hudson Bay Company Archives, Winnipeg; and the Tasmanian Archive and Heritage Office, Hobart. I am grateful to the participants at the Colonial Economies: Intimacy and Violence workshop at the University of Tasmania in November 2016 for their comments on the earlier version of this paper. I am deeply indebted to my advisor, Antoinette Burton, for all her guidance and forbearance. All errors are my own.

A. Jacobs (✉)
University of Tasmania, Hobart, TAS, Australia

© The Author(s) 2018
P. Edmonds, A. Nettelbeck (eds.), *Intimacies of Violence in the Settler Colony*, Cambridge Imperial and Post-Colonial Studies Series, https://doi.org/10.1007/978-3-319-76231-9_10

christened in our name'. The widowed polar explorer John Franklin had just returned from his third Arctic expedition, and had indeed named a 'Cape Griffin' in Jane's honour, and invited her to his house to find it on an oiled paper map. Together with Franklin's sister, Mrs. Booth, and his three-year-old daughter Eleanor, Jane looked at the map and 'saw names of a multitude of other friends—felt very nervous'.[1] Franklin came bearing other gifts. He stopped by Jane's house, 'begging acceptance of reindeer tongues and 3 prs shoes made by native Ind. [Indian] women' for her and her sisters.[2] For his daughter, Franklin brought a cornhusk doll made by a Mohawk woman, dressed in a beaded black wool skirt with beaded black leggings and a pink cotton dress.[3] He gave a raccoon skin (prepared by Dene women at Great Bear Lake) to his fellow Arctic explorer, William Edward Parry, as a wedding gift. Parry had just celebrated his marriage to Isabella Stanley under a silken flag that she sewed for his upcoming expedition to the North Pole, and they spent their honeymoon aboard Parry's ship HMS *Hecla* at Deptford. The raccoon skin ended up as a hearthrug.[4]

Tony Ballantyne has argued that historians need to assemble a full and rich understanding of the British colonial information order 'by identifying places of knowledge production, the role of "knowledgeable groups", changing shape of communication networks and technologies, and debates over the status of particular forms of knowledge'.[5] This chapter seeks to do so by exploring the interlinked economies of exploration, patronage, and marriage in Regency London and Arctic North America. Explorers' gifts of names, artefacts, and specimens were intrinsic to practices of Arctic exploration, scientific sociability, and the circulation of imperial knowledge. Within metropolitan 'Arctic Circles', wives and family members of explorers did not passively receive gifts (often made by Indigenous women) as either trinkets or tribute: they actively circulated and talked about them, together with field correspondence and scientific specimens. In doing so, they both acted as 'gatekeepers' of information within networks of imperial knowledge, and attested to the characters and stability of their long-absent relatives. This chapter draws on the insights of the 'new imperial history', which sees the intimacies produced by colonial encounters as crucial to the formulation of colonial knowledge and as a source of endemic anxiety for both colonial society and authorities.[6] It also understands the home as an imperial site, shaped by a 'permanent impermanence' of mobility and separation, where contests of authority were catalogued and historicised, part of the 'imperial lives' that were prisms of the British empire.[7] It sketches how educated women in the 1820s claimed a gendered authority over information as they helped their absent relatives secure credibility as rational observers, trustworthy travellers, and attached domestic men who were fundamentally unaltered by their experiences in the field. Finally, it examines how both women and men accommodated episodes of frontier violence and intimacy within their homes, families, and futures.

'Endeared to me by affliction': The Traumas of the First Land Arctic Expedition, 1819–1822

Captain Franklin was already famous when he began courting Jane Griffin in 1827, his name synonymous with the British search for the Northwest Passage. In 1817, the Second Secretary of the Admiralty, Sir John Barrow, argued that the search for the Passage would open up new whaling grounds for the British fleet, extend the British fur trade in North America, and forestall Russian incursions into British territory. Over the next decade, ten British naval expeditions attempted the Passage and the North Pole; all of them failed. Franklin led two overland expeditions across the Canadian Shield, while there were five attempts to take deep-draught vessels into Lancaster Sound (three of which were under Parry), one attempt to try the Passage from Bering Strait, and two attempts at the North Pole (one each by Franklin and Parry). While the expeditions had scientific aims and instructions, fundamentally the search was driven by access to natural resources and lucrative markets, and was conditioned by violence, distance, privation, and ignorance.[8]

On European maps, the circumpolar zone was a vast, tempting blankness. A Northwest Passage of trade and exchange already existed, however, as Inuit, Iñupiat, and Chukchi carried on a massive trade in goods and furs from Ostrovnoe in Siberia to the Mackenzie River Delta in what is now the Canadian Northwest Territory, and perhaps beyond.[9] Within this far-flung region and along its periphery, Indigenous geopolitics were destabilised by the fur trade and by introduced diseases. Control over trade, trading partners, routes, settlements, and hunting grounds exacerbated old hostilities and created new ones: between Dene Yellowknife and Slave (Hare) peoples on the Canadian Shield, between Dene and Gwich'in, between Dene and Inuit/Iñupiat groups across Alaska and Northern Canada, and between Iñupiat nations in northern Alaska.[10] On the fringes of this region, European fur companies (the Hudson's Bay Company, the North West Company, and the Russian American Company) vied for influence as they were themselves riven by conflict with each other and with Indigenous communities and middlemen.[11] Both the British and Russian fur trade depended upon mixed-race families, indentured labour, and Indigenous alliances to survive intensely cold winters, long supply chains, and the constant threat of starvation.[12] The territories through which many British and Russian expeditions passed were dangerous and unpredictable, requiring the patronage and support of powerful Indigenous leaders to survive.

It was in this context that John Franklin made his fame, but at a terrible cost. On his 1819–1822 overland expedition, Franklin, Dr. John Richardson, Lieutenants George Back and Robert Hood, seaman John Hepburn, Inuit interpreters Tattanouek ('Augustus') and 'Junius', and seventeen Canadian *voyageurs* ascended the Coppermine River to the 'Polar Sea'. They had the nominal support of the warring fur companies, the Hudson's Bay Company (HBC) and the North West Company (NWC), as well as the patronage of the powerful Dene Yellowknife leader Akaicho, who controlled the territory around Great Slave Lake. As the expedition retreated from the northern coast across the 'Barren Grounds' of the Canadian Shield in September 1821, it disintegrated into chaos as men died from starvation, from exhaustion, or at each other's hands. According to Richardson, one of the *voyageurs*, an Iroquois hunter named Michel Terohaute, murdered two men and deceived Richardson and Hepburn into eating them. When Terohaute later killed Lt Hood, Richardson shot him in the head. Richardson and Hepburn pressed on to Fort Enterprise, where they found Franklin and his companions starving. Hepburn would later recall that 'inarticulate sounds, issuing from the nose like grunts, were their only means of conversation', and Richardson wrote in his *Narrative*, 'the ghastly countenances, dilated eye-balls, and sepulchral voices of Captain Franklin and those with him were more than we could at first bear'.[13] On the brink of death, they were rescued by Yellowknife hunters. Franklin and Richardson saw them as superhuman; Franklin wrote: 'contrasted with our emaciated figures and extreme debility, their frames appeared to us gigantic, and their strength supernatural', while Richardson wrote to his wife: 'these savages, as they have been termed, wept upon beholding the deplorable condition to which we were reduced'.[14] After feeding, bathing, shaving, and nursing the emaciated men over several days (Franklin wrote that they 'fed us as if we had been children; evincing humanity that would have done honour to the most civilized people'), they were taken to Akaitcho's lodge to recover, alongside Akaitcho's niece, 'Greenstockings', who was nursing her infant daughter, whose father was the murdered Lt Robert Hood.[15]

For Franklin, Richardson, and Hepburn, the trauma of Fort Enterprise was transformative, and the basis of both intense religious conviction and fraternal friendship. As Jonathan Lamb has observed, afflictions like scurvy could cause 'despair and joy [to be] blended in a moment of suspense in which privation and pleasure were dilated to fantastic extremes'.[16] Franklin later wrote to his brother of his 'positive happiness from the comforts of religion as in the moments of greatest distress', while Richardson wrote to his wife that his imminent death 'produced a calmness of mind and resignation to His will … that I could not have previously hoped to attain'.[17] Franklin would say that the other men were 'endeared to me by affliction', particularly Richardson, whom he saw as a brother.[18] Indeed, in 1822 they wrote the manuscript of *Journey to the Polar Sea* together in London, where they were joined by Richardson's wife, Mary.[19] Over time, their families intertwined. After Mary's death in 1832, Richardson married Franklin's niece Mary Booth, and their first two sons (both of whom died in infancy) were named John Franklin and Henry Hepburn Richardson.[20] All of them repeatedly referred to their experiences on the Barren Grounds as a time of peace rather than horror; Franklin would often refer to his desire to enjoy the 'meditation and reflection' of Fort Enterprise; and years later, when Franklin took command of HMS *Rainbow* in the Mediterranean, Hepburn wrote to Richardson, 'I trust that He who was his comforter and guide on trackless barren Lands Will be very mindfull of his servant while crossing the Mighty Deep.'[21]

'HE A DISCOVERER, FORSOOTH!': NAVIGATING SCIENTIFIC SOCIABILITY AND POLAR MATRIMONY

There was a radical disjuncture between the profound vulnerability of the field and the glittering social world to which Franklin and his British companions returned, and where they also had to make their fame. The social world of polite science in Regency London thrived on Arctic voyages and on the 'curiosities' and 'lions' they produced. As James Secord, Gillian Russell, Samuel Alberti, and others have demonstrated, the public lectures, dinner parties, soirees, salons, and *conversationes* of the London Season were central to the discussion and diffusion of science.[22] As Russell has observed, the metropolitan gentility were able to 'assimilate and activate' information by 'circulating, talking about, and looking at' the 'curiosities' that explorers brought home.[23] Scientific soirees in the 1820s brought elite men and women together in conversation with celebrated travellers, writers, musicians, artists, and scientists, lending the aristocrats who invited them the ability to claim 'intellectual leadership for the nation'.[24] Historians of science see this exclusive world of scientific sociability as the genesis of the scientific institutions, networks that developed later in the century, which both demarcated the 'amateur' from the 'professional' and restricted (or eliminated) women's participation.[25] The acquaintances of explorers and their families in the 1820s included Maria Graham, Maria Edgeworth, Mary Somerville, Caroline Herschel, and many others. Within these circles, women could enjoy a degree of scientific and literary distinction—so long as they positioned themselves strategically, obtained the sponsorship of a male mentor, and constantly, as Mary Orr has put it, 'dressed [their] learning in the modesty of potential female error'.[26]

During the heyday of Arctic expeditions from 1818 to 1828, these social circles became Arctic circles. Ships bound for the Northwest Passage and the North Pole were equipped and dispatched at the height of the Season, and visiting them became one of its highlights. Franklin wrote to his sister Isabella Cracroft in 1818, 'Deptford has been covered with carriages and the ships with visitors every day since they were in a state to be seen'.[27] Jane Griffin was one of many who minutely inspected the crew's sleeping quarters on John Ross's departing expedition in 1818, while other young women flirted with the officers and watched the Inuit interpreter, Jack Saccheuse, paddling his *qayaq* in the Thames.[28] The visitations gave way to balls aboard the departing ships—in 1824, 320 guests crowded aboard Parry's HMS *Hecla*, beneath rigging hung with lanterns and flags.[29] When the ships and expeditions returned, leftover food was incorporated into dinner parties featuring Arctic delicacies like bison tongue, musk-ox steak, reindeer haunch, and pemmican, or lead-soldered tins of preserved meats opened decorously at the table.[30]

It was easy to put a foot wrong in the search for patronage. Naming geographical features after notable men could give rise to either pleasure or censure. Mary Russell Mitford privately condemned John Ross (who turned his ships around in Lancaster Sound in 1818 after sighting a mirage that he named the 'Croker Mountains' after the Secretary of the Admiralty), writing: 'He a discoverer, forsooth! All that he did was to go about christening rocks, capes, bays, and mountains after all the great men, dead and living, whom he thought to gain by, and then to come home and write a huge quarto about nothing.'[31] Furthermore, most of the Arctic officers had little education, for their late childhood and adolescence had been swallowed up by war. As Parry wrote to his parents in 1820, 'I begin to feel that a life spent at sea since 12 years of age does not qualify one altogether to write such an account as the public expect in print.'[32] Whether at intimate dinner parties, evening soirees and lectures, or private conversations, these were opportunities to fill in the blanks on the 'lion's' education, an opportunity provided by his own efforts to fill in blanks on maps.

In this milieu, Franklin's first wife, Eleanor Porden, wrestled with how to incorporate his Arctic trauma into both their marriage and their respective careers. Eleanor was an independently wealthy poet, who published under her own name with John Murray (who also published all official naval expedition narratives), was a member of the French Academy of Sciences and a frequent visitor to the Royal Society. In 1816, she had written a scientific epic, *The Veils*, which she followed with *The Arctic Expeditions* in 1818.[33] She ran her own salon, called 'The Attic Chest'. As both an author and as a fixture in circles of scientific sociability, she tried to help Franklin navigate these unknown shoals—but frequently found herself running hard up against both the trauma and the intimacies his expedition had wrought. On their return from North America in 1822, Franklin and Richardson eschewed the limelight as they huddled up together in their cramped quarters in Frith Street to write the narrative.[34] Before setting foot on British soil, Franklin wrote to Eleanor that he was dreading the 'disagreeable task' of writing the book.[35] He would later describe it as 'a sad plague', 'irksome', and 'a wearying task', even as Eleanor counselled him 'you write well enough if you would but fancy so, and would write ten times better if you did but like it. You want nothing but what you don't like—practice.'[36] Eleanor sent Franklin invitations to her parties, but he seldom attended them and, when he did, seemed constrained and out of sorts. He told her that while he enjoyed small circles of friends and improving conversation, he objected to insincere 'heterogeneous assemblages where forms and parade abound', where he might be tempted 'to assume individual merit for results ... [due to] the superintending blessing of a Divine Providence'.[37]

Shortly after Eleanor and Franklin were engaged in 1823, he and Richardson retreated to their apartments to write their accounts of the events on the Barren Grounds. Franklin would later write to his aunt, Ann Flinders, that 'the recollection of scenes which had been soothed by time and reflection, so distressed me that I felt quite unequal to correspondence with any of my friends'.[38] Eleanor responded to the long silence—and to the men's preference for each other's company—by writing them each a Valentine's poem in the name of 'Greenstockings' (Akaitcho's niece, and the mother of Robert Hood's child), titled 'The Esquimaux Girl's Lament'.[39] It included the stanzas:

> I through the snow & the Forest would guide thee
> On the ice-covered Lake I would gambol beside thee
> With the thongs of the Reindeer thy buskins would weave
> And dress thy light meal as thou slumber'st at Eve
>
> Nay Frown not! Thou knows't such moments have been,
>   Though cruel as False, thou could'st calmly depart,
> Thy Comrade too truly has pictured the scene
>   And my form—but thine own, it is drawn on my heart!
> Nor think in thy Green Isle some Fair one to wed,
> For in tempest and snow shall my vengeance pursue,
> My bidding at noonday shall darken the air,
> And the rage of my climate shall Follow thee there.

In the poem, Eleanor reckoned with Franklin's indebtedness to the Yellowknives as she imagined the labour of Indigenous women who made snowshoes and clothing for the expedition, alluded to their usefulness as guides and sources of geographical knowledge, and acknowledged their role as sexual partners. She was simultaneously trying to come to grips with Franklin's relationship with Richardson, which she signalled by sending him a duplicate Valentine—in which each man was the other's 'Companion' who also 'pictured the scene and my form'. At times, Eleanor blamed Richardson for Franklin's increasing religious severity and desire for seclusion, but they later became friends; when the Richardsons returned to Edinburgh in June 1823, Eleanor wrote to Franklin that she supposed the separation 'to be the most trying you ever encountered. You have been together so long and in such situations that he must be more than a brother to you.'[40] Ultimately, Eleanor seems to have concluded that as Franklin's future wife, she was one of a constellation of his companions, and that their marriage would always be relational to his other intimacies. She signalled as much on her own body on their wedding day in August 1823: She had her wedding dress embroidered with flowers taken from his narrative and named after Franklin, Richardson, and the dead Robert

Hood: the *Eutoca franklinii, Heuchera richardsonii,* and *Phlox hoodia.*[41] She died of tuberculosis five days after Franklin and Richardson left on their second expedition in February 1825. Months later, over Fort Franklin on Great Bear Lake, Franklin and Richardson unfurled the silken flag that Eleanor had sewn and wrote home to tell their relatives all about it.

'MY LETTERS TO *YOU* I CONSIDER ADDRESSED TO ALL': CORRESPONDENCE AND CREDIBILITY IN ARCTIC CIRCLES

Eleanor Porden Franklin was not alone in her struggle to reconcile frontier intimacies and traumas with domestic life and metropolitan society. Arctic explorers' wives and relatives acted as gatekeepers of information in the 1820s, and helped to establish explorers' trustworthiness and credibility as truthful, reliable, rational men within webs of scientific and imperial knowledge. As the authors of a recent collection have argued, correspondence was a vital media 'by which knowledge was exchanged and the credibility of the author or bearer of the letter was established', and field correspondence was especially important as a means of securing trust at a distance.[42] Explorers' perilous journeys could render them suspect as well as famous, especially when their success depended upon Indigenous intermediaries and vernacular agents. In their absence, relatives could attest to explorers' domesticity and respectability, brandishing letters and presents as evidence of their unchanged character. In doing so, they may have drawn on the role of maritime relatives in the naval, merchant, and fishing fleets, who often possessed both power over absent sailors' legal and financial affairs and also privileged information about their whereabouts and activities.[43] Relatives selectively shared field correspondence, conveying information to their social circles that would not be made public until the expedition narrative was published. Presents, souvenirs, and mementos that explorers sent home were distributed through families' social networks in a ceaseless search for patronage. The traffic went both ways, as family members shared important news and gossip in their own correspondence, sending books, domestic articles (from mittens to marmalade), and—importantly—gossip, to men in the field.

Private letters gave families privileged, early news of the expedition that only the Colonial Office or Admiralty might possess, and were therefore highly valuable in circles that thrived on the curious and unique. Explorers cautiously encouraged this practice. Parry wrote to his parents in 1818 that 'my letters to *you* I consider addressed to all' and urged them to circulate his letters to their friends and family. Correspondence sent via passing whaleships or birch-bark canoes was also a valuable insurance policy, a way to ensure that some version of the expedition's proceedings would circulate amongst friends and patrons.[44] On his third expedition in the winter of 1822–1823, Parry constructed a letter to his parents so that certain pages could be removed and shared with a select circle.[45] On the Second Land Arctic Expedition (1825–1827), Richardson asked Mary to pass along extracts of his letters to all of their family, to Franklin's family, and to his professional contacts (of whom Robert Jameson, Dr. William Hooker, and Mrs. Hooker were among the most important).[46] As a junior officer on the same expedition, Edward Kendall habitually asked his mother and sisters to share his letters, in particular with anyone who might be instrumental in getting him promoted.[47] One letter usually had to suffice for many—especially since, as Kendall reminded his mother, 'Paper is too precious in this part of the world to be wasted.'[48] This contributed to the intimate and privileged nature of the correspondence, reaffirming the importance of domestic ties stretched by time and distance.[49] It also made correspondence highly valuable. The press actively sought explorers' private letters, partly because they were thought to contain the most honest and truthful account of the events of the expedition, and partly because of the sense of intimacy they conveyed.[50] Franklin ordered his officers in 1825 to 'strictly prohibit their friends from publishing their accounts'.[51] Parry wrote to his parents on his second expedition in 1820: 'I *beg and intreat* you that this letter may only be shewn to your own circle of friends—but by no means published in any shape.'[52]

Explorers knew, however, that their letters were not the only accounts of their voyage that their families received. They also saw snippets of intelligence from vernacular and Indigenous sources. Over long winters, rumours about the expeditions circulated through both Yellowknife communities and the HBC's posts, and eventually filtered back to the London office in senior officials' correspondence.[53] Similarly, when whalers 'spoke' to each other in Davis Straits, men swapped stories, letters, parcels, and artefacts to be taken back to Britain—and, if they had it, news about Arctic exploring ships.[54] Even as they relied on vernacular agents, explorers cautioned their families that their intelligence was unreliable. Parry warned his parents in 1818 that the whalers carrying his letter 'may like to tell wonderful stories about us', and that 'every seaman's account of us will be greedily devoured and quickly circulated'.[55] In March 1821, Richardson urged Mary not to believe any of the rumours she might hear from the

HBC, since 'We have already been hemmed in by a nation which we have never seen and attacked by another which has not even heard of us, in short we have been disposed of a thousand different ways ... you are to believe nothing except what you have under my own hand.'[56] In 1825, Kendall cautioned his mother that 'this is the very country of exaggeration ... the most absurd falsehoods are circulated and credited, losing in their passage from fort to fort about as much as a snowball does in running downhill'.[57] After Franklin's first overland expedition, they had good reason to be wary. News of the starvation and cannibalism had preceded the survivors' return in 1822; Eleanor wrote to Franklin that 'it was enough to frighten all your friends'.[58]

Alongside these accounts, specimens and artefacts also made their way back to Britain via explorers' families. Like the expeditions and their officers, these travelling objects depended upon the domestic culture of the fur trade and its mixed-race families. Unions between fur traders and Indigenous or Métis women were ubiquitous in British North America, granting men access to widespread kinship and trading networks, as well as to women's skills and labour.[59] These families were indispensable to overland expeditions. Indigenous guides, translators, and European fur traders were all encouraged to bring their families to expedition forts so the women could make shoes and clothing. Dene women also gathered and prepared faunal specimens for Dr. Richardson. Before they left England in 1825, Franklin wrote to Peter Dease, George Simpson, and several of the chief factors to ask that 'the Indian women [procure] these specimens', because of their experience in dressing furs, adding 'the women know how to stuff them too well to need description from me'.[60] On the same expedition, Kendall later sent an 'Esquimaux woman's fur jacket' to his mother, with instructions to forward it to Dr. Tract at the Liverpool Institution, writing 'He is one of the Astronomical Society to which I hope to belong on my return and it may get me [his vote].'[61]

Most of the letters that family members sent to explorers in the field do not survive. Extracts of some of Mary Anne Kay's letters (copied out by Franklin in 1825–1827), however, give a tantalising glimpse into how Eleanor Porden Franklin's seventeen-year-old niece acted as a 'gatekeeper' of information for her uncle. As she built her own reputation as a young woman of taste, accomplishments, and connections, Mary Anne simultaneously gathered and circulated information for her uncle in the field. Scientists and naval officers visited her at her home in Greenwich and asked her to include excerpts of reviews and accounts of their experiments in her letters, which she combined with summaries of her own reading and notes on public lectures that she attended.[62] She scrupulously reported on the latest news of the Astronomical Society, the Royal Observatory, the court martial of a fellow Arctic explorer, Parry's debut as the Hydrographer of the Navy, and her own recent expedition prospecting for fossils at Folkstone. At Greenwich, she inspected departing exploring ships (including Phillip Parker King's to Australia) and passed judgement on them. She also passed on gossip, telling Franklin in one letter that Parry was trying to get up a new expedition to the North Pole (which she described as 'a six months trip founded in all essential points on a plan of yours laid down I believe in 1819') but the general opinion in Greenwich was that he was too sanguine, not least because 'he is grown enormously fat (of which he had no need) and has suffered a good deal with his head'.[63] Intriguingly, she also asked Franklin to 'give Miss Greenstockings a kiss' for her, flippantly acknowledging (as her aunt had) her uncle's cohabitation with and dependence upon Indigenous women.[64]

When family members circulated correspondence and information, they testified to absent explorers' credibility. They demonstrated to metropolitan social circles that even under duress, explorers' honour and moral integrity remained intact, and therefore their perceptions and observations could be trusted. This was enormously important, for the reason that formed the basis of the explorer's authority was often disordered by disease, by hunger, and by distance, isolation, and dislocation—precisely the kinds of perils that had attended Franklin's 1819–1822 expedition.[65] Yet the explorers' authority—and popularity—also partly derived from the fact that they placed themselves in peril for the sake of science. As Dorinda Outram has neatly put it, their bodily vulnerability was key to the moral economy of the knowledge they produced, as their physical suffering lent authenticity to their testimony about far-off places.[66] When their family members circulated explorers' private letters, they helped them walk this line, even while the men were in the field. Their correspondence could function as testimonials to their safety, competence, and detachment from the world they observed, while it served as valuable evidence of their authentic experiences.[67] This was augmented by the Arctic souvenirs and libraries that were a part of the family home, as sisters and nieces were enjoined to pull down a copy of Samuel Hearne or Alexander McKenzie's travels to compare Franklin and Richardson's progress on their maps— and, of course, show them to others, alongside letters marked with longitude and latitude in lieu of addresses.[68] These letters, with their embedded versions of the narrative yet to come, were valuable precisely because they were personal, presumably confidential, and fundamentally domestic. Amid both the mixed-race society of the forts and the homosocial society of their own chambers, explorers insisted that their compasses pointed resolutely 'home', with all of its grounding moral attachments. In this way, they helped establish the essential connection between truth, credibility, and gentlemanly status that was essential to securing trust in their observations.[69]

In their correspondence, explorers subsumed potential threats of intimacy and violence within both deprecating banter and professed longing for home and 'society'. In their letters from their second overland expedition from 1825–1827, Franklin, Richardson, and Kendall took pains to point out their ample provisions, domestic comforts, and good relationships with the Hudson's Bay Company and the Yellowknives, assuring their families and friends that their minds and bodies were intact.[70] Kendall wrote to his mother and sisters to describe the expedition's ascent up the Canadian river system: 'this hard marching agrees extremely well with me I assure you there is no extra fat on my bones nor any fear of appoplexy'.[71] Richardson wrote to Mary that at every trading post, they had been met 'with the utmost civility and attention', and that the abundance of provisions provided by the HBC meant that 'compared with our last journey this promises to be a party of pleasure'.[72] In one letter, he described how 'all the rank and fashion of Bear Lake' had attended a Christmas ball at Fort Franklin in 1825, 'their raven hair dripping with unguents prepared from the marrow of the rein-deer, and their expanded countenances ornamented with twin rows of ivory teeth gracefully contrasting with their lovely bronze features wheron streaks of lamp black and rudge were harmoniously blended'.[73] Franklin, for his part, characterised 'conversation' in North America to his sister-in-law Sarah Kay as:

> expatiating on travelling either in Canoe or on snowshoes—the arrival, the sending for, or the want of Meat or Fish—the driving of dogs—the appearance or going away of an Indian ... and perhaps the thread of these is stopped by the ... squalling of an unruly child—or the growling and fighting of some ungovernable dogs.[74]

In their private chambers, Franklin and Richardson told their families, they ate home-made pickles and marmalade, wore their home-knitted mittens, drank cherry brandy, swaddled themselves in woollen blankets, and played chess—all, Franklin wrote to Mary Anne Kay, 'so that we have daily mementos of you'.[75] As they assured readers of their longing for the 'Society' they had despised when they were actually at home, they simultaneously reassured their families that frontier domesticity was really defined by nostalgia for home and not by boisterous multi-ethnic families in the fur-trading fort at the edge of a continent.

Conclusion

In order to make their careers—and to survive—Arctic explorers and their families had to navigate the overlapping 'Arctic Circles' of London's scientific soirees and North America's polar regions. Within these circles, similar questions of trustworthiness attended exploration, marriage, friendship, and science, especially given the profound vulnerabilities that polar exploration laid bare. Their wives, families, and friends shored up explorers' reputations by sharing private correspondence, gifts, and specimens—the trinkets and snippets from the edge of the world that testified to their creditability as rational, domestic men. In doing so, families testified that up to this point, on this date, and at this place, the absent men were still whole and unaltered, trustworthy observers of all that they surveyed. As they operated this information economy, polar relatives claimed a tenuous authority over information. As privileged recipients of letters, they might know as much as the Admiralty or Colonial Office about explorers' plans and accomplishments, but they probably never knew the full extent of the traumas and liaisons of the field. As Eleanor Porden Franklin knew very well, any expectations of conjugality and domesticity were always and inherently relative to the relationships forged in the field, from the brother officers 'endeared by affliction' to Indigenous women and men upon whom they depended.

That these stories are legible today is due to the work of explorers' relatives as archivists. Families preserved volumes of correspondence, some of which they compiled privately for family histories, some of which they donated to other biographers, and some of which they kept for themselves but were later donated to polar and maritime institutions.[76] They also kept those artefacts that spoke in some way to traumas and stretched intimacies of the field. The corn-husk doll that Franklin brought home for his three-year-old daughter is one of them, now on loan to the National Maritime Museum in Greenwich.[77] Eleanor Porden's 'Greenstockings' poem, which evoked the faithlessness and abandonment that she, the Dene woman, and their daughters endured, is perhaps the most enigmatic of them all. Franklin and Richardson kept their copies carefully, as did their wives and descendants. More than two decades later, Franklin wrote it down from memory and sent it to his second wife, along with his last letter from HMS *Erebus* on his final, fatal attempt on the Northwest Passage in 1845.[78] His daughter, Eleanor, kept her own copy in Derbyshire, separate from the papers held by her estranged stepmother and cousin, Sophia Cracroft. Sophia's executors provided an excerpt of the *Erebus* version to Franklin's biographer, H.D. Traill, in 1896.[79] The three most important women in Franklin's life—his wife, his daughter, his niece—kept his first wife's powerful evocation of an abandoned Indigenous woman. It might have been simply a curiosity or a remembrance. But it might also have been because it hinted at the myriad vulnerabilities laid bare by environments, distances, violence, and unknown intimacies as a matter of course in British polar exploration.

Notes

1. Quoted in Frances J. Woodward, *Portrait of Jane: A Life of Lady Franklin* (London: Hodder and Stoughton, 1951), 156–158.
2. Woodward, *Portrait of Jane*, 158.
3. Cornhusk doll: Object ID AAA3777, National Maritime Museum Greenwich (hereafter NMM).
4. Ann Parry, *Parry of the Arctic: The Life Story of Admiral Sir Edward Parry, 1790–1855* (London: Chatto & Windus, 1963), 128; Francis Spufford, *I May Be Some Time: Ice and the English Imagination* (London: Faber and Faber, 1996), 96–97.
5. Tony Ballantyne, *Webs of Empire: Locating New Zealand's Colonial Past* (Wellington: Bridget Williams Books, 2012), 187.
6. Ann Laura Stoler, 'Tense and Tender Ties: The Politics of Comparison in North American History and (Post) Colonial Studies', *Journal of American History* 88, no. 3 (December 2001), 829–865; Stoler, *Carnal Knowledge*, 2002; Lynn Zastoupil, 'Intimacy and Colonial Knowledge', *Journal of Colonialism and Colonial History* 3, no. 2 (2002). https://doi.org/10.1353/cch.2002.0053; Tony Ballantyne and Antoinette Burton, eds. *Bodies in Contact: Rethinking Colonial Encounters in World History* (Durham and London: Duke University Press, 2005); Tony Ballantyne and Antoinette Burton, eds. *Moving Subjects: Gender, Mobility and Intimacy in an Age of Global Empire* (Urbana and Chicago: University of Illinois Press, 2009).

7. Antoinette Burton, *Dwelling in the Archive: Women Writing House, Home and History in Late Colonial India* (Oxford: Oxford University Press, 2003); Antoinette Burton, ed. *Archive Stories: Facts, Fictions, and the Writing of History* (Durham and London: Duke University Press, 2005); John Randolph, *The House in the Garden: The Bakunin Family and the Romance of Russian Idealism* (Ithaca: Cornell University Press, 2007); Elizabeth Buettner, *Empire Families: Britons and Late Imperial India* (Oxford: Oxford University Press, 2004), 1, 14; David Lambert and Alan Lester, eds. *Colonial Lives Across the British Empire: Imperial Careering in the Long Nineteenth Century* (Cambridge: Cambridge University Press, 2006), 26; Emma Rothschild, *The Inner Life of Empires: An Eighteenth Century History* (Princeton and Oxford: Princeton University Press, 2011); Desley Deacon, Penny Russell, and Angela Woollacott, eds. *Transnational Lives: Biographies of Global Modernity* (New York: Palgrave Macmillan, 2010); https://doi.org/10.1057/9780230277472; Ann Curthoys and Marilyn Lake, eds. *Connected Worlds: History in Transnational Perspective* (Canberra: ANU E Press, 2005), http://press.anu.edu.au?p=97101

8. Ann Savours, *The Search for the North West Passage* (New York: St Martin's Press, 1999), 39–55; Michael Bravo, 'Geographies of Exploration and Improvement: William Scoresby and Arctic Whaling, 1782–1822,' *Journal of Historical Geography* 32 (2006), 512–538. For appraisals of Barrow as a 'gatekeeper' and promoter of exploration, see Felix Driver, *Geography Militant: Cultures of Exploration and Empire* (Oxford: Blackwell Press, 2001), 31–32; I.S. MacLaren, 'John Barrow's Darling Project (1816–1846)', in *Arctic Exploration in the Nineteenth Century: Discovering the Northwest Passage*, ed. Frederic Regard (London: Pickering and Chatto, 2013), 19–36.

9. John Bockstoce, *Furs and Frontiers in the Far North: The Contest among Native and Foreign Nations for the Bering Strait Fur Trade* (New Haven and London: Yale University Press, 2009).

10. June Helm and Beryl C. Gillespie, 'Dogrib Oral Tradition as History: War and Peace in the 1820s', *Journal of Anthropological Research* 37, no. 1 (Spring 1981), 8–27; Shepard Krech III, 'Disease, Starvation, and Northern Athapaskan Social Organization', *American Ethnologist* 5, no. 4 (November 1978), 710–732; Ernest S. Burch, Jr., *Alliance and Conflict: The World System of the Iñupiaq Eskimos* (Lincoln and London: University of Nebraska Press, 2005).

11. Bockstoce, *Furs and Frontiers*, 115–224; Ilya Vinkovetsky, *Russian America: An Overseas Colony of a Continental Empire* (Oxford and New York: Oxford University Press, 2011), 52–72.

12. Sylvia Van Kirk, *Many Tender Ties: Women in Fur Trade Society, 1670–1870* (Norman, OK: University of Oklahoma Press, 1983); Jennifer S.H. Brown, *Strangers in Blood: Fur Trade Company Families in Indian Country* (Norman, OK: University of Oklahoma Press, 1996); Carolyn Podruchny, *Making the Voyageur World: Travelers and Traders in the North American Fur Trade* (Lincoln: University of Nebraska Press, 2006); Sonja Luehrmann, *Alutiiq Villages Under Russian and US Rule* (Fairbanks: University of Alaska Press, 2008).
13. Joseph Rene Bellot, *Memoirs of Lieutenant Joseph Rene Bellot*. (London: Hurst and Blackett, 1855), 263; John Richardson, 'Dr. Richardson's Narrative', in John Franklin, *Narrative of a Journey to the Shores of the Polar Sea, in the Years 1819–20–21–22*. 3rd ed. (London: John Murray, 1824), 348.
14. Franklin, *Narrative*, 1824, 359; John Richardson to Mary Richardson, April 1822, SPRI MS 1503/4/3.
15. John Franklin to George Back, Fort Enterprise, 21 November 1820: MS 395/70/2 BL, Scott Polar Research Institute, Cambridge (hereafter SPRI).
16. Jonathan Lamb, *Preserving the Self in the South Seas: 1680–1840* (Chicago and London: University of Chicago Press, 2001), 126.
17. John Richardson to Mary Richardson, April 1822: MS 1503/4/3, SPRI.
18. John Franklin to George Back, Fort Enterprise, 15 October 1821: MS 395/70/5, SPRI.
19. John Franklin to John Richardson, 24 October 1822: D3311/53/4, Derbyshire Record Office, Matlock (hereafter DRO).
20. Inscription on a memorial to John Franklin and Henry Hepburn Richardson, eldest and second sons of Dr. John Richardson, c. April 1838: MS 1503/19/21, SPRI.
21. John Hepburn to John Richardson, 20 December 1830: MS 1503/8/11, SPRI.
22. James A. Secord, 'How Scientific Conversation Became Shop Talk', in *Science in the Marketplace: Nineteenth-Century Sites and Experiences*, ed. Aileen Fyfe and Bernard Lightman (Chicago and London: University of Chicago Press, 2007), 23–25; Samuel J.M.M. Alberti, 'Conversaziones and the Experience of Science in Victorian England', *Journal of Victorian Culture* 8, no. 2 (Autumn 2003), 208–230; Gillian Russell, 'An "Entertainment of Oddities": Fashionable Sociability and the Pacific in the 1770s', in *A New Imperial History: Culture, Identity and Modernity in Britain and Empire, 1660–1840*, ed. Kathleen Wilson (Cambridge: Cambridge University Press, 2004), 48–70. See also Anne Secord, 'Botany on a Plate: Pleasure and the Power of Pictures in Promoting Early Nineteenth-Century Scientific Knowledge', *Isis* 93, no. 1 (March 2002), 28–57.

23. G. Russell, 'Entertainment of Oddities', 57.
24. James A. Secord, *Victorian Sensation: The Extraordinary Publication, Reception, and Secret Authorship of Vestiges of the Natural History of Creation* (Chicago and London: University of Chicago Press, 2000), 178–180.
25. Carl Thompson, 'Earthquakes and Petticoats: Maria Graham, Geology, and Early Nineteenth Century "Polite" Science', *Journal of Victorian Culture* 17, no. 3 (September 2012), 329–346; Jim Endersby, *Imperial Nature: Joseph Hooker and the Practices of Victorian Science* (Chicago and London: Chicago University Press, 2008), 1–30, 249–275; Evelleen Richards, 'Redrawing the Boundaries: Darwinian Science and Victorian Women Intellectuals', in *Victorian Science in Context*, ed. Bernard Lightman (Chicago and London: University of Chicago Press, 1997), 119–142.
26. Mary Orr, 'Pursuing Proper Protocol: Sarah Bowdich's Purview of the Sciences of Exploration', *Victorian Studies* 49, no. 2 (Winter 2007), 277–285.
27. H. Traill, *Life of Sir John Franklin, RN* (London: John Murray, 1896), 56.
28. Charlotte Grimston to Harriett Estcourt, 26 March 1818: MS 1145, SPRI.
29. John Franklin to John Richardson, 55 Devonshire Street, 24 April 1824: D3311/53/22, DRO.
30. William Edward Parry to his parents, 2 December 1820: MS 438/26/53, SPRI; Willingham Franklin Rawnsley, *The Life, Diaries, and Correspondence of Jane, Lady Franklin, 1792–1875* (London: E. Macdonald Ltd., 1923), 62; *A Brave Man and His Belongings: Being Some Passages in the Life of Sir John Franklin, R.N., First Discoverer of the Northwest Passage* (London: S. Taylor, 1874), 31; John Franklin to Sarah Kay, Lake Winnipeg, 3 June 1825: D3311/50/12, DRO.
31. Mary Russell Mitford, *The Life of Mary Russell Mitford, as Related in a Selection from Her Letters to Her Friends*, vol. 2, ed. Alfred Guy L'Estrange (London: Richard Bentley, 1870), 68.
32. William Edward Parry to Caleb and Sarah Parry, 2 December 1820: MS 438/26/53, SPRI.
33. For a discussion of Eleanor Porden's Arctic poetry, see Jen Hill, *White Horizon: The Arctic in the Nineteenth Century British Imagination* (Albany, NY: State University of New York Press, 2008), 53–87.
34. John Franklin to John Richardson, 24 October 1822: D3311/53/4, DRO.
35. In Edith Mary Gell, *John Franklin's Bride: Eleanor Anne Porden* (London: John Murray, 1930), 66–71.
36. Gell, *John Franklin's Bride*, 77–82, 86.

37. Gell, *John Franklin's Bride*, 82.
38. Quoted in Janice Cavell, *Tracing the Connected Narrative: Arctic Exploration in British Print Culture, 1818–1860* (Toronto and London: University of Toronto Press, 2008), 101.
39. The poem addressed to Franklin is in D3311/24/7, DRO. The poem addressed to Richardson is in MS1503/5/3, SPRI. As I discuss in the conclusion, the poem was memorised by many members of Franklin's family, and was alternatively called 'From Miss Greenstockings to her faithless admirer'. The original version is published in Gell, *John Franklin's Bride*, 97–98.
40. Gell, *John Franklin's Bride*, 145–149, 172, 279.
41. Correspondence on Eleanor Porden's Wedding Dress, D3311/12, DRO.
42. Innes M. Keighren, Charles W.J. Withers, and Bill Bell, *Travels Into Print: Exploration, Writing and Publishing with John Murray, 1773–1859* (Chicago and London: University of Chicago Press, 2015), 73.
43. Margaret Hunt, 'Women and the Fiscal Imperial State', in *A New Imperial History: Culture, Identity and Modernity in Britain and Empire, 1660–1840*, ed. Kathleen Wilson (Cambridge: Cambridge University Press, 2004), 29–47; Lisa Norling, *Captain Ahab Had a Wife: New England Women and the Whalefishery, 1720–1870* (Chapel Hill and London: University of North Carolina Press, 2000), 142–150; Margarette Lincoln, *Naval Wives and Mistresses* (London: National Maritime Museum, 2011), 50–57.
44. William Edward Parry to Caleb and Sarah Parry, H.M. Ship Alexander, 25 July 1818, Davis's Straits, Lat. 75, 30' North: MS 438/26/22, SPRI. For practices of circulating and reading letters aloud, see Dena Goodman, *Becoming a Woman in the Age of Letters* (Ithaca and London: Cornell University Press, 2009); Nichola Deane, 'Reading Romantic Letters: Charlotte Smith and the Huntingdon', *The Huntingdon Library Quarterly* 66, no. 3/4 (2003), 393–410.
45. W.E. Parry to his parents, H.M. Ship Fury, Island of Igloolik, North East Coast of America, 10 November 1822–3 July 1823: MS 438/26/63, SPRI.
46. John Richardson to Mary Richardson, Bas de la Riviere, Winnipeg, 29 May 1825: MS 1503/6/3, SPRI.
47. E.N. Kendall to Mrs. Kendall, Columbia New York, 15 March 1825; E.N. Kendall to Mrs. M.C. Kendall, Fort Alexander, Bas de la Riviere, the Borders of Lake Winnipeg, 18 June 1825; E.N. Kendall to Mrs. Kendall, Fort Franklin, Great Bear Lake, 18 January 1827: SSC/88/2, Royal Geographical Society, London (hereafter RGS).
48. E.N. Kendall to Mrs. Kendall, Fort Franklin, Great Bear Lake, 18 January 1827: SSC/88/2, RGS. Richardson to his mother, 6 September 1825, in

John McIlraith, *Life of Sir John Richardson* (London: Longman, Green and Co, 1868), 144.
49. For paper-based information systems in the colonial world, and especially their usage by Indigenous peoples, see Tony Ballantyne, 'Paper, Pen and Print: The Transformation of the Kai Tahu Knowledge Order', *Comparative Studies in Society and History* 53, no. 2 (2011), 232–260.
50. Cavell, *Tracing*, 33.
51. John Franklin's instructions to his Officers, 4 March 1825: John Franklin's Letter Book, 26 November 1823–12 May 1825, MS 248/281/1 BJ, SPRI.
52. William Edward Parry to his parents, 5 September 1820, SPRI MS 438/26/49.
53. See Fort Chipewyan Correspondence Books, 1822–26: B.38/1/2-4, Hudson Bay Company Archives, Winnipeg (hereafter HBCA); Robert MacVicar, Journals, Great Slave Lake, 1820–21 and 1822–23: B181/a/3-4, HBCA; Post Journal, Great Slave Lake, 1825–27: B.181/a/6-7, HBCA.
54. See William Scoresby, *An Account of the Arctic Regions, With a History and Description of the Northern Whale Fishery*, vol. 2 (Edinburgh: Archibald Constable and Co, 1820), 521–525.
55. W.E. Parry to his parents 25 July [1818]: MS 438/26/22, SPRI.
56. John Richardson to Mary Richardson, Fort Enterprise, 29 March 1821: MS 1503/4/1, SPRI.
57. Edward Kendall to Mrs. Kendall, Fort Chipewyan, 25 July 1825: SSC/88/2, RGS.
58. Gell, *John Franklin's Bride*, 71–72.
59. Van Kirk, *Many Tender Ties*, 61.
60. John Franklin Letter Book, John Franklin to James Keith, 9 March 1824: MS 248/281/1 BJ, SPRI.
61. E.N. Kendall to Mrs. M.C. Kendall, Fort Alexander, Bas de la Riviere, 18 June 1825: SSC/88/2, RGS.
62. See, for example, 'Extracts from Miss Kay afterwards the wife of Lieut. Kendall—to Captain Franklin' 25 May 1826: MS 248/432/2, SPRI.
63. Partial letter from Mary Anne Kay to John Franklin [17 February 1826]: D3311/30/3, DRO; 'Extracts …', 25 May 1826: MS 248/432/2, SPRI.
64. John Franklin to Mary Ann Kay, William Porden Kay, and Emily Kay, Fort Franklin, 6 February 1826: FRN1/10, NMM.
65. Johannes Fabian, *Out of Our Minds: Reason and Madness in the Exploration of Central Africa* (Berkeley and London: University of California Press, 2000), 180–208; Anne Salmond, *The Trial of the Cannibal Dog: The Remarkable Story of Captain Cook's Encounters in the South Seas* (New Haven: Yale University Press, 2003), xix–xxi; Lamb, *Preserving the Self*, 114–131.

66. Dorinda Outram, 'On Being Perseus: New Knowledge, Dislocation, and Enlightenment Exploration', in *Geography and Enlightenment*, ed. David N. Livingstone and Charles W.J. Withers (Chicago and London: University of Chicago Press, 1999), 281–294.
67. Gillian Beer, 'Travelling the Other Way', in *Cultures of Natural History*, ed. Nicholas Jardine, James Secord, and Emma Spary (Cambridge: Cambridge University Press, 1996), 323.
68. John Franklin to Sarah Kay, Lake Winnipeg, 3 June 1825: D3311/50/12, DRO; John Richardson to his sister Margaret Carruthers, in McIlraith, *Life of Sir John Richardson*, 133.
69. On correspondence as travel writing, and its epistemological importance, see Keighren, Withers, and Bell, *Travels Into Print*, 11–13.
70. John Richardson to Mary Richardson, Fort William, 12 May 1825, MS 1503/6/2, SPRI; John Franklin to Sarah, Kay, Fort Chipewyan, 23 July 1825, D3311/50/14, DRO.
71. Edward Kendall to Mrs. Kendall, Fort Chipewyan, 25 July 1825: SSC/88/2, RGS.
72. John Richardson to Mary Richardson, Fort William, 12 May 1825: MS 1503/6/2, SPRI; John Richardson to Mary Richardson, Fort Chipewyan, 20 July 1825: MS 1503/6/4, SPRI.
73. John to Mary Richardson, Fort Franklin, 6 February 1826: MS 1503/6/8, SPRI.
74. John Franklin to Sarah Kay, Fort Franklin, 12 June 1826: D3311/50/18, DRO.
75. John Franklin to Mary Anne Kay, Fort Franklin, Great Bear Lake, 8 November 1825: FRN/1/9, NMM; George Back to John Back, Great Bear Lake, 19 February 1827: SGB/1/4 RGS.
76. The most significant repositories are in SPRI, DRO, NMM, and the RGS, though there are considerable collections elsewhere in the United Kingdom and Australia.
77. Object ID AAA3777, NMM.
78. 'Miss Greenstockings to her faithless admirer': SJF/7/5, RGS. This version of the poem, in John Franklin's handwriting and in which several stanzas are transposed (as though it was written from memory), is identified as having been sent with Franklin's last letter from the *Erebus*.
79. The transposed stanzas in the RGS poem are replicated in the Traill version. H.D. Traill, *Life of Sir John Franklin, RN* (London: John Murray, 1896), 111–112.

CHAPTER 11

Mrs Milson's Wordlist: Eliza Hamilton Dunlop and the Intimacy of Linguistic Work

Anna Johnston

The poem 'The Aboriginal Mother' was first published in the *Australian* newspaper on 13 December 1838. The author, Eliza Hamilton Dunlop, highlighted settler colonial violence through its subtitle—'from Myall's Creek'—and imagined the perspective of an Aboriginal mother, sole adult survivor of the Myall Creek massacre,[1] speaking to her baby and mourning her dead child and husband, and the broader loss of culture:

> Now who will teach thee, dearest,
> To poise the shield, and speak,
> To wield the *koopin*, or to throw
> The *boommerring*, void of fear;
> To breast the river in its might;
> That mountain tracks to tread?
> The echoes of my homeless heart
> Reply—the dead, the dead![2]

The poem drew upon the court reports published in the *Sydney Monitor* of the trials of eleven stockmen for murder. In addition to an editorial, the

---

A. Johnston (✉)
University of Queensland, St Lucia, QLD, Australia

© The Author(s) 2018
P. Edmonds, A. Nettelbeck (eds.), *Intimacies of Violence in the Settler Colony*, Cambridge Imperial and Post-Colonial Studies Series, https://doi.org/10.1007/978-3-319-76231-9_11

paper published a two-page special supplement on the first trial held on 16 November 1838, and this provided detail that Dunlop used in her poetry.[3] The poem itself was published only four days before the public execution of seven of the perpetrators, and thus the geographical epigraph sufficed to invoke the massacre of about thirty Wirrayaraay people, 'struck down by English steel', and the burning of their bodies 'on the *stockmen's human fire*'.[4] Recently arrived in New South Wales, and having lost a child of her own, Dunlop graphically invoked the 'mother's torture': 'I saw my first-born treasure/lie headless at my feet'.[5]

The challenging colonial frontier in the 1830s contained some settlers who were sympathetic to the complex local circumstances faced by Aboriginal people under colonial conditions. Dunlop's poetic response to the Myall Creek massacre joined other political and affective representations that reveal several crucial issues about intimacy and violence and their representation in the early colonial print culture. First, violence was simultaneously committed, condoned, and critiqued from its initial instance, at least in cases that became public. Second, some colonists sought to publicise violent actions and engage witnesses both proximate to the event, and much further afield, particularly through textual means. Third, nineteenth-century print culture worked alongside the nascent law courts to transmit narratives of colonial violence. In so doing, print culture, legal systems, and religious networks became contextual and embedded sites through which humanitarianism was mediated and circulated, because of progressive interests in reforming both colonised peoples and imperial policy. These were the political and textual 'economies' of humanitarianism in settler colonies: such affective representations sought to move readers to action, to draw attention to the moral complexity of colonisation, and to advance their writers' reputations as witnesses to cultural change.

This chapter situates these testimonies condemning colonial violence in the 1830s alongside the collection of Aboriginal languages, often carried out by the same settler protagonists such as Dunlop and her near neighbour Reverend Lancelot Threlkeld. Both circulated narratives condemning violence and evidence of various local Aboriginal languages within overlapping legal, scientific, and literary realms, as part of early humanitarian activism in the Australian colonies.[6] Dunlop repurposed legal testimony in poetic form to bring attention to the plight of Indigenous peoples violently displaced by colonial expansion. Threlkeld used evangelical print circuits and missionary advocates to draw attention to colonial conditions. Both positioned their colonial work within global circuits of empire and humanitarianism. Here colonial missionary and humanitarian archives provide important antecedents for contemporary debates.

Humanitarian Discourses and Colonial Narratives

Humanitarian discourses have received increasing attention since the 1980s, as scholars seek to understand better the precursors to human rights movements and to account for major shifts in the relationship between metropolitan political actors and the distant others who became the target of philanthropic aid and attention.[7] The 'settler revolution' of the nineteenth century holds vital clues, for in the settler colonies the Anglophone world experimented with foundational terms for modern society—crucial ideas about the individual, society, the rule of law, race, sovereignty, and culture—and the complex suite of rights and responsibilities that underpin contemporary global formations.[8] James Belich's *Replenishing the Earth* (2009) emphasises exponential economic growth and mass migration in his advocacy for 'settlerism'. Yet questions about culture (which are largely absent from Belich's study) provide rich avenues for rethinking settler colonialism, considering the way that Indigenous cultures were simultaneously the subject of serious study and often violent administration by ambitious empires.[9] The mutually imbricated relationship between colonial expansion and modern knowledge production is generally acknowledged, but under-theorised and under-explored.[10] Alan Lester and Fae Dussart argue that settler colonies 'were the sites where the violence of colonialism was most integral to British life'.[11] British settlers were personally and profoundly implicated in conquest and dispossession, and in humanitarian amelioration. Settlers were also involved in either denying or preserving Indigenous culture and knowledge systems, given the intimacies of the colonial frontier.

Distinctive new forms of narrative provide insight into that duality in settler cultures. Thomas Laqueur emphasises the importance of studying the history and sociology of narrative forms, noting that humanitarian narratives from the late eighteenth century enabled a new question to be posed: 'Under what conditions can we speak of other individuals so as to care for them?'[12] Stefan-Ludwig Hoffmann notes that historians of genocide, refugees, nationalism, slavery, and/or humanitarianism and those in the comparatively new field of human rights history rarely overlap in practice or citation, and that this must change.[13] He calls for a focus on the long nineteenth century in human rights history, in order to temper claims for novelty in late twentieth-century activism and international law. So, too, we should insist on close attention to the cultural sphere to accompany fine-grained historical analyses of violence and conquest, in order to better understand the complexities of colonialism. While not underestimating the capacity of literature, arts, and music to support imperial expansion—jingoism thrives in popular forms[14]—it is also the case that cultural fields often recorded alternative visions of empire and colonial relations, and sought to bring about alternative modes of feeling and witnessing in their audiences. In this, the novel as a literary genre has been privileged, but both poetry and philological study were important forms of cross-cultural engagement, especially from the late eighteenth century onwards. These are different intimate 'economies' to those on plantations, mission stations, or pastoral holdings, but they are nonetheless productive and revealing sites of the intellectual history and political history of colonialism.

Romantic attitudes towards non-European others were reciprocally energised by the abolitionist movement, and poetry was an important genre through which progressive Europeans represented Indigenous cultures and sought to bring the reader into empathetic engagement.[15] As Tim Fulford argues of the central place of (imagined) Native Americans in British literature, exploration and empire gave rise to new forms of representation that have been retrospectively labelled as Romanticism, in which Indigenous peoples and cultures appear regularly as a foil to modernising Europeans.[16] Poetic attention to language and verisimilitude in Romantic poetry ensured that comparative philology (proto-linguistic study) was central. This was indubitably so in metropolitan literary circles; in colonial contexts, such writers found new source material and literary opportunities. They were also able to witness the reception of their work by colonial audiences (whose local experience often stood in opposition to the armchair philosophising of most Romantic writers and readers). In so doing, these settler artists and intellectuals engaged in important cross-cultural experiments in knowledge production and exchange. These were local and global in scale, and benefitted from the constant traffic of ideas, personnel, and artefacts around the routes opened up by empire.[17]

Poetry and Politics: Eliza Hamilton Dunlop's Colonial Career

Dunlop was a child of empire, born in Ireland to an Ulster Scots Protestant family. Her father Solomon was appointed advocate of the Supreme Court in Calcutta, India, in 1796, the year of his daughter's birth and his wife's death. Dunlop was brought up by her grandmother while her two older brothers accompanied their father to India, where Solomon was a barrister-at-law and a member of the Asiatic Society. She had an indulged childhood back in County Armagh, with access to her father's library and study. Dunlop described herself as possessing an 'early spirit of research', and she devoured astronomy and geography. Writing on her first trip in India in 1820, she recalled her childhood reading in ecstatic terms: she had read and re-read E. and J. Bruce's *An Introduction to Geography and Astronomy*, the voyage accounts of Anson, La Perouse, and Cook, the *Annual Register*, and the *Encyclopaedia* by the time she was twelve.[18] This access to education and a precocious intellect underpinned her literary ambitions and capacity for linguistic study. Only lightly supervised after her grandmother's death, Dunlop made an early marriage at age sixteen to the poet and astronomer James Sylvius Law, and they had two children.[19] By 1820, Dunlop was publishing articles and poems in small magazines, and in the same year she left to visit her family in India. On arrival, she discovered that during her voyage her father had died. She also found that she had two Anglo-Indian half-sisters whom her brothers did not acknowledge. Shortly afterwards, she returned to Ireland with some inheritance to support her independence. One year later, at age twenty-six, she married her friend David Dunlop, with whom she later had five children. Both Eliza and David Dunlop were active in local politics in Coleraine, which saw considerable upheaval during this period as the local Corporation was challenged by members of the Irish Society, who eventually got the Protestant reformer and London alderman William Copeland elected in 1831.[20] The Dunlops were closely linked to these Whiggish Protestant politicians, through whom Dunlop sought to get David a position in London; but by 1837 their capital and their connections were nearly exhausted, and the couple made a swift decision to emigrate to New South Wales.

The Dunlops arrived in Port Jackson in early 1838. Dunlop's social connections included the Irish-born physician and constitutional reformer Sir John Jamison and Lady Gipps, wife of the governor, Sir George Gipps;

and the couple were also in regular correspondence with Roger Therry, the Irish barrister who would later become a judge on the supreme court of New South Wales.[21] Gipps received David's credentials and appointed him a salaried police magistrate in Penrith. The Dunlops had arrived only weeks after the 'Australia Day' massacre of 1838, a punitive expedition of mounted police led by Major Nunn to suppress Kamilaroi resistance on the northwest frontier, in which over forty Aboriginal people were killed, and they lived in Sydney during the trials and execution of the Myall Creek perpetrators.[22] This abrupt introduction to the vicissitudes of settler colonialism and cross-cultural violence clearly influenced Dunlop's literary work and prompted her interest in Aboriginal culture.

Not only was Dunlop confronted by the evidence printed in the colonial newspapers about Myall Creek soon after she arrived, but she was taken aback by the response to her poem 'The Aboriginal Mother'. A barrage of criticism—numerous highly critical letters, supported by editorial comment in the papers—condemned her poem's content, ideology, and form.[23] When the poem was (widely) republished in 1841, the epigraph changed to: '"Only one female and her child got away from us." Evidence before the Supreme Court.'[24] Dunlop made clear here the movement of information between legal and poetic realms, and emphasised the factual evidence that underpinned her poetic testimony. The same year, Dunlop's poem was set to music by the recently arrived musician Isaac Nathan and performed by his daughter Rosetta.[25] In an extensive review of the concert, the *Sydney Gazette* praised the performances of many, declaring of Rosetta's performance: 'We were in spite of ourselves affected even to tears, and most of our neighbours from a similar state, were prevented observing our weakness.'[26] The reviewer in the *Sydney Herald* pointedly critiqued the 'misplaced' emotions attributed to the Aboriginal mother, and recommended disconnecting the words 'from their present black heroine—fancy her any one else, and a treat awaits you'. The words ascribed to the Aboriginal woman were 'pathetic, and display much poetic feeling', but they were more likely those of 'a North American Indian, but which a very slight acquaintance with the natives of this colony would enable any one to say never issued from the mouth of the woman who escaped from the New England massacre'.[27] Regardless, the reviewer was confident that the song would become a favourite, especially among liberal audiences in Britain. A number of negative letters from readers ensued.[28]

Dunlop did not resile from her poem's affective representation of an Aboriginal woman. Defiantly standing against the local opinion of '*Supers* and *Stock*-men', she claimed that the poem 'had its origin in the hope of awaking the sympathies of the English nation for a people whom it is averred, are rendered desperate and revengeful by continued acts of outrage'.[29] Here Dunlop explicitly linked politics and sympathy in her advocacy for recognising Aboriginal suffering and humanity. She noted that the central critique was that it was an anomaly to attribute 'the sweetest emotions of the heart—the feelings of mother and wife to an untutored savage—or moral courage to a wild denizen of nature's solitudes'. She refuted this entirely, citing both the Bible and an account of Aboriginal mourning practices by William Romaine Govett, who had witnessed women lamenting by graves.[30] She concluded with a damning indictment of those 'old hands licensed to cry havock beyond the boundaries'—settler elites who sought to influence imperial policy and opinion—and particularly the press:

> The author of the Aboriginal Mother did hope, that, even in Australia, the time was past, when the public press would lend its countenance to debase the native character, or support an attempt to shade with ridicule, ties stronger than death, which bind the heart of woman, be she Christian or savage.[31]

Unabashed, Dunlop went on to collaborate further with Isaac Nathan on new songs with Aboriginal themes, and continued to publish her own poetry, aided by her growing experience with Aboriginal people and their culture.[32]

Blanket Economies and Linguistic Labour

After a brief and intensely political period in Penrith, David Dunlop was appointed Police Magistrate and Aboriginal Protector at Wollombi. From 1839 to 1846, this new posting placed the Dunlops in the heart of contested land on the New South Wales colonial frontier. Located eighty kilometres inland from the coastal port and penal settlement at Newcastle, the upper Hunter River valley town of Wollombi was a traditional meeting place for the Wonaruah, Darkinyung, and Awabakal people, and its landscape remains rich with archaeological significance and spiritual meaning.[33] It was also linked to the region by the convict-built Great North Road, and David Dunlop's role as Police Magistrate ensured that their home 'Mulla Villa' was a clearing house for travellers and information. From these personal connections, Dunlop sought to learn about and record Indigenous language and cultural knowledge from local and visiting Aboriginal people, and from settlers with experience and interest.

The Dunlops were both keenly interested in Aboriginal language and culture and the plight of communities undergoing rapid and often violent change. Dunlop's knowledge of the colonial courts was heightened by her marriage to an agent of the colonial law. David constantly petitioned the governor for blankets for local Aboriginal people during the early 1840s. Blankets were a key resource in colonial contact zones: fostered by Governor Macquarie's annual feast and distribution, blankets had come to assume material and symbolic importance for Aboriginal people.[34] By the late 1830s, they had become a key mechanism for establishing statistical information for governments both local and imperial; they were central to census-taking and identifying local Aboriginal people. Experienced colonial operators pointed out that this was an imprecise measure—some years Aborigines did not turn up to collect blankets because of conflict, geographical, climatic, or supply variations—but, as Bob Reece suggests, blanket returns provided the only statistical information available about population trends at the local level, beyond anecdote.[35] Governor Gipps, however, sought to implement both budgetary prudence and an impetus for Aborigines to engage in the colonial economy by limiting blanket distribution from 1841. The effects on colonial relations and Aboriginal mortality were deleterious.[36] David Dunlop, having petitioned Gipps consistently, condemned the 'paltry saving', given the benefit the blankets brought to infants and mothers.[37] He wrote passionately about the function of blankets 'as a recognised tie between the ruler and the ruled'. They provided 'no sufficient recompense' for the loss of Aboriginal land, trees, and possums, but Aboriginal people 'accepted [them] from want'.[38] These kinds of transactions—non-financial but practical and freighted with material and symbolic value—are key indicators of the highly localised settler colonial economies and governance that collectively underpinned the spread of colonialism.

The gendered nature of elite colonial life meant that poetry and language study, rather than petitioning the governor, formed the basis of Eliza Dunlop's activist work with and on behalf of Aboriginal people.[39] Dunlop was acquainted with Lancelot Threlkeld, who lived less than eighty kilometres to the east at Lake Macquarie Mission, another site from which individual settlers sought to ameliorate colonial violence by providing alternative moral and material economies in which displaced Aboriginal people could engage.[40] Niel Gunson suggests that Dunlop was more closely engaged with Aborigines in the Hunter region than other interested settlers such as Threlkeld and Robert Dawson (Chief Agent of the Australian Agricultural Company at Port Stephens, 1826–1828), and equally involved with learning from elders about traditional knowledge.[41] Threlkeld had collected language from 1825, eventually building up sufficient material to publish *A Key to the Structure of the Aboriginal Language* (1850); later posthumously compiled and published by John Fraser, alongside Threlkeld's translations of Christian prayers and gospel texts, as *An Australian Language as Spoken by the Awabakal* (1892).[42] Gunson suggests that Dunlop's gender limited her capacity to contribute directly to Aboriginal affairs, yet the literary sphere clearly provided her with a voice to argue for humanitarian interests, particularly in relation to women. Her writing was supported by figures such as Threlkeld, who reprinted her poetry in his serialised *Reminiscences of the Aborigines of New South Wales* (1854).[43] Poetry was a socially acceptable form in which to mobilise feminine capacities 'for sympathetic identification to a relatively new category of social other, the Aborigine'.[44]

Dunlop's linguistic work did not fall so neatly within mid-century gendered norms, and it remains less well known than her poetry. Dunlop contributed an important Wollombi wordlist and transcribed Aboriginal songs, although few other sources remain of her ethnographic collection. Like many women's archives, Dunlop's papers are dispersed throughout family holdings, disaggregated and only partially deposited and identified. What has survived is known as 'Mrs Milson's Wordlist', now held in the Mitchell Library. It is part of a collection put together during the production of a celebratory biography of the prominent pastoralist James Milson.[45] (The Dunlops' daughter Rachel married into the Milson family; Rachel's continuation of her mother's work and curation of her papers ensured Dunlop's legacy.) What became known as 'Mrs Milson's Wordlist' is in fact Dunlop's linguistic work.

Colonial linguistic texts bear unmistakable traces of imperial ideas and colonial practice. Rachael Gilmour demonstrates how eighteenth- and early-nineteenth-century colonial linguistics, like other Western disciplines producing knowledge of people and culture, were imbricated with colonialism; founded upon practices of comparison, constructions of difference, and claims of scientific objectivity that were 'bound up with power relations enabled by, and enacted in, colonialism on a global scale'.[46] Linguistic representations were influential forms of colonial discourse, rendering colonial subjects intelligible by providing crucial information:

about the maintenance of colonial stability, the articulation and negotiation of colonial identities, the taxonomic classification and effective control of colonial subjects, [and] the capabilities of non-western peoples for spiritual, cultural, moral, and economic amelioration'.[47]

In broadly Foucauldian terms, then, we can see linguistics yoked with ethnography—both proto-anthropological forms of knowledge—as foundational in forming Western ideas about Europe's others.

Reading for these tropes in both the explicative material and the linguistic data proves instructive of the 'colonial situations' in which missionaries, poets, and Aborigines, for example, exchanged information about different languages.[48] Language collection shows us the intimate and entangled relationships that existed on the colonial frontier. Names for body parts are a standard feature of early wordlists, and the intricate details of these were generated by the knowledge seeker and their informants working in physical proximity, touching each other's bodies and fumbling towards a shared understanding of language and ideas. Dunlop's collection is distinctive because her vocabularies were accompanied by both transcripts of Aboriginal songs, and 'versifying' of Indigenous poetic or lyric forms.

The conditions of production of grammars, word lists, and language manuals are crucial, as are the ways in which they were received by contemporary readers and circulated through surprisingly diffuse reading communities. As Johannes Fabian suggests, perhaps the most interesting outcome of reading such texts is the ability to identify the ways in which certain issues or kinds of experience could 'pass from one discourse into another—from, say, religion into politics'.[49] Robert Dixon analyses this movement from one discursive regime to another by suggesting that texts circulate in 'domains of practice' that specify 'the different regions or economies within which representations circulate and have meanings'. Linguistic texts, for example, may originate in the domain of science, literature, or religion, but they take on considerable agency in the practice of colonial governance (especially the law). As Dixon argues, domains may be related or overlap, 'but they are certainly not one and the same thing, and an individual text needs to be theorised as participating in various ways and at various times in … different economies'.[50] With this in mind, it is useful to pay particular attention to the material production of the colonial linguistic texts, and the ways they respond both to local conditions of cross-cultural exchange and global currents of ideas and ideologies which swept through Wollombi on the way to London and on the way back.

Contemporary linguists find in the Wollombi wordlist evidence of both distinctive language groups and the overlapping nature of language families.[51] Yet these texts also provide documentary evidence of cross-cultural intimacy and exchange. The Wollombi wordlist is quite different to those early lists collected by Threlkeld only eighty kilometres east; that is, different in the nature of the words sought and recorded. Because of Threlkeld's involvement in the colonial courts and his desire to publicise cross-cultural violence, his wordlists often revolve around terms of violence and conflict. By far the largest set of examples in Threlkeld's *An Australian Grammar* (1835) revolve around being struck or speared: at first, these are mostly to do with spearing fish and shooting birds, but the examples become much less benign with a five-page section on being beaten or beating someone else. There is also a related section about permitting, compelling, or causing people to die, being left to die, or killing. As a poet, trained to hear and transcribe cadence and dialect, Dunlop's language collection is both meticulous and provisional. Her notes on her work make clear the precision of the process:

> The flights of the lyric Poets are marvellously short perhaps the beauty of sentiment supplies the apparent deficiency—if not, repetition must—for all the aboriginal songs I have heard are frequently repeated, I am told by Mr Somerville who sings all these songs in concert with the Blacks that they are very difficult to be translated.
>
> N.B. I find I have frequently written Qui and Quia for <u>Gni</u> & <u>gnia</u>. In each poem the resemblance in the original between q and g ... I have corrected some, others remain as when written.[52]

Like most early language collectors, Dunlop had no formal linguistic training, yet her literary interests gave her particular skills.

The Wollombi wordlist is a relatively short three-page source.[53] It begins with two lists of female and male names, which may reflect the informants with whom Dunlop conversed. Its careful delineation of gender from the outset suggests that Dunlop became aware of different kinds of knowledge that she could gain from different interlocutors. Animal names are next in the list (opossum, mullet, squirrel, wild duck, bandicoot), including some careful distinctions between kangaroo, black kangaroo, wallaroo, and wallaby. There is some vocabulary about catching or spearing, but more about food collection. Words for plants (Warratan—the gigantic lily) or phrases for collecting particular things continue: 'give me the tomahawk', 'cut me some bark', 'get me some honey', 'we must go long way', 'Where are we going to camp', 'Cooleman, a hollow dish cut off the apple tree', or 'I will give you bread'. These kinds of terms suggest the practices of cross-cultural exchange: local travels with Aboriginal women, collecting food, naming the items and the means of subsistence. These are the intimate spaces and experiences in which language learning took place: Dunlop moving amidst Aboriginal women and sharing their daily pursuits and domestic economies. These are suddenly interrupted on page three with a phrase in bold, underlined script transcribed as: 'Do not be angry; or, we do not wish to fight.' This latter, she noted, was 'of the Liverpool and Wollombi tribes'. Dunlop's notes record that some terms are linked to the 'Northwest Cumeleroy Tribe'. Repeated terms in the wordlist suggest that Dunlop may have asked different individuals the same question, triangulating her data and getting more precise in her orthography (thus three different recordings of 'honey': coutiong; couyon; coutiyon). It reveals too that she recognised the diversity of contiguous language groups and the multilingual skills of her informants. This is significant evidence of Dunlop's acuity, for it had taken Threlkeld over a decade of research to acknowledge that the particular language he was collecting was neither a pan-Aboriginal national language nor merely a local dialect.

Indeed, Dunlop retrospectively created a comparative table of 'Different languages spoken in seven of the upper districts', delineating the terms for water, fire, sun, and moon across these seven. This later linguistic work follows 'Murree gwalda or Black's Language of Comileroi', a much more detailed three-page vocabulary and phrase list than the Wollombi wordlist.[54] Dunlop's table describes the district naming system she is working from, and reflects upon its source: an 1839 'Question and Answer between Mr Somerville, Mr Cox, and the Tribes'. That meeting was most likely between Morris Townshend Somerville (a Hunter landowner who had been employed as an overseer in the nearby Wallis Plains since 1828), William Cox, junior (a pastoralist with stations in Muswellbrook and Warialda, very close to the site of the Myall Creek massacre), Dunlop, and Boni (a senior man in the Wollombi clan of the Darkinyung people), perhaps also with visiting Aboriginal people, and must have taken place at the very beginning of the Dunlops' Wollombi posting. The 'district' terms Dunlop records are nascent and imprecise, but they mostly bear a phonetic relationship to the language groups that are now listed under the designated AIATSIS category 'Gamilaraay/Gamilaroi/Kamilaroi language (D23) (NSW SH55-12)'.[55] The points to be made here are, first, the various and improvisational ways that Europeans attempted to categorise Aboriginal languages and, second, the effort made by curious and engaged interlocutors such as Dunlop to begin to understand Indigenous social, cultural, and linguistic knowledge systems and to render these in forms accessible to Anglophone audiences. In these forms, colonial Indigenous knowledges could be incorporated in transnational, Empire-wide, intellectual economies and literary contexts.

Conclusion: Poetry, Linguistics, and Settler Colonialism

Eliza Dunlop's language lists informed linguistic, ethnographic, and poetic forms of knowledge transfer and poetic creation. Hovering eaglehawks had featured in some of the testimony about the Myall Creek massacre site, and Dunlop's keen intellect and poetic eye quickly made a connection to the importance of the bird: the eaglehawk is central to the Awabakal nation, for instance. Her personal version of the song 'The Eagle Chief'—libretto by Dunlop and music by Nathan (1842)—recorded a local word, 'Bibiga', as the 'name given to the Falcon-Hawk by the Tribe of the Wollombi. The bird is of snow-white plumage it is a noble looking, strong, and bold bird'.[56] Her published note, which preceded the music score, explained that she had learnt that some senior men wore 'a piece of crystal' carried in a possum-skin girdle that women were forbidden to see, and that she herself had had to abide by the dictum of 'the Wollombi Chief', despite her curiosity. Boni was named by Dunlop as her advisor in her manuscript poetry collection, where she quoted his description of the sacred stones as like 'one bit of the sun's eye'. Her account of Boni's refusal—'who not refusing absolutely yet evaded compliance, by sundry "wreathed smiles" and mysterious sentences, implying a secret and indefinable affinity between "Ladies' eyes" and *"bad luck* belong it"'—suggests a relationship of considerable mutual respect. Dunlop links this knowledge protection to 'hibernian' (that is, Irish) traditions and declares that 'that single phrase comprised a host of argument quite powerful in deterring me from any further effort to obtain view of the magic gem, which is I believe either a symbol of right to govern; or an object of reverence, as being to the privileged holder, a mean of communication with a great mysterious power whose anger they dread'.[57] When published in the newspaper, the *Sydney Herald* condemned the cultural anachronism of sacred stones being brandished in a public ceremony, while the *Australian* instead pointed to 'Mrs. Dunlop's well written and interesting note, as published on the title-page of the "Eagle Chief" as a significant contribution to understanding Aboriginal culture'.[58] Dunlop's representation of what Deborah Bird Rose calls the 'gendered geography' created by men's and women's Dreamings is incomplete and partial, yet she makes intuitive sense of it and considers this information worth communicating to her readers.[59] The published version of this note is brief, but its inclusion was important in demonstrating Dunlop's interest in and respect for cross-cultural knowledge and custom, including her respect for secret, sacred knowledge practices, unlike her contemporary critic in the *Sydney Morning Herald* who, in order to debunk Dunlop's poetry, explicitly breaches a promise to an Aboriginal man to keep information private because it was exclusively Aboriginal men's business.[60] Dunlop's note also provided evidence of her ongoing commitment to use literary forms to further understanding between Indigenous and non-Indigenous cultures.

If we see Eliza Dunlop as a precursor to settler women writers such as Katherine Langloh Parker—whose *Australian Legendary Tales* (1896) were published in London with an introduction by renowned folklorist Andrew Lang—it is possible to hold her representations of Aboriginal people and cultures to account for cultural appropriation, as those later writers have been.[61] Whether the act of translation is inherently acquisitive and colonising, or that such translations can be co-opted to consolidate colonial or imperial power, it is unarguable that culture can be implicated in colonisation.[62] It is not necessary to concede to the racism of the *Sydney Herald*'s dismissal of Dunlop's Aboriginal protagonists and her adaptations of Aboriginal culture to acknowledge that her writing was highly influenced by Romantic literary fashion and global trends in Anglophone publishing. It is understandable that some critics condemn her Aboriginal-themed poems for plundering traditional knowledge for personal literary advancement and accuse Dunlop of being more interested in advancing her writing career than cross-cultural curiosity and engagement.[63]

Yet perhaps it is more productive to utilise Dunlop's literary experiments to map the 'critical geography' of the settler imagination, as Jeanine Leane suggests of later settler historical fiction featuring an Aboriginal presence.[64] Creating more culturally grounded readings of both settler-

and Indigenous-authored works, as Leane calls for, requires reconstructing the asymmetrical collaborations between people on the colonial frontier. Those intimacies—as Jan Critchett notes, often as close as the person sharing one's bed—were complex and shifting.[65] They were often dangerous, as the Myall Creek massacre revealed, when familiarity offered little protection when external agents or interests dominated. Yet as Dunlop's poem 'The Aboriginal Mother' showed, settler cultures also contained those uneasy about rapid settler expansion, who questioned its collateral effects on Indigenous communities and cultures, and who sought to challenge derogatory assumptions by learning and disseminating translations of Indigenous knowledge.[66] There is a fine line between retrieving the work of—and analysing the motivations of—those who operated in this sphere on the one hand, and seeking to write settler apologetics that create sanitised foundation narratives on the other.[67]

When we link the poetry to the wordlists, we can see that Dunlop came to linguistic study through an affective and politically engaged response to colonial violence. Arguably, Dunlop's collection of linguistic and poetic forms was motivated by the antagonistic reception of her poem 'The Aboriginal Mother'. The crucial intervention she made in publishing that poem was not about European emotions, but about Indigenous ones. 'The Aboriginal Mother' conjured up universal 'motherhood' emotions: it did so to invoke white readers' sympathies, but its most disruptive effect was to imbue the imagined Aboriginal mother with the capacity to grieve, lament, and rage at her loss of family and culture. Lynn Hunt argues that human rights are so difficult to identify because their definition 'depends on emotions as much as on reason … we are most certain that a human right is at issue when we feel horrified by its violation'.[68] Dunlop's poetic and performative testimony sought to activate humanitarian responses, affective and political, in local communities and in a far-flung imperial diaspora of correspondents, policymakers, and readers. This was central to evangelical ideas of humanitarian reform: 'an interweaving of empiricism and emotion, reason and sentiment'.[69] Her work also provides an opportunity to connect local colonial experience with the global cultural history of humanitarianism. In order to pursue this, it is necessary to bring together diverse sources and consider how ideas moved across discursive regimes. We can see Dunlop's engagement with her Wollombi informants as a concerted process to gather the evidence to refute her critics. In collecting and incorporating Aboriginal languages in Romantic literary forms, and in transcribing and circulating Aboriginal lyric songs, Dunlop quietly but determinedly disproved the newspaper critics who had declared Aboriginal people incapable of cultural richness, emotion, or humanity.

This linguistic and poetic archive (albeit dispersed) provides insight into the formation of settler society, the visibility of debates about the morality of colonisation, and the thick and contested local knowledge about relationships between Indigenous people, settlers, and the law. This colonial knowledge was significant at the time and has ongoing resonance. Dunlop's work continues to inform linguistic research and language reconstruction.[70] For example, the Wollombi wordlist was included in a 2008 project generated by the Muurbay/Many Rivers community and the linguist Caroline Jones, a collaboration that created an accessible version of Darkinung grammar and diction, subtitled 'revitalizing a language from historical sources'.[71] These contemporary usages contribute both to the increasing scholarly and general public appreciation of the richness and diversity of Aboriginal languages, and to crucial community projects of reclaiming and revitalising Aboriginal languages and cultures. Twenty-first-century speakers of their traditional language frequently and powerfully attest to the personal and communal transformative impact of speaking language, and making it live in contemporary communities.[72] It is a profoundly affective and political experience, as Jakelin Troy describes, on weeping when for the first time she spoke in her language in front of a large gathering of people.[73] Such are resonant afterlives of colonial texts, which provide testimony of the troubled and violent intimacies of the past yet also serve as vital sources available for Indigenous co-option and repurposing.

Notes

1. For a comprehensive account of the massacre, see Roger Milliss, *Waterloo Creek: The Australia Day Massacre of 1838, George Gipps and the British Conquest of New South Wales* (Melbourne: McPhee Gribble, 1992); see also Jane Lydon and Lyndall Ryan, eds. *Remembering the Myall Creek Massacre, 1838–2018* (Sydney: NewSouth, forthcoming 2018).
2. Eliza Hamilton [E.H.D.] Dunlop, 'Original Poetry: Songs of an Exile (No. 4.) the Aboriginal Mother', *Australian*, 13 December 1838, lines 41–48.
3. See 'Slaughter of the Blacks', *Sydney Monitor and Commercial Advertiser*, 19 November 1838; 'Supplement to the Sydney Monitor and Commercial Advertiser', *Sydney Monitor and Commercial Advertiser*, 19 November

1838. For further discussion of Dunlop and her verse, see Margaret de Salis, *Two Early Colonials* (Sydney: n.p., 1967); Katie Hansord, 'Eliza Hamilton Dunlop's "The Aboriginal Mother": Romanticism, Anti Slavery and Imperial Feminism in the Nineteenth Century', *JASAL* 1, no. 1 (2011); John O'Leary, '"Unlocking the Fountains of the Heart": Settler Verse and the Politics of Sympathy', *Postcolonial Studies* 13, no. 1 (2010); Elizabeth Webby, 'Biographical Note', in *The Aboriginal Mother and Other Poems*, ed. Eliza Hamilton Dunlop (Canberra: Mulini Press, 1981).

4. Dunlop, lines 12 and 73 (emphasis in original).
5. Dunlop, lines 10, 25–26.
6. See Anna Johnston, 'The Language of Colonial Violence: Lancelot Threlkeld, Humanitarian Narratives and the NSW Law Courts', *Law & History* 4, no. 2 (2017), 72–102.
7. Tony Ballantyne, 'Humanitarian Narratives: Knowledge and the Politics of Mission and Empire', *Social Sciences and Missions* 24 (2011); Tony Ballantyne, 'Moving Texts and "Humane Sentiment": Materiality, Mobility and the Emotions of Imperial Humanitarianism', *Journal of Colonialism and Colonial History* 17, no. 1 (2016); Roland Burke, 'Flat Affect? Revisiting Emotion in the Historiography of Human Rights', *Journal of Human Rights* (2015); Penelope Edmonds and Anna Johnston, 'Empire, Humanitarianism and Violence in the Colonies', *Journal of Colonialism and Colonial History* 17, no. 1 (2016); Thomas L. Haskell, 'Capitalism and the Origins of the Humanitarian Sensibility, Part 1', *American Historical Review* 90, no. 2 (1985); Thomas L. Haskell, 'Capitalism and the Origins of the Humanitarian Sensibility, Part 2', *American Historical Review* 90, no. 3 (1985); Stefan-Ludwig Hoffmann, 'Human Rights and History', *Past & Present* (2016); Lynn Hunt, *Inventing Human Rights: A History* (New York: W.W. Norton, 2007); Lynn Hunt, 'The Long and the Short of the History of Human Rights', *Past & Present* 233, no. 1 (2016); Sam Hutchinson, 'Humanitarian Critique and the Settler Fantasy: The Australian Press and Settler Colonial Consciousness During the Waikato War, 1863–1864', *Settler Colonial Studies* 4, no. 1 (2014); Zoë Laidlaw, '"Aunt Anna's Report": The Buxton Women and the Aborigines Select Committee, 1835–37', *The Journal of Imperial and Commonwealth History* 32, no. 2 (2004); Zoë Laidlaw, 'Breaking Britannia's Bounds? Law, Settlers, and Space in Britain's Imperial Historiography', *The Historical Journal* 55, no. 3 (2012); Thomas W. Laqueur, 'Bodies, Details, and the Humanitarian Narrative', in *The New Cultural History*, ed. Lynn Hunt (Berkeley: University of California, 1989); Alan Lester, 'Colonial Networks, Australian Humanitarianism and the History Wars', *Geographical Research* 44, no. 3 (2006); Samuel Moyn, *The Last Utopia: Human Rights in History* (Cambridge, MA: Harvard University Press, 2010); Samuel

Moyn, 'The End of Human Rights History', *Past and Present* (2016); Amanda Nettelbeck, 'Colonial Protection and the Intimacies of Indigenous Governance', *History Australia* 14, no. 1 (2017); Rob Skinner and Alan Lester, 'Humanitarianism and Empire: New Research Agendas', *The Journal of Imperial and Commonwealth History* 40 no. 5 (2012).
8. James Belich, *Replenishing the Earth: The Settler Revolution and the Rise of the Anglo-World, 1783–1939* (Oxford: Oxford University Press, 2009).
9. Dror Wahrman, 'The Meaning of the Nineteenth Century: Reflections on James Belich's *Replenishing the Earth*', *Victorian Studies* 53, no. 1 (2010), 91–99.
10. Notable exceptions include Warwick Anderson, *The Cultivation of Whiteness: Science, Health, and Racial Destiny in Australia* (Melbourne: Melbourne University Press, 2005); David Armitage et al., *The Ideological Origins of the British Empire*, Ideas in Context (Cambridge: Cambridge University Press, 2000); Bain Attwood and John Arnold, eds. *Power, Knowledge and Aborigines* (Melbourne: La Trobe University Press, 1992); Tony Ballantyne, *Orientalism and Race: Aryanism and the British Empire*, Cambridge Colonial and Postcolonial Studies (Basingstoke: Palgrave, 2002); Tony Ballantyne, 'Colonial Knowledge', in *The British Empire: Themes and Perspectives*, ed. Sarah Stockwell (Malden: Blackwell, 2008); C.A. Bayly, *Empire and Information: Intelligence Gathering and Social Communication in India, 1780–1870* (Cambridge: Cambridge University Press, 1996); Frederick Cooper and Ann Laura Stoler, *Tensions of Empire: Colonial Cultures in a Bourgeois World* (Berkeley and Los Angeles: University of California Press, 1994); Dipesh Chakrabarty, *Provincialising Europe: Postcolonial Thought and Historical Difference* (Princeton: Princeton University Press, 2000); Lorraine Daston, 'The Sciences of the Archive', *Osiris* 27, no. 1 (2012); Michel Foucault, *The Order of Things: An Archaeology of the Human Sciences* (London and New York: Tavistock Publications, 1970).
11. Alan Lester and Fae Dussart, *Colonization and the Origins of Humanitarian Governance: Protecting Aborigines Across the Nineteenth-Century British Empire* (Cambridge: Cambridge University Press, 2014), 14–15; see also Angela Woollacott, *Settler Society in the Australian Colonies: Self-Government and Imperial Culture* (Oxford: Oxford University Press, 2015), 8–9.
12. Thomas W. Laqueur, 'Bodies, Details, and the Humanitarian Narrative', in *The New Cultural History*, ed. Lynn Hunt (Berkeley: University of California, 1989), 202.
13. Hoffmann, 'Human Rights and History'.
14. John M. MacKenzie, ed. *Imperialism and Popular Culture* (Manchester: Manchester University Press, 1986).

15. See John O'Leary, *Savage Songs and Wild Romances: Settler Poetry and the Indigene, 1830–1880* (Amsterdam: Rodopi, 2011).
16. Tim Fulford, *Romantic Indians: Native Americans, British Literature, and Transatlantic Culture 1756–1830*, Romantic Indians (Oxford: Oxford University Press, 2006).
17. Tony Ballantyne, *Orientalism and Race: Aryanism and the British Empire* (Basingstoke: Palgrave, 2002), 3.
18. George Anson, *A Voyage Round the World in the Years 1740 ... 1744* (London: Knapton, 1748); E. and J. Bruce, *An Introduction to Geography and Astronomy* (Newcastle: Longman et al., 1805); the *Annual Register* was a year-by-year record of British and world events, published from 1758.
19. Despite considerable research, it has not been possible to verify either the date of divorce proceedings or Law's death, due to the vagaries of Irish Protestant recordkeeping at this time. Eliza remarried at Portpatrick, Scotland, in 1823. Niel Gunson, 'Dunlop, Eliza Hamilton (1796–1880)', *Australian Dictionary of Biography* (Canberra: National Centre of Biography, Australian National University, 1966), http://adb.anu.edu.au/biography/dunlop-eliza-hamilton-2007/text2455
20. http://www.historyofparliamentonline.org/volume/1820-1832/constituencies/coleraine#footnote32_4g9e720
21. C.H. Currey, 'Sir Roger Therry (1800–1874)', *Australian Dictionary of Biography* (Canberra: National Centre of Biography, Australian National University, 1966), http://adb.anu.edu.au/biography/therry-sir-roger-2723
22. See Roger Milliss, *Waterloo Creek: The Australia Day Massacre of 1838, George Gipps and the British Conquest of New South Wales* (Melbourne: McPhee Gribble, 1992).
23. Duncan Wu claims that the criticism directed at Dunlop was unprecedented: Wu, '"A Vehicle of Private Malice": Eliza Hamilton Dunlop and the *Sydney Herald*', *The Review of English Studies* 65, no. 272 (2014), 898.
24. Eliza Hamilton Dunlop, 'The Aboriginal Mother', *Sydney Herald*, 15 October 1841.
25. Dunlop, 'The Aboriginal Mother'; 'Concert', *Australian*, 30 October 1841; 'Nathan's Grand Concert', *Australasian Chronicle*, 28 October 1841.
26. 'Mr. Nathan's Concert', *Sydney Gazette and New South Wales Advertiser*, 30 October 1841.
27. *Sydney Herald*, 15 October 1841, 2. On the *Herald*'s highly partisan reporting of the massacre and the role of newspapers in defining settler identity, see Rebecca Wood, 'Frontier Violence and the Bush Legend: The *Sydney Herald*'s Response to the Myall Creek Massacre Trials and the Creation of Colonial Identity', *History Australia* 6, no. 3 (2009).

28. For example, 'Thorough-Bass', 'Original Correspondence', *Sydney Herald*, 3 November 1841; 'Mr. Nathan's Concert', *Sydney Herald*, 29 October 1841.
29. Eliza Hamilton Dunlop, 'The Aboriginal Mother', *Sydney Herald*, 29 November 1841.
30. William Romaine Govett, 'Sketches of New South Wales', which includes Govett's watercolour 'Native Women Weeping over a Grave', *Saturday Magazine*, 5 November 1836, 184.
31. Govett, 'Sketches of New South Wales', 184.
32. Indeed, Dunlop and Isaac also collaborated on 'The Aboriginal Father: A Native Song of the Maneroo Tribe' (Sydney: Thomas Bluett, 1843). This used Aboriginal musical forms, albeit bowdlerised. See Graeme Skinner, 'The Invention of Australian Music', *Musicology Australia* 37, no. 2 (2015).
33. Helen Brayshaw, *Aborigines of the Hunter Valley: A Study of Colonial Records* (Scone, NSW: Upper Hunter Historical Society, 1986); Denis Mahony and Joe Whitehead, eds. *The Way of the River: Environmental Perspectives on the Wollombi* (Wollombi, NSW: Wollombi Valley Landcare Group in assoc. with the University of Newcastle Department of Community Programmes, 1994); W.J. Needham, *Burragurra, Where the Spirit Walked: The Aboriginal Relics of the Cessnock-Wollombi Region in the Hunter Valley of NSW* (Cessnock, NSW: Bill Needham, 1981).
34. R.H.W. Reece, 'Feasts and Blankets: The History of Some Early Attempts to Establish Relations with the Aborigines of New South Wales, 1814–1846', *Archaeology and Physical Anthropology in Oceania* 2, no. 3 (1967), 190.
35. Reece, 'Feasts and Blankets', 199.
36. Reece, 'Feasts and Blankets', 200–203.
37. Reece, 'Feasts and Blankets', qtd. 203.
38. Reece, 'Feasts and Blankets', qtd. 205.
39. When newspapers attacked David Dunlop's efforts to break the stranglehold of non-stipendiary magistrates who had pastoral interests, Eliza became the target of public ridicule. Inferring that David was ruled by his wife, the *Australasian Chronicle* published a letter by a correspondent who claimed that while David was providing a ruling, 'Mrs Dunlop mounted the bench, interrupted Mr. Dunlop, and said that for her part she would have "the bible, the whole bible, and nothing but the bible"': 'Wollombi', *Australasian Chronicle*, 22 March 1842. Having a clever and outspoken wife was often a way that colonial officials could be attacked or have their careers stymied by detractors.
40. Sarah Threlkeld, née Arndell, had brought substantial cattle holdings to the marriage, as well as an inherited land claim to 150 acres at Caddie on

the Hawkesbury River. In the 1830s, Threlkeld's eldest son from his first marriage, Joseph Thomas, took up a station in the Gwydir district with his step-uncle James Arndell, Sarah's younger brother. In 1840, Threlkeld defied the AAC's monopoly and opened a coal seam at Belmont that he had discovered in 1834; the Ebenezer Coal Works continued under his son-in-law, G.A. Lloyd. Each of these enterprises at times employed Aboriginal and convict labourers, and ensured that Threlkeld's family was thoroughly enmeshed in emergent colonial economies.

41. Niel Gunson, 'Introduction', in *Australian Reminiscences and Papers of L.E. Threlkeld, Missionary to the Aborigines, 1824–1859*, ed. Niel Gunson (Canberra: AIAS, 1974), 7.
42. See my analysis of Threlkeld's linguistic studies in Anna Johnston, *The Paper War: Morality, Print Culture, and Power in Colonial New South Wales* (Perth: University of Western Australia Press, 2011), chapter 2.
43. L.E. Threlkeld, 'Reminiscences. Aborigines—The Muses—Poetry', *The Christian Herald, and Record of Missionary and Religious Intelligence*, 11 November 1854: Q205/C, Mitchell Library, State Library of New South Wales, Sydney (hereafter ML).
44. Ann Vickery, '"A Lonely Crossing": Approaching Nineteenth-Century Australian Women's Poetry', *Victorian Poetry* 40, no. 1 (2002), 35.
45. Published as Roy H. Goddard, *The Life and Times of James Milson* (Melbourne: Georgian House, 1955). The manuscript is Mrs. David Milson [Eliza Hamilton Dunlop], 'Mrs. David Milson Kamilaroi Vocabulary and Aboriginal Songs, 1840', Wollombi (NSW), 1840: A1688, ML.
46. Rachael Gilmour, *Grammars of Colonialism: Representing Languages in Colonial South Africa* (Basingstoke: Palgrave Macmillan, 2006), 6.
47. Gilmour, *Grammars of Colonialism*, 2.
48. G.W. Stocking, Jr., 'Colonial Situations', in *Colonial Situations: Essays on the Contextualization of Ethnographic Knowledge*, ed. G.W. Stocking, Jr. (Madison, WI: University of Wisconsin Press, 1991), 5.
49. Johannes Fabian, *Language and Colonial Power: The Appropriation of Swahili in the Former Belgian Congo 1880–1938* (Cambridge, Cambridge University Press, 1986), 79.
50. Robert Dixon, *Prosthetic Gods: Travel, Representation and Colonial Governance* (Brisbane: University of Queensland Press, 2001), 7, 8.
51. See Caroline Jones, *Darkinyung Grammar and Dictionary: Revitalising a Language from Historical Sources* (Nambucca Heads: Muurrbay Aboriginal Language and Culture Co-operative, 2008); Caroline Jones and Shawn Laffan, 'Lexical Similarity and Endemism in Historical Wordlists of Australian Aboriginal Languages of the Greater Sydney Region', *Transactions of the Philological Society* 106, no. 3 (2008).
52. Milson, 'Kamilaroi Vocabulary'.

53. Milson, 'Kamilaroi Vocabulary'.
54. Assessing the different context of this later linguistic study is the subject for further study.
55. AIATSIS, 'Language Thesaurus', accessed June 2017, http://www1.aiatsis.gov.au/
56. Dunlop, 'The Vase, Comprising Songs for Music and Poems by Eliza Hamilton Dunlop'. This word (for 'white hawk') is also listed in Dunlop's wordlist; as is the word Matiyan for eagle hawk, which was used in the note to the published version of 'The Eagle-Chief'. Milson, 'Kamilaroi Vocabulary'; Eliza Hamilton Dunlop and Isaac Nathan, 'The Eagle Chief', *Sydney Gazette and New South Wales Advertiser*, 21 April 1842.
57. Dunlop, 'The Vase, Comprising Songs for Music and Poems'.
58. 'The Eagle Chief: An Australian Melody by I. Nathan', *Australian*, 19 April 1842.
59. Deborah Bird Rose, 'Gendered Substances and Objects in Ritual: An Australian Aboriginal Study', *Material Religion* 3, no. 1, 2007, 37.
60. See 'Domestic Intelligence: New Music', *The Sydney Herald*, 18 April 1842; also Anon. 'Aboriginal Poems Attacked: Eliza Dunlop Criticised', *Margin* 42 (1997), 32–34.
61. For indicative readings of appropriation by Parker, see Tanya Dalziell, *Settler Romances and the Australian Girl* (Perth: University of Western Australia Publishing, 2004); Nancy E. Wright and Brooke Collins-Gearing, 'The Rhetoric of Benevolence as an Impediment to the Protection of Indigenous Cultural Rights: A Study of Australian Literature and Law', *Journal of Australian Studies* 85 (2005); Judith Johnston, 'The Genesis and Commodification of Katherine Langloh Parker's *Australian Legendary Tales* (1896)', *Journal of the Association for the Study of Australian Literature* 4, no. 2 (2006).
62. On translation, see Talal Asad, 'The Concept of Cultural Translation in British Social Anthropology', in *Writing Culture: The Poetics and Politics of Ethnography*, ed. James Clifford and George E. Marcus (Berkeley, Los Angeles, and London: University of California Press, 1986); Tejaswini Niranjana, *Siting Translation: History, Post-Structuralism, and the Colonial Context* (Berkeley: University of California Press, 1992).
63. See O'Leary, *Savage Songs and Wild Romances*.
64. Jeanine Leane, 'Tracking Our Country in Settler Literature', *JASAL: Journal of the Association for the Study of Australian Literature* 14, no. 3 (2014), 1, citing Toni Morrison, *Playing in the Dark: Whiteness and the Literary Imagination* (Cambridge, MA: Harvard University Press, 1992).
65. Jan Critchett, *A 'Distant Field of Murder': Western Districts Frontiers, 1834–1848* (Melbourne: Melbourne University Press, 1990), 23.

66. See Henry Reynolds, *This Whispering in Our Hearts* (Sydney: Allen and Unwin, 1998).
67. Leane, 'Tracking Our Country in Settler Literature', 15.
68. Hunt, *Inventing Human Rights*, 26.
69. Tony Ballantyne, 'Humanitarian Narratives: Knowledge and the Politics of Mission and Empire', *Social Sciences and Missions* 24 (2011), 242.
70. See Jones, *Darkinyung Grammar and Dictionary*; Jones and Laffan, 'Lexical Similarity'.
71. Jones, *Darkinyung Grammar and Dictionary*.
72. See Jane Simpson, 'Brand New Day for the Darkinyung Language', *Transient Languages and Cultures*, 19 December 2008, accessed 15 June 2016, http://blogs.usyd.edu.au/elac/2008/12/brand_new_day_for_the_darkinyu_1.html
73. Jakelin Troy, 'The First Time I Spoke in My Own Language I Broke Down and Wept', *The Guardian*, 1 December 2015, https://www.theguardian.com/commentisfree/2015/dec/01/the-first-time-i-spoke-in-my-own-language-i-broke-down-and-wept

CHAPTER 12

'A Frivolous Prosecution': Allegations of Physical and Sexual Abuse of Domestic Servants and the Defence of Colonial Patriarchy in Darwin and Singapore, 1880s–1930s

Claire Lowrie

Historians of domestic service have long asserted that exercising domestic mastery over colonised servants was considered to be an expression and a symbol of coloniser status. At the same time, intimate physical contact between 'native' servants and their employers could destabilise hierarchical distinctions, thereby threatening the stability of colonial rule.[1] The potential for intimate relationships between employers and servants to affirm or contest colonial hierarchies has been richly demonstrated in the small body of work on violence within the colonial domestic service relationship. Historians of colonial Africa and the Pacific have illustrated

---

I would like to thank the anonymous reviewer for the critical and helpful feedback on this chapter. Thanks also to my research assistant on this project, Claire Wright.

C. Lowrie (✉)
University of Wollongong, Gwynneville, NSW, Australia

© The Author(s) 2018
P. Edmonds, A. Nettelbeck (eds.), *Intimacies of Violence in the Settler Colony*, Cambridge Imperial and Post-Colonial Studies Series, https://doi.org/10.1007/978-3-319-76231-9_12

how (real and imagined) incidents of physical and sexual assault of white employers by Indigenous and Asian domestic servants were interpreted as an attack on white colonial power.[2] At the same time, scholarship on India and Australia has considered how the notions of racial superiority on which colonial societies rested enabled and excused the physical and sexual abuse of Indigenous servants by their white employers.[3] Gender has been a key concern within the literature on violence and domestic service, with much of the scholarship exploring how white women became the focus of colonial anxieties, either as victims of assault or as perpetrators of violence.

This chapter takes the literature in a new direction by exploring the relationship between domestic service, violence, and colonial masculinities in the settler colony of Darwin and the exploitation colony of Singapore between the 1880s and the 1930s. By analysing the representations of assault and abuse of domestic servants by their British, white Australian, and Chinese masters, the chapter aims to illuminate the ways in which violence could challenge or sustain colonial patriarchy. Colonial legitimacy in Darwin and Singapore—similarly with European colonial projects all over the world—rested on the belief that white men were inherently righteous and benevolent rulers of the home and the colony.[4] Instances of white male violence towards colonised servants had the potential to unsettle such assertions.

My argument in this chapter is that the ways in which violence towards Chinese and Aboriginal servants was either justified or ignored by the press, colonial officials and ordinary colonists reflected an underlying agenda to protect the reputation of ruling-class men and the colonial venture as a whole. At the same time, I illustrate how the different status of Darwin as a part of a settler colony and Singapore as an exploitation colony ensured that the maintenance of colonial patriarchy played out in different ways. In Darwin, the aim of creating a white settler society ensured that the image of white men as firm yet fair employers of Chinese and Aboriginal servants prevailed despite evidence to the contrary. In Singapore, too, British masters were depicted as civilising and good even as they were convicted of assault of their Chinese houseboys. They were not, however, the only men whose kindly image was safeguarded. In Singapore, where the stability of colonial rule relied upon the cooperation of Chinese elites, the press and the government downplayed the abuse of young Chinese bonded servants (*mui tsai*) employed in Chinese homes.

By comparing representations of violence, gender, and domestic mastery in Darwin and Singapore, this chapter aims to illuminate the shared and particular preoccupations and processes which underpinned settler and non-settler colonial projects. Specifically, I argue that race was the most important determiner of coloniser status in Darwin, while in Singapore class and masculinity were more important. Thus, in Singapore, middle- and upper-class Chinese men were depicted, alongside British men, as worthy masters and colonisers, whereas in Darwin, that status was reserved for white men and women only.

The level of documentation of violent assault by or towards domestic workers in Darwin and Singapore differs significantly. Research for this chapter uncovered a mere seven accounts of violence involving servants reported in Northern Territory newspapers, including the *Northern Territory Times*, the *Northern Standard,* and (in the South Australian period) the *Register* between 1880 and 1930. This compares with thirty-eight incidents in Singapore's English-language press, including the *Straits Times*, the *Singapore Free Press and Mercantile Advertiser*, and the *Malaya Tribune*. The differences in the number of reported court cases reflects the larger size of the domestic-servant workforce in Singapore.[5]

The reported accounts of assault and abuse examined in this chapter probably reflect only a small proportion of the violent altercations between employers and servants that took place. The unequal power dynamic at the heart of the master–servant relationship mediated against servants reporting their employers to the police for physical abuse. Even if they did take them to court, the balance of the law was not in the servants' favour. Under Masters and Servants laws, for example, judges had the power to fine employers for mistreatment of servants, but they tended to be more concerned with prosecuting servants who failed to deliver 'faithful service'.[6] Even so, Chinese servants in Darwin and Singapore (like their counterparts in India and Hong Kong) sometimes turned to the law to redress their abuse by employers.[7] Aboriginal servants in Darwin, it seems, did not. I uncovered no court cases brought by Aboriginal servants against their employers.

While the record is sparse and one-sided, a critical reading of the cases of physical and sexual assault reported in the press and discussed by colonial officials, together with an analysis of oral histories and memoirs from servants and employers, gives a good indication of how central violence was to the domestic-service relationship. The ways in which violence perpetrated by white-Australian, British, and Chinese masters was reported, policed, and remembered, as well as the ways in which it was ignored, erased, and forgotten, provides insights into the relationship between colonial patriarchy and domestic service in settler and non-settler colonies.

Settlers and Servants in Darwin and Singapore

In some ways, Darwin and Singapore were very different colonies. Singapore's colonial history began in 1819, following the signing of a formal treaty with the Sultan of Johore. Singapore was an exploitation colony in which the aim of colonisation was to generate profits by extracting resources and exploiting migrant labour.[8] In contrast, the Northern Territory of Australia, of which Port Darwin was the capital, was intended to be a 'settler colony' in which the permanent settlement of British and white Australian colonists was pursued through the violent dispossession of the traditional owners of the land.[9] In contrast to the negotiation of a treaty in the case of Singapore, the Northern Territory was considered to be a 'wilderness for the taking', and Aboriginal people were treated accordingly.[10] The contrasting objectives of British colonialism in Singapore and Darwin was solidified with Australian Federation in 1901, after which point the Northern Territory ceased to be a British colony and was subsumed into the Commonwealth of Australia.

While the underlying intentions of colonisation in Darwin and Singapore were very different, as neighbouring ports situated in the Southeast Asian region the colonies nonetheless had a good deal in common. The establishment of a settlement at Palmerston (as Darwin was originally called) in 1869 was the fifth attempt to establish a northern trading outpost. The early residents of the town optimistically declared that Darwin would become the 'Singapore of Australia', and the port was initially exempt from customs duties in order to promote it as a free port like Singapore.[11] The grand aspirations for Darwin did not eventuate, with economic recession and population decline setting in by the 1890s. While Singapore rose to become one of the most successful port cities in Asia, Darwin remained a backwater.[12] Nonetheless, Darwin and Singapore remained connected by the movement of migrants, tourists, and trade along the steamship lines which linked the ports (see Fig. 12.1).

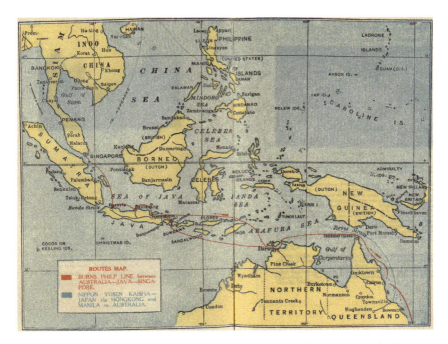

Fig. 12.1 Burns Philp Steamship Line between Singapore and Darwin. *Picturesque Travel*, Burns Philp and Company, no. 6, 1925, National Library of Australia

The different levels of success that Darwin and Singapore enjoyed as trading ports was reflected in the sizes of their populations. In 1911, Singapore's population reached 303,321, while Darwin's was a mere 1387. Yet there were similarities in the ethnic compositions of the populations. In 1911, ten years after the introduction of the White Australia Policy, Darwin's population, like that of Singapore, was multi-ethnic, with the Chinese population still the largest ethnic group resident in the town.[13] The ethnically diverse nature of Darwin's population calls into question its status as a white settler colony. While distinctions between settler and non-settler colonies might illuminate the intentions of colonial projects, such categorisations do not always reflect the realities on the ground.[14]

The nature of Singapore's population also illustrates the unfixed and ambiguous nature of categories such as 'settler' versus 'exploitation' colonies.[15] Many of the Chinese migrants who came to Singapore ended up settling permanently in the colony.[16] By 1911, the Chinese population of Singapore had stabilised at 72 per cent of the total population.[17] Like Asian migrants resident in other European colonies, the Chinese community of Singapore was certainly oppressed by the white colonial state. Yet they were also colonists in their own right and were implicated in the colonial project.[18] As advisors to the administration, Chinese elites in Singapore played a critical role in colonial governance, helping to keep the majority Chinese labouring population in check.[19]

The history of connection between Darwin and Singapore—their common status as tropical colonies and the similar nature of their multi-ethnic populations—facilitated the development of a common colonial culture. In both sites, colonial prestige was marked by the presence of numerous Asian and Indigenous servants in elite colonial homes. Chinese houseboys predominated in domestic service in Darwin and Singapore between the 1880s and the 1910s. In Darwin by the 1920s, Aboriginal men and women as well as young mixed-descent girls came to dominate the servant class. In Singapore in the same period, Chinese female servants called *amahs* gradually replaced Chinese men in service. In Chinese homes in Singapore, *mui tsai* (girl slaves) were also employed throughout the period between the1880s and 1930s.[20]

As will be explored in the following discussion, the common ways in which violence by white male employers was legitimised or ignored in the two colonies illustrates the 'connective tissue' of gendered ideologies and the ways in which colonialism as a system rested on the maintenance of patriarchy.[21] At the same time, however, the condemnation of Chinese employers of servants in Darwin, compared with the respect Chinese masters were accorded in Singapore, illustrates how conceptions of race and class shaped patriarchy in different ways in settler and exploitation colonies.

A 'Slight Kick': Justifying White Men's Violence Against Chinese Houseboys, 1880s–1910s

Between the 1880s and the 1910s, accounts of violence by white men towards their Chinese servants were relatively common. In both sites, white men were charged and convicted for beating, slapping, and kicking Chinese houseboys and other servants employed in the home. In Darwin in 1885, a police constable by the name of Robert Stott defended himself against a charge of assault on his Chinese houseboy, Ah Lung, by claiming that his 'slight kick' was provoked by Ah Lung 'using a certain closet in a filthy manner'. Stott's use of the racist trope of Chinese people as dirty and unhygienic worked in his favour, with the judge fining him a mere one pound for the assault and the newspaper dismissing the case as 'a most trumpery affair'.[22] In Singapore, a similar emphasis on white masters' violence as justified prevailed. Cases of white men slapping or beating their Javanese and Chinese servants with belts and fishing rods were reported in sympathetic terms. Convictions for assault were described by journalists as 'frivolous prosecution[s]', while acts of violence were dismissed by judges as 'quite justified' or a result of 'grave and sudden provocation'.[23]

First-hand accounts from the Chinese servants who worked for British and white Australian men are incredibly rare. One of the only accounts that I am aware of is an oral history interview with Lim Ming Joon, a Hainanese man who worked as a servant in Singapore in the 1920s and 1930s. His account contests the idea that British men only responded with violence when justifiably provoked. Lim recalled a British male employer who became 'very angry' and 'threw a fit' when he was a few minutes late for work. Lim was forced to defend himself with a knife.[24]

Attitudes toward violence in colonial societies were complex and often contradictory. From the mid-nineteenth century in Britain and in the empire, respectable servant management involved a 'retreat from violence'.[25] At the same time, the use of violence to discipline native servants was viewed in some circles as necessary and even appropriate.[26] In the Philippines, Americans were forthright when it came to describing the use of force against their Filipino servants. They did not view violence in opposition to their stated goal of 'tutelage' and 'benevolent assimilation'.[27] By the early twentieth century in British colonies, however, displays of violence were seen by colonial officials to call into question the legitimacy of the civilising mission and to violate the maintenance of physical distance between coloniser and the colonised.[28] Displays of 'vulgar abuse' by white men also had the potential to unsettle the assertion that Anglo-Saxon men were biologically destined to rule, due to their innate rationality and restraint.[29] In this context, the emphasis on white male violence as justified can be interpreted as an attempt to shore up white colonial and patriarchal authority.

The depiction of white masters as firm yet fair was reinforced by representations of acts of violence by white mistresses. In both Darwin and Singapore, violence on the part of white women tended to be attributed to hysterical bursts of rage, particularly if the woman involved was working-class.[30] Such depictions reflected the anti-white women rhetoric which was aired across the tropical colonial world. The increasing numbers of white women visiting and settling in colonies across India, Africa, Asia, and the Pacific from the late nineteenth century was viewed by colonial administrators as a welcome development. The imperialist and nationalist rhetoric of the era emphasised that white women's supposedly innate maternal influence would 'civilise' white colonial men and 'native' others. In the popular press, however, these women were often represented as 'idle memsahibs' who were incapable of managing 'native' servants and, by association, were ill equipped for colonial rule.[31]

The depiction of white male violence as justified also expressed and sought to resolve broader fears about the large and supposedly lawless Chinese populations of Darwin and Singapore. During the 1880s and 1890s, colonial authorities in both sites depicted Chinese labourers as a criminal class. In Singapore, anxiety centred upon Chinese labourers' membership in so-called 'secret societies' (*kongsi*). In both sites, petty and violent crime in the colonies was attributed to the Chinese labouring classes and, in particular, their recreational activities, which included opium consumption, gambling, and frequenting brothels.[32] In Darwin, concerns about crime were conflated with angst about growth of the Chinese population in what was supposed to be a 'white mans [sic] country'.[33] In 1888, the Chinese population of the Northern Territory reached seven thousand, outnumbering white colonists by four to one.[34]

As the labourers with whom Australian and British colonists were most intimate, Chinese houseboys came to embody white anxieties about the Chinese population. One of the attractions and obligations of the colonial venture for white men travelling to places like Darwin and Singapore was the experience of exercising 'personal authority' over colonised subjects.[35] In their fictional accounts and travel stories, British and white Australian men described how the colonial experience, and their mastery over Asian and Indigenous servants in particular, transformed them from perfectly ordinary men into white masters. In Somerset Maugham's short story 'The Outstation', set in the remote jungles of Malaya and published in the 1920s, a newly arrived British colonist, Warburton, revelled in the fact that 'he was no longer the sycophant craving the smiles of the great, he was the master whose word was law'.[36] Likewise, in *Capricornia*, his novel based on his time working as the Chief Protector of Aborigines in Darwin in the 1920s, Xavier Herbert cynically described how middle-class men from the southern regions of Australia transformed themselves into aristocratic gentlemen after arriving in the town by engaging Chinese domestic staff and by acquiring the appropriate tropical attire. As he put it: 'Within two dozen hours of landing they were wearing solar topees … Within a hundred hours they came forth in all the glory of starched white linen clothes. Gone was their simplicity forever.'[37]

The British and white Australian men who constituted the main employers of Chinese male servants in this era did not, however, always encounter the loyal and devoted Chinese houseboys of colonial imaginings (see for example Fig. 12.2). Chinese male servants were regularly accused of stealing from and, occasionally, violently assaulting their white male employers.[38] In Singapore, accounts of Chinese servants 'running amok', attacking and sometimes murdering their Chinese employers, reinforced a general fear of the Chinese servant class.[39] In Darwin, too, the potential of disgruntled servants to lash out at their employers was the subject of press comment.[40] As much as it was a means through which white masculinity was affirmed then, the colonial experience also exposed its vulnerability and insecurity.[41] In Darwin and Singapore, white men's anxieties about their own violence and potential violence from their Chinese male servants was resolved by employing the same strategy. As we have seen, white men were depicted in newspaper accounts of violence against servants as rational bearers of justice whose discipline was directed at taming savage Chinese men. While the rhetorical strategies for dealing with the perceived problem of Chinese criminality were the same, the governmental responses to this issue were very different and reflected the divergent aims of settler and exploitation colonialism.

In the Northern Territory, the introduction of immigration restriction by the South Australian administration in 1888 and the passing of the White Australia Policy in 1901 ensured that the Chinese population declined dramatically.[42] The beginning of the Commonwealth administration in 1911 brought with it new mechanisms designed to marginalise the Chinese labouring community economically, as well as diminishing their numbers through strict adherence to immigration restriction.[43] As the Chinese servants who had been such an essential part of white households were largely forced from the town, discussions of violence by and towards Chinese male servants disappeared. While a number of white Territorians lamented the decline of Chinese houseboys, occasional reports of acts of violence by the remaining few Chinese servants resident in the Northern Territory and by those employed in other parts of Australia and Asia

Fig. 12.2 *Chinese Boy on Duty*, Lambert and Co, Singapore, c. 1900, Royal Netherlands Institute of Southeast Asian and Caribbean Studies

perhaps soothed other white Territorians into thinking that their 'Chinese problem' had been resolved.[44]

In Singapore, rather than alienating and excluding the entire Chinese population, the colonial government sought to assert control over labouring Chinese by collaborating with elite Chinese merchants (*towkays*) and the English-speaking Straits Chinese community.[45] In addition, the government banned *kongsi* organisations in 1890 and began regulating brothel prostitution and the production and sale of opium.[46] The administration also targeted the Chinese servant class specifically, attempting to introduce the registration of domestic servants in 1888 in order to provide employers with information about their servants' personal and criminal histories.[47] Further calls for the introduction of servant registration followed, but it was never instituted. While in Darwin concerns about the Chinese servant class disappeared from public commentary, in Singapore a new threat of politically inspired violence by Chinese male servants emerged during the 1920s.[48] Like colonial administrators in Darwin, the ruling elite of the Straits Settlements sought to deal with this 'Chinese problem' through immigration control. Rather than creating a nation for the white man, however, the intention was to exclude those 'likely to promote sedition or to cause a disturbance of public tranquillity', with Chinese male servants signalled for particular attention.[49]

'... A FORM OF CRUELTY NOT EASILY DETECTED': IGNORING THE ABUSE OF ABORIGINAL SERVANTS IN WHITE AUSTRALIAN HOMES AND *MUI TSAI* IN CHINESE HOMES, 1910s–1930s

Between the 1880s and the 1910s, popular representations of violence by British and white Australian masters emphasised assault and abuse as a legitimate means of disciplining unwieldy Chinese servants. By the 1920s, strategies for defending ruling-class men's violence had changed. The period of the 1920s and 1930s was a time of growing humanitarian critique, with the alleged exploitation of Aboriginal servants employed in white homes in Darwin and the abuse of *mui tsai* (girl slaves) working in Chinese homes in Singapore targeted for comment. Rather than confront the allegations, government officials and the local press remained silent in order to protect and defend the reputation of white Australian men in Darwin and middle-class Chinese men in Singapore. Preserving the image of these men as good masters and good colonisers was essential to achieving the settler colonial project in Darwin and to ensuring the long-term stability of exploitation colonialism in Singapore.

From the 1910s, governmental efforts to transform Australia's multi-ethnic north into a bustling site of white settlement stepped up pace.

While immigration restriction had largely solved the perceived problem of Chinese settlement in the Northern Territory, the persistence of Indigenous communities and the emergence of a mixed-race population were seen as an obstacle to achieving a white Australia in the north.[50] The Commonwealth government's Aboriginal Ordinances of 1911 and 1918 sought to resolve the so-called 'half-caste problem' by removing mixed-descent children from their families and communities and assimilating them into white society. In aid of this objective, mixed-descent boys were trained as farm labourers, while girls were recruited into domestic service. Prospective white employers had to apply for a license to employ Aboriginal and mixed-descent servants in their homes (see Fig. 12.3).[51]

While this system of Aboriginal employment was lauded by the Commonwealth administration as the ideal means of 'protecting' Aboriginal people and assimilating the mixed-descent community, it was criticised by some commentators within Australia and overseas. The fact that Aboriginal and mixed-descent servants were compelled to work as

Fig. 12.3 Margaret Gilruth sitting on steps outside Government House with an unnamed Aboriginal maid servant and Billy Shepherd, Darwin, c. 1912–1918, Jean A. Austin Collection, Northern Territory Library

servants for white employers and received little or no remuneration for their work ensured that the licensing system was condemned in London and Europe as one of 'slave certificates'.[52] Australian missionaries and feminists also condemned the conditions of Aboriginal employment as 'analogous to slavery' and warned of the potential for violence against, and sexual abuse of, mixed-descent servant girls by white male employers.[53]

Despite the national and international context of debate, instances of abuse of Aboriginal domestic workers were not discussed by the press in the Northern Territory and were only rarely the subject of official comment. Nor did employers (either at the time or later in oral-history accounts) acknowledge violence and exploitation.[54] Where the issue of violence or abuse involving Aboriginal and mixed-descent domestic servants was raised, it was in relation to their alleged abuse by Chinese employers prior to introduction of the South Australian administration's Aborigines Act of 1910, which first banned the employment of Aboriginal and mixed-descent people by 'Asiatics'.[55] In contrast to Chinese masters, white Australian mistresses in particular were depicted as civilizing and protecting.[56] As Victoria Haskins has shown, this image of the kindly white mistress was used by government officials in the Northern Territory and across Australia to justify both the forcible removal of Aboriginal children from their communities and their so-called 'apprenticeship' in white homes.[57] The image of the benevolent and paternal white employer was also of vital importance in justifying the pursuit of a white Australia in the tropical north. This is illustrated by the ways by which white male violence towards Aboriginal servants was intentionally obscured in Darwin.

The attempt to ignore and silence accounts of violence by white men towards their Aboriginal servants in the Northern Territory is demonstrated by the story of an Aboriginal man called Romula employed on Oenpelli Station. In 1917, Romula was convicted of attempting to murder his employer, Patrick Cahill, and the entire Cahill family, by adding strychnine to the butter. While the case was briefly discussed in the Annual Report for the Northern Territory in 1917, it received no coverage in the local press.[58] The entire incident might well have been forgotten were it not for the Royal Commission on corruption in the administration of the Northern Territory, which ran from 1920 to 1921. While the local press in Darwin continued to ignore the case, journalists elsewhere detailed the failure of the justice system to adequately defend Romula. Newspaper articles from around Australia also documented Cahill's violent response to the poisoning, describing how he had chained and whipped Romula and the mixed-descent cook, Jimmy Ah Foo.[59]

The reluctance to discuss the case in the Northern Territory reflects the anxieties that surrounded Aboriginal men who transgressed the role of passivity and powerlessness which colonial discourses had allocated them.[60] While we do not know Romula's motivation in poisoning Cahill, his attempt to murder the mission manager would surely have been read as a challenge to colonial power in the Northern Territory. On the other hand, other cases where the behaviour of Aboriginal men exposed the myth of their harmless and passive nature did receive attention in the local press.[61] The key reason for the reluctance to engage with this case related to the actions of Cahill. The image of a white employer chaining and whipping his Aboriginal and Chinese servants was the absolute opposite of restrained civility and fatherly care befitting a white master and coloniser. It seemed to confirm the accusations levelled at white employers of Aboriginal servants that they acted like, in effect, slave owners. In a report to the government, Cahill attempted to restore his reputation as a kindly white master by claiming that Romula had poisoned him because he was trying to stamp out the practice of 'wife beating' amongst the Aboriginal men on the station. The *Northern Territory Times*'s support for this version of events is illustrated by their decision to republish the report.[62]

An inclination to protect the image of white men in the Northern Territory can also be seen in the reporting of instances of sexual abuse of mixed-descent girls in service. Oral-history accounts from women who worked as domestic servants in Darwin indicate that the threat of sexual abuse was part of life as a domestic servant.[63] Public awareness of the issue of sexual abuse is demonstrated by the campaigns of feminist groups for white women to be appointed as Aboriginal Protectors and to be given powers to inspect the conditions in which mixed-descent girls were employed.[64] The reluctance of the Commonwealth administration to act on such requests illustrates the wish to avoid the implication that, as Fiona Paisley puts it, 'white men were the problem on the frontier'.[65] In Darwin, the reluctance to discuss potential and actual incidences of abuse of Aboriginal servants in white homes reflects a desire to protect the image of white men as good masters, good colonisers, and the rightful inheritors of the land.

The only article I have located that delved into the issue focused not on the sexual exploitation of Aboriginal servants, but on a 'rumour' that a named mixed-descent woman had murdered her newborn baby. Implied within the discussion of the article was the suggestion that mixed-descent Aboriginal servants were regularly involved in sexual relationships with their male employers, though there was no suggestion of coercion.[66] The widely accepted view of white Australians in this period that mixed-descent women were sexually promiscuous served to absolve white employers of guilt.[67] That the article was published in 1935, at a time when assimilation took on increasingly eugenic undertones with the aim of breeding out colour, perhaps also explains the lack of public outrage and action.[68]

While humanitarian critique in Darwin surrounded Aboriginal employment in white homes, in Singapore the position of *mui tsai* employed in Chinese homes was subjected to intense international scrutiny. The *mui tsai* practice was a tradition that Chinese migrants had brought with them to Singapore; it involved impoverished Chinese families selling their daughters into servitude. On reaching puberty, *mui tsai* were married off, became concubines, or were resold—sometimes to brothels.[69] During the 1920s and 1930s, the Chinese republican government, the League of Nations slavery committees, the British Aborigines Protection League, and various missionary organisations based in London and China labelled the practice child slavery and called for its abolition within the Straits Settlements, Malaya, and Hong Kong.[70] The Straits Settlements government sought to 'remove any vestige of doubt … that slavery … is tolerated in this Colony' by making superficial changes to transform the system into a form of domestic apprenticeship.[71] The most significant piece of legislation was the Mui Tsai Ordinance of 1933, which required the registration of all existing *mui tsai*, the payment of a small wage, and regular inspections of their working conditions. The legislation failed to bring the practice to an end, with owners disguising their *mui tsai* as family members or simply refusing to register them.[72] Further action was taken with the commissioning of a report on the *mui tsai* in 1937, in which it was argued that most *mui tsai* now worked for their employers as free servants and were generally well cared for. In contrast to the 'Majority Report', Edith Picton-Turbervill's 'Minority Report' maintained that the system and its abuses were ongoing. Picton-Turbervill gave evidence that beating *mui tsai* was commonplace and, while it was difficult to document that 'form of cruelty not easily detected', the notions of ownership on which the practice rested increased the potential for sexual abuse.[73]

Very few of the oral histories and memoirs from Chinese people who employed *mui tsai* in 1920s and 1930s Singapore detail any abuse, with most maintaining that *mui tsai* were treated as part of the family.[74] Yet the accounts of former *mui tsai*, such as Janet Lim, confirm Picton-Turbervill's assessment that because the *mui tsai* was a 'slave' who 'had been purchased', 'the master could do whatever he pleased with her'.[75] *Mui tsai* who suffered physical and sexual abuse had little opportunity for redress, as the Chinese patriarchal system allocated women roles as domestic drudges, child-bearers, and sex objects.[76]

Despite the international anti-*mui tsai* campaign, which drew attention to the systematic abuse of these servants, there was reluctance in Singapore to condemn the Chinese employers of *mui tsai*. In Singapore during the 1920s and 1930s, the reporting of murder, attempted murder, battery, and sexual assault variously perpetrated by Hainanese houseboys, British *memsahibs*, or Eurasian masters was at a peak.[77] In Hong Kong, stories of 'callous mistress[es]' violently abusing *mui tsai* were occasionally featured in the local European newspapers.[78] In Singapore, however, there was a marked absence of accusations of abuse of servants within Chinese homes. Journalists, like government officials and even anti-*mui tsai* campaigners, were influenced by the arguments made by Chinese employers that the *mui tsai* were treated as family members rather than slaves and were rarely abused.[79]

While upper- and middle-class Chinese employers of servants were generally spared the critical gaze of newspaper reporters, one incident involving the beating of a 'Chinese servant maid' who may have been a *mui tsai* was reported in the *Straits Times* in 1909. The focus of the case and the article was not, however, on the assault of Wee Ah Hoh by her Chinese master Hoh Sang Lim, a wealthy *towkay* (merchant). Rather, the case was brought against Wee for attempting suicide. She was convicted and sentenced to fourteen days' imprisonment.[80]

It was not until 1937 in the context of Picton-Turbervill's minority report and subsequent publications on abuses of *mui tsai* by Sir George Maxwell, a former colonial administrator in Malaya, that the *Straits Times* acknowledged a previous 'indifference' towards the *mui tsai* issue. The paper resolved to bring to light 'allegations of shocking cruelty' and the 'dangers and evils that are inherent in this custom'.[81] The Straits Settlements government too made further attempts to end the *mui tsai* practice with the Children's Ordinance of 1938–1940. However, the outbreak of World War II and the resultant dissolution of the British empire ensured that it was never instituted.[82]

Sarah Paddle attributes the lack of hysteria during the *mui tsai* controversy to the 'internationalist and racially aware' Western feminist movement.[83] For the press and the colonial government in Singapore, the display of cultural sensitivity also had a practical purpose. The reluctance of the British to condemn respectable Chinese for keeping *mui tsai* needs to be read in the context of a majority Chinese population and Chinese elite with close ties to the government. For European colonisers, to be a good and worthy master was to be a good and worthy coloniser. To exclude the Chinese from the status of respectable mastery was to exclude them from coloniser status. This would allocate the British a long-term moral responsibility for the colony, a situation that was not consistent with their colonial objectives. As Acting Secretary of the Straits Settlements Hayes Marriott put it in 1921, it was the Chinese community rather than the British who 'look upon this Settlement as their home' and 'form a permanent population' in Singapore.[84] The cultural sensitivity displayed by the British in Singapore was in their own best interests, providing a means to maintain colonial stability and business as usual.

Conclusion

The representation of violence perpetrated by British, white-Australian, and Chinese men against their servants in Darwin and Singapore underwent considerable change between the 1880s and the 1930s. During the 1880s and to the 1910s, convictions of white men for assault of their Chinese houseboys were regularly reported in the local papers. In the context of widespread anxiety about the large numbers of Chinese labourers within the colonies and their supposed predilection for crime, beating, slapping, and kicking Chinese servants was envisioned as an appropriate form of servant discipline and a reasonable means of demonstrating white men's status as rulers. Thus, despite the contrasting objectives of settler colonialism in Darwin and exploitation colonialism in Singapore, the potential threat that white male violence presented to the colonial civilising mission was conceived of and resolved in very similar ways. Ultimately, the colonial governments of Darwin and Singapore also sought to resolve the perceived problem of Chinese criminality in the same way, using immigration controls to exclude the migration of Chinese male workers. In Darwin, however, the intent of immigration restriction was to create a 'white man's country' while in Singapore the aim was to achieve political stability so that profits might keep flowing back to London.

By the 1920s and 1930s, the reporting of violence by white masters disappeared almost entirely. In the context of widespread humanitarian critique of colonialism, government officials and the press in both Singapore and Darwin were careful to protect the reputation of white masters as representatives of colonial legitimacy. Thus, the press in Darwin refused to engage with the allegations of white men violently assaulting and sexually abusing Aboriginal servants that were reported in newspapers in southeastern Australia and overseas. In Darwin, discussing the potential for white men to abuse Aboriginal servants was seen to risk the future of the colony. The justification for the domestic indenture of Aboriginal and mixed-descent people rested upon white colonial patriarchy with a paternalistic white master and a kindly white mistress responsible for assimilating Aboriginal people into the white settler nation.

In Singapore in the 1920s and 1930s, the racialised and gendered image of British men as good masters and good colonisers was reinforced by salacious accounts of savage white memsahibs and uncivilised Eurasian masters abusing their servants. At the same time, there was marked silence in the press regarding allegations that were being aired in Hong Kong and London of exploitation and abuse of *mui tsai* in Chinese homes. In Singapore, condemning Chinese masters for abusing *mui tsai* had the potential to alienate the elite Chinese on whom colonial stability in part rested, and thus risked the future of the colony.

An analysis of the ways in which violence by employers of servants was represented by the press, colonial governments, and ordinary colonists illustrates the central yet distinct way in which colonial patriarchy operated in settler and non-settler colonies. In Darwin, colonial legitimacy rested upon defending white men from accusations of violence. In Singapore, middle- and upper-class Chinese men were also represented as respectable and restrained masters and, by implication, worthy colonisers.

Notes

1. Ann Laura Stoler, *Carnal Knowledge and Imperial Power* (Berkeley: University of California Press, 2002), 6, 8.
2. Jeremy Martens, 'Settler Homes, Manhood and "Houseboys": An Analysis of Natal's Rape Scare of 1886', *Journal of Southern African Studies* 28, no. 2 (2002), 369; Prinisha Badassy, '"And my blood became hot!": Crimes of Passion, Crimes of Reason: An Analysis of the Crimes of Murder and Physical Assault against Masters and Mistresses by Their Indian Domestic Servants, Natal, 1880–1920', *Journal of Natal and Zulu History* 23, no. 1 (2006), 73–106; Amirah Inglis, *The White Women's Protection Ordinance:*

Sexual Anxiety and Politics in Papua (London: Sussex University Press, 1975), 54–55, 65–66.
3. Jordanna Bailkin, 'The Boot and the Spleen: When Was Murder Possible in British India?', *Comparative Studies in Society and History* 48, no. 2 (2006), 472–488; Fae Dussart, '"Strictly Legal Means": Assault, Abuse and the Limits of Acceptable Behaviour in the Servant/Employer Relationship in Metropole and Colony 1850–1890', in *Colonization and Domestic Service: Contemporary and Historical Perspectives*, ed. Victoria Haskins and Claire Lowrie (New York: Routledge, 2015), 153–171; Victoria Haskins, '"Down the Gully and Just Outside the Garden Walk": White Women and the Sexual Abuse of Aboriginal Women on a Colonial Frontier', *History Australia* 10, no. 1 (2013), 11–15.
4. Mrinalini Sinha, 'Giving Masculinity a History: Some Contributions from the Historiography of Colonial India', *Gender and History* 11, no. 3 (1999), 447.
5. In Singapore in 1921, 19,369 domestic servants were employed. This compares with 212 servants in the Northern Territory. This figure does not include the substantial number of Aboriginal servants employed in the Northern Territory who were not counted in the census. J.E. Nathan, *The Census of British Malaya 1921* (London: Waterlow and Sons, 1922), 118; Chas. H. Wickens, *Census of the Commonwealth of Australia 1921: Part XVII Occupations*, 1250.
6. B.W. Higman, *Domestic Service in Australia* (Melbourne: Melbourne University Press, 2002), 175–181.
7. Christopher Munn, 'Hong Kong, 1841–1870: All the Servants in Prison and Nobody to Take Care of the House', in *Masters, Servants, and Magistrates in Britain and the Empire, 1562–1955*, ed. Douglas Hay and Paul Craven (Chapel Hill: University of North Carolina Press, 2004), 366, 387; Dussart, '"Strictly Legal Means"', 159.
8. Ann Laura Stoler, 'Tense and Tender Ties: The Politics of Comparison in North American History and (Post) Colonial Studies', *Journal of American History* 88, no. 3 (2001), 456.
9. Haunani-Kay Trask, *From a Native Daughter: Colonialism and Sovereignty in Hawai'i* (Honolulu: University of Hawai'i Press, 1993), 25.
10. Alan Powell, *Far Country: A Short History of the Northern Territory* (Melbourne: Melbourne University Press, 1988), 52.
11. Alfred Searcy, *In Northern Seas* (Darwin: Northern Territory Department of Education, 1984), 70.
12. David Carment, '"A De Facto Australasia": Darwin, Asia and the Australian Identity', *Northern Perspective* 18, no. 1 (1995), 8; C.M. Turnbull, *A History of Singapore, 1819–1975* (Kuala Lumpur: Oxford University Press, 1977), 88–91.

13. 'Census Figures for Darwin, 1911': A1/15, 11/16191 (1911), National Archives of Australia, Canberra (hereafter NAA).
14. Adele Perry, 'The State of Empire: Reproducing Colonialism in British Columbia, 1849–1871', *Colonialism and Colonial History* 2, no. 2 (2001).
15. Daiva Stasiulis and Nira Yuval-Davis, 'Introduction: Beyond Dichotomies', in *Unsettling Settler Societies: Articulations of Gender, Race, Ethnicity and Class*, ed. Daiva Stasiulis and Nira Yuval-Davis (London: Sage, 1995), 3.
16. Christopher Lloyd and Jacob Metzer, 'Settler Colonization and Societies in World History: Patterns and Concepts', in *Settler Economies in World History*, ed. Christopher Lloyd, Jacob Metzer, and Richard Sutch (Leiden: Koninklijke and Brill, 2013), 3.
17. Hayes Marriott, 'The Peoples of Singapore: Inhabitants and Population', in *One Hundred Years of Singapore*, ed. Walter Makepeace, Gilbert Brooke, and Roland Braddell (Singapore: Oxford University Press, 1991), 360.
18. Ann Curthoys, 'An Uneasy Conversation: The Multicultural and the Indigenous', in *Race, Colour and Identity in Australia and New Zealand*, ed. John Docker and Gerhard Fischer (Sydney: University of NSW Press, 2000), 32.
19. Edwin Lee, *The British as Rulers Governing Multiracial Singapore 1867–1914* (Singapore: Singapore University Press, 1991), 91–92, 288.
20. Claire Lowrie, *Masters and Servants: Cultures of Empire in the Tropics* (Manchester: Manchester University Press, 2016), 29–32.
21. Penny Edwards, 'Mixed Metaphors: Other Mothers, Dangerous Daughters and the Rhetoric of Child Removal in Burma, Australia and Indochina', *Balayi: Culture, Law and Colonialism* 6 (2004), 42.
22. 'News and Notes', *Northern Territory Times and Gazette*, 17 January 1885.
23. *Singapore Free Press and Mercantile Advertiser*, 22 September 1891; 'A Frivolous Prosecution: Justification for Striking a Javanese Servant', *Straits Times*, 21 June 1909; 'Taiping Topics', *Malaya Tribune*, 15 May 1914; 'A Troublesome Amah', *Singapore Free Press and Mercantile Advertiser*, 7 May 1915; 'A Technical Assault', *Singapore Free Press and Mercantile Advertiser*, 4 July 1923.
24. 'Transcript of Interview with Lim Ming Joon': ACC 000334/07, 25–6, National Archives of Singapore (hereafter NAS). Translated from Mandarin to English by EthnoLink Language Services, certified by the National Accreditation Authority for Translators and Interpreters (NAATI), http://www.ethnolink.com.au/translation/naati-accredited-certified-translations-australia
25. Dussart, '"Strictly Legal Means"', 157.
26. Bailkin, 'The Boot and the Spleen', 463–464.

27. Sarah Steinbock-Pratt, '"We were all Robinson Crusoes": American Women Teachers in the Philippines', *Women's Studies* 41, no. 4 (2012), 382–384.
28. E.M. Collingham, *Imperial Bodies: The Physical Experience of the Raj, c. 1800–1947* (Cambridge: Polity Press, 2001), 110–111.
29. John Thomson, *The Straits of Malacca, Indo-China and China* (London: Sampson, Low, Marston, Low and Searle, 1875), 71–72; John Tosh, *Manliness and Masculinities in Nineteenth Century Britain: Essays on Gender, Family and Empire* (New York: Pearson Longman, 2005), 193–197.
30. For Darwin, see 'Law Courts: Police Court, Palmerston', *Northern Territory Times and Gazette*, 14 January 1882. For Singapore, see 'Labu Assault Case: European Lady Charged', *Singapore Free Press and Mercantile Advertiser*, 1 April 1924; *Straits Times*, 13 January 1927; '"Mem" Fined for Striking Cook', *Straits Times*, 19 June 1937.
31. Claudia Knapman, *White Women in Fiji, 1835–1930: The Ruin of Empire?* (Sydney: Allen and Unwin, 1986), 19; Lowrie, *Masters and Servants*, 136–143.
32. Carl Trocki, *Opium and Empire: Chinese Society in Colonial Singapore, 1800–1910* (Ithaca: Cornell University Press, 1990), 11.
33. 'Letter to the Editor', *Northern Territory Times and Gazette*, 12 February 1881; *Northern Territory Times*, 6 October 1883; 'European or Chinese Labor', *Northern Territory Times and Gazette*, 4 May 1889.
34. Glenice Yee, *Through Chinese Eyes: The Chinese Experience in the Northern Territory, 1874–2004* (Parap: Glenice Yee, 2006), 38.
35. Tosh, *Manliness and Masculinities*, 199–200; Powell, *Far Country*, 123–124.
36. Somerset Maugham, *The Casuarina Tree: Six Stories* (London: Heinemann, 1926), 117.
37. Xavier Herbert, *Capricornia* (Sydney: Angus and Robertson, 1987), 8, 10.
38. For Darwin, see 'Legal Information: Police Court', *North Australia*, 18 March 1888; 'Chinese Secret Societies', *South Australian Register*, 23 July 1891; 'Opium Smuggling: Chinese Cook Heavily Fined', *The Advertiser*, 19 May 1909; 'Inspector of Police to Government Resident', 1887, Government Resident of the Northern Territory (South Australia), List of Inwards Correspondence, 1870–1911: NTRS829, A9768, Northern Territory Archives Service, Darwin (hereafter NTAS). For Singapore, see Jonas Daniel Vaughan, *The Manners and Customs of the Chinese of the Straits Settlements* (Singapore: Mission Press, 1879); 'A Dishonest Boy', *Straits Times*, 4 July 1899.
39. Ong Siang Song, *One Hundred Years' History of the Chinese in Singapore* (Singapore: Oxford University Press, 1984), 265; 'A Ferocious "Boy"',

Straits Times, 1 July 1899; 'Three Tragedies: Angus Street Murder', *Singapore Free Press and Mercantile Advertiser*, 17 June 1909; 'Murderous Assault: Hylam Servant Attacks Master', *Malaya Tribune*, 26 September 1919.
40. 'Law Courts: Police Court, Palmerston', *Northern Territory Times and Gazette*, 14 January 1882.
41. Warwick Anderson, 'The Trespass Speaks: White Masculinity and Colonial Breakdown', *The American Historical Review* 102, no. 5 (1997), 1343.
42. Henry Reynolds, *North of Capricorn: The Untold Story of Australia's North* (Sydney: Allen and Unwin, 2003), 107.
43. Powell, *Far Country*, 156.
44. 'Murdered by a Chinese Cook: Waiter's Head Beaten In', *The Advertiser*, 5 March 1906; 'Seven Persons Killed: A Cook's Revenge', *Northern Standard*, 29 April 1930; 'Station Hand Shot: Chinese Cook Imprisoned', *The Advertiser*, 21 April 1926.
45. Ching-Hwang Yen, 'Class Structure and Social Mobility in the Chinese Community in Singapore and Malaya 1800–1911', *Modern Asian Studies* 21, no. 3 (1987), 427.
46. Trocki, *Opium and Empire*, 183–185.
47. Song, *One Hundred Years*.
48. Lowrie, *Masters and Servants*, 143–147.
49. Joyce Ee, 'Chinese Migration to Singapore, 1896–1941', *Journal of Southeast Asian History* 2, no. 1 (1961), 42.
50. Tony Austin, '"A Chance to Be Decent": Northern Territory "Half-Caste" Girls in Service in South Australia 1916–1939', *Labour History* 60 (1990), 52–53.
51. Austin, '"A Chance to Be Decent"', 52–53.
52. 'The Black Man's Burden', *Sunday Express*, 3 June 1934; 'Alleged Ill-Treatment of Natives Nt—Reports by Foreign Newspapers': A1/15, 1934/8852 (1934), NAA.
53. Mary Montgomerie Bennett, *The Australian Aboriginal as a Human Being* (London: Alston Rivers, 1930); Alfred H. Brown, *Report on Some Problems of Northern Australia* (Australia: Religious Society of Friends (Quakers) in Australia, 1914), 131.
54. Of the sixteen employers' accounts that I accessed, only two mentioned violence between Aboriginal servants, and none suggested employer–servant violence. 'Transcript of Interview with Betty Dangerfield': NTRS 226, TS 187 (1982), tape 1, 9, NTAS; 'Transcript of Interview with W.E (Bill) Eacott': NTRS 226, TS 758 (1992), tape 1, 11–12, NTAS.
55. 'Annual Report of the Northern Territory' (Commonwealth Government of Australia, 1912), 48; 'The Discouragement of White Labor: Cruelty to Natives', *Northern Standard*, 25 April 1922; 'Starving Blacks: To the Editor', *Northern Standard*, 19 April 1925.

56. Claire Lowrie, 'The Transcolonial Politics of Chinese Domestic Mastery in Singapore and Darwin 1910s–1930s', *Journal of Colonialism and Colonial History* 12, no. 3 (2011).
57. Victoria Haskins, 'Domestic Service and Frontier Feminism: The Call for a Woman Visitor to "Half-Caste" Girls and Women in Domestic Service, 1925–1928', *Frontiers* 28, no. 1/2 (2007), 127.
58. Northern Territory of Australia: Report of the Administrator for the Years 1915–1916 and 1916–1917: nla.obj-54061288, 45, 47, National Library of Australia, Canberra (hereafter NLA).
59. See, for example, 'The Natives: Revelations at Federal Inquiry', *Sydney Morning Herald*, 20 January 1920; 'In Territoria: Trial of Prisoners, Peculiar Court Methods', *Daily Standard*, 31 March 1917; 'Darwin Doings: Missing Documents, an Aborigines Plea', *Register*, 1 January 1920; 'The Darwin Inquiry: Investigation Regarding Administration', *Queenslander*, 10 January 1920.
60. Victoria Haskins and John Maynard, 'Sex, Race and Power: Aboriginal Men and White Women in Australian History', *Australian Historical Studies* 126 (2005), 42.
61. For example, the attempted sexual assault on a white woman by an Aboriginal courier called Packsaddle in 1938. Fiona Paisley, 'Race Hysteria, Darwin 1938', *Australian Feminist Studies* 16, no. 34 (2001), 43.
62. 'Oenpelli Blacks: Gins Get a Few Strokes', *Northern Territory Times and Gazette*, 3 January 1920.
63. 'Transcript of Interview with Dolly Bonson': NTRS 266, TS 429/2 (1982), tape 1, 12, NTAS; 'Transcript of Interview with Hilda Muir', NTRS 226, TS 793 (1993), tape 1, 5, NTAS.
64. Ann McGrath, *Born in the Cattle: Aborigines in Cattle Country* (Sydney: Allen and Unwin, 1987), 142.
65. Fiona Paisley, *Loving Protection: Australian Feminism and Aboriginal Women's Rights, 1919–1939* (Melbourne: Melbourne University Press, 2000), 70–91.
66. 'Half Caste Woman', *Northern Standard*, 1 February 1935.
67. Auber Octavius Neville, *Australia's Coloured Minority: Its Place in the Community* (Sydney: Currawong Publishing Company, 1947), 183.
68. Victoria Haskins, '"A Better Chance"?—Sexual Abuse and the Apprenticeship of Aboriginal Girls under the NSW Aborigines Protection Board', *Aboriginal History* 28 (2004), 33–35.
69. Ah Eng Lai, *Peasants, Proletarians and Prostitutes: A Preliminary Investigation into the Work of Chinese Women in Colonial Malaya* (Singapore: Institute of Southeast Asian Studies, 1986), 46–47.
70. Susan Pederson, 'The Maternalist Movement in British Colonial Policy: The Controversy over "Child Slavery" in Hong Kong, 1917–1941', *Past and Present* 171 (May 2001), 163.

71. 'Mui Tsai in the Straits: Why It Must Be Banned by Statute', *Straits Times*, 27 January 1932.
72. Lai, *Peasants, Proletarians and Prostitutes*, 50–53.
73. Edith Picton-Turbervill, 'Minority Report', in *Mui Tsai in Hong Kong and Malaya*, ed. W.W. Woods and C.A. Willis (London: His Majesty's Stationery Office, 1937), 233.
74. See, for example, 'Transcript of Interview with Miu Ling Lee': ACC 001917/02/03 (1997), 37–38, NAS. The exception is Lucy Lum's account of her grandmother abuse of a *mui tsai*. Lucy Lum, *The Thorn of Lion City: A Memoir* (London: Fourth Estate, 2007), 160.
75. Janet Lim, *Sold for Silver: An Autobiography of a Girl Sold into Slavery in Southeast Asia* (Singapore: Monsoon Books, 2004), 35, 38.
76. Maria Jaschok and Suzanne Miers, 'Women in the Chinese Patriarchal System: Submission, Servitude, Escape and Collusion', in *Women and Chinese Patriarchy: Submission, Servitude and Escape*, ed. Maria Jaschok and Suzanne Miers (Hong Kong: Hong Kong University Press, 1994), 9.
77. On Hainanese houseboys, see 'The Limit: Lade Threatened with Axe by Hylam Servant', *Malaya Tribune*, 29 September 1922; 'End of the Assizes: Last Case Being Heard Today', *Malaya Tribune*, 25 January 1926; 'Onan Road Murder: Hylam Boy Guilty', *Malaya Tribune*, 16 September 1933. On white mistresses, see 'Labu Assault Case: European Lady Charged', *Singapore Free Press and Mercantile Advertiser*, 1 April 1924; '"Mem" Fined for Striking Cook', *Straits Times*, 19 June 1937. For violence by Eurasian men, see 'Girl Witness Collapses: Poignant Scenes in Police Court, Eurasian on Murder Charge', *Malaya Tribune*, 17 January 1931; 'Amah's Alarming Experience: Eurasian's Escapade in Field', *Straits Times*, 8 January 1932.
78. 'Cruelty to Mui Tsai: Story of a Callous Mistress, a Shocking Case', *South China Morning Post*, 9 May 1930.
79. Victor Purcell, *The Chinese in Malaya* (London: Oxford University Press, 1948), 79, 181; Picton-Turbervill, 'Minority Report', 214, 231–233.
80. Between the 1880s and the 1930s, I located only two other newspaper accounts of assault on servants by Chinese employers.
81. 'A Register of Girls', *Straits Times*, 19 August 1937; 'Sir George Maxwell on the Mui Tsai Problem II: "Registration Was Very Badly Done". "Worse in Malaya Than in Hong Kong"', *Straits Times*, 6 August 1937.
82. Lai, *Peasants, Proletarians and Prostitutes*, 53.
83. Sarah Paddle, 'The Limits of Sympathy: International Feminists and the Chinese "Slave Girl" Campaigns of the 1920s and 1930s', *Journal of Colonialism and Colonial Studies* 4, no. 3 (2003).
84. Marriott, 'The Peoples of Singapore', 353, 360.

Index[1]

Subject headings

A

Aboriginal (Australian)
  ceremonies, 143, 238
  child removal, 128
  children, 14, 27, 51, 63n12, 91, 99, 102, 117, 118, 120, 122, 125, 127–129, 131, 132, 145, 261
  clans and nations, 29, 36, 37, 50, 56, 236
  employment policy, 28, 39, 40
  extermination of, 39, 40
  forced removal, 39, 261
  guides, 25, 29, 34, 37, 38, 51, 52
  language, 125, 226, 232, 237, 239, 240
  resistance, 95, 117, 124
  warriors, 29, 38, 165
  weapons, 55
  women, abduction of, 29, 67
  workers, 27, 49, 51, 53, 89, 90, 92, 95
Aborigines Department, 70, 71, 73, 76, 78–80
Agricultural labourers, 51
Anti-slavery movement, 32, 102, 111n70
Australian Agricultural Company (AAC), 9, 10, 25–43, 233, 245n40
Authority, 12, 38, 68, 72–74, 78, 81n2, 84n16, 93, 96–98, 103, 110n59, 124, 160, 164–166, 204, 205, 214, 216, 255, 256

B

Ben Lomond massacre, 123–128
Black War, *see* Vandemonian War
Blankets, 126, 215, 231–237

[1] Note: Page numbers followed by 'n' refer to notes.

C

Cannibalism, 213
Cape Grim massacre, 26, 29, 34
Captivity narratives, 12, 141, 142
Chartered companies, 27
Chinese people, 255, 263
Christianity, 46, 53, 61, 175, 185
Class, 11, 12, 31, 48, 50, 151, 153, 159, 171, 251, 254, 256, 257, 259
Colonial archive, 79, 122, 180
Colonial governance
    Land Purchase Officers, 182
    licensed interpreters, 182
    Native Land Court, 183
    resident officials, 179, 185, 194
Colonialism
    exploitation, 6, 68, 257, 259, 265
    settler, 3, 4, 6, 7, 11, 14, 15, 45–48, 118, 131, 227, 230, 237–240, 265
Colonial justice, 168
"Contact zone," 45, 124, 140, 232
Convict labour, 27, 30, 75, 245n40
Convict workers, 28, 36, 38
Corporal punishment, 77, 99
Correspondence, 39, 67, 68, 70, 76, 77, 96, 181, 188, 204, 210–216, 230
Credibility
    in exploration, 214
    in relationships, 47
Criminal trials, 166, 174, 225
Curiosities, 53, 57, 207, 208, 217, 237, 238

D

Disease, 205, 214
Dispossession, 2, 3, 5, 7, 9, 10, 13, 14, 45, 51, 71, 80, 81, 90, 118, 120, 124, 128, 179–199, 227, 252
Domestic
    service, 33, 78, 249–252, 254, 260
    violence, 11, 13, 14, 117–120, 132, 171–173, 249–251, 261
    workers, 251, 261
Domesticity, 2, 13, 118, 119, 121, 123, 124, 211, 216
    See also Home; Homely

E

Emotional economy, 4, 12, 188
Ethnography/anthropology, 13, 98, 99, 148, 234
Exploration, explorers, 2, 4, 12, 13, 15, 101, 204, 216, 217, 228
Extermination policies and practices, 39

F

First Land Arctic Expedition (1819–1822), 205–207
Flogging, 89–112
Friendship, 2, 131, 163, 192, 207, 216
Frontier, 2, 7, 8, 10, 14, 15, 39, 46, 47, 49–51, 55, 56, 60, 62, 68, 70, 71, 74, 81, 82n5, 82n6, 90, 91, 115–137, 139–161, 165, 166, 168, 181, 182, 189, 205, 211, 216, 226, 227, 230, 231, 234, 239, 262
Frontier violence, 14, 39, 56, 62, 91, 119, 124, 168, 205
Fur trade, 205, 206, 213

G

Gendered violence, 5, 103, 254
Gender relations, 53, 57, 146, 171

H

Home, 13, 14, 117–124, 127–132, 140, 144, 152, 166, 171, 173, 180, 186, 188, 190, 193, 204, 205, 208, 211, 213–216, 231, 250, 254, 259–266
Homely, unhomely (*unheimlich*), 117
Hudson's Bay Company (Canada), 205, 206, 215
Humanitarianism, 15, 34, 126, 226, 227, 239
Humanitarian movement, 227
Human rights, 227, 228, 239

I

Imperial knowledge, 203–223
Incarceration, 106n10, 132
Indenture, 79, 266
Interracial sex, 55, 56, 60, 142

K

Kīngitanga (Māori King Movement), 180, 182, 191
Knowledge production, 203–223, 227, 228

L

Labour relations, 2, 3, 5, 9, 10, 12, 25–43, 68, 69, 71
Land, 3, 5, 8, 14, 30, 34, 36, 37, 39, 40n7, 47, 50, 52, 55, 60, 61, 70, 71, 91, 96, 98, 101, 116–119, 121–125, 127, 128, 131, 132, 136n53, 141, 146, 150, 161, 164, 165, 167, 171, 174, 180, 182, 183, 185, 189–192, 194, 231, 232, 244n40, 252, 262
Land transactions, 164
Languages, Aboriginal/Indigenous, 125, 226, 232, 237, 239, 240
Law, 8, 11, 38, 49, 61, 68, 69, 73–79, 81, 97, 99, 100, 128, 161, 164, 165, 168–170, 174, 175, 182, 226–228, 232, 234, 240, 251, 256
Legislation, 31, 69, 72–75, 81, 85n37, 263
Linguistics, 10, 118, 225–247
Literature, 228, 234, 250

M

Magistrates, 31, 38, 52, 70, 72, 75, 76, 78, 82n6, 165, 170, 191, 230, 231, 244n39
Māori land
  dispossession, 180, 189
  gold prospecting, 180
  leasing, 183
  sales, 180
Māori–Pākehā relationships
  emotional economy, 4, 12
  entanglement, 186
  social networks, 180
  strategic intimacies, 5
Māori tikanga
  atawhai, 186
  manaakitanga, 186, 190
Maritime, 2, 211, 216
Marriage, 56, 69, 80, 121, 146, 148, 171, 190, 204, 209, 210, 216, 229, 232, 244n40
Masculinities, 93, 250, 251, 257
Massacres, 26, 29, 34, 39, 90, 94, 123–128, 137n76, 167, 225, 226, 230, 236, 237, 239
Masters, 11, 38, 48, 69, 75, 77, 80, 85n37, 98, 130, 137n76, 144, 152, 194, 250–252, 254–256, 259, 261, 262, 264–266
Material culture, 4, 171
Members of Parliament (MPs), 30–33
Middle ground, 124, 161, 163, 168, 170

Mining, 3, 68, 70, 78, 180, 182, 183, 191
Missionaries, 98, 100, 125, 136n54, 154n6, 162, 164, 174, 184, 227, 234, 261, 263
Modernity, 4–6
Moral ambiguity, 47, 50, 51, 56, 61, 62
Moral economy, 4, 10, 48, 49, 62, 96, 214

N
'Native mind,' 89–112
Native police, 51, 160, 163, 164, 166, 170, 175
Newspapers, 91, 92, 95, 98, 101–103, 124, 160, 166–169, 174, 225, 230, 238, 240, 251, 255, 257, 261, 264, 266

O
Overstraiters, 115–137

P
Pastoral companies, 9–10, 70
Pastoralism, 9, 10, 45, 47–49, 55, 56, 60–62, 70, 94, 117, 120
Pastoral station, 2, 71, 124
Pearling, 68, 70–73, 85n34
Poetry, 226, 228–233, 237–240
Police, 33, 46, 51, 68, 75, 77, 78, 81n2, 82n6, 98, 101, 102, 104, 121, 125, 160, 163–166, 170, 174, 175, 187, 230, 233, 251, 254
Power, 2, 3, 9, 12, 13, 15, 26, 33, 38, 60, 68, 70, 71, 74, 79–81, 92, 95, 97, 100, 117, 119, 120, 124, 126, 132, 148, 161, 164–166, 170, 182, 189, 211, 233, 238, 250, 251, 262

Print culture, 226
Prostitution, 56, 69, 80, 259
Protection, 4, 10, 28, 32, 34, 36, 37, 68–70, 75, 76, 78–80, 85n28, 164, 189, 237, 239
Proximity, 1–21, 49, 50, 53, 55, 61, 98, 118, 163, 166–171, 195n1, 234

R
Race, 5, 10–12, 15, 55, 81, 95, 100, 103, 141, 142, 159, 165, 166, 180, 192, 227, 251, 254
Race relations, 10, 142, 165, 180
Remuneration, 26, 261
Representation, 101, 141, 152, 226, 228, 230, 233, 234, 238, 250, 251, 255, 259, 265
Respectability, 78, 92, 122, 171, 211
Royal Commission, 91, 92, 94, 95, 97, 106n10, 261

S
Scandal, 69, 89–112
Scientific sociability, 204, 207–211
Sealers, 36, 37, 125, 164
Second Land Arctic Expedition (1825–1827), 212
Servants, 11, 13, 14, 29, 31, 37, 48, 51, 52, 57, 67, 70, 72, 74–81, 85n37, 86n47, 86n56, 100, 116, 120, 122, 137n76, 180, 186, 207, 249–272
Settler colonialism, 3, 4, 6, 7, 11, 14, 15, 45–48, 118, 131, 227, 230, 237–240, 265
Settler colonies, 3, 45, 120, 128, 226, 227, 250, 252, 253
Settler morality, 46

Settlers, 1–21, 29, 31, 34, 36, 45–65, 69–71, 75–77, 79, 80, 85n37, 89–112, 116–124, 127, 128, 131, 132, 140, 141, 159, 168, 181, 185, 190, 225–228, 230–233, 237–240, 250–254, 257, 259, 265, 266
Sexual violence, 55, 60, 82n5, 103, 146
Shareholders, 30–32, 39
Slavery, 46, 56, 73, 102, 103, 227, 261, 263
See also Anti-slavery movement
Sovereignty, 3, 98, 165, 227
Specimens and specimen-gathering, 13, 204, 213, 216
Stolen Generations, 136n59
Structural violence, 181, 194
Surveillance, 74, 80
Surveyors, 34, 37, 38, 180, 184, 195n1

T
Trade, 5, 11, 50, 72, 93, 162, 174, 205, 206, 213, 252
Trading relationships, 162
Treaties, 116, 164, 175, 252
Trust and trustworthiness, 26, 147, 207, 211, 215, 216

U
Unhomely (*unheimlich*), 14, 115–137

V
Vandemonian War, *see* Black War
Van Diemen's Land Company (VDLC), 9, 10, 25–43

Vernacular agents and authority, 211, 212
Violence
  bureaucratic, 8, 118
  colonial, 1, 5–8, 10, 11, 70–73, 89–93, 104, 118, 124, 181–185, 225, 226, 232, 239
  disciplinary, 105, 255, 257
  emotional, 62, 127
  frontier, 14, 39, 56, 62, 91, 119, 124, 168, 205
  gendered, 5, 103, 254
  intimate, 3, 9, 60, 67–87, 90, 171–173
  martial, 6
  necessary, 10
  sexual, 55, 60, 103, 146
Voyageurs, 206

W
Wages, 48, 72, 75, 85n37, 182, 263
Warfare, 46, 60, 62, 117, 118, 128, 132, 168
Whalers, 125, 212
Women
  cross-cultural relations, 139–158
  Indigenous, 10–13, 68–74, 77–81, 82n6, 142, 143, 153, 154, 204, 210, 214, 216
  Irish, 120, 121
  middle class, 142
  Māori, 13, 165, 190, 194
  white, 12–14, 56, 100, 103, 118, 147, 152, 154, 250, 255, 256, 262
  women's work, 139–158, 172
  working class, 256
Wool industry, 26

People mentioned

A
Aburda, 145, 150
Adey, Stephen, 35, 43n51
Akaitcho, 206, 207, 210
Aldwell, Sophia, 171
Aldwell, William, 171
Alika, 145
Allen, John or 'Jacky,', *see* Lurnerminner or Meelerleeter
Anstey, Thomas, 125, 126, 136n56, 136n57
Arthur, George, 39, 86n47, 111n70, 121, 122, 129
Ashton, Jennifer, 168, 177n39

B
Back, George, 206, 219n15, 219n18, 223n75
Backhouse, James, 28, 41n14, 130
Bairstow, Deirdre, 41n8
Baldwin, Charles, 32, 94, 98, 107n22, 109n46
Ballara, Angela, 56, 165, 176n20, 176n24–26, 176n30
Barclay, Charles, 32
Barnard, Edward, 31
Barrow, Sir John, 205, 218n8
Batman, Eliza, 115–137
Batman, Elizabeth, 132n1, 133n2
Batman, John, 14, 115, 117, 120–123, 125, 126, 128, 132, 132n1, 133n2, 136n50, 136n56, 136n57
Batman, John (Aboriginal boy), 116, 130, 131
Batman, John Charles, 115
Batman, Pellenominer Frances Darling, 130, 131

Beckham, Thomas, 165, 170
'Ben Lomond' or 'Benny,', *see* Rolepana
Bennet, Henry Grey, 31
Bigge, John Thomas, 30, 31
Birtles, Francis, 89, 92, 100–103, 110–111n63, 111n68, 111n70, 112n79
Bischoff, James, 33, 39, 41n7, 43n72, 43n73
Bob, Worimi man, 25, 36, 232
Boni, Darkinyung man, 236, 237
Bosanquet, Charles, 32
Brabant, H.W., 184
Brierly, Oswald, 142, 144–147, 150, 152, 155n9, 156n19–21, 156n25–34, 157n35, 157n37–46, 158n60, 158n61, 158n64–67, 158n71, 158n72, 158n74, 158n75
Brogden, James, 31
Bunce, Daniel, 131, 137n75
Burns, Joseph, 12, 160, 161, 171–175, 253

C
Cahill, Paddy, Jr. (Neyingkul), 93
Cahill, Patrick (Paddy), 90, 94, 107n18, 107n22, 107n26, 261
Callaghan, Elizabeth, *see* Batman, Eliza
Churton, Reverend, 173
Close, Edward Charles, 31
Collins, David, 34
Compton, Charles, 32
Cook, Captain James, 164, 229, 262, 269n30, 269n38, 270n44, 272n77
Cooke, Nicola, 131
Copley, John, 32
Corallis, Joseph, 147
Cox, William, 236
Cripps, Joseph, 33, 34

Crook, Johnny, 125, 131, 136n53
Cubit, James, 38
Curr, Edward, 26, 29, 30, 33–35, 37–39, 40n5, 41n16, 42n44, 42n45, 43n49, 43n50
Curtis, John, 142, 143, 149, 153, 155n8, 155n10, 156n14, 157n58, 158n78

D

Darling, J.W., 129
Davis, Charles, 166
Davis, James (Duramboi), 147
Davis, Richard Hart, 32
Dawson, Robert, 25, 26, 28, 30, 32–34, 36, 38, 40, 40n1, 42n37, 60, 65n35, 233
Dearle, Charles, 190
Dumaresq, Edward, 36, 40n3
Dunlop, David, 229, 231, 232, 244n39
Dunlop, Eliza Hamilton, 225–247

E

Eliza (wife of Wilkinson, also known as Raiha, or Piki), 186, 187

F

FitzRoy, Governor Robert, 163
Fossey, Jospeh, 38
Franklin, Eleanor (Porden), 209, 211, 213, 216, 220n33, 221n41
Franklin, Eleanor Anne, 220n35
Franklin, Jane, nee Griffin (Lady), 119, 120
Franklin, John (Captain, Governor), 119, 204, 206, 207, 219n13, 219n15, 219n18–20, 220n29, 220n30, 222n51, 222n60, 222n63, 222n64, 223n34, 223n68, 223n70, 223n74, 223n75, 223n78
Fraser, Eliza, 139–158

G

Gameema, 150
Gilfallan family, 167
Gill, Richard, 185
Gillespie family, 167
Gipps, Lady Elizabeth, 229
Gipps, Sir George, 229
Goldie, Alexander, 35, 43n51
Grant, Sir Alexander Gray, 32, 54
'Greenstockings,' 207, 210, 214, 216, 221n39, 223n78
Grey, Earl, 167
Grey, Governor George, 163, 167

H

Haldimand, William, 32
Hannah, Mark, 27, 41n8
Hariata, 186
Harrison, George, 31, 32
Hellyer, Henry, 34, 38, 43n48
Hepburn, John, 207, 219n20
Herbert, Xavier, 256, 269n37
Hodgson, Frederick, 32
Hood, Robert, 206, 207, 211
Hughes, Henry, 31

I

Inskip, George, 144, 156n22, 158n73

J

Johnson, Henry Dunbar, 189, 190
Jorgenson, Jorgen, 43n61, 43n62

K

Karnerbutcher, 129
Kay, Mary Anne, 213, 216, 222n63, 223n75
Kenny, Nepean, 189
Kingi, 167, 187
King, John, 185
King, Philip Gidley, 31
King, Phillip Parker, 31, 36, 214
Kirkland, Katherine, 56–62, 64n28–31, 65n32–34, 65n36

L

Law, James Sylvius, 229
Lewis, T.W., 196n12, 198n78, 198n82, 198n88
Lind, Jenny, 67–71, 73, 76–81, 86n52
Lurnerminner, 116, 118, 122, 123, 129, 131
 See also Meelerleeter 'John Allen' or 'Jacky'
Lushington, Stephen, 32

M

Macarthur, John, 33
Macarthur, John Jnr, 32
Mackay, James, 189, 190
Macquarie, Lachlan, 31, 35, 232
MacQueen, Thomas Potter, 31, 42n30
Mair, W.G., 191
Maketu, Wiremu Kingi, 167
Makiwi, 186, 197n44
Manakau, Rawinia, 190
Maniapoto, Rewi, 191, 192
Marakara, Nipper, 96
Martin, Chief Justice William, 172
Massingberd, Peregrine, 122, 123, 129, 135n38–40, 137n67
Masson, Elsie, 94, 95, 107n24, 108n36, 109n47

Mathinna, 119
Maugham, Somerset, 256, 269n36
McKay, Alexander, 38
McLean, Sir Donald, 182, 196n11
Merea (wife of Wilkinson), 180, 186, 188–191, 193, 195, 197n59, 199n93, 199n96
Meredith, Louisa, 119, 120, 134n18
Meremana, Hemaima, 190
Miller, Olga, 142, 154n5, 156n16, 156n17, 157n51, 157n53, 157n54
Mulgrave, P.A., 121

N

Nathan, Isaac, 230, 231, 237, 243n25, 243n26, 244n28, 246n56, 246n58
Nathan, Rosetta, 230
Nelson, Charles, 167, 185
Ngākiore, 186
Ngamuka, 169, 170
Ngāonewhero, Raiha, 186–188

O

Otter, Charles, 141, 148

P

Paraone, 193
Parker, Katherine Langloh, 238, 246n61
Parry, Sir William Edward, 36, 204, 220n30, 220n32, 221n44, 221n45, 222n52, 222n55
Patuone (Eruera Maihi/Edward Marsh), 12, 163–166, 168, 172, 174, 176n20, 176n24–26, 176n30
Pearse, John, 33, 34

INDEX

Pellenominer (Pellonymyna), 130, 131, 137n74
Pemberton, Pennie, 30, 31, 41n20–22, 42n25–29, 42n31, 42n32, 42n35, 42n36
Pequi, 144
Perkins, John, 27, 41n8
Petchey, John, 121
Petrie, Hazel, 162, 175n9, 176n12–16, 176n22
Pevay (Tunnerminnerwait), 37
Picton-Turberville, Edith, 263, 264, 272n73, 272n79
Pigeon, 125, 131, 133n3, 136n53
Pope, Alan, 27, 41n10
Porden, Eleanor (later Franklin), 209, 211, 213, 216, 220n33, 221n41
Prinsep, Henry, 69–71, 73, 74, 76, 78, 80, 81n1, 83n8, 83n9, 85n29, 85n31–85n33, 86n44, 86n45, 86n49, 86n53, 86n54, 87n59, 87n60, 87n62, 87n64

R
Rapana, Miriama Te Kiritahanga, 190
Raurau (wife of Wilkinson), 180, 186–188, 190–195, 197n44, 199n96
Reardon, Margaret, 160, 161, 171–175
Richardson, Dr. John, 43n72, 206, 219–19–21, 219n13, 219n14, 219n17, 219n20, 220n29, 220n34, 221n46, 222n56, 223n68, 223n70, 223n72
Richardson, Mary, 219n14, 219n17, 221n46, 222n56, 223n70, 223n72, 223n73
Roberton family, 167
Robina, 149

Robinson, George Augustus, 129
Rolepana, 'Ben Lomond' or 'Benny,' 116, 118, 122, 123, 126–132, 133n3, 137n76
Romula, 95–97, 261, 262
Rutherford, Danilyn, 181, 190, 195n7

S
Scott, Helenus, 31
Scott, Robert, 31
Scott, William, 32, 218n8, 222n54
Shaw, Benjamin, 32
Short, Henry, 31
Smith, William, 32
Snow, Hannah, 160
Snow, Lieutenant Robert, 160
Somerville, Morris Townshend, 236
Sorell, William, 34
Spence, George, 32
Spencer, Baldwin, 94–96, 98, 100, 107n22, 108n35, 108n37, 108n39, 108n40, 109n45, 109n46, 110n58
Stewart, David, 190

T
Tahipapa, 186, 187
Taipari, W.H., 189
Takarangi (Riria/Lydia), 164
Tapua, 163, 164
Taraia, 169
Tattanouek (Augustus), 206
Tāwhiao (second Māori king), 182, 191–193
Te Kotuku, 190
Te Mimiha, Hoera, 190
Te Momotu Rangimiria, 184
Te Okowai, 186, 188
Te Rangihaeata, 167
Te Rauparaha, 167

Te Wahanui, 191
Te Wairingiringi (daughter of Wilkinson and Raurau), 194
Te Wairingiringi (living in Wilkinson's house), 194
Te Wherowhero, 163, 167, 168, 170, 175
Teetoreric, or May Day, 127
Terohaute, Michel, 206
Thompson, Barbara (Giom), 12, 139–158
Thornton, Henry, 32
Threlkeld, Reverend Lancelot, 226
Tomagagu, 145
Tony, Worimi man, 25, 28, 33, 35–37, 39
Tooke, Thomas and William, 32
Traill, Henry, 32, 220n27
Tukukino, 182
Turner, Annie and Sophie, 32
Twining, George and Richard, 32

U
Urdzanna, 145

W
Walker, George Washington, 28, 130
Wedge, John Helder, 38, 127
Weenie, 145, 146
Wetherill, William, 31
Wilberforce, William, 32
Wilkinson, Catherine, 181
Wilkinson, George Thomas, 181
Wilkinson, Henry, 181
William IV, King, 164
Williams, Henry, 164
Wittenoom, Frank, 67, 69–71, 73, 74, 76–78, 81n1, 83n9, 83n11, 83n12, 84n14, 85n33, 86n45, 86n51, 86n53
Woodhouse, William, 32

Y
Yuri, 150, 151

Tribal groups mentioned

A
Awabakal people, New South Wales, 231

B
Badu, 145, 146
Butchulla, 140, 141, 143, 147–149, 153

D
Darkinyung people, New South Wales, 236
Dene Yellowknife (Canada), 205, 206

G
'Gamilaraay/Cumeleroy/Gamilaroi,' New South Wales, 237
Gundungurra nation, New South Wales, 33
Gunwinjgu people, 93, 96

I
Inuit (Canada), 205, 206, 208
Iñupiat (North and Northwest Alaska), 205

K
Kabi-Kabi, 140, 147–149, 153
Kaurareg, 139, 141, 142, 144–147, 150–153, 155
Kaurna, 55

Kulin Nation, southeastern Australia, 116
Kulkulaga, 146

M
Moner balug clan, 56

N
Ngâti Hako, 182, 183
Ngâti Hao, 163
Ngâti Koe, 182
Ngâti Maniapoto, 191, 192
Ngâti Maru, 182
Ngâti Paoa, 164, 165, 182
Ngâti Ruru, 169
Ngâti Tamaterâ, 182
Ngâti Toa, 167
North Nation, Tasmania, 37
North West Nation, Tasmania, 37

P
Parperloihener clan, North West nation, Tasmania, 36, 37
Peramangk, 55
Plairhekehillerplu clan, North West nation, Tasmania, 37
Plangermaireener Nation, Tasmania, 121

T
Tarkiner clan, North West nation, Tasmania, 37
Tommeginer clan, North West nation, Tasmania, 37

W
Wathaurong people, 56, 57
Wirrayaraay people, 226

Wonaruah, New South Wales Darkinyung, and Awabakal, 231
Worimi Nation, New South Wales, 25

Place Names

A
Arctic circle, 203–223
Auckland, New Zealand, 12, 160–175, 182, 184, 192, 197n39

B
Barren Grounds (Canada), 206, 207, 209
Bass Strait, southeastern Australia, 82n5, 116, 125
Bay of Plenty, New Zealand, 162, 181, 182, 189
Ben Lomond, Tasmania, 116, 121–128, 130, 131
Boolardy, Western Australia, 67, 69, 71, 73, 74, 77, 79, 83n11
Bribie Island, Queensland, 141
British Empire, 4, 15, 89, 92, 95, 102, 103, 163, 204, 264

C
Camden Estate, New South Wales, 33
Cape Grim, Tasmania, 26, 29, 34
Cape York, Queensland, 139, 141, 145
Circular Head, Tasmania, 37, 38
Cirencester, Gloucestershire, 33
Colonial Office, London, 31, 34, 73, 95, 211, 216
Coppermine River, Canada, 206
Coromandel, New Zealand, 162, 164, 182, 184

D
Darwin, Northern Territory of Australia, 11, 15, 94, 100, 249–272
Davis Strait, 212
Devonport, New Zealand, 165

E
Emu Bay, Tasmania, 37, 38

F
Flinders Island, Tasmania, 39, 129, 130
Fort Enterprise, Canada, 206, 207

G
George Town, Tasmania, 38, 121
Great Bear Lake (Canada), 204, 211
Great Slave Lake (Canada), 206
Greenwich (UK), 203, 213, 214, 216

H
Hampshire Hills, Tasmania, 28, 37
Hauraki, 169, 180, 182, 183, 190, 191, 193
Hauraki Gulf, New Zealand, 164
Hobart, Tasmania (Van Diemen's Land), 121, 129, 131, 203
Hokianga, New Zealand, 164
Hunter River, New South Wales, 36, 231
Hunter Valley, New South Wales, 31
Hutt Valley, New Zealand, 167, 168

I
India, 46, 48, 50, 51, 181, 229, 250, 251, 256
Ireland, 171, 229

J
Japanese Empire, 162

K
Kangaroo Island, South Australia, 36
K'gari (Fraser Island), Queensland, 140, 143, 147, 148, 153
King Country, New Zealand, 180, 182, 191, 192
Kingston, Tasmania (Van Diemen's Land), 121–124, 126–129, 132

L
Lake Macquarie, 232

M
Mackenzie River, Canada, 205
Manning River, New South Wales, 36
Mechanics Bay, New Zealand, 163
Melbourne, Victoria, 56, 57, 59, 94, 98, 99, 101, 115–117, 120, 131, 133n3
Moreton Bay, Queensland, 141, 147
Mowkero (Maukoro), New Zealand, 169
Muralag (Prince of Wales Island), Queensland, 139, 141, 145, 151, 153
Myall Creek, 225, 226, 230, 236, 237, 239
Myall Lakes, New South Wales, 36

N
Nagir (Mount Ernest Island), Queensland, 146
Newcastle penal settlement, New South Wales, 35, 231

New South Wales (NSW), 25, 26, 29–35, 46, 55, 101, 103, 121, 124–127, 131, 132, 165, 171, 172, 226, 229–231, 233, 237
Ngurapai (Horn Island), Queensland, 141
Norfolk Plains, Tasmania, 38
Northern Territory, Australia, 40n7, 89–112, 251, 252, 256, 257, 260–262, 267n5
North Shore, Auckland, New Zealand, 160, 161, 164, 171, 172, 174
Northwest Passage (Canada and Alaska), 205, 208, 217

O
Oenpelli, Northern Territory, 93–97, 261
Ōkahu, New Zealand, 162
Ottoman Empire, 162

P
Parramatta, New South Wales, 125
Piako River, New Zealand, 169
Port Macquarie, New South Wales, 35
Port Phillip, New South Wales, 115–137
Port Stephens, New South Wales, 25–28, 35–37, 233

Q
Queensland, 11, 71, 72, 93, 139–158

R
Robbins Island, Tasmania, 37

S
Sandy Cape, Tasmania, 37
Singapore, 11, 15, 249–272
South Australia, 27, 49, 53, 54, 189
Surry Hills, Tasmania, 37
Sydney, NSW, 100, 116, 121, 122, 125, 132, 141, 164, 230

T
Table Cape, Tasmania, 37
Takapuna Beach, New Zealand, 165
Tasmania (Van Diemen's Land), 36, 40, 50, 115, 125, 126
Torres Strait, Queensland, 139, 140, 144, 146

V
Van Diemen's Land, 9, 10, 25–43, 115–137, 160, 172, 174
See also Tasmania (Van Diemen's Land)
Victoria, 49, 50

W
Waikato, New Zealand, 163, 168, 169, 180–182, 189, 191, 192
Waitangi, New Zealand, 164
Western Australia, 49–52, 56, 67, 70, 72, 79
Whakatāne, New Zealand, 162, 193
W(h)anganui, New Zealand, 167, 168
Wollombi, 231, 233, 235–237, 239, 240
Woodford, Essex, 33

CPSIA information can be obtained
at www.ICGtesting.com
Printed in the USA
LVHW07*2044300518
578991LV00003B/3/P